The Cambridge Edition of the Works of Immanuel Kant is a venture that when complete (14 volumes are currently envisaged) will offer translations of all Kant's published works and a generous selection of his unpublished writings in a uniform format suitable for Kant scholars.

This volume is the first ever English translation of Kant's last major work, the so-called *Opus postumum*, a work Kant himself described as his "chef d'oeuvre" and as the keystone of his entire philosophical system. It occupied him for more than the last decade of his life.

Begun with the intention of providing a "transition from the metaphysical foundations of natural science to physics," Kant's reflections take him far beyond the problem he initially set out to solve. In fact, he reassesses a whole series of fundamental topics of transcendental philosophy: the thing in itself, the nature of space and time, the concept of the self and its agency, the idea of God, and the unity of theoretical and practical reason. Though never completed, the text reaches a logical, albeit not fully developed, conclusion.

Professor Förster's introduction places the text in the context of Kant's earlier writings and provides a comprehensive account of the remarkable history of the manuscript from Kant's death to its eventual publication in the 1930s. There are extensive explanatory notes and a helpful glossary.

THE CAMBRIDGE EDITION OF THE WORKS OF IMMANUEL KANT

IMMANUEL KANT
Opus postumum

THE CAMBRIDGE EDITION OF THE WORKS
OF IMMANUEL KANT

General Editors: Paul Guyer and Allen W. Wood

Advisory Board: Henry Allison
Lewis White Beck
Reinhard Brandt
Mary Gregor
Ralf Meerbote
Charles D. Parsons
Hoke Robinson
Eva Schaper
J. B. Schneewind
Manley P. Thompson

IMMANUEL KANT

Opus postumum

EDITED, WITH AN INTRODUCTION AND NOTES, BY
ECKART FÖRSTER
TRANSLATED BY
ECKART FÖRSTER AND MICHAEL ROSEN

CAMBRIDGE
UNIVERSITY PRESS

Published by the Press Syndicate of the University of Cambridge
The Pitt Building, Trumpington Street, Cambridge CB2 1RP
40 West 20th Street, New York, NY 10011-4211, USA
10 Stamford Road, Oakleigh, Melbourne 3166, Australia

First published 1993

First paperback edition 1995

Printed in the United States of America

Library of Congress Cataloging-in-Publication Data
Kant, Immanuel, 1724–1804.
Opus postumum / Immanuel Kant: translated by Eckart Förster and
Michael Rosen; edited by Eckart Förster
p. cm . – (The Cambridge edition of the works of Immanuel
Kant)
Includes bibliographical references and index.
Translation of: Opus postumum.
ISBN 0-521-26511-8 (hbk)   ISBN 0-521-31928-5 (pbk)
1. Transcendentalism. 2. Physics – Philosophy. I. Förster, Eckart.
II. Series: Kant, Immanuel, 1724–1804. Works. English. 1992.
B2794.062E5   1993
193 – dc20   92-14088
                                                                   CIP

A catalog record for this book is available from the British Library.

ISBN 0-521-26511-8 hardback
ISBN 0-521-31928-5 paperback

Contents

General editors' preface

Within a few years of the publication of his *Critique of Pure Reason* in 1781, Immanuel Kant (1724–1804) was recognized by his contemporaries as one of the seminal philosophers of modern times – indeed, as one of the great philosophers of all time. This renown soon spread beyond German-speaking lands, and translations of Kant's work into English were published even before 1800. Since then, interpretations of Kant's views have come and gone and loyalty to his positions has waxed and waned, but his importance has not diminished. Generations of scholars have devoted their efforts to producing reliable translations of Kant into English as well as into other languages.

There are four main reasons for the present edition of Kant's writings:

1. Completeness. Although most of the works published in Kant's lifetime have been translated before – the most important ones more than once – only fragments of Kant's many important unpublished works have ever been translated. These include the *Opus postumum*, Kant's unfinished *magnum opus* on the transition from philosophy to physics; transcriptions of his classroom lectures; his correspondence; and his marginalia and other notes. One aim of this edition is to make a comprehensive sampling of these materials available in English for the first time.

2. Availability. Many English translations of Kant's works, especially those that have not individually played a large role in the subsequent development of philosophy, have long been inaccessible or out of print. Many of them, however, are crucial for the understanding of Kant's philosophical development, and the absence of some from English-language bibliographies may be responsible for erroneous or blinkered traditional interpretations of his doctrines by English-speaking philosophers.

3. Organization. Another aim of the present edition is to make all Kant's published work, both major and minor, available in comprehensive volumes organized both chronologically and topically, so as to facilitate the serious study of his philosophy by English-speaking readers.

4. Consistency of translation. Although many of Kant's major works have been translated by the most distinguished scholars of their day, some of these translations are now dated, and there is considerable terminological disparity among them. Our aim has been to enlist some of the most accomplished Kant scholars and translators to produce new translations, freeing readers from both the philosophical and literary preconceptions of previous generations and allowing them to approach texts, as far as possible, with the same directness as present-day readers of the German or Latin originals.

In pursuit of these goals, our editors and translators attempt to follow several fundamental principles.

1. As far as seems advisable, the edition employs a single general glossary, especially for Kant's technical terms. Although we have not attempted to restrict the prerogative of editors and translators in choice of terminology, we have maximized consistency by putting a single editor or editorial team in charge of each of the main groupings of Kant's writings, such as his work in practical philosophy, philosophy of religion, or natural science, so that there will be a high degree of terminological consistency, at least in dealing with the same subject matter.

2. Our translators try to avoid sacrificing literalness to readability. We hope to produce translations that approximate the originals in the sense that they leave as much of the interpretive work as possible to the reader.

3. The paragraph, and even more the sentence, is often Kant's unit of argument, and one can easily transform what Kant intends as a continuous argument into a mere series of assertions by breaking up a sentence so as to make it more readable. Therefore, we try to preserve Kant's own divisions of sentences and paragraphs wherever possible.

4. Earlier editions often attempted to improve Kant's texts on the basis of controversial conceptions about their proper interpretation. In our translations, emendation or improvement of the original edition is kept to the minimum necessary to correct obvious typographical errors.

5. Our editors and translators try to minimize interpretation in other ways as well, for example, by rigorously segregating Kant's own footnotes, the editors' purely linguistic notes, and their more explanatory or informational notes; notes in this last category are treated as endnotes rather than footnotes.

We have not attempted to standardize completely the format of individual volumes. Each, however, includes information about the context in which Kant wrote the works that have been translated, an English–German glossary, an index, and other aids to comprehension. The general introduction to each volume includes an explanation of specific principles of translation and, where necessary, principles of selection of works included in that volume. The pagination of the standard German edition of Kant's works, *Kant's gesammelte Schriften,* edited by the Royal Prussian (later German) Academy of Sciences (Berlin: Georg Reimer, later Walter deGruyter & Co., 1900–   ), is indicated throughout by means of marginal numbers.

Our aim is to produce a comprehensive edition of Kant's writings, embodying and displaying the high standards attained by Kant scholarship in the English-speaking world during the second half of the twentieth century, and serving as both an instrument and a stimulus for the further development of Kant studies by English-speaking readers in the century to come. Because of our emphasis on literalness of translation and on information rather than interpretation in editorial practices, we hope our edition will continue to be usable despite the inevitable evolution and occasional revolutions in Kant scholarship.

PAUL GUYER
ALLEN W. WOOD

Acknowledgments

Preparing this edition of Kant's *Opus postumum* has taken more years than I now like to recall. Alan Montefiore first suggested the project to me on a memorable walk in London when I was still a graduate student at Balliol College, Oxford. The final product owes much to his enthusiasm and encouragement over the years.

Part of the research for this edition was made possible by a fellowship from the American Council of Learned Societies and by three research grants from the Pew Memorial Trust. A fellowship at the Stanford Humanities Center gave me a year's leave from teaching and provided a most congenial environment at a later stage of my work on Kant's text. This fellowship was made possible in part by a challenge grant from the National Endowment for the Humanities.

I am grateful to Peter Frank and his staff at Green Library, Stanford, for cheerfully and indefatigably providing me with all the books, journals, microfilms, and photocopies that I needed.

I also owe thanks to K. Schmidt, R. Essi, and R. Hayn of the *Arbeitsstelle der Akademie der Wissenschaften zu Göttingen: Index der deutschsprachigen Zeitschriften des 18./19. Jahrhunderts (1750–1815)* for allowing me to use their resources and facilities for a week in July 1987 and for making that week such an enjoyable one.

I am grateful to the Warden and Fellows of Merton College, Oxford, for their hospitality when I stayed in Oxford in the summer of 1985 to translate parts of the text with Michael Rosen.

Albrecht Krause, the owner of Kant's *Opus postumum*, was kind enough to let me inspect parts of the manuscript at first hand, and to give permission for the reproduction of a page from it.

Special thanks to my friends at Marburg – Reinhard Brandt, Werner Stark, and Burkhard Tuschling – who have been an unfailing source of inspiration. Stark's expertise in all matters relating to Kant's life, and Tuschling's suggestions and advice when it came to making the final selection of Kant's text, proved invaluable.

Special thanks also to Michael Friedman, whose interest in Kant's *Opus postumum* often provided welcome stimulation. He also helped generously with problems of translation, as did Taylor Carman.

In ways too numerous to list, this edition benefited from the knowledge and advice of Manfred Baum, Alan Code, Edward Courtney, John Dupré, Peter Galison, Mary Gregor, Sir Stuart Hampshire, the late Ingeburg Heidemann, Dieter Henrich, Wilbur Knorr, Helmut Müller-Sievers, Wolfgang Ritzel, Marleen Rozemond, Sir Peter F. Strawson, David Wellbery, and Margaret D. Wilson.

I should also like to express my gratitude to the secretarial staff of the Stanford Philosophy Department for their unflagging help with the preparation of the manuscript through its various stages: Teal Lake, Nancy Steege, and Eve Wasmer.

But my greatest thanks go to Ingrid Deiwiks – who knows what for.

Stanford, August 1992   E. F.

I should like to thank Professors Nancy Cartwright and Stuart Hampshire for their hospitality during a visit to California, a visit made possible thanks to financial support from the British Academy. I should also like to thank John Allen of the library at University College, London.

Oxford, August 1992   M. R.

Introduction

Almost two centuries after Immanuel Kant's death, one of his major works is still virtually unknown in the English-speaking world; this in itself is remarkable and calls for an explanation. It cannot be explained entirely by the fact that Kant did not live to prepare the text for publication, leaving a stack of several hundred pages on his desk at the time of his death. For though unedited, the manuscript is not unfinished in the sense that its argumentation breaks off midway; rather, the train of thought running through it is brought to what seems to be a logical, if not fully worked out, conclusion.

Kant's literary executor, however, thought the text unfit for publication, with the result that it soon disappeared among the possessions of Kant's heirs. When it resurfaced half a century later, influential philosophers such as Kuno Fischer thought they could dismiss it without inspection, as a product of senility – after all, had not Kant himself completed the critical philosophy with his *Critique of Judgment?*

But more sympathetic thinkers, too, found it difficult to make sense of Kant's text, for the various sheets and fascicles of the manuscript were not preserved in the order of their composition, making it seem impossible to determine the chronological (and logical) order of his reasoning.

Nevertheless, an edition of the *Opus postumum* was begun in 1882 by Rudolf Reicke – only to come to an abrupt end two years later, when the manuscript was sold by Kant's heir to an uncooperative buyer. Quarrels with the new owner – which reached the highest court in the country – also prevented inclusion of the text in the newly started Academy edition of Kant's works. When these quarrels were finally overcome twenty years later, disagreements within the Academy further delayed its publication for more than a decade.

Eventually the entire manuscript was published in 1936–8, on the eve of World War II. Again a considerable amount of time went by before the first major studies based on this new edition came out. Only in the second half of the twentieth century, it seems, has Kant's text begun to attract the philosophical attention one would expect, with translations of it being published in French (1950 and 1986), Italian (1963), and Spanish (1983).

As the extraordinary history of Kant's *Opus postumum* has never been told in its entirety, I describe it in some detail in the next section of this introduction. Then follows a brief account of the format and composition of the manuscript, together with the features that permitted Erich Adickes, in 1916, to reestablish its chronological order. Adickes's chronology is generally accepted today, and I have adopted it for the present edition (with one minor exception) even though the Academy editors decided not to follow it. In the third section, I attempt to locate the *Opus postumum* in the context of Kant's other writings and to suggest the reasons why, so late in his life, he decided to engage in another major work. A brief account of the development of Kant's argument in the *Opus postumum* concludes this introduction.

THE HISTORY OF THE MANUSCRIPT[1]

During the last years of Kant's life, only a few of his colleagues and table companions knew that he was working intensely on another major critical work. In 1790, in the preface to his *Critique of Judgment*, he had written: "With this, then, I bring my entire critical undertaking to a close. I shall hasten to the doctrinal part, in order, as far as possible, to snatch from my advancing years what time may yet be favorable to the task."[2] Yet eight years later Kant writes in a letter to Christian Garve of a "pain like that of Tantalus" on seeing before him "the unpaid bill of my uncompleted philosophy" while he was convinced of the possibility of its completion. "The project on which I am now working . . . must be completed," he writes, "or else a gap will remain in the critical philosophy."[3]

This remaining "gap" in the critical undertaking is also mentioned a month later in a letter to Kant's former pupil Kiesewetter. "The transition from the metaphysical foundations of natural science to physics," Kant explains here, as a special part of *philosophia naturalis*, "must not be left out of the system. . . . [W]ith that work the task of the critical philosophy will be completed and a gap that now stands open will be filled."[4]

Kant's first plans for such a "Transition," however, apparently date back several years earlier. For in June 1795 Kiesewetter had already reminded Kant that "for some years now" he had promised to present the public "with a few sheets which are to contain the transition from your *Metaphysical Foundations of Natural Science* to physics itself."[5]

It was apparently not until 1796, however, that Kant, who retired from teaching in the same year, began to work systematically on the projected "Transition." From then on, this task occupied him virtually until his death. His table companions of these years, who usually gathered in Kant's study before lunch, often found him still writing on their arrival. One of them, J. G. Hasse, later reported that for "several years" he saw on Kant's desk a huge pile of closely written folio sheets, and that he was allowed occasionally to leaf through the papers. Hasse also mentioned that in their familiar circle Kant often spoke of his manuscript as "his 'chief work, a *chef d' oeuvre*,' " which was "an (absolute) whole completing his system [and] only needed to be edited (which he still hoped to be able to do himself)."[6]

R. B. Jachmann, a former pupil of Kant's and one of his early biographers, gives a similar account: "The immortal man often spoke to me with true enthusiasm of his last work which, according to him, was to be the keystone of his entire system, and which was to demonstrate conclusively the tenability and real applicability of his philosophy."[7]

Kant's enthusiasm was not untroubled, however. In 1798, he expressed doubts in a letter to Lichtenberg about whether his deteriorating strength would permit him to complete his project.[8] And E. A. C. Wasianski, Kant's executor and a frequent visitor in the philosopher's house during the last years of his life, recalls that Kant was undecided about the future of his manuscript: at times believing that it was almost completed and only required brushing up, at other times requesting that it be burned after his death. Wasianski, too, reports Kant's conviction that this was "his most important work," but adds that "his weakness probably played a great part in this judgment."[9]

After Kant's death, Wasianski presented the manuscript to Johann Schultz, professor of mathematics and court chaplain in Königsberg, whom Kant had once described as his best interpreter.[10] On examination of the text, Schultz advised against publication on the grounds that it was "only the first beginning of a work whose introduction was not yet completed, and which was incapable of being edited."[11] To Hasse he explained that he found "nothing in it of what the title promised."[12] Both these remarks suggest that Schultz's examination of the text was anything but thorough. However, his advice was followed, and the manuscript disappeared for several decades in the possession of Kant's heirs. When Kiesewetter returned to Königsberg only three years after Kant's death, this time fleeing from Berlin with his king, Friedrich Wilhelm III, in the face of the rapidly invading Napoleonic troops, he used the opportunity to search for Kant's last work – without success. The whereabouts of the manuscript seemed to be unknown, and remained so for half a century.[13]

Wasianski had delivered the papers to Carl Christoph Schoen, Kant's brother Johann Heinrich's son-in-law, who lived in the Russian province of Kurland. After Schoen's death fifty years later, his daughter discovered Kant's work in her father's library, hidden under piles of books.[14] With it, she found the remains of Schoen's own attempts to edit and revise the text for publication – a task he apparently had soon abandoned. Now the family decided that the manuscript should be sold. As they wished to remain anonymous, an agent in Berlin was entrusted with the task of finding an appropriate buyer. Soon several local papers advertised the "discovery" of a new Kantian manuscript, and a year later, in 1858, two renowned Kant scholars published short descriptions of its size and outward appearance.[15]

Yet these efforts did not bear fruit: Potential buyers – among them the *Königliche Bibliothek* in Berlin – found the price to be greatly in excess of their means, with the result that the manuscript soon disappeared once again from the scene.

Meanwhile rumors began to circulate that Kant's last work was a product of senility. In this vein, one of the most influential philosophers of the time, Kuno Fischer, wrote in his *Geschichte der neuern Philosophie* (1860):

One may doubt the value of this [i.e., Kant's last] work . . . without previous inspection if one considers both the frail state Kant was in at the time, and the completion to which he himself had brought the philosophy which he had founded. . . . Competent men who read the very voluminous manuscript just after Kant's death have testified that it merely repeats the contents of the earlier works in a form which bears the marks of decrepitude.[16]

In 1864, finally, the Königsberg librarian Rudolf Reicke learned of the whereabouts of the manuscript, and a few months later Schoen's daughter agreed to lend it to him for publication. A scholarly edition of Kant's unfinished work seemed at last assured. Yet for sixteen years nothing happened. Eventually Reicke reported his possession of the manuscript in the *Altpreussische Monatsschrift*. His initial hope to extract from the various fascicles one coherent text, he wrote, had on closer inspection met with serious difficulties; his endeavors were set aside until better days and "eventually forgotten in favor of other tasks." In the end he abandoned his plan to work the various papers into a book; "instead," he now wrote, "the entire manuscript will appear in this journal in a series of articles."[17]

Not the least of the difficulties that frustrated Reicke's initial hopes of editing Kant's text was the fact that the chronological order of the various sheets and fascicles had been hopelessly corrupted: Over the years, many people had taken sheets from the manuscript for inspection and returned them to the wrong places,[18] and an unusual amount of dirt on one fascicle suggests that the manuscript may have fallen to the ground at one time, and then been shoved together again in an arbitrary way.[19] The arrangement of the text in Reicke's hands in no way corresponded to the order of its composition, and this, together with the fact that it was unedited, made its comprehension virtually impossible.

So why did Reicke decide, after sixteen years, to publish the text after all? Fortunately, we know from the correspondence of his close friend Emil Arnoldt of the circumstances that surrounded this decision.[20] Meanwhile, Schoen's grandson Paul Haensell had inherited Kant's manuscript from his mother and presented Reicke with an ultimatum: Reicke must either publish the text immediately or return it to its owner so that another scholar who had expressed interest in the task could be entrusted with it.

Reicke called on Arnoldt for help, and soon they reached the following agreement: Reicke was to provide a transcript of the text (a task for which he enlisted the help of his son and a cousin) and Arnoldt was to prepare the transcript for publication. Furthermore, it was decided that the text should appear in a number of installments in the *Altpreussische Monatsschrift*, of which Reicke was an editor.[21] Beginning in January 1882, there appeared over the next two years the XIIth, Xth, XIth, IInd, IXth, IIIrd, Vth, Ist, and VIIth fascicles (in that order).

In many ways, the edition was a fiasco. Arnoldt had adopted the editorial principle of making Kant appear "as dignified [*würdig*] as seems possible" while at the same time preserving some of the text's peculiarities. To this end, he deleted passages from Reicke's transcript and changed the punctuation and occasionally entire sentences – without always indicating his emendations, and without once consulting the original. Not surprisingly, he himself regarded his edition as "merely provisional." At his request, only Reicke's name appeared as editor in the *Altpreussische Monatsschrift*. As Arnoldt later put it in a letter to Kuno Fischer:

One must consider the way in which the text is edited: no one knows the content of the manuscript exactly; in what order the fascicles are to be printed is determined almost entirely by external criteria. . . . And now emendations are provided in the text by someone who has not inspected the manuscript as a whole, nor could have done so, since one cannot make sense of the manuscript as we have it – by someone, that is, who does not in the least know beginning, middle, or end of the manuscript. How can good emendations result from such treatment of the text?[22]

The publication, in a provincial journal with a limited readership, caused no sensation; virtually no one took any notice – except Albrecht Krause, a pastor and amateur philosopher in Hamburg. In June 1883, Krause wrote to Reicke to suggest a separate edition of Kant's text in the form of a book, to facilitate its study. Reicke, grateful for the sign of interest in his undertaking, nevertheless declined. Because of the "repetitiveness" of the material, he now wrote to Krause, no more than about two-fifths of Kant's text would be published in the *Altpreussische Monatsschrift;* a separate edition was not intended.[23]

Immediately Krause wrote to the Prussian minister for cultural affairs. He reminded the minister that Kant had dedicated his *Critique of Pure Reason* to a predecessor in the minister's office. Krause urged him to initiate an unabridged edition of Kant's last work in one volume, and to provide Reicke with the time and means to carry out the task. Although only twenty sheets had thus far appeared in the *Altpreussische Monatsschrift*, Krause was confident that the *Opus postumum* was "the deepest and most far-reaching of all of Kant's writings," and he concluded: "Your Excellency, such a manuscript must not be the possession of an individual, nor its content the possession of a library."[24]

At the same time, Krause prepared a polemical attack on Kuno Fischer.

The result, published in 1884, bore the title *Immanuel Kant wider Kuno Fischer, zum ersten Male mit Hülfe des verloren gewesenen Hauptwerkes: Vom Übergang von der Metaphysik zur Physik verteidigt*. What the book did not mention was the fact that Krause had already "defended" Kant against Fischer on a previous occasion, although at that time anonymously and without the help of Kant's "*Hauptwerk*." To his earlier claim that Fischer failed to comprehend fundamental aspects of Kant's theory, Krause now added the charge that Fischer had "neither the will, nor the diligence, nor the objectivity"[25] required to comprehend it: Although several fascicles of the *Opus postumum* had meanwhile become accessible, the third edition of Fischer's *Geschichte*, published in 1880, repeated almost verbatim the first edition's negative assessment of Kant's last work, and Fischer's *Kritik der kantischen Philosophie* of 1883 did not even mention it.

Fischer responded immediately with *Das Streber- und Gründerthum in der Literatur: Vade mecum für Herrn Pastor Krause in Hamburg*,[26] a booklet every bit as shrill and personal as Krause's onslaught. Again, Fischer was unwilling to reconsider his *a priori* assessment of the *Opus postumum*, and largely because of this, in the end, Krause appeared to have the edge in the dispute. Although the philosophical weights were quite unevenly distributed between the two of them, Krause presented himself not without skill as Kant's sole defender against the charge of senility – indeed, as the only person who at that time recognized the importance of Kant's last work – and as such he has lived on in the literature. His true motives in his dispute with Fischer have never been questioned.[27]

Before these two texts appeared, however, another turn of events had further complicated the situation.[28] When Reicke returned the first published fascicles to their owner, Haensell indicated that he might sell the manuscript after its complete publication to the British Museum. Reicke secretly contacted Krause and proposed that he buy the manuscript for 800 marks to prevent it from going abroad. Unknown to anyone else, Krause and Haensell entered into negotiations. As the pastor requested to see the manuscript before committing himself, Haensell and Reicke sent him their respective fascicles, except two that Reicke was currently copying. Krause decided at once: He sent 800 marks to Haensell and thus became the new owner of the *Opus postumum*. Immediately he advertised his acquisition in the local papers and announced a new, unabridged edition of Kant's text, although a clause in the contract had stipulated that Reicke should complete his publication in the *Altpreussische Monatsschrift*, and to this end keep the unedited fascicles for three more years. Haensell attempted unsuccessfully to annul the contract, and although Reicke, with the help of a lawyer, received two more fascicles from Krause, Arnoldt decided to take no further part in the edition. The last installment of the *Opus postumum* in the *Altpreussische Monatsschrift* (1884) ends with the cryptic remark: "To be continued – when is still uncertain." It was never continued. Four years later, Krause published his own text: not, indeed, the unabridged edition he had promised, but a "popular presentation" of parts of the manuscript, with excerpts from Kant and his own interpretations thereof on opposite pages.[29]

It was only a few years later (1894) that the Royal Prussian Academy of Science decided on a critical edition of Kant's complete works under the direction of Wilhelm Dilthey. It was conceived in four divisions: published works, correspondence, *Nachlass,* and lectures. Planned as a long-term project, the edition was designed to include previously unpublished, newly discovered, or perhaps still-unknown material.[30] In 1896, the Kant Kommision of the Academy publicly announced its plan and called for help from those in possession of *Kantiana.* It seemed that the *Opus postumum* would at last receive its overdue scholarly publication. These hopes were soon disappointed. In return for his cooperation, Krause requested the right to decide who should edit Kant's text.[31] The Academy, which in 1896 had appointed Erich Adickes as editor of Kant's *Nachlass,* was unwilling to make this concession. When further negotiations proved fruitless, it brought a lawsuit against Krause to establish its right to publication. The Academy won at the trial level, but the decision was reversed by the intermediate court of appeals, and shortly before his death in 1902, Krause's victory was upheld by the highest court in the country. This whole incident is not without irony, for the Royal Academy was represented in court by the Prussian minister of cultural affairs[32] – the successor in office to the man to whom Krause had written nineteen years before: "Your Excellency, such a manuscript must not be the possession of an individual, nor its content the possession of a library."

After Krause's death, things once again quieted down. Meanwhile, the Academy edition was beginning to take shape; the first volume had appeared in 1900 (Correspondence); the first *Nachlass* volume came out in 1911.

Editing the handwritten notes and reflections that Kant had recorded over more than half a century was a task for which Adickes had initially allotted four years; it was to occupy him until his death thirty-two years later. The sheer complexity of the material, and the wealth of allusions to, and quotations from, texts and figures familiar to Kant but mostly forgotten in the meantime, made it seem necessary to Adickes to complement his edition with three monographs that brought this background to light again. Work on one of them, *Kant als Naturforscher,* led Adickes to the *Opus postumum.* Reicke's edition soon proved to be inadequate; many problems in Kant's text could only be solved, Adickes realized, if the order of its composition could be reconstructed. He therefore contacted Krause's widow, and in the summer of 1916 Adickes was able to travel to Hamburg to inspect the manuscript at first hand. During the four weeks available to him, he succeeded in the immensely important task of reestablishing the chronological order of the various fascicles – "to an extent and with a degree of certainty that far exceeded my wildest expectations."[33] In particular, Adickes realized that the commencement of Kant's work on the "Transition" fell into a period when his philosophical powers could not be in question; further neglect of this work by Kant scholars was, therefore, entirely without justification.

Adickes reported his results to the Academy and urged it to try once again to have Kant's text included in its edition. The Kant Kommission, meanwhile led by a new generation of scholars, responded negatively.[34] Three years later, Adickes was approached by a publisher who had heard of the *Opus postumum* and was eager to publish it. Before making contact with the Krause family, Adickes wrote to the Academy again, urging it to reverse its decision and offering his services as a go-between in negotiations with the Krauses.[35]

Only after another letter from Adickes did the Academy respond. Feeling that on the whole "most scholarly *opera postuma* had better remain unpublished," it preferred to wait for its final decision until after the publication of Adickes's announced study of the *Opus postumum*.[36] That study appeared the following year (1920). In it, Adickes emphasized once more that "an unabridged, diplomatic publication of the entire material, according to strict philological criteria," was an "urgent scientific desideratum" and an "obligation of honor towards Kant." And, he pointed out, the chronological reordering of Kant's text that he presented here for the first time now provided "the previously missing basis for such an edition."[37] It took another three years, however, before the Academy decided that it would indeed be desirable to include the text in its edition.

These three years of indecision also happened to be the years of the great inflation that crippled Germany in the aftermath of World War I, leaving virtually no household unaffected. So, when the Kant Kommission finally decided to act in 1923, it found to its surprise that the Krause family had sold the rights of publication of the *Opus postumum* for 1,000 gold marks to de Gruyter, the press that also published the Academy edition.[38]

This set the stage for the final round of complications. De Gruyter was determined to publish the work, if necessary outside the Kant edition. To avoid this, the Academy had to meet the press's requirements, the most important of which was that the *Opus postumum* remain in Berlin where it had been insured for 12,000 gold marks. The Academy, on the other hand, wished to secure the involvement of Adickes, who was editing Kant's other *Nachlass* in Tübingen. Eventually the Academy and the publisher reached an agreement: Both Adickes and Artur Buchenau, the consultant and editor for the press who had brought about the deal with Krause's heirs, would be responsible for preparing the manuscript for publication – Buchenau in Berlin, Adickes in Tübingen. The provision that Adickes was to superintend the process and have the final decision at all stages, as the president of the Kant Kommision had assured him in writing,[39] was not included in the final contract between the publisher and the Academy, nor in that between de Gruyter and Buchenau.[40]

Problems soon developed. To copy the manuscript, Buchenau employed a 23-year-old scientist, Gerhard Lehmann, as his assistant. Lehmann's transcript was completed in 1924; in December 1924 Buchenau began to compare it with the original and with the previous transcriptions of Reicke and Krause. As Adickes's correspondence with Buchenau shows, he was not satisfied with some of the transcripts that were sent to him. He also considered it extremely unprofessional that Buchenau and Lehmann published separately, under the title *Der alte Kant*, Kant's personal notes from fascicles VII and I – notes that, as they put it in their preface, "all previous editors have regarded as proof of the senile character of Kant's last work."[41] But more serious tensions developed when Buchenau informed Adickes in the summer of 1925 that he intended to deviate from the editorial principles on which Adickes had based the previous volumes of Kant's *Nachlass*. Most important, Buchenau planned to keep the fascicles in the order in which he had received them, rather than rearrange the material in accordance with Adickes's chronology. Adickes, who had been assured in writing by the Academy that his editorial principles would be adopted for the *Opus postumum*,[42] saw no further basis for his involvement with the project. On June 19, 1926, he informed the Kant Kommission of the Academy that he resigned from his "superintendence" of the edition of the *Opus postumum*.[43]

The disagreements between Buchenau and Adickes left their permanent mark on the Academy edition. Initially announced for 1925,[44] the *Opus postumum* eventually appeared in 1936 and 1938 – almost a decade after Adickes's death in 1928 – as Volumes 21 and 22 of the edition, sandwiched between two volumes of "Vorarbeiten und Nachträge." Several passages are printed twice: in the *Opus postumum* and as *Reflexionen* in the volumes edited by Adickes; the transcriptions differ substantially.[45] Most important, the editors of the *Opus postumum* broke with the editorial principles that governed all previous *Nachlass* volumes. They did not do so consistently, however, with the result that conflicting editorial principles are at work even in the *Opus postumum* itself: The various leaves of the IVth fascicle are reproduced in the chronological order that Adickes established for them.[46]

More than 130 years after Kant's death, the text of his *Opus postumum* was finally available for serious study. Although one perhaps need not agree with Lehmann that "dark forces dominated the fate of Kant's last work,"[47] human failings clearly contributed as much to its long-delayed reception as did the special nature and format of the text.

THE COMPOSITION OF THE MANUSCRIPT

Early descriptions of the *Opus postumum* vary as to its format; the original manuscript seems to have been more extensive. A number of sheets that clearly belong to the manuscript but were not contained in it when the Academy undertook its transcription were subsequently published in Volume 23 of the Academy edition as "Ergänzungen zum Opus Postumum" (1955). Adickes also knew of various loose leaves in the possession of libraries in Berlin and in Königsberg of which Lehmann and Buchenau did not make use.[48] These leaves were lost during World War II. A few have since been rediscovered;[49] others may be lost forever.

The manuscript as it has been handed down to us consists of thirteen fascicles. The last one contains only a single sheet with notes for *The Conflict of the Faculties* (1798); it is not part of the "Transition" project and hence does not belong to the *Opus postumum* proper.

All fascicles consist of folios, varying between one (XIII) and thirteen (V) in number. In addition, the Vth, VIIth, and Xth fascicles contain some quartos; a number of small leaves (address pages of letters, etc.) are contained in the IVth and Xth fascicles. Kant also wrote on the wrappers of the Ist and IVth fascicles. All in all, the transmitted manuscript contains 527 written pages (1,161 pages in the Academy edition).[50]

To a large extent, Kant's text reflects the working style he appears to have found congenial throughout his career, which he also recommended in his lectures to his students: "First one writes down all thoughts as they come, without any order. Thereafter one begins to coordinate and then to subordinate."[51] That is to say, Kant typically wrote thoughts, notes, excerpts, or simply key words on whatever paper he might have available at the time – on loose leaves, in the margins of books or manuscripts, in the empty spaces of letters he received, and so forth – which he later worked into drafts of a continuous text. These drafts were then revised and incorporated into a clean copy (*Reinschrift*), which was still further revised. The next stage was for an amanuensis – usually one of Kant's students – to copy the text (*Abschrift*). In this Kant made further, often important, emendations, changes, and deletions in order to improve the text. Either this corrected version or a new clean copy was then sent to the printer. Depending on his time and involvement with the material, Kant might correct the proofs himself or delegate the task. (For example, he had Kiesewetter read the proofs of the third *Critique*.)[52]

The *Opus postumum* reflects all but the last two stages of this process, from loose leaves and marginal notes to an amanuensis's copy of part of the manuscript (sheets VIII, IX, and X of the Vth fascicle), including Kant's corrections thereof. Unlike his published works, which only present the reader with the polished end product of his labors, the *Opus postumum* therefore shows Kant at work over a number of years, providing us with a unique insight into the genesis of a major text.[53]

As a consequence, the text that we have is often repetitious, reflecting Kant's seemingly ceaseless attempts to find ever better formulations for his thoughts. Moreover, his emendations of, or additions to, what he had previously written sometimes resulted in truly monstrous sentences. One sentence in the Xth fascicle, for instance, contains no fewer than 225 words but only one comma – obviously unproblematic for Kant, a genuine test of the interpretive skills of the reader, a nightmare for the translator. The many later additions in the text also show that Kant frequently returned to the material he had written earlier – often months after its original conception.

In all this, the *Opus postumum* does not differ significantly from preserved drafts of Kant's earlier works. The "Duisburg'sche Nachlass," for example, a 1775 preliminary sketch for the *Critique of Pure Reason*, was characterized by its first editor in terms that apply equally to Kant's last work:

Kant's working style in the early '70s [was] one unbelievably slow in progression. . . . It is characteristic of these unpublished papers . . . that he sought to find, and did find, the proper expression, even for ideas already conceived in thought, by means of continuously revised, *written* formulations. This accounts for the endless repetitions in his unpublished manuscripts; and his published writings too, above all the critical [writings], provide ample evidence of this working method in the very manner of their conception.[54]

Kant's *Reflexionen* on physics, also written in the 1770s, exhibit the same features.[55]

In writing the *Opus postumum*, Kant usually left margins of an inch and a half at the top and on at least one side (sometimes on all sides) of his sheets; in this he wrote key words as reminders for a later, lengthier treatment of a certain topic,[56] corrections of the main text, or alternative formulations – also additional thoughts, occasionally, at a later time and on different topics. The margins thus functioned *quasi* as Kant's notebook, whereas the main part of the sheet contains his drafts for a continuous text – or discontinuous text, for it is noteworthy that on the folios – huge sheets of paper that were folded once to yield four pages – Kant hardly ever carried over a sentence from one sheet (or even page) to the next. With only a few exceptions, each sheet/page was intended to contain a complete thought or set of paragraphs – most likely to facilitate a later comparison of various drafts or sketches on the same topic.[57] This is also suggested by the fact that Kant left parts of pages or whole pages empty, to be filled later with the text that should be there, using only the margins at the time to record key words. If, on the other hand, space became scarce in the process of developing a thought, Kant would begin to write smaller and smaller or between the lines and paragraphs of the page; if a new page *had* to be used, he would continue in its margin rather than in the main part of the page, and connect the continuation with the previous page by means of any of various signs.[58]

The later fascicles also contain in the margins occasional notes on household affairs,[59] lists of potential luncheon guests with their favorite dishes, reminders for conversation topics, and such like. These notes were often deleted after they had fulfilled their function.

The main text is, in Adickes's words, "written almost throughout in his best, broad handwriting, in the style of letters and official records (which Kant kept as rector, for example) – current or later additions in the margins usually considerably sketchier."[60]

Kant used various papers as wrappers for the different fascicles; they were later numbered consecutively ("Ist fascicle," etc.) by an unknown hand. The wrappers are, in the order of the fascicles:

    I Invitation to a commemorative address for the Prussian secretary of state Jacob Friedrich von Rohd, May 22, 1801

    II Invitation to celebrate the king's birthday, August 3, 1803

    III Waste sheet of a sermon: "Anhang: Das pflichtmässige Verhalten eines Christen gegen Feinde, Hasser und Widersacher"

    IV Medical doctor's diploma for T. M. Hübschmann, a student of Kant's colleague K. G. Hagen, *Quasimodogeniti*, 1798

    V Page of *Königsberger Intelligenz-Blatt*, August 10, 1799

    VI Page of *Königsberger Intelligenz-Blatt*, April 14, 1800

    VII Page of *Königsberger Intelligenz-Blatt*, July 11, 1801

    VIII Page of *Königsberger Intelligenz-Blatt*, February 4, 1799

    IX Doctor's diploma in philosophy for G. F. Parrot, signed (by the dean J. G. Hasse) *Quasimodogeniti*, 1801

    X Page of *Königsberger Intelligenz-Blatt*, October 7, 1799

    XI Poem composed by Professor Poerschke in honor of the birthday of King Friedrich Wilhelm III on August 3, 1801

    XII Page of *Königsberger Intelligenz-Blatt*, June 24, 1799

Although almost all of the wrappers contain dates, they do not permit an inference as to the time when the sheets they hold together were composed. In some cases they seem to have replaced older, and probably damaged wrappers; more often than not they contain sheets that were composed at different times and ended up together by mistake or oversight. Adickes's chronological rearrangement of Kant's text had to rely on a number of different criteria. To some extent it was facilitated by the fact that Kant marked the sequence of several sheets with various designations. Thus it is likely that draft "Übergang 11," for example, precedes "Übergang 12," whereas draft "C" was almost certainly written later than draft "A." A few sheets contain dates; several others permit reliable dating because they contain notes for existing letters or are written on letters to

Kant, references to or excerpts from recently published books or reviews, or drafts for Kant's own publications. Others can sometimes be seen to fit between datable drafts on the basis of textual criteria, representing a stage between a first recognition of a problem and its eventual solution. Where such criteria were unavailable, Adickes compared the ink and writing pattern in the *Opus postumum* with other datable material from Kant's *Nachlass* that was available to him.[61] His results – which he emphasized are "approximations" – are as follows:

Approximate Dates	*Designations, etc.*
1786–96	23 leaves (IVth fascicle)
1796–7	*Oktaventwurf*
July 1797 – July 1798	"A–C," "α-ε"
April–October 1798	Wrapper, IVth fascicle
August–September 1798	4 leaves (IVth and IInd fascicles)
	Sheet 3 (IInd fascicle)
	"a–c"
September–October 1798	"No.1–No.3η,"
	"1" (Sheet 2, Vth fascicle)
October–December 1798	"Elem. Syst. 1–7"
December 1798 – January 1799	"Farrago 1–4"
January–February 1799	"A, B Übergang"
February–May 1799	"A Elem. Syst. 1–6"
May–August 1799	"Übergang 1–14"
August–September 1799	"Redactio 1–3"
August 1799 – April 1800	Xth/XIth fascicles
April–December 1800	VIIth fascicle
December 1800–3	Ist fascicle
1803	Wrapper, Ist fascicle

With one small exception,[62] I have seen no reason to diverge from the chronological *order* Adickes established, although his characterization of the different periods needs amendment in at least two cases.

1. Adickes divides the early leaves of the IVth fascicle into two groups: (a) 18 leaves from 1786–95, "which stand in no relation to the Op. p."; (b) 5 leaves from 1795–6 with "*Vorarbeiten* to the Op. p." The *Opus postumum* proper, according to Adickes, begins with the *Oktaventwurf* of 1796–7.[63]

Adickes's reason for excluding the leaves under (a) from the *Opus postumum* altogether is that they contain no mention of a proposed science of "Transition" – the first such mention is in leaf number 36 – even though they treat the same problems as the later drafts.

This view, it seems to me, is built on a questionable assumption as to the type of "work" the *Opus postumum* in fact is. More important, it seems to conflict with the fact that, as I mentioned, Kiesewetter reminded Kant in June 1795 that "for some years now" Kant had promised to present the public "with a few sheets which are to contain the transition from your *Metaphysical Foundations of Natural Science* to physics itself." Kiesewetter had studied with Kant in 1788–9 and again visited him for one month in the fall of 1790. Kant must have mentioned his project of a "Transition" to Kiesewetter on one of these occasions, for shortly after Kiesewetter's return to Berlin in 1790, Kant broke off his relations with Kiesewetter, and he did not write to him again until December 1793.[64] There is no mention of a "Transition" in this letter, and a later communication that could have been lost would not fit Kiesewetter's expression "for some years." The tone of Kiesewetter's letter also rules out the possibility that he had heard of Kant's project from a third person. It seems, therefore, that Kant must have had the plan to write a "Transition" at least in the fall of 1790, if not already in 1788–9. The early leaves of the IVth fascicle from that period, therefore, cannot globally be excluded from the "Transition" project, especially as they address the same problems as Kant's later drafts.[65]

2. The second amendment concerns Kant's last fascicle. As Adickes writes, his limited time in Hamburg did not permit him to inspect this fascicle closely; his attempt to date it is based entirely on Reicke's edition. Pointing out that notes on the wrapper indicate that Kant worked as late as 1803 on this fascicle, he adds: "Its main part, however, the first nine sheets, probably originates entirely in the year 1801."[66] This assumption is confirmed by the text of the Academy edition, which provides, or allows one to establish, the following dates for the Ist fascicle:

Sheets I–III:		none
Sheet IV:		"Saturday, March 21" [1801]
Sheet V:		after March 1801
Sheet VI:		none
Sheet VII:		"Monday, July 27" [1801]
Sheet VIII:		before "Michaelis" [Sept. 29, 1801]
Sheet IX,	page 1:	mid-November 1801
Sheet X,	page 1:	January 1802
	page 3:	April 1802
Sheet XI,	page 4:	June 3, 1802
Sheet XII,	pages 1–3:	none
Wrapper,	page 1:	April 1803.

The *Opus postumum* was thus virtually completed by the middle of 1801, a time when Kant still enjoyed a fair degree of physical and mental strength. Reports on his condition agree that it began to deteriorate during that year.[67] The biographies by Hasse and Wasianski on which the standard view of the "old" Kant is based cannot be used to assess the quality of the *Opus postumum:* They record the time after 1801.[68] Kant's last work must be judged entirely on its own merits.

THE PLACE OF THE MANUSCRIPT
IN KANT'S WORK

Whatever degree of importance one ultimately ascribes to the *Opus postumum* will depend, in large measure, on the extent to which one sees it as relating to Kant's other major writings, and as taking up problems previously unsolved or unaddressed in his philosophy. These relations are not obvious or in plain view; it may therefore be helpful to sketch here some of the reasons that led Kant to think, so late in his career, that another major work was required to complete his philosophical system. Such a sketch, clearly, can only be subjective and reflect the editor's interpretative viewpoint. The reader who wishes to approach Kant's text with as few preconceptions about it as possible is encouraged to skip this section.

Kant himself saw his unique contribution to philosophy in having asked for the first time whether metaphysics was possible at all – that is, whether and how it was possible to extend our knowledge by means of thinking alone, unaided by experience. In view of the absence of any clear progress in the long history of metaphysics, this question had to be settled, Kant insisted, before any further engagement in this field could be justified: "The world is tired of metaphysical assertions; it wants [to know] the possibility of this science, the sources from which certainty therein can be derived, and certain criteria by which it may distinguish the dialectical illusion of pure reason from truth."[69]

To this end, as Kant wrote to Lambert, a "quite special, though purely negative science"[70] was required; a new science that preceded metaphysics and, by means of a critical self-examination of reason, first of all established the origin, limit, and extent of possible *a priori* knowledge.

This project is carried out in Kant's *Critique of Pure Reason* (1781). Not the least of the fascination this text has exercised ever since stems from the considerable methodological problem it addresses and overcomes. For if the very *possibility* of metaphysics is to be examined, the investigation cannot itself be metaphysical: It cannot itself adopt or follow the metaphysical method; nor can the ground plan for such a "negative science," the "idea" according to which it is to be executed, be derived from any of the traditional systems of metaphysics – "the worst was," Kant recalled afterward, "that metaphysics, such as it then existed, could not assist me in the least."[71] On the other hand, without such an idea or plan the project is doomed from the start: "No one attempts to establish a science unless he has an idea upon which to base it" (A834).

Kant was, of course, acutely aware of this unique methodological challenge. When after more than a decade of intensive reflection the *Critique* had finally appeared, he wrote in proud awareness of the novelty of his undertaking that, in order to solve the problem of metaphysics, a "completely new science" had been required of which "previously not even the idea was known."[72]

The "idea" on which Kant based his investigation is the "idea of a transcendental philosophy" (A1, A13), "which may serve for a critique of pure reason" (A11) and thus help determine the fate of future metaphysics. More precisely, it is the idea of a particular kind of self-examination, or self-cognition, of reason: a special type of "knowledge which is occupied not so much with objects [*Gegenstände*] as with our *a priori* concepts of objects in general [*Gegenstände überhaupt*]." (A11–12)

Because metaphysics purports to be *a priori* knowledge of *objects*, the transcendental investigation must inquire into the possibility of such non-empirical reference to objects and must elucidate the conditions on which it depends. The concept of an "object in general" in Kant's definition of transcendental knowledge is consequently even wider in scope than the concept of logical possibility: It signifies the (as yet) indeterminate object of a judgment, the accusative of a thought (A290–2). Because thought in its judgments is always directed toward something, it inevitably has an intentional object, a *Gegenstand überhaupt*. The task for the transcendental inquiry is then to determine the conditions under which this concept of an "object in general" can become the concept of an object of our *a priori knowledge*. The *Critique of Pure Reason* thus establishes the criteria any metaphysics must meet to lay claim justifiably to knowledge of its objects.

To this end, it "isolates" the human cognitive faculties and examines their role in possible knowledge; it "abstracts from all objects that may be given" (A845) and in this sense differs from all metaphysical knowledge. But, more important, the "idea of transcendental knowledge" also "serves for a critique of pure reason" and yields the plan on which to base such a critique: Because we have three types of concepts that refer *a priori* to objects, namely, the concepts of space and time as forms of our sensibility (A85), the categories of the understanding (A85), and the ideas of reason (A338), there emerges in rough outline the plan for a *Critique of Pure Reason* in three divisions – transcendental aesthetic, transcendental analytic, and transcendental dialectic. In each of these divisions we have to ask whether the concepts in question refer to *Gegenstände überhaupt* – which have to be distinguished into phenomena and noumena (A294) – or only to one of the domains of this dichotomy.

Aware of the brilliance and novelty of his undertaking, Kant also knew that the plan on which he based his investigation into the possibility of metaphysics was likely to appear dark and obscure to the unprepared reader. Even before the *Critique* was completed, he reflected on another and more perspicuous way of presenting his results.[73] And the book had hardly left the press when Kant decided to publish a brief account of his results, based this time on a different plan – "a plan," he wrote, "according to which even popularity might be gained for this study."[74] The result is the *Prolegomena to Any Future Metaphysics* of 1783. In its preface, we read:

Something more belongs to a sound plan of a general critique of pure reason than one may generally assume. [Yet] a mere plan preceding the *Critique of Pure Reason* would be unintelligible, unreliable, and useless; it is all the more useful, [however], as a sequel. . . . With that work complete, I offer here a plan based on the analytic method, while the *Critique* itself had to be executed in the synthetic style.[75]

Accordingly, in the *Prolegomena* Kant adopts a different procedure. In order to answer the question of "whether such a thing as metaphysics [is] at all possible," he starts out from the synthetic *a priori* propositions of mathematics and the natural sciences – propositions, Kant alleges, that are uncontested. He then asks how these propositions are possible, in order to deduce from the principle that makes *them* possible the possibility of all other synthetic *a priori* propositions.[76] Because the propositions of metaphysics are synthetic and *a priori*, the conditions of the possibility of metaphysics must be elucidated in the course of this "regressive" or "analytic" procedure, just as they were in the course of the first *Critique*. Here in the *Prolegomena*, however, the rational sciences of the objects of experience (mathematics and physics) provide the criterion any science of nonempirical objects (metaphysics) has to meet.

To understand Kant's further development, it is essential to realize that he was working on the *Prolegomena* when the first review of the *Critique of Pure Reason* came to his attention. This review, published anonymously in the *Göttingischen Gelehrten Anzeigen*, had a significant impact on Kant's thinking. For it brought home to him the fact that the special sense he had given to the term "transcendental" had not been understood: "The word 'transcendental,' the meaning of which is so often explained by me [is] not once grasped by my reviewer."[77] Rather, the reviewer saw in Kant's position a "higher idealism" and allied it to Berkeley's idealism about *things*. This must have been especially painful to Kant, given that "the word 'transcendental,' which *with me* never means a reference of our knowledge to things, but only to the cognitive faculty, was meant to obviate this misconception."[78] In other words, the novelty of Kant's transcendental undertaking, the "idea" underlying the *Critique of Pure Reason* and especially the point of taking the concept of a *Gegenstand überhaupt* as the "supreme concept" (A290) of transcendental knowledge, had not been understood.

Kant's distress is clearly visible in the *Prolegomena*. He even considered retracting the term "transcendental" altogether and calling his philosophy "critical idealism" instead.[79] In the end, he did not do that; nevertheless, Kant drew an important lesson from the misunderstanding of his work. With the *Critique* executed and completed, Kant decided *post festum* to play down the idea that underlay it and that caused such difficulty for the reader, and to make the "plan" of the *Prolegomena* the defining paradigm of transcendental knowledge. Hence it is no longer the *a priori* reference to *Gegenstände überhaupt* with which transcendental knowledge is concerned, but the reference to possible experience: "The word 'transcendental' . . . does not signify something passing beyond all experience but something that indeed precedes it *a priori*, but that is intended simply to make knowledge of experience possible."[80] In other words, transcendental philosophy now becomes exclusively a theory that discerns the *a priori* conditions of possible experience.

To this shift of emphasis within Kant's account of transcendental knowledge there eventually must correspond one on the side of metaphysics too: Metaphysics proper is the science of the *supersensible* and thus is concerned with objects that lie beyond all boundaries of experience. Rational physics, the philosophy of corporeal nature, can no longer be a part of the metaphysical system, to which the first *Critique* had assigned it (see A846–7). It has to be treated separately and as independent of the system of general metaphysics – a task Kant carried out in the *Metaphysical Foundations of Natural Science* (1786). As he stated in its preface:

Metaphysics has engaged so many heads up till now and will continue to engage them not in order to extend natural knowledge . . . but in order to attain to a knowledge of what lies entirely beyond all boundaries of experience, namely God, freedom and immortality. If these things are so, then one gains when one frees general metaphysics from a shoot springing indeed from its own roots but only hindering its regular growth, and plants this shoot apart.[81]

Treating rational physics as a separate "shoot" also allowed Kant to counter the charges of the Göttingen review in a more appropriate manner than had previously been possible for him. The reviewer had compared Kant's idealism with that of Berkeley – a misunderstanding that seemed "unpardonable and almost intentional" to Kant. For unlike himself, Kant insisted in the *Prolegomena*, Berkeley could not even distinguish truth from illusion, because he regarded space as merely an empirical representation, not as *a priori* in origin, as one must. Perhaps not fully convincing in its initial formulation, during the next few years this argument, which culminates in the Refutation of Idealism of the second edition of the *Critique*, is further refined. The underlying thought remains the same: All empirical truth, that is, all experience, involves change. As such it requires something "permanent in perception" in relation to which the alterations can be determined. Time, the form of inner sense, does not make such determination possible – it has no metrics. Rather, what allows us to represent something as abiding during change is the *simultaneity* of its manifold. Yet we can only represent a manifold as simultaneous, Kant insists against Berkeley and all empirical idealists, because we have an *original*, that is, nonempirical, representation of space.[82]

Consequently, the *Metaphysical Foundations of Natural Science*, by laying out the *a priori* principles and forms of external intuition in their entirety, provides an "excellent and indispensable service" to transcendental philosophy itself: By providing "instances (cases *in concreto*) in which to realize the concepts and propositions of the latter (properly, transcendental philosophy), [it gives] to a mere form of thought sense and meaning." For we "must always take such instances from the general doctrine of body, i.e. from the form and principles of *external* intuition, and if these instances are not at hand in their entirety, [one] gropes, uncertain and trembling, among mere meaningless concepts."[83]

The *Metaphysical Foundations of Natural Science* provides this indispensable service by providing the "fundamental determination of a something that is to be an object of the external senses."[84] To this end the concept of an object of outer sense in general – matter – is carried through all the four functions of the categories, a new determination of matter being added with each chapter.[85]

Such a "fundamental determination of a something that is to be an object of the external senses," if it is conducted *a priori*, must correspond to the "rational," or *a priori*, part of the scientific study of the objects of the external senses, that is, physics – if physics indeed has, or requires, such a rational part. Kant is in no doubt that it does. Every science that deserves the name, he argues, must exhibit not only systematic unity but also necessity. Because all laws learned from experience are contingent, natural science, properly so called, requires a pure part on which its apodictic certainty can be based.

This pure part involves a dynamical theory of matter according to which all filling of space, that is, matter of any density, is possible only as a product of the interplay of two conflicting forces: attraction and repulsion. The mechanical, or atomistic, theory of matter, which tries to explain the filling of space in terms of impenetrable atoms and interspersed empty spaces, is claimed to be untenable. Although this theory has the admitted "advantage" of being able to explain with ease the differences of density in different types of matter, the price it has to pay for this advantage is intolerably high. With the concepts of absolute impenetrability and absolute emptiness, atomism lays at its foundation two concepts that can be confirmed by no experiment; moreover, it gives up all the proper forces of matter, thus functioning in effect as a barrier to the investigating reason of the physicist.[86] The dynamical theory of matter, by contrast, makes attraction and repulsion equally necessary and fundamental: With only the former, Kant argues, all matter would coalesce into a single point, leaving space empty; with only the latter, it would expand to infinity, again leaving space empty.

It is from this work, the *Metaphysical Foundations of Natural Science,* Kant later argues, that a transition to physics is required. In 1786, there is as yet no indication of such a plan. On the contrary, his remark in its preface that "I believe that I have completely exhausted this metaphysical doctrine of body, as far as such a doctrine ever extends"[87] seems to suggest that at that time he ruled out the possibility of further philosophical achievement in this field. And in the chapter entitled "Dynamics," Kant even warns that "one must guard against going beyond what makes the universal concept of matter in general possible."[88]

So why a "Transition" after all? An answer emerges if we attend once more to the two features that, according to Kant, any doctrine of nature must exhibit in order to qualify as a science: apodictic certainty and systematic unity. Whereas the *Metaphysical Foundations* had accounted for the apodictic certainty associated with the fundamental laws of physics, it did not, nor could it, provide insight into the possibility of the systematicity of physics. Yet neither necessity nor systematicity can be gained empirically. No mere collection of empirical data, no aggregate of perceptions, can yield the systematic unity we expect to find among the various laws and propositions of physics. Such unity is of *a priori* origin; consequently, its possibility must be explained philosophically. For physics to be possible as a science, then, philosophy must provide principles for the investigation of nature; it must provide *a priori topoi* for the systematic classification of those specific forces of matter that can only be given empirically.

The *Metaphysical Foundations of Natural Science* did not suffice for this task – for two reasons. Although itself drawn up in a systematic way, it had merely analyzed the concept of "matter in general" in accordance with the table of categories. Hence it dealt only with attraction and repulsion in general. This does not supply physics with a guideline for a systematic investigation of the specific forces of nature. As Kant later wrote in the *Opus postumum:* "The transition to physics cannot lie in the *Metaphysical Foundations* (attraction and repulsion, etc.). For these furnish no specifically determined, empirical properties, and one can imagine no specific [forces], of which one could know whether they exist in nature, or whether their existence be demonstrable."[89]

But second, for the classification of the specific forces of nature, it is not enough that philosophy provide *a priori topoi* for their systematic investigation. We must also have *a priori* reason to expect that nature permits such classification; for "it is clear that the nature of reflective judgment is such that it cannot undertake to *classify* the whole of nature by its empirical differentiation unless it assumes that nature itself *specifies* its transcendental laws by some principle."[90]

Yet such a principle of nature's appropriateness to our cognition only emerged clearly when Kant addressed the problem of pure judgments of taste in the *Critique of Judgment* (1790). There he wrote, "Independent natural beauty reveals [*entdeckt*] to us a technic of nature that allows us to present nature as a system in terms of laws whose principle we do not find anywhere in our understanding: the principle of a purposiveness directed to our use of judgment as regards appearances."[91]

The analysis of judgments of taste for the first time showed the power of judgment to be a separate cognitive faculty with its own *a priori* principle: Nature, for the sake of judgment, specifies its universal laws to empirical ones, according to the form of a logical system.[92] This principle allowed Kant to regard as purposive and hence systematic the part of nature that from the standpoint of the first *Critique* and the *Metaphysical Foundations* had to be regarded as contingent.

The principle thus yields the precondition under which a systematic empirical doctrine becomes *a priori* thinkable. Only when this principle of a formal purposiveness of nature is set alongside Kant's general theory of matter does a "Transition" from the metaphysical foundations of natural science to physics become possible – indeed necessary, if his philosophy of nature is to be complete: "Judgment first makes it possible, indeed necessary, for us to think of nature as having not only a mechanical necessity but also a purposiveness; if we did not presuppose this purposiveness, there could not be systematic unity in the thoroughgoing classification of particular forms in terms of empirical laws."[93]

The principle of a formal purposiveness of nature, of nature as art, then, is not itself part of the "Transition"; rather it prepares the ground for the latter. By itself, this principle gives us no clue as to how we have to investigate nature in order to be systematically instructed by it. This principle "provides no basis for any theory, and it does not contain cognition of objects and their character any more than logic does; it gives us only a principle by which we [can] proceed in terms of empirical laws, which makes it possible for us to investigate nature."[94] In other words, there remained a task to be completed in the philosophy of nature – a task to be completed by the new work with the title, "Transition from the Metaphysical Foundations of Natural Science to Physics." It had to specify a method of bringing about the systematic knowledge of physics by providing the outline of a system of all objects of the outer senses.

If this reconstruction of the origin of Kant's plan for a "Transition" is correct, its initial conception could have been as early as the winter of 1787–8. For it was in December 1787, in a letter to K. L. Reinhold, that Kant first reported on his work on the third *Critique*. And since we can assume that Kant informed Kiesewetter of his plan to write a "Transition" during one of their conversations in Königsberg, we can be reasonably certain that it cannot have been much later, for Kiesewetter visited Kant for the last time in the fall of 1790.

Nevertheless, Kant did not begin to work systematically on the project until at least 1796. We do not know for certain whether it was largely academic duties and his other literary projects that prevented him from doing more at the time than record reflections on various leaves. But at least two theoretical problems may have contributed to the slow start of the "Transition."

The first problem is mentioned in Kant's correspondence with Jacob Sigismund Beck, who had taken on the task of preparing "Erläuternde Auszüge" of Kant's major writings. In a letter of September 8, 1792, Beck asks how he may understand the differences of density in matter on the basis of Kant's dynamical theory. Kant covers Beck's letter with extensive reflections on this problem.[95] In his answer of October 16, he writes, after acknowledging the importance of the question:

I would expect a solution to this problem in the following: that attraction (the universal, Newtonian) is originally the same in all matter, and only the repulsion of different [types of matter] is different and thus accounts for the specific differences of their density. But this leads in a way into a circle that I cannot get out of, and about which I still have to try to come to a better understanding.[96]

The explanation of the differences in density Kant gives here is the same that he gave in the *Metaphysical Foundations of Natural Science,* and it is not difficult to see where he locates the circle. The repulsive force, he had argued, acts only at the surface of contact – it being "all the same whether behind this surface much or little . . . matter is found." It may thus be originally different in degree in different types of matter.[97] The attractive force, on the other hand, goes beyond the surface and acts directly on all parts of a matter. It is "a penetrative force and for this reason alone is always proportional to the quantity of matter."[98] Yet this seems to lead into the circle that Kant laments in his letter to Beck, for his dynamical theory of matter also requires that only "[b]y such an action and reaction of *both* fundamental forces, matter would be possible by a determinate degree of the filling of space," hence by a determinate quantity.[99] In other words, attraction depends on density; and density, on attraction.

In his next letter, Beck suggests his own solution, which, however, does not find Kant's approval. In his reply of December 4, Kant writes:

By the end of the winter, before you begin with your *Auszug* of my *Metaphysical Foundations,* I shall inform you of the efforts I undertook in this regard [on the differences of density in matter] during the writing of this [book], but which I rejected, [and I] shall shortly send you my [first] introduction to the *Critique of Judgment.*[100]

That Kant intended to send the reflections on matter only several months later suggests that he hoped in the meantime to find a solution to his problem. On April 30, 1793, Beck reminds Kant of the two manuscripts he had promised to send – "one, which concerns the *Critique of Judgment,* and another one which concerns the metaphysics of nature."[101] On August 18, Kant sends Beck, "in accordance with my promise," only the first introduction to the third *Critique.*[102] Beck responds immediately, pointing out that he does not understand Kant's "concept of the quantity of matter." Kant does not reply.[103] Almost a year later, Beck writes again, reporting that he finally succeeded in understanding the *Metaphysical Foundations of Natural Science;* his "Erläuternder Auszug" of that work (and of the third *Critique*) appears in the fall of the same year.

All of this suggests that early in the 1790s, Kant's thinking on the philosophy of nature went through a transitional period. If this is correct, it would hardly be surprising if he wanted "to try to come to a better understanding" before embarking on the new project of a "science of transition."

The second problem that might account for the slow start of the project is more general. It can be felt clearly throughout the early drafts of the *Opus postumum.* In a way, the situation is not unlike the one Kant had faced years earlier when the possibility of metaphysics was at stake. Now the possibility of physics as a system needed to be accounted for. To this end, it had to be preceded by a "special science," namely, the "Transition from the Metaphysical Foundations of Natural Science to Physics." But this "science of transition," in turn, requires an "idea" or "plan" according to which it is to be executed. What can function as such an "idea"? This idea cannot be derived from physics itself, any more than the "idea of a transcendental philosophy" could be derived from metaphysics. Nor can it be derived from the *Metaphysical Foundations* from which the "Transition" commences: The concepts of attraction and repulsion "furnish no specifically determined, empirical properties, and one can imagine no specific [forces], of which one could know whether they exist in nature, or whether their existence be demonstrable."[104]

For a while, Kant hoped to achieve the desired systematic result by "follow[ing] the clue given by the categories and bring[ing] into play the moving forces of matter according to their quantity, quality, relation and modality."[105] But this turned out not to be enough, and Kant's struggle with the problem is palpable in the earlier fascicles of the text. And yet, perhaps more than anything else, it accounts for the unique fascination the *Opus postumum* exerts on the reader that, in the course of his reflections, we see Kant taken far beyond the problem he initially set out to solve. We are allowed to witness how his project develops in such a way that fundamental issues of transcendental philosophy have to be re-addressed, until in the end the title of a "Transition from the Metaphysical Foundations of Natural Science to Physics" is no longer adequate. Kant's efforts culminate in sketches of a new title for this, his last work – a work that, according to the testimony of his early biographers, he now regards as the keystone of his entire system.

It remains to outline briefly the development of Kant's argument in the *Opus postumum*.

THE DEVELOPMENT OF KANT'S ARGUMENT

Early leaves and Oktaventwurf

Perhaps the oldest part of Kant's manuscript is an excerpt from an anonymous review (1786) of his *Metaphysical Foundations of Natural Science* in which the reviewer questions the introduction of repulsion as a fundamental force of matter. The following leaves show Kant returning to such problems as cohesion, density, solidification, dissolution, fluidity, and heat: "My *Metaphysical Foundations etc.* already undertook several steps in this field, simply as examples of their [the *Foundations' a priori* principles'] possible application to cases from experience." Now these problems stand at the center of Kant's interest. Their renewed examination leads to several modifications of his earlier position that are worth mentioning.

1. Whereas in 1786 Kant was noncommittal as to the existence of an ether and regarded cohesion as a physical, not a metaphysical, property, which does not pertain to the possibility of matter in general,[106] he now argues that the possibility of cohesion, hence the possibility of matter of a particular *form*, depends on the living force (impact) of a universally distributed ether or caloric. Its supposition thus becomes "an inevitably necessary hypothesis, for without it, no cohesion, which is necessary for the formation of a physical body, can be thought." Contrary to Kant's previous explicit assertion, then, the *Metaphysical Foundations* cannot have been a "doctrine of body [*Körperlehre*],"[107] but only a theory of matter in general.

2. Because both fluid and rigid matters cohere, Kant in 1786 explained the difference between them in terms of a possible replacement of their respective parts: Unlike a fluid matter, a rigid matter resists the displacement of its parts due to their friction.[108] But friction already presupposes the property of rigidity, and it was for this reason that Kant admitted: "How rigid bodies are possible, is still an unsolved problem; in spite of the ease with which ordinary natural science believes itself to dispose of it."[109] In the early leaves and the *Oktaventwurf* of the *Opus postumum*, Kant begins to develop a theory of the rigidification of previously fluid matters in an effort to overcome the problem of the *Metaphysical Foundations*.

3. In the *Metaphysical Foundations of Natural Science*, Kant had declared that the quantity of matter must be estimated in comparison with every

other matter by its quantity of motion at a given velocity, hence by impulse and velocity.[110] But this explanation, because it makes quantity a mechanical property rather than a dynamical one, can hardly be plausible in a dynamical theory of matter that insists on attraction's being essential to matter, and constitutive of it. In the early drafts of the "Transition," Kant's position is consequently revised: The principal method of estimating a quantity of matter can only be by way of gravitation, that is, through weighing. Before long, this shift will lead to a special consideration of the instrument of weighing.

4. Does Kant now escape the "circle" in his theory of matter that he lamented in the letter to J. S. Beck of October 1792? Although he does not mention it explicitly in the *Opus postumum*, and although a complete answer to this problem only emerges later, it is possible to see even in these early drafts how he hopes to avoid the circle – namely, by treating attraction and repulsion both as superficial forces (cohesion and elasticity) and as penetrative forces (gravitation and heat), ultimately grounded in the unceasing pulsations (*alternating* attraction and repulsion) of a universally distributed ether or caloric.

The *Oktaventwurf* ends with drafts of a preface to the new work, explaining the requirement of a "Transition from the Metaphysical Foundations of Natural Science to Physics."

Towards the elementary system of the moving forces of matter

The topics from the early leaves and the *Oktaventwurf* are further developed in the following drafts ("A–C," "α–ε," "a–c," "No. 1 – No. 3η," "1"). Proper chapter headings and a continuous numbering of paragraphs reflect Kant's renewed optimism. The investigation, as Kant makes very clear, is to proceed according to the table of categories. Yet his efforts repeatedly come to a halt before the category of modality is reached. Quality, under which the aggregate states of matter are discussed, gives rise to a discomforting problem: Caloric [*Wärmestoff*], which keeps all matter fluid and whose escape causes matter to rigidify, can itself be neither fluid nor rigid. "How one can call it a fluid is unintelligible"; it is "*qualitas occulta.*"

Thus Kant is repeatedly forced to start all over again (a feature of the manuscript that could only be preserved to a small extent in a selection of the text). While problems of detail lead to an impasse in his theory, Kant continues to assure himself of the inescapable need for a "Transition," in the form of prefaces and introductions to the work at hand.

A significant change occurs in the following drafts, which now also receive a proper title: "Elementary System 1–7." Returning once again to a discussion of the quantity of matter, Kant introduces a new thought that foreshadows the epistemological turn his investigations are soon to take.

The concept of ponderability presupposes gravitational force, which makes a body heavy, but it *also* presupposes "an instrument for the measurement of this moving force" – scales and a lever-arm that are rigid and exert a repulsive force to resist the pressure of the heavy body. In fact, "the moving force of cohesion underlies all mechanism," hence all physical powers, and "even ponderability . . . will require the assumption of [an ether or caloric]."

With ponderability thus described, Kant has found a concept that properly belongs to the provenance of the elementary system, and hence to the "Transition from the Metaphysical Foundations of Natural Science to Physics." For it is a concept that is both *a priori* and "physically conditioned," requiring the assumption of a (relatively) imponderable matter responsible for the rigidity of the instrument of weighing.

This thought leads quickly to an expansion of the original "Transition" project. Because *any* physical body can be regarded as a system of the moving forces of matter, there seems to be no further reason to exclude the concept of *natural* machines, or living organisms, from the "complete division of the system of forces in general" (as Kant had done up to this point): "Organic bodies are natural machines, and, like other moving forces of matter, must be assessed according to their mechanical relationship, in the tendency of the metaphysical foundations of natural science."

The ether proofs

The sheets "Übergang 1–14" occupy a central position in the *Opus postumum*. On the one hand, Kant now provides *a priori* proofs of the existence of the ether, which, with its attributes, yield the long-sought idea or "principle" of the elementary system. On the other hand, the manuscript contains an amanuensis's copy of "Übergang 9, 10, 11" (with the "Introduction" to the "Transition") – usually one of the last steps before a text was sent to the publisher.

So, does the ether (or caloric) exist? The ether is not a hypothesis feigned to explain certain physical phenomena, Kant now argues, but a "categorically given material," because without it, no outer experience would be possible. Because empty space cannot be an object of experience, space, in order to be sensible, must be thought of as filled with a continuum of forces extended through the entire cosmos: The ether is the "hypostatized space itself." The unity of possible experience, which reason demands *a priori*, presupposes all moving forces of matter as combined in collective, not just distributive, unity. The ether is therefore also the "basis (first cause) of all the moving forces of matter," and as such the material condition of possible experience. And because experience can only be one (cf. A110), we must also presuppose a constant motion of all matter on the subject's sense organs, without which no perception would take place. In sum, the ether is "identically contained for reason, as a categorically and *a priori* demonstrable material."

Kant follows his proofs with reflections on their "strangeness" and "uniqueness," and with a repeated self-assurance that it is the singularity and uniqueness of this world-material that allows for an *a priori* demonstration of its existence. Yet the reader will not fail to notice a certain ambiguity on Kant's part as to whether his proof really establishes the existence of such a material "in itself" and outside the idea of it, or merely "in idea," and thus as a "thought-object."

How is physics possible? How is the transition to physics possible?

The ether proofs were meant to complete the elementary system of the moving forces of matter, and to pave the way for the subsequent "world-system." Yet, on the subsequent sheets "A–Z" and "AA–BB," Kant's thoughts take a different direction. Physics is to be a system; but we cannot know a physical system as such, except insofar as we produce it ourselves, in the combination of perceptions according to *a priori* principles. That is, the *topic* of concepts (of the moving forces of matter) "does not yet, on its own, found an experience"; rather, what has been "analytically investigated" (the elementary system) must also be "synthetically presented." But how? "How is physics possible?"

The first thing to realize, Kant emphasizes, is that the aggregate of the moving forces of matter is only appearance; the object of physics, the thing [*Sache*] in itself that the subject constitutes, is indirect appearance, or appearance of an appearance. "The objects of the senses, regarded metaphysically, are appearances; for physics, however, these objects are things [*Sachen*] in themselves." Hence, there arises the threat of an amphiboly, namely, to take what is given empirically ("appearances in the subject") for one and the same as what the subject makes: experience of an object, or the appearance of an appearance. But physics is constituted not *from* experience but *for* experience. The objective element in appearance presupposes the subjective element in the moving forces: "The doctrinal element in the investigation of nature in general presupposes in the subject an organic principle of the moving forces in [the form of] universal principles of the possibility of experience": "The moving forces of matter are what the moving subject itself does with its body to [other] bodies. The reactions corresponding to these forces are contained in the simple acts by which we perceive the bodies themselves."

How, then, is the transition to physics possible? It becomes possible, Kant now realizes, if we focus our attention on the moving subject, rather than on the object that moves. It is because the subject is conscious of agitating its own moving forces that it can anticipate the counteracting moving forces of matter. More precisely, a "Transition" becomes possible "insofar as the understanding presents its own acts – being the effects on the subject – in the concepts of attraction and repulsion, etc., in a whole of experience produced formally thereby."

In this act the subject constitutes itself as an empirical object – it becomes an appearance of an object for itself. Herewith space and time likewise become sensible. For, Kant writes, the positing of moving forces through which the subject is affected must precede the concept of the spatial and temporal relations in which they are posited. And it is the subject's own motion (its act of describing a space in a certain time) that combines both and makes them into a sense object. "The subject which *makes* the *sensible* representation of space and time for itself is likewise an object to itself in this act. Self-intuition. For, without this, there would be no self-consciousness of a substance."

The Selbstsetzungslehre

The theory of the subject's original self-positing is further developed in the VIIth fascicle. In its course, the notion of a thing in itself is also reexamined. The positing subject is a thing in itself because it contains spontaneity, but the thing in itself $= x$, as opposed to, or corresponding to, the subject, is not another object, Kant now argues, but a thought-entity without actuality, merely a principle: "the mere representation of one's own activity." It is the correlate of the pure understanding in the process of positing itself as an object. Its function is to "designate a place for the subject"; it is "only a concept of absolute position: not itself a self-subsisting object, but only an idea of relations."

Self-consciousness is the "act" through which the subject makes itself into an object. This act is at first merely a logical act, a thought without content. The "first progress in the faculty of representation" is that from pure thought in general to pure intuition: the positing of space and time as pure manifolds. Space and time are "products of our own imagination, hence self-created intuitions." Space is then determined by problematically inserting into it forces of attraction and repulsion, and by determining the laws according to which they act: "The forces already lie in the representation of space."

These forces are what affect the subject and allow it to think of itself as receptive and determinable. For only insofar as the subject can represent itself as affected can it appear to itself as corporeal, hence as an object of outer sense. It then progresses to knowledge of itself in the thoroughgoing determination of appearances, and of their connection into a unified whole. "The understanding begins with the consciousness of itself (*apperceptio*) and performs thereby a logical act. To this the manifold of outer and inner intuition attaches itself serially, and the subject makes itself into an object in a limitless sequence."

Practical self-positing and the idea of God

Yet the subject does not just constitute itself as an object of outer sense. It also constitutes itself as a person, that is, a being who has rights and duties. By determining its will in accordance with the categorical imperative, the subject can raise itself above all merely sensuous beings and become the "originator of his own rank." Thoroughgoing determination of my existence in space and time is consequently not the only thoroughgoing determination of myself: "*Every human being* is, in virtue of *his freedom* and of the law which *restricts* it, made subject to necessitation through his moral-practical reason."

Kant's main interest now, however, is in the idea that moral-practical reason inevitably generates in order to constitute itself as a person: the idea of God as the highest moral being. For it is through the categorical imperative that all rational world-beings are united, as standing in mutual relations of right and duty. But a command, to which "everyone must absolutely give obedience, is to be regarded by everyone as from a being which rules and governs over all. Such a being, as moral, however is called God. So there is a God."

The idea of God thus lies "at the basis" of the categorical imperative; the concept of unconditional duty is contained "identically" in the concept of a divine being: All human duties are prescribed as (if they were) divine commands. Whether God exists as a substance different from man, as a world-being, cannot be known; but for moral-practical reason, the *idea* of God is indispensable and inevitably given with the categorical imperative. Just as there is an all-comprehending nature (in space and time), there is also "an all-embracing, morally commanding, original being – a God." Like "the world," this original being is a maximum and can only be one. "The subject determines itself (1) by technical-practical reason, (2) by moral-practical reason, and is itself an object of both. The world and God."

What is transcendental philosophy?

The last fascicle Kant wrote – but which has been called the first fascicle because it lay on top of the manuscript – is the summation of his years of labor. Again there are clear indications (although now, increasingly, coupled with signs of decrepitude) of Kant's belief that his work could finally be completed: The name of the amanuensis to be used is recorded in the margin, and various sheets contain versions of a new title, of the table of contents, and of an introduction. The initial title "Transition from the Metaphysical Foundations of Natural Science to Physics" is no longer sufficient for the work at hand. This does not mean that the "Transition" is abandoned or that Kant at this time has plans for a second volume; the initial "Transition" is to become one of the parts of the larger work Kant now wants to call, for example, "The Highest Standpoint of Transcendental Philosophy in the System of Ideas: *God,* the *World,* and *Man* in the World, Restricting Himself Through Laws of Duty" – or, more simply, "System of Transcendental Philosophy in Three Sections."

Kant's account of theoretical and practical self-positing culminates in the ideas of world and God. These ideas, however, are thoroughly heterogeneous and stand in "real opposition." If philosophy is to be systematic and complete, they must be combined into one whole: "In this relation there must, however, be a means of the combination of both [ideas] into an absolute whole – and that is *man* who, as a natural being has at the same time personality – in order to connect the principles of the senses with that of the supersensible." Man, as a sense object, belongs to nature; as a person, capable of rights and duties, he must have freedom of the will and hence be a citizen of the noumenal realm. These three ideas (or ideals, as they each express a maximum and are unique) belong together and form a system: "If *God* is, he is only one. If there is a *world* in the metaphysical sense then there is only one world; and if there is *man* he is the *ideal,* the *archetype* (*prototypon*) of a man adequate to duty." Whether these objects exist, "is not here decided" – it is not a question for transcendental philosophy.

What, in Kant's final analysis, is transcendental philosophy? It is, first, synthetic *a priori* knowledge *from concepts.* This is the "negative" definition, which sets it apart from mathematics. But Kant now adds a positive characterization, which explains the possibility of such knowledge: "Transcendental philosophy is the act of consciousness whereby the subject becomes the originator of itself and, thereby, also of the whole object of technical-practical and moral-practical reason in one system." In other words, transcendental philosophy becomes the theory of self-positing, of reason's self-constitution in the light of three original and necessary ideas or "images" that supply it with the material for synthetic knowledge from concepts: "I must have objects of my thinking and apprehend them; otherwise I am unconscious of myself." Reason (or the "spirit in man") therefore inevitably creates these ideas (God, world, duty) in the process of positing itself, of becoming conscious of itself as both a natural being and a person. Or, finally, already on the wrapper of this fascicle, among the last words Kant wrote: "Transcendental philosophy precedes the assertion of things that are thought, as their archetype, [the place] in which they must be set."

NOTE ON THE SELECTION AND TRANSLATION

The present edition is based on the text of the *Opus postumum* in Vols. 21 and 22 of the Academy edition of *Kant's gesammelte Schriften.* Its aim is to provide a selection from the *Opus postumum* that both illustrates the nature of Kant's last work and gives a comprehensive representation of its main ideas. I harbor no illusions that there can be a perfect approach to this task: Different editors would make – and have made – different selections. Nevertheless two principles of selection suggest themselves, both of which I have adopted.

First, as was noted, Kant tended in his last manuscript to adjust his writing to the paper in front of him, and to try to fit a thought or a set of paragraphs on a single sheet (sometimes even page), rather than freely to carry over his sentences from one to the next. The reason for this seems to have been his wish to have sheets (or sometimes pages) form self-contained units that could easily be compared with other drafts on the same topic and then reworked or amended at a later time if desired. The present selection is an attempt to preserve as far as possible this feature of the manuscript. It therefore reproduces entire pages rather than specific passages from those pages. Although I have not felt it necessary to adhere to this principle unswervingly, I have deviated from it only rarely, and only to avoid excessive repetition or to include in a selection a passage that seems crucial to the unfolding of Kant's argument, but that only occurs in the context of an otherwise unimportant or already much belabored discussion. I have not extended the principle to the margins of the pages, where Kant recorded alternative phrasings, reminders for a later treatment of a particular topic, and so forth. Kant's marginal notes are included when they seemed to contribute to an understanding of the argument on the page itself (or on other pages); otherwise they were omitted.

The second principle of selection is dictated by what Kant tried to achieve in his last work. Because the manuscript was begun with the intention of producing a "Transition from the Metaphysical Foundations of Natural Science to Physics" and reflects his long struggle with this problem and its implications, the selection should contain those pages that best represent the unfolding of the argument, as well as the various modifications and transformations the original plan underwent in the course of his deliberations. For this reason, otherwise interesting reflections that Kant recorded in the manuscript but that do not bear on his project – drafts of the prefaces to the *Critique of Practical Reason* and to R. B. Jachmann's *Prüfung der Kantischen Religionsphilosophie,* for example, or Kant's thoughts on a smallpox epidemic or on the alleged *Fortschritt zum Besseren* of the human race – had to be excluded from the selection.

This second principle also implies, it seems to me, that the selection should reflect the logical and chronological order of Kant's thought and thus use the chronology that Adickes established for the *Opus postumum*. This makes a comparison of the present text with the German original more complicated, but it makes Kant's argument vastly more intelligible. So as not to complicate the comparison beyond necessity, the present edition reproduces the inconsistencies in the arrangement of the text in the Academy edition, which provides Kant's marginal notes sometimes before the main text and sometimes after and includes his personal jottings from the margins sometimes in the apparatus to the text, sometimes on the page itself. The sole exception to this policy is Kant's marginal reflections on page 2 of sheet II of the Ist fascicle. The Academy edition prints them after page 3 of that sheet; I have included them immediately after the main text of page 2.

Whereas the responsibility for making selections from Kant's text lay entirely with the editor, the translation has been a collaborative effort* in the fullest sense: We established early on that the demands of the text (relative, at least, to our capacities) were such that the only possible way of proceeding was for us to translate each individual sentence together from scratch.

In general, we tried to render the text as intelligible as possible without imposing on it our own interpretation of what Kant is trying to say, or artificially eliminating its fragmentary, digressive, and repetitious character. But when faced with Kant's often jumbled and overlong sentences, their many parentheses, and not infrequently the complete absence of punctuation, a translator at times has no choice but to make a decision, guided only by an intuitive sense of what Kant wants to convey, as to which parts of a sentence belong together, or to which of many possible subjects a verb refers. We also often found it necessary, because the English language does not tolerate the large number of dependent and subdependent clauses that German can accommodate, to rearrange Kant's sentence structure and to disentangle and decompose his more convoluted constructions into more manageable units. In so doing, we did not hestitate to replace where necessary Kant's relative pronouns with the substantives to which we felt he must be referring, and which offered the best chance of making sense of the words in question.

Nevertheless, we were left with many sentences whose complexity still stretches the resources of the language. For this we make no apology: The English already represents a considerable simplification of the original, and to go farther would be to produce not a translation but a reconstruction of Kant's text.

In relation to Kant's words themselves we attempted to act much more conservatively. The problems here are ones that all of Kant's translators must face. For he is, notoriously, one of those philosophers who introduce into their work a great deal of novel terminology that has no familiar role (either in English or in German) outside its original context. The problem for the translator, however, is to determine how far Kant's terminology is

---

* All translations in the Introduction, the Notes to the Introduction, and the Factual Notes are by Eckart Förster unless otherwise indicated.

intended in this technical way (in which case the proper procedure must be to find a single equivalent) and how far it admits of flexibility in its sense.

A case in point is the words *Objekt* and *Gegenstand*, on the one hand, and *Ding* and *Sache*, on the other. (In ordinary German, all four words can be used interchangeably, with certain restrictions applying to *Sache*.) Whereas some scholars maintain that the first two words represent, for Kant, different ideas, we found no evidence in the *Opus postumum* to support this view. Rather, in this text, he seems to be using both terms interchangeably; we therefore translated both terms as "object," without distinction.

The case is different, however, with *Ding* and *Sache*, both of which are commonly translated as "thing." This seemed unacceptable to us in the *Opus postumum*, where Kant frequently speaks of a *Sache an sich* in a way that does not appear to be synonymous with the *Ding an sich* – the "thing in itself" familiar from his earlier writings. Whether this appearance is correct or not, it seemed important to us to alert the reader to such possible nuances in Kant's meaning. Consequently, wherever Kant uses the term *Sache*, we have translated it – for want of another term – as "thing [*Sache*]," to distinguish it from "thing" proper, or *Ding*.

Such decisions as to when terms do and do not demand a unique English equivalent are recorded in the Glossary. In addition, where the decision is of substantial philosophical significance, it is discussed in the Factual Notes at the appropriate place.

Finally, as regards the rendering of the principal terms, we have adapted ourselves, as far as we felt we reasonably could, to the existing standard translations. For the *Opus postumum* this means two translations in particular: Norman Kemp Smith's translation of the *Critique of Pure Reason* and James W. Ellington's translation of the *Metaphysical Foundations of Natural Science*. Especially from Kemp Smith's translation of terms we deviated only reluctantly – usually because we felt he treated too flexibly a term that needed a consistent equivalent.

In sum, our policy in translating Kant's *Opus postumum* has been conservative (as far as possible) with respect to words while being free with respect to word order and sentence structure. Although we are aware that this is a compromise – and one that reasonably could have been made otherwise – we hope that the reader will appreciate that it is a compromise that has been made in good faith. The resulting text is one that, we know, the English-speaking reader will often find extremely demanding. But no legitimate principles of translation – however free – could make the *Opus postumum* read like smooth, polished English. Our regulative principle has been that, where the text could not be made to read like English, it should, as far as possible, read like Kant.

ECKART FÖRSTER

Notes to the Introduction

1   For the history of the *Opus postumum*, see also E. Adickes, *Kants Opus postumum dargestellt und beurteilt* (*Kant-Studien Ergänzungsheft* Nr. 50), Reuther & Reichard: Berlin 1920, pp. 1–35, and G. Lehmann, "Einleitung," in AK 22:751–73.

2   AK 5:170; see also AK 10:494.

3   Kant to C. Garve, September 21, 1798, AK 12:257.

4   Kant to J. G. C. C. Kiesewetter, October 19, 1798, AK 12:258.

5   Kiesewetter to Kant, June 8, 1795, AK 12:23.

6   J. G. Hasse, *Letzte Äusserungen Kants von einem seiner Tischgenossen*, Friedrich Nikolovius: Königsberg 1804, p. 22.

7   R. B. Jachmann, *Immanuel Kant geschildert in Briefen an einen Freund*, reprinted in F. Gross (ed.), *Immanuel Kant: sein Leben in Darstellungen von Zeitgenossen*, Wissenschaftliche Buchgesellschaft: Darmstadt 1978, p. 128.

8   Kant to G. C. Lichtenberg, July 1, 1798, AK 12:247.

9   E. A. C. Wasianski, *Immanuel Kant in seinen letzten Lebensjahren*, reprinted in F. Gross (ed.), *Immanuel Kant*, p. 294.

10   "Erklärung gegen Schlettwein," AK 12:367. Hasse reported that the manuscript was to be published after Kant's death by J. F. Gensichen, to whom Kant had also bequeathed his library. (See J. G. Hasse, *Letzte Äusserungen*, p. 22n.)

11   E. A. C. Wasianski, *Immanuel Kant*, p. 294.

12   J. G. Hasse, *Letzte Äusserungen*, p. 22n.

13   Kiesewetter consulted J. F. Gensichen and C. J. Kraus, but apparently failed to contact Wasianski. Kiesewetter writes of his search in his introduction (1808) to an annotated edition of Kant's *Metaphysical Foundations of Natural Science*, which he planned to publish but which did not materialize. Kiesewetter's preface and introduction to this planned work are now in the Biblioteka Jagiellońska, Krakau (Poland). I am grateful to Dr. Marian Zwiercan of the Bibliotheka Jagiellońska for providing me with a microfilm of the texts.

14   See P. Haensell's letter of December 23, 1883 to A. Krause, printed in A. Krause, *Das nachgelassene Werk Immanuel Kant's: Vom Uebergange von den metaphysischen Anfangsgründen der Naturwissenschaft zur Physik mit Belegen populär-wissenschaftlich dargestellt*, Moritz Schauenberg: Frankfurt a. M. und Lahr, 1888, p. xvi.

15   F. W. Schubert, "Die Auffindung des letzten grösseren Manuskripts von Immanuel Kant," *Neue preussische Provinzialblätter* LVIX, 1 (1858), pp. 58–61; and R. Haym (anonymous), "Ein ungedrucktes Werk von Kant," *Preussische Jahrbücher* 1 (1858), pp. 80–4. Both scholars declined, however, to pass decisive judgment on the manuscript on the basis of their brief encounter with it.

16 Kuno Fischer, *Geschichte der neuern Philosophie*, Friedrich Bassermann: Mannheim 1860, vol. 3, p. 83.

17 *Altpreussische Monatsschrift* 19 (1882), pp. 67–8.

18 The first was perhaps Kant himself: "Insertion V" of the VIIth fascicle is clearly of a later origin than the rest of this fascicle, and is probably mixed up with the "Insertion V" that is now in the Xth fascicle. That this is Kant's own doing is suggested by Kant's note next to the heading "Insertion VI" on page 1 of the seventh sheet of fascicle VII: "N.B. Should perhaps be V" (AK 22:65.33).

19 This was suggested by Albrecht Krause, *Das nachgelassene Werk*, p. xv; and by Julius von Pflugk-Harttung, "Paläographische Bemerkungen zu Kants nachgelassener Handschrift," *Archiv für Geschichte der Philosophie* II 1 (1888), p. 41.

20 See Emil Arnoldt, *Gesammelte Schriften*, Nachlass Band IV, Bruno Cassirer: Berlin 1911, Part II, pp. 342–81.

21 Arnoldt to Kuno Fischer, June 20, 1884, in ibid., p. 378.

22 Ibid., p. 380.

23 Reicke's letter is reprinted in part in A. Krause, *Immanuel Kant wider Kuno Fischer, zum ersten Male mit Hülfe des verloren gewesenen Kantischen Hauptwerkes: Vom Übergang von der Metaphysik zur Physik verteidigt*, Moritz Schauenburg: Lahr 1884, p. 24.

24 Krause to von Gossler, June 30, 1883, reprinted in ibid., p. 25. Although the minister showed interest, the project did not materialize. Arnoldt, who for political reasons had been denied an academic position at a Prussian university, categorically refused to collaborate with a representative of the government; yet without the help of his friend, Reicke was unwilling to undertake the task.

25 Krause, *Immanuel Kant wider Kuno Fischer*, p. 3.

26 Cotta'sche Buchhandlung: Stuttgart 1884.

27 Thus Adickes writes that Krause's attack on Fischer was caused by his anger at Fischer's failing to revise his earlier dismissal of the *Opus postumum* in his *Kritik der kantischen Philosophie* of 1883: "A. Krause was so infuriated by this that he took pen in hand for a pointed attack on Fischer" (E. Adickes, *Kants Opus postumum*, p. 17). Gerhard Lehmann and others followed Adickes in this assessment (see G. Lehmann, "Einleitung," AK 22:765). Yet this is not even half the story.

In 1876, Krause published a book entitled *Die Gesetze des menschlichen Herzens wissenschaftlich dargestellt als die formale Logik des reinen Gefühls* [The Laws of the Human Heart, Scientifically Presented as the Formal Logic of Pure Feeling], M. Schauenburg: Lahr 1876, in which he claimed to have extended the principles of Kant's first *Critique* to the realm of human feelings and emotions. Contrary to Kant's claim that there can be no philosophical knowledge in rational psychology, Krause purported to show that this discipline had its own "synthetic *a priori* judgments," such as, for instance, "The present lasts only for a moment" (p. 44), or, "If fear induces a motion, it is the motion of flight" (p. 75). Such judgments can be proved, he insisted, if one adds to Kant's "insufficient" table of categories such "categories" as "*Wenigkeit*" (fewness), "*Separation*" (separation), and "*Zufälligkeit*" (contingency).

Krause sent a dedication copy of his book to Kuno Fischer with the inscription: "To the *Geheimen Rath* Kuno Fischer, his highly esteemed teacher, with deep gratitude, the author" (see K. Fischer, *Das Streber- und Gründerthum*, p. 63). Fischer, like the rest of the literary world, ignored the book. Convinced that this neglect by professional philosophers must be due to a failure to understand the Kantian principles on which his book was based, Krause next wrote a "popular" account of the *Critique of Pure Reason*, published appropriately in the centennial year 1881.

Again, there was virtually no response from the academic community. Krause now took more desperate steps. Together with a friend and ally, A. Claasen, he approached the editors of *Die Grenzboten*, a popular journal for politics, literature and arts, and asked for space in the journal's pages for the popularization and discussion of Krause's Kant interpretation. This was granted, and for the next three years, in a number of articles and book reviews, Krause and Claasen pursued their task. Heralding Krause's writings as "the first and only progress in the theory of knowledge since Kant," they explicitly set out to rescue the "true" Kant from the "trash of professorial wisdom [*Schutt der Professorenweisheit*]." Accordingly, they charged the "professors of philosophy" with either "arrogantly ignoring" or with "plagiarizing" Krause's work – the latter with respect to a book by Kurd Lasswitz, a later editor of the Academy edition, which had just been awarded a literary prize for the best popular account of Kant's theory of the ideality of space and time. See *Die Grenzboten* 42,2 (1883), pp. 190–7; see also 40,4 (1881), pp. 231–6; 41,1 (1882), pp. 113–17; 41,3 (1882), pp. 396–404; 41,4 (1882), pp. 10–17; 42,1 (1883), pp. 166–8; 42,2 (1883), pp. 348–9, pp. 650–62; 43,2 (1884), pp. 218–24.

Although their anger was directed against the community of professional philosophers as a whole, Krause and Claasen singled out Kuno Fischer for special attack from the start. See "Kant und die Erfahrungswissenschaft," 40,4 (1881), p. 232; "Kant und Kuno Fischer," 41,4 (1882), pp. 10–17; "Kuno Fischer und sein Kant" 42, 3 (1883), pp. 549–64.

Fischer eventually responded in the preface to his *Kritik der kantischen Philosophie*, Fr. Bassermann: München 1883. Lamenting the trend to publish on Kant without understanding him, he refers to an "immature and confused book" of a few years ago that could not have had a better fate than to sink into oblivion, but which was now heralded as the first and only progress in the theory of knowledge since Kant. Without mentioning Krause or Claasen by name, Fischer voiced his opinion of them in the form of a quotation from the Walpurgisnight scene of Goethe's *Faust:* " 'Ein Dilettant hat es geschrieben!' Und Freund Servibilis ruft: 'Mich dilettirt's, den Vorhang aufzuziehen!' " (Fischer, p. vi).

Now Krause writes his book *Immanuel Kant wider Kuno Fischer*. And although he is silent in the book as to the circumstances that led up to it, his true motives are nevertheless revealed in the introduction: "It is not only the love of Immanuel Kant which makes me carry out the present project, but it is also the drive of self-preservation which compels me to do so" (p. 3). Kant's *Opus postumum* clearly came in handy as a new weapon in Krause's struggle for "self-preservation."

28 The following incidents are reported in Arnoldt's letter to Fischer of June 6 and 7, 1884. See E. Arnoldt's *Gesammelte Schriften*, pp. 371–3.

29 A. Krause, *Das nachgelassene Werk Immanuel Kants*. In the preface Krause writes, no doubt to the surprise of those familiar with the circumstances: "As far as possible, I have only chosen passages that have already been published in Dr. Reicke's edition" (p. xvii).

In 1902, Krause complemented this with a publication about the first fascicle: *Die letzten Gedanken Immanuel Kants: Der Transzendentalphilosophie höchster Standpunkt: Von Gott, der Welt und dem Menschen, welcher beide verbindet*, Lahr 1902. Like Hans Vaihinger and Karl Vorländer, Krause subscribed to the *Zwei Werke* theory, that is, the view that Kant's *Opus postumum* contains the plan and the material for two different works. Although disproved by Adickes in 1920, this view has recently been revived in W. H. Werkmeister, *Kant's Architectonic*, Open Court: La Salle and London 1980, pp. 112, 173.

30 For the history of the Academy edition, see G. Lehmann, "Zur Geschichte der Kantausgabe 1896–1955," in Lehmann, *Beiträge zur Geschichte und Interpretation der Philosophie Kants*, de Gruyter: Berlin 1969, pp. 3–12; Paul Menzer, "Die Kant-Ausgabe der Berliner Akademie der Wissenschaften," *Kant-Studien 49* 4 (1957–8), pp. 337–50; and Werner Stark, "Nachforschungen zur Herausgabe von Kants handschriftlichem Nachlass," unpublished manuscript, Marburg 1983.

31 See B. Guttmann, "Der Kampf um ein Manuskript," *Frankfurter Zeitung und Handelsblatt*, Nr. 321, 47. Jahrgang, 19. November 1902, Erstes Morgenblatt.

32 Ibid.

33 E. Adickes, *Kants Opus postumum*, p. iv.

34 B. Erdmann to E. Adickes, December 22, 1916. This and the following letters from Adickes's correspondence are part of the so-called *Ingelheimer Papiere* – a portion of Adickes's *Nachlass* that Werner Stark located in 1982 (see W. Stark, "Mitteilung in memoriam Erich Adickes," *Kant-Studien 75* 3 [1984], pp. 345–9) and that is now in the Kant Archiv of the Philipps Universität Marburg. I am grateful to Werner Stark for permitting me to quote from the *Ingelheimer Papiere*.

35 E. Adickes to H. Diels, February 10, 1919 (*Ingelheimer Papiere*).

36 H. Diels to E. Adickes, June 6, 1919 (*Ingelheimer Papiere*).

37 E. Adickes, *Kants Opus postumum*, pp. 854, 34, iv, 854.

38 H. Maier to E. Adickes, November 9, 1923 (*Ingelheimer Papiere*). See also G. Lehmann, "Zur Geschichte der Kantausgabe," p. 8.

39 H. Maier to E. Adickes, November 9, 1923 (*Ingelheimer Papiere*).

40 I owe this information to Werner Stark.

41 A. Buchenau and G. Lehmann (eds.), *Der alte Kant*, de Gruyter: Berlin und Leipzig 1925, p. 3. Bound together with Kant's notes is a reprint of Hasse's *Letzte Äusserungen Kants*. Adickes expressed his negative assessment of *Der alte Kant* in his letter to A. Buchenau of May 4, 1926, and in a letter to Lehmann of June 2, 1926 (*Ingelheimer Papiere*), where he spoke of his "disgust" with their way of handling their editorial task.

42 H. Maier to E. Adickes, January 8, 1924; see Adickes's letter to Buchenau, June 30, 1925 (*Ingelheimer Papiere*).

43 E. Adickes to H. Maier, June 19, 1926 (*Ingelheimer Papiere*).

44 See P. Menzer, "Die Kant-Ausgabe," p. 347.

45 See AK 18:679.1–9 (R 6352a) and 21:337.23–338.05; 18:305.2–18 (R 5652a) and 21:440.16–441.2; 19:310.17–311.7 (R 7314) and 21:446.2–12; 18:659.9–665.21 (R 6338a) and 21:454.21–461.12; 15:972.14–974.14 (R 1552) and 22:295.22–297.11, 298.6–8, 298.15–17; 15:974.17–976.18 (R 1553) and 22:302.6–304.12, 304.16–18, 304.22–305.3.

46 The leaves of the IVth fascicle have been transmitted in the following order (as of 1986): nos. 22 (with the *Octaventwurf* inserted in it), 8, 25, 29, 23, 24, 26/32, 30, 27, 31, 28, 33, 35, 39/40, 36, 37, 38, 41, 42, 44, 43/47, 45, 46, 3/4, 7, 5, 6, 3. The editors also deviated from the principles of a "diplomatic" edition in the IXth fascicle, where they reversed the order of the pages of draft "B Übergang" (AK 22:233–46).

47 G. Lehmann, *Beiträge*, p. 48. Thirty years later Lehmann still recalled the "string of difficulties, even nastinesses" that accompanied the interactions between him, Buchenau, and Adickes; see ibid., p. 38.

48 See E. Adickes, *Kants Opus postumum*, p. 153n.

49 See, e.g., Wolfgang G. Bayerer, "Ein verschollenes Loses Blatt aus Kants Opus postumum?" *Kant-Studien* 58 (1967), pp. 277–84; *idem.*, "Bemerkungen zu einem neuerdings näher bekannt gewordenen Losen Blatt aus Kants Opus postumum," *Kant-Studien* 72 (1981), pp. 127–31; Hans-Joachim Waschkies, "Eine neu aufgefundene Reflexion Kants zur Mathematik (Loses Blatt Leningrad 2)," *Kant-Forschungen* 1 (1987), pp. 229–78; Werner Stark, "Loses Blatt Leipzig 1. Transkription und Bemerkungen," in: Forum für Philosophie Bad Homburg (ed.), *Übergang: Untersuchungen zum Spätwerk Immanuel Kants*, Klostermann: Frankfurt am Main 1991, pp. 146–55.

50 For a detailed description of the various sheets of the manuscript, see AK 22:773–89 and Julius von Pflugk-Harttung, "Paläographische Bemerkungen zu Kants nachgelassener Handschrift."

51 Kant's logic lecture of 1772 ("Logik Philippi"), §436, AK 24:484.

52 See the correspondence between Kant, Kiesewetter, and Lagarde, November 19, 1789 to May 1790, AK 11:107–67.

53 For another illustration of Kant's working style at the time, see G. Baum, W. G. Bayerer, R. Malter, "Ein neu aufgefundenes Reinschriftfragment Kants mit den Anfangstexten seines Entwurfs 'Zum ewigen Frieden,'" *Kant-Studien* 77 (1986), pp. 316–37.

54 T. Haering, *Der Duisburg'sche Nachlass und Kant's Kriticismus um 1775*, J. C. B. Mohr (Paul Siebeck): Tübingen 1910, pp. 2ff.

55 E. Adickes, who edited the physics *Reflexionen* in the Academy edition, described them thus: "stylistic monster-sentences, anacolutha, unclear formulations of thoughts themselves unclear" (*Kants Opus postumum*, p. 23; see AK 14:xviii–xix).

56 According to Wasianski, it was Kant's habit to write down in the evenings key words for topics he planned to develop the next day. See Wasianski, *Immanuel Kant in seinen letzten Lebensjahren*, p. 225.

57 For this reason, Vittorio Mathieu characterized the manuscript as "zellenartig" – cellular. See *Kants Opus postumum*, Klostermann: Frankfurt am Main 1989, p. 61.

58 For a fairly typical page of Kant's manuscript, see the facsimile of page 1 of the first sheet of fascicle IX in this volume.

59 In this respect, too, the *Opus postumum* does not differ from Kant's *Duisburg'sche Nachlass* of 1775; see AK 17:651.

60 E. Adickes, *Kants Opus postumum*, p. 36.

61 Adickes's general method of dating Kant's *Nachlass* (see his "Einleitung" to AK 14:xvii–lxii) has not gone uncriticized. His plan to "verify" his method in the last *Nachlass* volume of the Academy edition was prevented by his early death. For the *Opus postumum*, however, this dispute is of only secondary importance. Here one must distinguish between the *order* in which the various drafts were composed, and their exact dating. Adickes established the former, by and large, in a manner that leaves little room for doubt; this order is generally accepted today. As for the exact dating of the various sheets and leaves, a complete answer could only come, if at all, from a scientific analysis of the papers used, the inks, the watermarks, etc. As long as the manuscript remains in private possession and inaccessible to scholarship of this kind, this is out of the question. However, Kant's text contains enough dates and references to datable events to permit reliable dating for most of the drafts (hence a margin of error of not more than several months for the others). Whenever possible, such dates or references are given in the Factual Notes.

62 For this deviation, see Factual Note 30.

63 See E. Adickes, *Kants Opus postumum*, pp. 36–54.

64 Kiesewetter had published with Kant's publisher a *Grundriss einer allgemeinen Logik nach Kantischen Grundsätzen* (F. T. Lagarde: Berlin 1791) in which he made liberal use of material Kant had unwittingly "dictated" to him, as Kiesewetter later put it (see AK 11:267, 254). Kant, who himself had plans for a *Logic* as a compendium for lectures, was infuriated, especially because he did not learn of this book through Kiesewetter himself but through their publisher. Kant wrote again only after Kiesewetter sent him a small cask of *Teltower Rüben* – a type of carrots Kant was particularly fond of – in December 1793. The letter in which Kiesewetter reminds Kant of his intended "Transition" is from June 8, 1795, AK 12:23.

65 In this context it is worth noticing that several of the early leaves, which Adickes dates between 1786 and 1790, address topics that are also the subject matter of some of the so-called *Kiesewetter-Aufsätze* – short essays in which Kiesewetter recorded his discussions with Kant. See, e.g., on "the moment of a speed": nos. 31, 37, 38, 41, 33 (AK 21:426, 429, 431, 432, 435–7) and R 67 ("Loses Blatt Kiesewetter 6," 14:495–6); and "On miracles": no. 35 (21:439.18–22) and R 5662 ("Loses Blatt Kiesewetter 2," 18:320–2).

66 See E. Adickes, *Kants Opus postumum*, p. 153.

67 See, e.g., F. T. Rink's letter to Charles de Villers of June 1, 1801: "The condition of our dear Kant is rapidly deteriorating." (Quoted from Hans Vaihinger, "Briefe aus dem Kantkreis," *Altpreussische Monatsschrift* 17 [1880], p. 292.)

68 See J. G. Hasse, *Letzte Äusserungen Kants*, pp. 4–5: "During the last three years [of Kant's life] I was his guest once or twice per week." Wasianski began to look after Kant almost daily in the winter of 1801–2, when he took

over the philosopher's financial affairs and found a new servant for him in January 1802. At this time, Kant wrote in the *Opus postumum:* "(Herr deacon [Wasianski]) daily" (AK 21:126.2, not included), and, soon after, "Receive the Herrn deacon, politely [*mit Geschmack aufzunehmen*]" (AK 21:134.13, not included).

69 *Prolegomena to Any Future Metaphysics*, AK 4:377 (translated by Carus/Beck). References to the *Critique of Pure Reason* are given in the text with the usual 'A' and 'B' numbering for the first and second edition, respectively.

70 Kant to J. H. Lambert, September 2, 1770, AK 10:98.

71 *Prolegomena*, AK 4:260.

72 Ibid., 262.

73 See Kant to Marcus Herz, January 1779, AK 10:247.

74 Kant to Herz, after May 11, 1781, AK 10:269.

75 *Prolegomena*, AK 4:263.

76 See ibid., 275.

77 Ibid., 373n.

78 Ibid., 293. Italics added.

79 See ibid.

80 Ibid., 373n.

81 *Metaphysical Foundations of Natural Science*, AK 4:477, translated by James W. Ellington.

82 See also Kant's *Reflexionen* 6311–16, AK 18:607–23.

83 *Metaphysical Foundations of Natural Science*, AK 4:478; see also A244–5 and B288–92. Italics added.

84 *Metaphysical Foundations of Natural Science*, AK 4:476.

85 The first chapter (Phoronomy) treats of "matter as the movable in space"; the second chapter (Dynamics) of "matter as the movable insofar as it fills a space"; the third chapter (Mechanics) of "matter as the movable insofar as it as such has a moving force"; and the fourth (Phenomenology), finally, of "matter as the movable insofar as it can as such be an object of experience."

86 See *Metaphysical Foundations of Natural Science*, AK 4:525, 532–3.

87 Ibid., 473.

88 Ibid., 524.

89 AK 22:282.

90 First introduction to the *Critique of Judgment*, AK 20:215, translated by James Haden.

91 AK 5:246, translated by Werner S. Pluhar.

92 First introduction, AK 20:216.

93 Ibid., 219, translated by Werner S. Pluhar.

94 Ibid., 204–5.

95 AK 11:361–5.

96 Ibid., 376–7.

97 *Metaphysical Foundations of Natural Science*, AK 4:524.

98 Ibid., 516.

99 Ibid., 521.

100 AK 11:396.

101 Ibid., 426.

102 Ibid., 441. The first introduction was published by Beck under the mislead-

ing title "Anmerkungen zur Einleitung in die Kritik der Urteilskraft" as an appendix to the second volume of his *Erläuternder Auszug aus den critischen Schriften des Herrn Prof. Kant*, Hartknoch: Riga 1794, pp. 543–90.

103　This is clear from the opening lines of Beck's next letter to Kant, June 17, 1794, AK 11:508–9.

104　AK 22:282.

105　AK 21:311.

106　See AK 4:518, 526, 563–4.

107　See ibid., 473: "I believe that I have completely exhausted this metaphysical doctrine of body, as far as such a doctrine ever extends"; see also 470, 477, 478, etc.

108　See AK 4:527.

109　Ibid., 529.

110　Proposition 1, Mechanics, AK 4:537.

Bibliography

I. EDITIONS

(arranged chronologically)

Reicke, Rudolf (ed.). "Ein ungedrucktes Werk von Kant aus seinen letzten Lebensjahren: Als Manuscript herausgegeben." *Altpreussische Monatsschrift* XIX (1882): 66–127, 255–308, 425–79, 569–629; XX (1883): 59–122, 342–73, 415–50, 513–66; XXI (1884): 81–159, 309–87, 389–420, 533–620.

Krause, Albrecht (ed.). *Das nachgelassene Werk Immanuel Kant's: Vom Uebergange von den metaphysischen Anfangsgründen der Naturwissenschaft zur Physik mit Belegen populär-wissenschaftlich dargestellt.* Moritz Schauenberg: Frankfurt am Main und Lahr, 1888.

Kant's gesammelte Schriften. Herausgegeben von der Preussischen Akademie der Wissenschaften. Vols. 21, 22. Walter de Gruyter & Co: Berlin und Leipzig, 1936, 1938.

Kant, Emmanuel. *Opus postumum.* Textes choisis et traduits par J. Gibelin. Vrin: Paris, 1950.

Kant's gesammelte Schriften. Herausgegeben von der Deutschen Akademie der Wissenschaften zu Berlin. Vol. 23 ("Ergänzungen zum Opus Postumum"). Walter de Gruyter & Co: Berlin, 1955, 477–88.

Kant, Emanuele. *Opus postumum: Passaggio dai principi metafisici della scienza della natura alla fisica.* A cura di V. Mathieu, Zanichelli: Bologna, 1963.

Bayerer, Wolfgang G. "Ein verschollenes Loses Blatt aus Kants 'Opus Postumum'?" *Kant-Studien* LVIII (1967), 277–84.

Bayerer, Wolfgang G. "Bemerkungen zu einem neuerdings näher bekannt gewordenen Losen Blatt aus Kants Opus Postumum." *Kant-Studien* LXXII (1981), 127–31.

Kant, Immanuel. *Transición de los principios metafísicos de la ciencia natural a la física.* Edición preparada par F. Duque, Editora Nacional: Madrid, 1983.

Kant, Emmanuel. *Opus postumum: Passage des principes métaphysiques de la science de la nature a la physique.* Traduction, présentation et notes par F. Marty, Presses universitaires de France: Paris, 1986.

Waschkies, Hans-Joachim. "Eine neu aufgefundene Reflexion Kants zur Mathematik (Loses Blatt Leningrad 2)," *Kant-Forschungen* 1 (1987), Meiner: Hamburg, 1987, 229–78.

Stark, Werner. "Loses Blatt Leipzig 1," in *Übergang: Untersuchungen zum Spätwerk Immanuel Kants.* Herausgegeben vom Forum für Philosophie Bad Homburg, Klostermann: Frankfurt, 1991, 146–55.

2. SECONDARY SOURCES

For a nearly complete bibliography of the secondary literature on Kant's *Opus postumum* up to 1990, see Karin Beiküfner, "Literatur," in *Übergang: Untersuchungen zum Spätwerk Immanuel Kants.* Herausgegeben vom Forum für Philosophie Bad Homburg, Klostermann: Frankfurt 1991, 233–44.

Editor's note

The following text has been broken up into seven chapters corresponding to the major themes in Kant's argument. The chapter headings are provided by the editor.

In addition, four symbols have been used to indicate special features of the text:

• •	means	added later by Kant.
{ }	means	deleted by Kant.
[...]	means	editor's omission.
[ ]	means	translators' insertion.

KANT'S
OPUS POSTUMUM

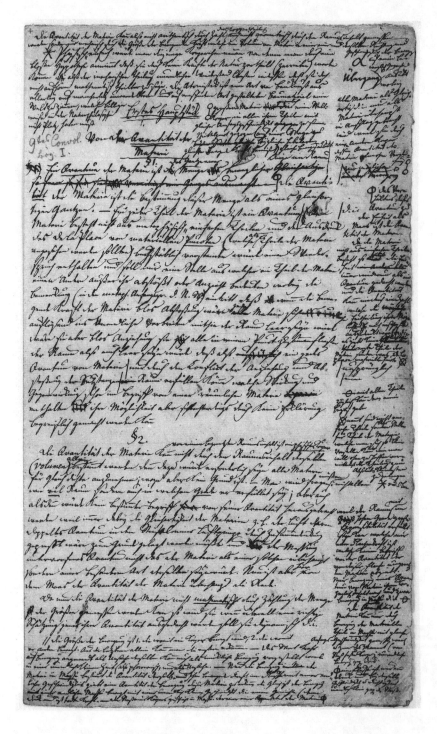

IXth fascicle, sheet I, page 1

[Early leaves and Oktaventwurf*]*

GÖTTINGISCHE ANZEIGEN NO. 191, 1786

Phoronomy contains only the previously mentioned proposition concerning composite motion. Reviewer confesses that he has not [found] the present topic there, or, if, perhaps, he has overlooked it, does not comprehend how it could follow from the previously mentioned proposition.² (N.B. The *phoronomic proposition* was cited by me to support the claim that nothing can abolish motion save motion in the opposite direction.) A body which has motion certainly remains in exactly the same place in absolute space if the plane on which it rests is moved with equal speed in the opposite direction, but *must* every case of remaining in one place be thought of in the same way? *Must* one think of a moving force in a wall, because, at the wall, one cannot progress further? It is not even clear how Phoronomy, which merely treats of motion without considering force (from which the motion arises) could lead to moving force.

[Bottom margin]
   On the doctrine of repulsive forces.

[IVth fascicle, leaf 25, page 2]
   Because repulsion is a superficial force (does not proceed immediately from one part to all parts in a given quantity of matter) the quantity of matter is not equal to the repulsion; not even density is proportional to the latter (in different kinds of matter). So the quantity of matter can be very unequal, for the same repulsion (without empty intermediary spaces), but, for the same attraction (at the same distance) it is always equal – which is   21:416
not the case when attraction is itself not true attraction but only approach through impact or pressure, for, then, it is only a superficial force, like cohesion.
   N.B. Whether, in cohesion, the attracting parts also attract those which are not in contact?

[IVth fascicle, leaf 26/32, page 1]

[. . .]³

21:417

COHESION

The question is whether cohesion be possible through inner forces of matter (like gravity). The moment of acceleration of the attracting parts would have to relate to gravity as the weight of a wire, which breaks through its gravity, does to the weight of that small piece of matter which immediately exerts the attraction; and since its parts attract only in the inverse square ratio, as a third of the latter's weight. It would follow from this that small pieces of matter (which would be smaller than the distance amounted to) would have that much less cohesion.

[. . .]

[IVth fascicle, leaf 23, page 2]⁴   21:453

DISSOLUTION

What is chemistry? The science of the inner forces of matter.

Dissolution (chemical) is the separation of two types of matter, penetrating each other through attraction. It is either quantitative – if the matter is divided into homogeneous matters – or qualitative if it is divided into its heterogeneous (specifically different) matters. (a) Water into vapor (b) into two types of air. The latter is called analysis, properly speaking.

Quantitative but yet chemical division takes place, for example, through evaporation of the lighter [matter], etc.

Dissolution requires a medium (*menstruum*) which must always be fluid and which dissolves either another fluid or a solid matter (*menstruum universale*).

The question is whether the dissolution of a solid body takes place through the attraction of the fluid [*menstruum*] or merely through the   21:454
neutralization [*Aufhebung*] of the attraction of the parts of the solid [matter] among one another. If the latter is merely diminution, [its] effect is swelling as in wooden wedges or the growth of trees.⁵

Whether the theory of capillary tubes is valid here.

Attraction is a force moving the matter outside of a body. Because the spaces from which the motions of the body in its approach commences are in various distances as the squares of the distances, the attraction is also in this ratio. Cohesion can indeed, according to its effect, be considered as attraction; since, however, it involves no diminishing attraction – at least not that according to the squared ratio – cohesion is therefore not the effect of one body approaching another but rather the effect of such matters which extend much farther than the two bodies, hence pressure or impact. However, it cannot be pressure for a fluid [matter] has cohesion. Through pressure, however, the fluid [matter] would conserve any figure if it is equally compressed on all sides. Therefore, cohesion is only possible through [the] living force of impact.

[IVth fascicle, leaf 39/40, page 1]⁶

Magnitude is the determination of an object according to which the apprehension of its intuition is represented as possible only through the repeated positing of what is the same – elucidation by space and time as *a priori* magnitudes.

Thus magnitude is for us merely a predicate of things as objects of our senses (for only through the senses is intuition possible for us). The concept of the magnitude of a thing in general would, if I omit the restriction to sensible intuition, read thus: It is the determination by which what is manifold and homogeneous together makes one. But one cannot

21:455 comprehend the possibility of a thing according to these concepts; in consequence one does not know whether the definition has explained a thing or a nonentity [*Unding*] – this general concept of magnitude is not an element of knowledge.

The above concept of magnitude is not an empirical concept, for it contains the conditions of apprehension in general and the unity of the concept according to its rule, from which alone empirical concepts can arise. Thus it also contains *a priori* intuition and a concept of the understanding, [that is, a concept of] the synthetic unity of its manifold in apperception.

•A definition which has no relation to application *in concreto* is transcendent (without meaning).•

Theorem: All objects of the senses have extensive magnitude. For space and time, as that in which alone their manifold can be intuited, are knowable only as magnitudes. This proposition is a principle of the possibility of experience; namely, to produce perceptions according to it and to combine them into the unity of the knowledge of the object.

Categories of magnitude (quantity). (1) Unity (mathematical, not qualitative; measure – this itself regarded as magnitude and a part of it*ᵃ* used as a measure of other magnitudes). (2) Plurality (multitude, counting – largeness and smallness). Nothing is absolutely large. Indeterminate multitude. The largest and the smallest. Infinite progression. (3) Totality. Number – aesthetic comprehension, uniting the multitude. Infinite magnitude thereof (the absolute totality [*All*] is the largest). Regression to infinity. Continuity. The infinitely small $\frac{1}{\infty}$.

To describe God as infinite is to regard him as of the same kind as his creatures, only beyond all measure as regards magnitude (aesthetic value of the description). Totality of reality is a better description and one and the same as unlimited.

21:456 The things which occupy time and space can only be known in experience, according to the conditions of the apprehension of their manifold, and of the unity of their combination, which conforms to the *a priori*

ᵃ Reading *ihm* for *ihnen.*

concepts of this unity. For this reason, laws of all objects of possible experience must hold, because empirical knowledge is only possible by this principle. •Quanta are all continua. Multitudes are not quanta. Where the unity is specifically determined – as sheep, for example – it is no quantum but rather a multitude.•

QUALITY

In the case of [quality], sensation is combined, but not connected, with intuition to yield an empirical apperception; that is, the intuition is empty, or partly empty and partly sensible. Every sensation can be thought of as gradually vanishing; that is, as decreased from a strong to a weaker, declining to nothing. Equally it can be increased. Thus it, and the reality of the object corresponding to it, has a degree.

The sensation is represented subjectively as unity, namely in regard to empirical apperception, which, however, vanishes as magnitude, but not by division.

[IVth fascicle, leaf 39/40, page 2]

The concept of magnitude is not a concept derived from experience. It lies *a priori* in the understanding, although only in experience do we develop it. What cannot be *perceived* in the object cannot be derived from experience either. Now the concept of magnitude contains that which the understanding performs for itself, namely, to produce an entire representation through the synthesis of repeated addition. Therefore, nothing is contained in it which would require a perception; it hence presupposes no experience, although it is contained in all of them. Thus it can be applied 21:457 *a priori* to the intuitions [of] space and time. It is not derived even from these, however, but is only applied to them and receives by way of them objective reality with respect to things in space and time. It contains nothing further than the synthetic unity of consciousness, which is required for a concept of an object in general, and insofar is an element of knowledge, but is not yet knowledge save when applied to pure or empirical intuition.

(1) *Concept.* (2) Its origin. Synthetic division (*a priori*). (3) Domain ([applies] only to objects of the senses). (4) Principle (under this concept). *Predicables* (possibility of pure mathesis).

A
CONCEPT OF MAGNITUDE

(1) Explanation and synthetic division. (2) Origin of the concept. (3) Domain. (4) Principle – then predicables.

B
CONCEPT OF QUALITY

(1) Explanation and synthetic division. Explanation: The quality of a thing is the determination which represents it as a something or as a mere lack, i.e. whose concept contains a being or a nonbeing.

Division. Reality, negation and limitation. (Possibility of *dynamics*.)

C
CONCEPT OF RELATION

21:458

Definition: It is the real relation of one thing to something else, which may be its own predicate or that of other things. . . . The former is internal relation, the latter external relation. A real relation is opposed to the merely formal, for it is a relation of reality to another reality (possibility of physics). Everything as a demonstrable science from *a priori* principles.

N.B. One can give no proof of these propositions, valid for all things in general. For, in seeking the pure category, one cannot know if something such as it could apply to any thing at all. Taking the conditions of intuition in space and time, one does not know whether they can be presupposed in all things. For it is not as concepts that one comprehends their necessity; they are just conditions under which we must represent things for ourselves.

Quality is the determination of a thing insofar as it is not increased in number, although the thing itself is enlarged, e.g. figure. Understanding in contrast to the senses. Gravity in contrast to weight. Infinite divisibility in contrast to extension. Reality in contrast to negation.

[IVth fascicle, leaf 39/40, page 3]

The object in general: (1) According to the form of intuition without something which this form contains (space and time). (2) The object as something (*aliquid est objectum qualificatum*) is the occupation of space and time, without which both are empty intuitions. This something is posited *in* space and time in the second class of categories. (3) This real [something], determined in space and time according to its relations, or thought *a priori* for relations in space and time. (4) Something as the object of empirical consciousness of a thing outside me (of the immediate). Against idealism. Hence, something as object of the senses, not just of the imagination.

Transcendental philosophy or ontology [*Wesenlehre*] is followed by the (metaphysical) physiology of objects of experience according to *a priori* principles: doctrine of body and doctrine of soul. Then cosmology and theology.

QUALITY   21:459

Is that internal determination of a thing by which it can be distinguished from others as a unity. It is opposed to magnitude which is the internal determination of a thing by which it can be distinguished from others as a plurality. Plurality, however, is that determination of a thing which can no more be explained as unity. The quality of a thing, which distinguishes it as a something from mere form, is reality, to which corresponds sensation.

Quality is that internal determination which, without enlargement or diminution of the thing, can become greater or lesser; e.g. weight (given the same gravity) is not a quality since it can only be increased by enlargement of the thing, but gravity is a quality because it can grow without growth in the body according to its mass. Continuity is quality, velocity, finally sensation (reality), between a and o.

The relation of things to empty space is not an object of possible experience. No more [that] to empty time.

The combination of reality with the concept of magnitude is intensive; this absolute unity of reality can itself have no magnitude. What, however, has no reality but is absolute unity (the point) has no magnitude. Of the bounds of reality in contrast to the limits of space. Of boundless – of infinite reality. That all manifoldness of things as things in general consists only in the extension of the totality of reality, which presupposes a unified being. That all negations are mere boundaries: transcendental theology. These are mere ideas which concern the constitution of our thought without being regarded as knowledge of things.

Of the manifoldness of things in accordance with all the united categories 21:460
insofar as the concepts of them are to have objective reality, e.g. magnitude (1. transcendental definition, 2. metaphysical).
[. . .]

[IVth fascicle, *Oktaventwurf*][7]

I TRANSITION FROM THE METAPHYSICAL
FOUNDATIONS
OF NATURAL SCIENCE TO PHYSICS

From the moving forces, by which matter in general is possible, to those which give it a determinate connection (which is alterable by other natural forces), that is:

(1) density, (2) cohesion, (3) movability •or comparative
immovability•
of the parts which cohere.

Alteration of density is either by heat or by cold, by which alone all matter without distinction can be penetrated. The former is dissolution; opposed to it is attraction, i.e. cohesion – either involving rest (the equality of reaction of forces in contact), that is, an *immediate* cohesion, or involving approach [of separated bodies to one another], that is, *mediated* cohesion as in magnets and electricity. The latter is only possible by the dissolution of types of matter which are combined with other non-separable ones. The cohesion which resists only the separation but not the displacement of all parts is fluidity; that which resists only displacement but not separation, is friability. The cohesion which resists both is solidity (*rigiditas*). Flow.

Cohesion is thus the first thing which requires explanation (the pressure of the ether through gravity),[8] and original difference of density, which arises therefrom [as] its consequence. The second is fluidity, i.e. the free movability of a matter in a dense medium, irrespective of the cohesion of the latter's parts. For, without this, bodies cannot penetrate one another.

2   This fluidity must be original; for, without it, the derivative forces of dissolution and expansion (by heat) do not allow of explanation. It also depends on the mechanical necessity for a continuous matter, to exercise equal pressure in all directions – of a degree equal to that in which it is pressed in one direction.

Hence, solidity must be a derivative property, consisting in an internal resistance which counteracts this sort of pressure to displacement (and thus does not require a counterpressure on the part of the surrounding space).

Such resistance must arise from the same force as creates cohesion, which, as in the case of a drop of water, preserves by its pressure the abiding position of each part. This [disposition], however, cannot be derived from the pressure alone (which would permit movability to all sides). [Hence], it is only possible by original perpetual vibration of the ether, whose repulsive forces differ from those of other types of matter in manifold ways. The vibration of the ether must, in the absence of heat, give

cohesion to all the scattered types of matter, according to the difference of their specific gravities (that is to say, in inverse proportion to their repulsive forces, given the same quality of matter). The vibration confers on the parts of matter a certain texture, so that they are combined into that figure in which their own oscillations are able to resist completely the oscillations of the ether. For it is not in all figures that the oscillations of the denser types of matter can resist the lightest. It is as if [configurations of matter] were to have a tone (counting pitch and volume together) which is in tune with a certain texture of their parts (the figure of the whole is irrelevant here) – whether they are in thin laminae or long fibers and the manner in which lighter and heavier types of matter are combined. So arranged, [3]   21:375
they resist all displacement of their parts; they must, however, be separated from one another by intermediate spaces filled with lighter matter. Such solid types of matter can be fractured, having been previously stretched, for as long as their counteroscillation (together with their weight) is smaller than the oscillations of the ether; this is possible when different types of matter are mixed.

Where the repulsive force of the parts decreases strongly, at small distances, but, at the same time, the pressure pressing them against one another remains the same, the force required to separate them increases – assuming that the parts cannot displace one another without making smaller oscillations than would be possible, according to their length and thickness, for a given impact of the ether. It is only a maximum of stretching.

That ponderosity must belong to all matter – that is, that all matter in a determinate volume is a mass – can be recognized *a priori*. For, otherwise, it would be able neither to resist the motion of another impacting [body] nor to communicate motion. That, however, the ponderability in bodies, which uniformly fill an equally large space, may yet be different, precisely in consequence of the specific differences of types of matter, apart from their figure and texture [*breaks off*]

To repel at a distance and to attract in contact, so that the one is the condition of the possibility of the other, is contradictory, except by means of an intermediary matter which must surround all bodies.

    A. Ponderosity

1. Cohesion and elasticity of the types of matter without determinate inner form
2. Fluidity and solidity
3. Heat and cold
4. Dissolution and decomposition (precipitation). Full and empty space

    1. Expansibility and heat
    2. Cohesion and solidity
    3. Ponderability and quantity of   21:376
       matter

    4. Penetrability and coercibility

11

IMMANUEL KANT

Universal synthetic properties of matter

1. Extension realistically regarded: *vis expansiva* – volume
2. Ponderosity: reality of intensive magnitude *versus* absolute lightness – *massa*
3. The reciprocal action in the motion of one body by another versus the *vis inertiae* of the one
4. Full space as an object of experience versus empty. In organized beings.
a. Vital force.⁹ Seed
b. Nourishment and development also in seeds *per intussusceptionem*
c. External and internal growth to manhood
d. Propagation – either alternative or communicative
[. . .]

21:378   [5]   An inwardly merely expansive (aerial) matter is so either *originally* (*originarie expansiva*) or only derivatively (*derivative expansiva*). One could call the former the ether, but not as an object of experience; rather, merely as the idea of an expansive matter whose parts are not capable of any greater dissolution, because no attraction of cohesion is to be found in them. Expansibility through heat is already derivative, for heat itself depends upon a particular matter (caloric). To assume such a matter filling cosmic space is an inevitably necessary hypothesis, for, without it, no cohesion, which is necessary for the formation of a physical *body*, can be thought.

All matter, however, is originally combined in a whole of world-attraction through universal gravitation, and thus the ether itself would, however far it may extend, be in a state of compression, even in the absence of all other matter. Such compression must, however, be oscillating, because the first effect of this attraction in the beginning of all things must be a compression of all its parts toward some midpoint, with consequential expansion, and which, because of the elasticity [of the world-matter], must hence be set in continuous and everlasting oscillation. The secondary matter distributed in the ether is thereby necessitated to unify itself into bodies at certain points and so to form cosmic bodies. This universal attraction, which the matter of the ether exerts upon itself, must

21:379   be thought of as a limited space (a sphere), consequently as the one universal cosmic body, which compresses itself in a certain degree through this attraction. It must, however, be regarded, just in virtue of this original compression and expansion, as eternally oscillating, and, hence, all cohesion can only have been produced (or be produced further) by the living force of impact, not the dead force of pressure.
[. . .]

21:386   13   *Progress (progressus)* in knowledge (*qua* science in general) begins with the collection of the elements of knowledge, then connects them [in the]

12

manner in which they are to be arranged (systematically). For the division of this enterprise into a doctrine of elements and a doctrine of method constitutes the supreme division; the former presents the concepts, the latter their arrangement in order to found a scientific whole.

The transition (*transitus*) from one form of knowledge to another must be a step (*passus*) only, not a leap (*saltus*); that is, the doctrine of method requires one to *pass* from the metaphysical foundations of natural science to physics – from concepts of nature given *a priori* to empirical ones which yield empirical knowledge. The rule herein will be (as in a philosopher's[10] jesting remark) to proceed like elephants, which do not put one of their four feet a step further until they feel that the other three stand firm. All physical forces are, however, contained in the concept of motion as active cause; their effect is, consequently, capable of being sensed and, as an element of experience, they are based upon the empirical [concept of motion]; their cause cannot be given *a priori*, unlike the form of the different relations in which they must be placed in order to act.

21:387

[*Bottom margin*]

   Attraction and repulsion, both as superficial force (*cohaesio et expansio*)
   Attraction and repulsion, both as •penetrative• bodily force (*gravitatio et caloricum*)
   Fluid and rigid matter
   Dissolution in a liquid into homogeneous parts (*solutio*)
   Decomposition into nonhomogeneous (*decompositio*)
   Free progressive and oscillating motion (of light)
   Of cohesion in distinction to adhesion (of *continui* or *interrupti*) of homogeneous, not amalgamated *intermediary types of matter*, e.g. water or smooth surfaces of solid bodies in contact.

14   All matter can be known as such by experience (that is, as a quantum in space) only if it is moved by the external force of a body whose influence penetrates it (i.e. by weighing); more precisely, by the reciprocal universal *attraction* at a distance, *gravitation*. But, were a type of matter expansive and at the same time *incoercible* (as one conceives magnetic matter, and perhaps also the ether in general), it would, as a result, be *imponderable* also; i.e. one would be incapable of knowing it and its weight by any experience. *Ponderosity* is the quantity of matter known by its degree, and differs according to the difference of the inverse proportion of the square of the distances of the gravitating bodies: the further from the earth, the smaller. Caloric, because it is expansive matter and yet at the same time incoercible, must, therefore, be regarded as imponderable, just as is magnetic matter (although the latter not absolutely but only relatively, in regard to all types of matter except iron).

21:388

15   Physics itself does not contain
                      a further transition from merely mechanical
                  to organic nature (founded on the concept of purpose)
             {which [transition], and according to which causal laws these
                 [purposes] could be explained, exceeds the insights
                                of human reason}
            because [physics] itself here makes a leap, [*margin:* namely to
          a nature which can be thought possible only through purposes];
                          for no bridge is placed for us
                            to reach from one bank
                                 to the other.

I

OF THE MECHANICAL COMBINATION OF
INDIVIDUAL
WORLD-MATERIALS

2

OF THE MECHANICAL FORMATION OF THE
COSMOS

[*Margin,*   Quantity   ⎫
next to "2"]   Quality   ⎬
                  Relation   ⎬   of the Transition
                  Modality   ⎭

21:389   Since the cohesive force of solid bodies is finite, the thickness of the
          attracted segment must be infinitely small; for, otherwise, such a body or
          wire would not be capable of being broken apart. Consequently, the
          attraction does not go beyond the surface in contact.

          If one imagines a quantity of water [*Wassermasse*], floating freely in the
          air, and pressed by it with the usual weight of the atmosphere, then its
          figure cannot be altered by this pressure. Just as little can this body do so
          by its own attraction, for that always acts only in a perpendicular direction
          toward the surface, which resists it in the same direction. Thus [the
          alteration of its figure] can occur, not through dead, but only living force
          (impact).
          [. . .]

21:402   PREFACE

[20] The concept of a *science of nature* (*philosophia naturalis*) is the systematic representation of the laws of motion of outer objects in space and

14

time, insofar as these [laws] can be known *a priori* (thus as necessary). For empirical knowledge of them concerns only contingent knowledge of these outer appearances, only to be acquired by experience; and it is not philosophy, but merely an aggregate of perceptions – yet its completeness, as a system, is, nonetheless, an object for philosophy.

The supreme division of the science of nature according to its content can be none other than that between its *metaphysical foundations,* which are founded entirely on concepts of the relation of motion and rest of outer objects, and *physics,* which systematically orders the content of empirical knowledge of them, and which, as stated, has the task of moving toward *completeness* in its elements – although it cannot count on this with certainty.

{Nevertheless, there can be a relationship of the one form of knowledge to the other which rests neither entirely on principles *a priori,* nor on   21:403 empirical principles, but simply on the transition from one to the other; [it shows] how it is possible for us to collect and order the elements of a doctrine of nature to be based on experience, and to arrange them with the completeness required for systematic classification. Thus one attains a *physics* which is a comparatively complete whole}[b] and which, being neither metaphysics of nature nor physics alone, contains simply the transition from the former to the latter and the step which connects both banks.

Physics of mineral or organic nature. Only the former do we treat according to *a priori* principles.

[Next page, top margin]

Solid bodies, if they were fluid, form themselves in *fibers, laminae,* and *blocks.*[11]

[Main text]

I.
THE QUANTITY OF MATTER

It is known only insofar as it is moved in mass – either by impact, by pressure, or by traction. (The pressure of a fluid, not in mass, [but] by successive impact on a rigid object, is to be regarded as an impact.) Impact is a living force, pressure and traction dead ones. The former is infinitely large in comparison with the latter.

All matter as such must be thought as in itself ponderable, because of the universal world-attraction, although the latter is not ponderable physically.

---

[b]   Kant rephrased this deleted passage as: "There remains, however, a task for the philosophy of nature."

15

2.
QUALITY

Insofar as it is mutually attractive with respect to the inner parts or repulsive; it is both: (1) originally (for without repulsion no space would be filled, without attraction no quantity of matter would be knowable – gravitation) (2) derivatively by heat.

Fluid and rigid. Both in the cohesion of matter.

21:404 Specifically, by its dissolution by means of heat (whose material, however, is neither fluid nor solid but produces [*hinwirkt*] the one as well as the other).

[*Left and right of "3," below*]

Whether light rays may be returned by general attraction.

Of the dissolution of matter into light and ether, also the first formation [of matter] by the attraction [of the ether]. Regeneration.

3.
RELATION

Cohesion, i.e. attraction in contact and attraction at a distance (world-attraction), crystallization in the rigidification of fluid as either water or heat escapes rapidly.

[*Left of "4," below*]

•A physical point: an impossibility.•[12]

4.
MODALITY

Motion at a moment: (a) as merely possible but prevented motion (dead force); (b) as actual [motion] – an accelerated or uniformly retarded motion with the same moment; (c) as necessarily continuing in motion, through the fall from a certain height, not by increase in the degree of the moment, but only in the degree of the motion by means of the moment; and continuing necessarily bound up with the latter, and as terminating itself in an ascent. Likewise the constancy of gravity; thus the necessity of remaining in the same degree of motion for the same quantity of matter. Not a gradual extinction of [the motion], as may be the case with the existence of the soul.

[*Right of "Appendix," below*]

•Of nature as art: (1) without determinate purpose, (2) as for other natural beings, (3) as purpose of the thing for itself. Organized beings.•

16

APPENDIX:
OF THE WHOLE OF NATURE
IN SPACE AND TIME

In the investigation of nature, human reason is not content to pass from metaphysics to physics; there lies within it an instinct (which, though 21:405 fruitless, is not inglorious) to transcend even the latter, to fantasize in a hyperphysics, and to create for itself a whole of nature of still greater extent, namely, in a world of ideas, according to outlines directed toward moral ends – as if God and the immortality of the soul alone (the former as *natura naturans*, the latter as *natura naturata*)[13] could entirely encompass our desire for knowledge in regard to nature in general.

21 According to the order of the categories. A. Quantity of matter.

A.

Ponderability (*ponderabilitas*) differs from *ponderosity* (*ponderositas*) in that the latter signifies greater than average weight in comparison with other [types of matter] of the same volume.

Body is a quantity of matter of a certain shape (figure), insofar as it is moving in *mass*, that is, all its parts which occupy one mathematical-bodily space have[c] power of motion with the same velocity and at the same instant (simultaneously).

Quantity of matter can be known only [through] the *vis acceleratrix* of all its parts, by means of the attraction of another body, as a force that penetrates [this matter]. Gravitation is not a specific but a general attraction and has as its basis a moment, at the initial velocity of fall – a moment which, for the same distance and the same quantity of matter in the attracting *body*, always remains the same and does not pass through different moments according to degree. As such, the velocities increase in proportion to time; distances covered, however, as the square of velocities (or times).

The quantity of the moment of gravitation is proportional to the square of the distance from the attracting body (regarded as a point in which all its matter is represented as being contained), given that the height of its 21:406 fall may be treated as infinitely small in comparison with the distance to the central body.

In this uniformly accelerated motion the fall of the body passes through all degrees of velocity from that in the moment (= 0) which is infinitely small; but not through all the greater moments which can be thought

<hr>

[c] Reading with Lehmann *haben* for *hat*.

between that in the initial instant of the fall and the final velocity; for otherwise it would not be *motus uniformiter acceleratus*.

The question is whether the moment of attraction at an infinitely small distance (i.e. in contact, which is then merely a superficial force) does not contain a finite velocity. Given a separation equal to that attraction, a moment of finite velocity would yield an infinite velocity, in no matter how short a time. And, in that case, were a wooden stake or iron wire, for instance, whose parts attract one another only in contact, to be broken apart by appending a weight [to them], then the compression of this matter, due to its own inner attraction, would transform itself into an explosion of unlimited velocity. Now, since this is impossible, the cohesion of types of matter whose moment of acceleration is infinite against that of gravitation, cannot rest on their inner force of attraction; especially as the thickness of the plate (gold-plating) causes no lesser attraction.

[*Right margin*]

The quantity of matter can be estimated, not by the number of its parts, nor by volume (if they are not homogeneous), nor even by mere comparison with others, but only by gravitation. The material point of Laplace is an impossibility.[14]

Physics (*elementaris*) is the science of the influence of types of matter on one another according to universal laws. If these laws are of the sort that concern only matter as such, and hence presuppose no representation of purposes, then this forms the doctrine of elements of nature, as containing inorganic productions. If, however, they are such that they require the idea of purposes for the comprehension of a law and of the possibility of a product of nature, then nature is here being regarded as organic. In the Transition we attend only to the former.

21:407

Physica generalis is not set alongside *physica specialis*, but rather, as *elementaris*, alongside *physica specifica*, in which different forms of the composition of matter are represented not as elements but as fabrications of nature.

[*Next page, main text*]

PREFACE

The *science of nature* (*philosophia naturalis*) turns upon two hinges, the one being its *metaphysical* foundations (that is, bound *a priori* in a system), the other containing universal principles based on experience (that is, empirical principles) of its application to objects of outer sense, which is called *physics*.

This physics is, in turn, divided into *general physics* (*physica generalis*), which expresses only the properties of *matter* in outer objects of experience, and that (*physica specialis*) which attends to bodies formed from this matter in a particular way, and which draws up a system of them – for example, regarding the difference between organic and inorganic bodies.

If it is introduced by no relationship, the progress from one system to the other is not a transition (*transitus*) but a *leap* (*saltus*), which entirely destroys what is systematic, and, hence, what is scientific in a doctrine; it cannot be tolerated in a philosophy such as physics ought to be, for the fragmentary treatment of its objects carries with it no connection of concepts and does not amount to a whole even for memory.[15]

Physica generalis thus contains the necessity of the transition from the metaphysical foundations of natural science to physics, in virtue of the relationship which is to be found between *a priori* rules and the knowledge of their application to empirically given objects; this [transition] restrains itself from continuing upon the ground onto which it has passed (which would yield a special physics) but only determines and completely displays the foundations for progress in this science.   21:408

My *Metaphysical Foundations etc.* already undertook several steps in this field, but simply as examples of their possible application to cases from experience, in order to make comprehensible by examples what had been stated abstractly.

I

QUANTITY
OF MATTER

It can only be measured by weighing, i.e. by compression of an elastic matter (e.g. a steel spring) or, and chiefly, by means of a balance (with lever-arms of equal length). The weight which indicates this quantity of matter is a pressure, which the matter exercises due to the fact that the earth, as a cosmic body, attracts it. The quantity of the earth itself (which attracts) can only be estimated by the swings of a pendulum and the number of the small arcs of its oscillation. Thus it cannot be measured directly but only inferentially. The moment thereof. The latter is different at different heights; it is not a specific velocity but rather produces such a velocity in the fall of bodies, and, in virtue of this, all bodies on earth (insofar as it can be regarded as a sphere) have their *gravities,* which are everywhere the same, but different *weights.* Yet, it is dubious whether the gravity [of bodies] on the earth would always remain the same, even were the period of the earth's rotation on its axis to remain constant, because of the imperceptible shrinkage of the earth and its diminishing radius. This gravitation is an attraction at a distance, the possibility of which has been defended by me.[16] It must be a penetrative force in order that each element of matter be drawn specifically and in the same degree into falling. Ponderosity indicates a great quantity of matter in a small volume.   21:409

19

Whether there is here a limit (in *universo*) one cannot know. Platinum has the greatest, until now. Absolute lightness would mean a matter without gravity, which contradicts the concept of a *mobilis*.

The quantity of matter can be judged neither by its volume, nor by a determinate measure in itself; for only the attraction of the whole mass by gravitation can determine it relative to other types of matter (as weight) when placed at the same height as another body. Thus the scale of a balance, which is at the same height as the other, would no longer be in equilibrium if the one scale were suspended one mile higher than the other. (It is the same for measures of spatial dimension.) Everything must be compared with the earth. A small sphere which impelled a greater one (the whole earth) upward with a certain velocity, etc.

[Right margin, bottom half]

At different distances of a body from the midpoint of the earth there are different moments of acceleration; but, taking a certain height, however far from the earth it may be, at which the difference of these moments can be regarded as insignificant (e.g. the height of a tower), the moments are to be regarded as equal, and the square of the velocity acquired by the fall is proportional to its height.

If the attraction of the internal cohesion in matter were suddenly to cease completely, matter would extend itself infinitely, and, if repulsion ceased, matter would coalesce into one point.

[Next page, main text]

II

21:410

QUALITY

Fluid or solid, rigid. The former is either *expansive-fluid*, by *repulsion*[d] of all its parts, or *attractive-fluid*, internal to both. Matter has the tendency to globosity. *Original* repulsion would be that without heat. *Derivative* that by heat. Whether there exists a specific caloric or whether heat is merely the internal vibration of all matter in cosmic space?[17] If the former, whether caloric must be bound by every other type of matter – yet in such a way that a proportion is free for expansion (and sensation)?

All merely expansive matter appears to presuppose heat as cause of expansion. Is heat itself, then, an expansive *fluidum*? Since all fluidity requires heat, and since, however, the generation of all cosmic bodies requires a preceding fluid state, and, since this latter is now preserved (at least) by the light of the sun, one may regard the fire-element as a type of

[d] Addition in margin: •Whether it is not necessary to assume this as a particular force, but as given merely through the concept of elementary particles?•

20

matter which moves and is contained in all bodies; by means of heat and light it is the cause of all fluidity.

III
INTERNAL RELATION

a. Of cohesion of fluid matter in itself, of solid with fluid, finally, of solid in itself. In the first relation the attraction of the fluid on the surface determines its figure. In the second [it determines it] to an elevation in or around a solid pipe. In the third to a lowering of the fluid in the pipe or outside it.

   b. In the dissolution of matter (solid as well as fluid) and precipitation.

   c. In crystallization and evaporation, in fluid or solid form.   21:411

IV
MODALITY

The principle of *a priori* knowledge of the *existence* of things (actuality of existence), i.e. of experience in general, in thoroughgoing determination according to Leibniz's Dyadic: *omnibus ex nihilo ducendis sufficit unum*,[18] by which the unity of all determinations in the relation of all things emerges.

[*Left margin*]
   No two mutually repelling or attracting particles are nearest material points, but between each point there is always another, and matter is a continuum.

   At different distances from the midpoint of the earth the moment of acceleration is different. Nevertheless motion is said to be uniformly accelerated when it is produced [*getrieben*] at small heights, by the same moment [of acceleration], be it repulsive or [*breaks off*]

   Attraction in contact by which a matter becomes rigid is cohesion, as dead force. The moment of attraction is here *finite* and would, in the shortest possible time, produce an infinite velocity, were it not resisted.

   Adhesion is a displaceable cohesion, as, for instance, when slippage on a smooth inclined plane meets a resistance, which is called friction and which has a smoothing effect. Even a mirror-smooth surface has such a friction which gradually wears away the solid matter which is rubbed, whether that be the matter of the moving and slipping body or of what supports it.

   A rigid surface on a rigid, though mirror-smooth, surface still resists displacement as a moment of impact. But *gutta cavat lapidem*.[19]

   Rigid bodies rubbed against one another give heat. Is not, perhaps, all heat a mere state of extension and reciprocal attraction by vibration? That   21:412
all rigid and brittle bodies (glass), although the surface of their breakage

fits together, are yet no longer internally cohesive, but only as surface force. Thus, in the form of fragments, though organized so as to fit together, they [yet] have a greater volume.[*]

* A *quantum* of matter is the multitude of the movable *in* space insofar as, united and moving together, it forms a whole. *Quantity* is its determination as a homogeneous whole. All matter is a quantum; that is, no matter consists of simple parts (physical points). [There is no corresponding * in the text.]

[Toward the elementary system of the moving forces of matter]

"A"

INTRODUCTION
OF THE MOVING FORCES
OF MATTER

§1

Physics is the science of nature founded on experience; its object is matter in general insofar as it has moving force according to empirical laws.

§2

All moving forces are either attraction or repulsion; for one matter has a tendency (*nisus*) to approach or distance itself from another – or a part of it from another part. This tendency to begin a motion in a particular 21:308 direction or its opposite, with a certain velocity, is called the moment of the motion. For it takes time to reach a finite (measurable) velocity by continual accumulation of these infinitely small quantities of motion. This increase is called acceleration (*acceleratio*) which, if it increases through nothing but equal moments, is called uniformly accelerated motion (*motus uniformiter acceleratus*) – from which, then, uniformly retarded motion (*motus uniformiter retardatus*) can be directly understood.

§3

All repulsion of the parts of matter (by which it becomes expansive) is superficial force; i.e. a greater quantum of the latter does not move matter which is outside it with a greater velocity than would a smaller quantum, for it exercises moving force only in contact. On the other hand, the attraction of a greater quantum of matter can impress a greater velocity at a moment on another external to it, because it (like the force of gravity) does not just affect the surface but also the inside – or, at least, *can* affect

23

it. Thus one [may] profitably use the division of moving forces into superficial force and penetrative force for the distinction of physical force.

Note. Expansion as superficial force cannot be uniformly accelerating; for its moment always diminishes with increased expansion. On the other hand, attraction (e.g. by the force of gravity) can very well be uniformly accelerating because it acts upon the inside of matter *immediately.* Expansion, by contrast, acts directly only on the surface of the matter in contact; it has internal influence only by mutually canceling action and reaction.

[*Right margin*]

21:309   The apparent attraction and repulsion in capillary tubes. Crystallization: in ice-rays, in lines; in snow flakes, in ice-surfaces; and in ice-blocks.

Of cohesion of and with fluid; and of capillary tubes.

Of the cohesion of the rigid.

4th category. Of the connection of all matter with the totality thereof. The totality of community regarded absolutely. Actuality knowable from possibility, i.e. necessity.

Of stratification (*stratificatio*) of the diverse as cause of rigidity.

Crystallisatio

textura: fibrosa, laminea, truncalis

3rd category – Relation. Cohesion of rigid types of matter among themselves.

Of watery or fiery origin. Earths and metals. The luster of the latter.

The *Transition* contains only concepts of thinkable moving forces of matter and their laws, whose objective reality is still left undecided; and it founds a system of concepts according to form, to which experience can be adjusted.

Of expansion, which is not so uniformly accelerating as attraction by gravity.

The attraction of fluid also acts upon the bare surface.

[IIIrd fascicle, sheet VI, page 2]

4
OF THE DIFFERENCE
BETWEEN THE LIVING AND DEAD FORCES
OF MATTER IN MOTION

I call motion which is exercised by impact against a *body* living force; that by pressure, as only a moment of motion, dead force. Here, however, I call a (physical) body in distinction from matter in general [*breaks off*]

21:310   The continual sequence of impacts and counterimpacts in an intermediate space I call pulsations (*pulsus*).

All matter must have repulsive forces, since otherwise it would fill no space; but attractive force must also be attributed to it, since otherwise it would disperse itself into the infinity of space – in both cases space would be empty. Consequently, one can think of such alternating impacts and counterimpacts [as existing] from the beginning of the world, as a trembling (oscillating, vibrating) motion of the matter which fills the entire universe, includes within itself all bodies, and is both elastic and at the same time attractive in itself. These pulsations constitute a living force, and never allow dead force by pressure and counterpressure (i.e. absolute rest inside this matter) to occur.

An elastic fluid in the state of internal vibration necessarily occupies a greater space than in the state of rest. Thus is brought about, as the effect of a living force, the extension of matters in cosmic space, as well as that of the corporeal things contained in it insofar as they are penetrated by those matters.

The reason to assume such a hypothesis is that, in the absence of such a principle of the continual excitation of the world-material, a state of lifeless stasis would come about from the exhaustion of the elastic forces in the unceasing universal attraction, and a complete cessation in the moving forces of matter would occur.

The doctrine of the laws of the moving forces of matter, insofar as they are known *a priori*, is called metaphysics; insofar as they can only be derived from experience, physics. That doctrine, however, which envisages only the *a priori* principles of application of the former, rational [doctrine] to [the latter] empirical one, can form the transition of the philosophy of nature from the metaphysics of corporeal nature to physics.   21:311

Thus, for example, the doctrine of attraction at a distance in general, and its magnitude in inverse proportion to the square of the distance, as these concepts can be thought *a priori*, belong to the metaphysical foundations of natural science. The doctrine of gravity, as it and its laws are observed at different heights, [belongs] to physics. But, in a philosophy of nature, the two require a combination and the step necessary for it, which, like everything reason connects by the unity of the object, cannot be a leap. Thus there must be mediating concepts which [enable] the transition from the one doctrine of nature to the other, i.e. the application of *a priori* concepts to experience in general; just as the principles of the possibility of experience in general must themselves be given *a priori*.

I believe that I could not better reach the completeness of a system in the composition of this work, than if here, too, I were to follow the clue given by the categories and bring into play the *moving forces* of matter according to their *quantity*, *quality*, *relation* and *modality* in turn. Herein, the opposites, which one thinks of in relation to each of them, are not to be thought of as *logical* (as between A and non A), but as *real* (as between A and $-$A); for

25

they are to be taken as forces effective in space which (like attraction and repulsion) affect one another by opposite direction of motion.

Category 3. Of the internal attractive and expansive force of matter. Of cohesion and caloric. Relationship of substances with one another.

21:312   That caloric penetrates all bodies and that every body in warm space must also be warm, belongs to the category [of] necessity.

Whether it can be said of caloric that, although it is something movable in space, it *fills* space, for it penetrates whatever occupies space, and, consequently, is ubiquitous?

That which moves everything but is itself not movable in mass. Exists only inherently, but not subsistently. *Principium motionis.*

The prime matter is that which is originally moving (*motrix*) but is not itself movable (*mobilis*) since it contains the totality of what is movable. It is reciprocally attractive and repulsive, not fluid (*fluidum*) but that which renders everything fluid.

At this point [treatment] of heat, whether a particular material or mere motion, whether spread out everywhere in the world?

Of motion in mass or in flow (by pressure or by impact)

[. . .]

"α Übergang"

FIRST CHAPTER
OF THE QUANTITY OF
MATTER

§1

A *quantum* of matter is the whole of a multitude of movable things in space. The *quantity* of matter is the determination of this multitude as a homogeneous whole. Each part of matter is a quantum, i.e. matter does not consist of metaphysically simple parts, and Laplace's talk of material *points* (which were to be regarded as parts of matter) would, understood literally, contain a contradiction; it should signify only a position from which a part of matter repels or attracts another which is external to it. Here there occurs (in the *Metaphysical Foundations of Natural Science*)[20] the remark that, were repulsion the sole moving force of matter, every matter would dissipate itself into infinity; consequently, space would be *empty*. But were it attraction alone, all [matter] would coalesce into a single point and space would also be empty. So each quantum of matter can originally fill a space only through the conflict of attraction and repulsion of substances – an action and reaction which is already contained in the concept of a spatial matter, but whose possibility can be made comprehen-   22:206
sible by no explanation whatsoever.

§2

The quantity of matter cannot be determined by its volume alone, for that would require the assumption of all matter as equally dense – for which, however, there is no reason. One will have to ask not only: How *much* space? but, also: To what *degree* is it filled? But, even then, no determinate concept of its quantity would be generated, because the homogeneity of the types of matter (e.g. the air, a double quantum of which is compressed in the barrel of an air pump) would always have to be assumed, and a quantum subjected to measurement would not be a quantum of matter as such but of a specific type of it. But here we are concerned with the measure of the quantity of matter in general.

Since the quantity of matter cannot be measured *mathematically*, by enumerating the multitude of the magnitudes, it must, if a correct estimate of its quantity is to be conceivable at all, be estimated dynamically (i.e.[a] by

---

[a]   The sentence is continued on page 2, top.

the quantity of motion which one matter impresses on another with a velocity that is the same by nature). For, in that case, the quantity of matter must necessarily stand in proportion to the quantity of motion which it produces under this condition.

22:207 [*Right margin*]
The relation of this quantum to unity as measure is the quantity of matter.

Since matter does not consist of simple parts, its unity must always be thought of as a quantum, and [its] quantity can never be expressed by a number which would exhaust [its] possible division. That is, there are no absolutely primary parts of matter; what Laplace terms "material points" are not simple parts but, rather, mere positions for parts of matter, which one may imagine as small as one pleases, without hope of reaching, by means of division, the absolutely smallest.

[*Top margin*]
One would call those corpuscles physically simple of which one assumes, by a mere hypothesis, that they can be divided (ground down) by no natural forces; thus offering an infinite resistance to mechanical division, without ceasing to be mathematically divisible. Atomism is a sort of construction method [*Baukunst*] for putting a world together out of all kinds of immutable and differently formed material; properly, it must have no place in the philosophy of nature.

The quantity of matter can thus be measured neither arithmetically, by the number of corpuscles, nor geometrically, by volume, but only mechanically, by the quantity of the moving force which a volume of matter exercises in one direction and at one velocity of motion upon a movable object. Herein all matter is treated as homogeneous, i.e. as matter in 22:208 general, since it is attracted in all its parts, with equal initial velocity and equal motion, to the midpoint of another body – a cosmic body, indeed, whose quantity of matter [is] incomparably greater (on a balance manifesting equal moving force through arms of equal length).

[*Right margin, bottom*]^b
The quantity of matter can only be measured through motion of the material parts *in mass* with the same initial velocity, that is, through its moment (of the impact of solid bodies in infinite motion, in contrast to pressure).

[*Bottom margin*]
The quantity of motion is (1) that with which a body is moved, (2) that

---

^b The Academy edition leaves out the following two notes in the margin.

with which it moves others. From the latter alone the former can be known. The word "force," applied to motion as its cause, can also be represented as a real motion in an infinitely small time (that is, phoronomically, only as cause). Only the motion of matter *in mass* determines its quantity. Its moving force in flow with a finite velocity allows a quantity of motion to be known for this matter, which is equal to the motion of a finite mass, moved with an infinitely small velocity, that is, equal to a weight (pressure), and is dead force. The impact of a body occurs in mass; that of a quantity of matter in flow is only a pressure and is, for the same velocity and density, infinitely small in relation to impact.

[IXth fascicle, sheet I, page 2]

§4ᶜ

Weighing is the only general and dynamical means for the precise determination of the quantity of matter, of whatever type it be; and an absolutely imponderable matter would be one for which there would exist no assignable quantity.

Weighing is an experiment: the pressure by which a heavy body, by the quantity of its matter, opposes the sinking of another, whereby both bodies remain equally movable around a stable point (*hypomochlium*). For weighing, there is required equality of the moment of velocity in the fall of all bodies toward the midpoint of a cosmic body, the equality of distance from this midpoint, and, finally, the world-attraction, called gravitation, which penetrates all matter. This moment of acceleration by gravity differs according to different distances from the center; in experiments [of weighing] which we can perform, however, inasmuch as they concern the same place, [acceleration] can be taken as uniform. Attached to a lever with arms of equal length, the horizontal line, intersecting the direction of gravity at right angles, and passing through the center of gravity, is the proof of equilibrium.

An estimate of the quantity of matter can, thus, only be made by means of an original moving force, which instantaneously penetrates all bodies at all distances, and which, at the initial instant, is termed the *moment* of acceleration. 22:209

To this centripetal force can be opposed another centrifugal force, [striving] to distance itself from the midpoint with the same moment [of motion]; this, however, results from real motion, namely the rotation in a circle of an attracted body. Yet this motion is not conceived of as accelerating (like a sling-stone, swinging in a circle) but only as a continuous resistance against the moment of gravitation; resistance which does not [belong] to matter's own [forces] but rests on their combination with real

---

ᶜ There is no §3.

motion. Of the same kind is the centrifugal force of a body moving freely in a circle by being thrown along its tangent which has the same moment as gravity, but which is not accelerating, and, although opposed to gravity, does not belong to the original, and thus naturally inherent, forces of matter.

From an equal number of the swings of a pendulum in small unequal arcs the *weight* of the body appended to it cannot be known, without [the use of] scales (for the size and the material content of the body makes no difference to these swings). What can be known, however, is the gravitation and the moment of fall of bodies at different distances from the attracting central body – even, in fact, the quantity of the matter of individual parts of the central body, which [causes] the direction of gravity to deviate noticeably, and so makes measurable, the relation of a mountain, for example, to the earth as a whole.[21]

[Top and left margin]

So all matter must be regarded as ponderable, for otherwise one could have no determinate concept of its quantity. The more matter a body contains in the same volume the *heavier* it is, and this condition is called its ponderosity. The cosmic body, upon which we conduct this estimation of the quantity of matter, acts upon all bodies, at the same distance, by the immediate attraction of all its parts, with equal initial velocity (which is called the moment of gravitation), toward the midpoint; consequently, there cannot be any absolutely and completely (*simpliciter*) imponderable matter. At most there could be such under certain conditions opposed to the moment of gravitation (*secundum quid*).

22:210

Of such a kind is the tendency of a freely moving body, rotating in a circle, to distance itself from the midpoint, which contains a moment of motion, but not of acceleration. It continues to distance itself by the initially impressed motion without being accelerated, [i.e.] centrifugal force, which is no particular property of matter.

The accelerative force of gravity is determined by a number of swings in small arcs. Quantity of matter, however, by a balance or a spring. The first demonstrates the weight by the opposed attraction of the balance, the second by repulsion of the weight.

Living force (by impact) (*vis viva*) is different from the *vivifying* force (*vis vivifica*). The latter, in a separate world-system (and its generation), is perhaps the cause of *plants* and *animals*.

Modality. What rests upon hypotheses, observations and inferences, which count all of this as experience.

That which is thinkable in the concept, that which exists in sensation, that which is necessary and knowable *a priori*.

Pressure, impact and cohesion belong under the categories of relation.

30

Of moving force by pressure and impact. 22:211

Initiated motion by attraction or merely *imparted* [motion] by pressure and impact. Dead and living force. The latter is to be found in the cohesion of the rigid or the fluid. Whether heat is imponderable, whether incoercible, and whether absolutely *simpliciter* or only *secundum quid?*

[IXth fascicle, sheet I, page 3]

SECOND CHAPTER
OF THE QUALITY OF
MATTER

§5

Besides the *attractive* forces, there also belong to the possibility of matter in general *repulsive* forces; and that both must be found together in every type of matter may be developed from the mere concept of matter. For matter is something which fills space. If *attraction* alone were to belong to the parts of the world-matter, then they would all coalesce into one point and space would remain empty. On the other hand, were *repulsion* the only mode of action of its parts on one another, it would dissolve and disperse its parts into infinity, and cosmic space would remain equally empty. Thus, the existence of matter is nothing other than a greater or lesser whole of material points, which, as they repel, but yet also at the same time attract one another, *fill* a space (extensively and intensively).

•A constantly alternating attraction and repulsion, as resulting from the primordial formation of matter (*undulatio, vibratio*), would be the third [element], and the matter for it the ether.•

§6 22:212

Matter does not consist of simple parts, but each part is, in turn, composite, and atomism is a false doctrine of nature. Corpuscular philosophy [is adopted] to account for [*herausklügeln*] the difference in the density of matter. It is in vain to conceive of matter, not as a continuum, but as a whole, separated by empty, intermediate spaces (*interruptum*), whose parts would thus have a certain form by means of the empty space between them (in order not to require repulsion, as a special force to account for the difference of density). For such primitive corpuscles (*corpuscula*) would, in turn, always have to consist of parts which repel one another – otherwise they would fill no space physically.

The void cannot be *thoroughly* interspersed in the plenitude of matter. Otherwise matter would fill no space. And, since the material parts must, at least, have repulsive forces in order to *fill* their space (the filling of space just amounts to this), matter will not fill the volume of a certain quantity of matter merely by its own existence (without requiring particular repulsive forces); but always by a repulsive force opposed to attraction.*

[*Next to the above*]
Gehler[22]

[*Right margin*]
That the more rapid vibrations of the glass, in contact with the water, make it lighter (because they further expand the water, although without increase of the caloric) is a sufficient explanation for the rising [of water] in capillary tubes – even without assuming a ring of attraction at a distance.[23] In the same fashion, water rises against the glass outside the tubes, although not so high, for it does not [rise] between two close surfaces beside the [*breaks off*]

22:213   [IXth fascicle, sheet I, page 4]

§7

The first division of matter in regard to its quality can be only this: It is either *fluid* or *solid* – which latter quality is better expressed, with Euler,[24] as *rigid* (*materia rigida*).

The principle of all fluidity is generally attributed to heat, whose escape must have rigidification as its inevitable consequence. This rigidification, if it takes place from a still fluid state, results in a certain *texture* (*textura*), as experience teaches. Under the name of *crystallization* (*crystallisatio*), it regularly forms *fibers* (*fibras*), *plates* (*tabulas*) and *blocks* (*truncos*), according to the three geometrical dimensions.[25] The escaping heat, however, does not always escape in substance; possibly the greatest portion is merely bound (made latent). The caloric serves all of this as a vehicle, and even as a formative means [*Bildungsmittel*], if only nothing mechanically prevents this regularity.

Formations in the three realms of nature all begin from the fluid state, hence from heat; and one may now ask whether the caloric is a fluid matter. Its transition from one body to another is warming (heating). It cannot exist in isolation, but acts only by its penetration into all matters, without exception, with greater or lesser velocity; and it increases the volume of those which become fluid by it. It renders matters elastic, which, previously, in combination with others, were not (e.g. hydrogen gas), without itself being elastic – for that, in turn, would require heat.

* [The space for this note is left empty.]

32

•textura fibrosa, laminea et truncalis.•

§8

22:214

If one assumes an *originally* elastic matter, it would have to be so without caloric. {. . .}. Or else the latter would be only one of the names for a material which permeates all bodies universally; a material which, in one case, would be called caloric, but, when represented according to another quality, light-material – in both cases, ether. Hence, heat and light would be only two modifications of one and the same repulsive matter, •but• not different materials. The ether would, thus, be the only *originally* elastic matter; the name of fluid would not, however, apply to it. For, in contrast to rigidity, which can be abolished only by caloric (acting directly or indirectly), fluid has here, as yet, no application. This ether, moving as elastic matter in straight lines, would be called light-material; when absorbed by bodies, and expanding them •in all three dimensions,• it would be called caloric. This is so, regardless of the fact that, in the latter condition, it is neither a fluid nor repulsive, but only makes fluid and expands their matter.

[*Left margin*]

Repulsion can act as a superficial force, or as a penetrative force (but not one acting at a distance, like gravitation). In the latter case, the repulsion of all internal material parts of all bodies is heat.

One could call the ether empyreal air – although not in Scheele's[26] sense, 22:215 by which it means a respirable form of air, but, rather, as an expansive matter whose penetration contains the ground of all the forms of air.

A lump [of matter] which can be shifted by human hands, exercises no significant attraction on another body (unless it is magnetic). Schegallien.[27]

Two smooth and rigid surfaces attract each other – and I can raise the one slab by means of the other. In that case they attract each other at a distance. Rigidity on a polished (i.e. ground) surface passes gradually into fluidity.

What is fluid, what is rigid? For rigidity there must be friction, without which there would be no slippage.

Attraction in contact (not that of gravitation or magnetism), i.e. cohesion, counteracts the expansive forces.

In magnetism and electricity there occurs an attraction at a distance – through an intermediary matter, however. But, in cohesion, immediately, in contact.

[*Bottom margin*]

Heat can only be thought as inherence, not as subsistence for itself, in space. One must first assume matter in space, which can become expansi-

33

ble by heat, before one can think of warming or the elimination [*Ausschei-dung*] of heat (cooling) in it. For the latter are determinations belonging only to the modality of the ether, namely, expansibility of the ponderable matter, expansion, and the unified filling of space necessary for such an effect. The caloric, which is the ether itself,[d] is imponderable in this universal medium, for its attraction in all directions is combined with an equal repulsion; another matter must first be given which gravitates in some direction in this space. It is incoercible, i.e. all-penetrating, partly in resistance, as in electricity, partly without resistance, by magnetism.

[. . .]

21:521   [Vth fascicle, sheet IV, page 1]

"ε"

OF THE RELATION OF TYPES OF MATTER
TO ONE ANOTHER BY HEAT

Heat is always regarded as merely inherent; caloric, however, as something subsistent. If, however, a material is assumed for elasticity, heat is required, in turn, to turn it into gas. But it is difficult to imagine that this material could assume a figure and, like all matter, form a body by itself, in isolation from all other matter and placed by itself in empty space. Especially because one assumes that heat penetrates all bodies without exception, and none which is completely lacking in heat could be thought. The causality of heat is that it expands all bodies, weakens their cohesion, and renders them fluid; that it is the cause of all elasticity, which is thus fundamentally derived from it (although it cannot itself be called elastic, for, for that, another heat would, in turn, be required); and, since it is incoercible, its material content cannot be estimated by weight. How one could call it a fluid is unintelligible. For, in order to be an elastic fluid, it would itself require heat; to be a fluid absorbed [*eingesogen*] by other bodies, it requires cohesion within itself and with other types of matter.

NO DROPLET-FORMING FLUID IS POSSIBLE
WITHOUT THE LIVING FORCES OF A MATERIAL
PENETRATING ALL MATTER

1. Attraction in contact produces no motion, for matter resists the attracted particle in the direction of contact as much as the latter is attracted by the former. Thus water, mercury, etc. would form no droplets by their

---

[d] The sentence is continued on page 1 of sheet xii, IInd fascicle.

own forces. Neither can this occur by pressure (that is, not by a dead   21:522
force), but only by an impact which, rather than moving the whole body of
water in a certain direction, unceasingly moves it in all its parts, in all
directions, by pulsation. In this way one can understand that the fluid
must yield to all these impacts until the contact of its parts among one
another is at its maximum, and their contact with empty spaces at its
minimum; for only then is the resistance equal to the moving forces, and
the body of water in a permanent condition.

This matter can be regarded as that which we call caloric; its motion, as
that of an elastic material, is called heat.

The rising of water in capillary tubes is the effect of the greater attraction of the glass, and of the increased repulsion of the parts of the fluid
among one another, due to the contact of the fluid with the glass. Consequently, also, it is an effect of the thinning of the fluid by the inner
vibrations, by means of which the fluid becomes lighter and, in this way, is
raised. The sinking of mercury below the waterline [*Wasserpass*] is to be
derived from the greater attraction of mercury among its parts and the
lesser contact with the vessel (the glass).

When caloric, or a part of it (whose vibration was responsible for mixing
together the species of fluid matter) escapes, a moderate form of this
vibration of heterogeneous, but, yet, reciprocally resolved, elementary
materials, now produces stratification (*stratificatio*). This is a texture in
which the tremblings of those (fibers, laminae) which are not in accord
separate themselves from those which are. Thus they form fascicles which
resist redisposition of their layers, in that their parts cannot (unlike a fluid)
be displaced in all directions without resistance.

It can be seen from the texture of fibers, laminae and blocks, which is   21:523
formed by crystallizing minerals – indeed in the configurations formed
undisturbed by metals – that this [escape of caloric] is the cause of rigidity. Here the vibrating quality of the caloric sets the tone, as it were, for
this formation. Euler's pulsations of the ether are to be applied here not
just to light but also to the motion of heat.[28] The peculiar luminosity of
metals. The beating of metals produces simultaneously the melting and
the alignment in fibers of their parts.

[*Right margin*]
The increase of caloric without increase of heat is latent heat.

Heat is everywhere, in empty space as much as in full space, incoercible
and imponderable. It is not elastic, for the reason that it is incoercible,
and, in expansion, is only delayed, not wholly prevented. Is it a fluid?

The concept of rigidity is here understood as in the transition of a fluid
matter, in a state of rest, from complete fluidity to a solid state, and the
form it takes on in it.

What is to be remarked first is that heat (whether great or small in degree) means a universal state of vibration of all world-matter, which, for that reason, is fluid.

The reason why caloric is elastic remains inexplicable.

The *stratification* of the different elements of a fluid, with the gradual decrease of the heat which, previously, had amalgamated everything.

For one of these amalgamated matters, more caloric is required than for another in order to remain fluid; thus heat is latent in its different [elements], and the whole, although equally *warm*, is *rigid*.

21:524

[Vth fascicle, sheet IV, page 2]

Preface

{Philosophical treatments do not deserve the name of philosophy as science unless they are presented as combined in a *system*. Fragmentary philosophizing means only the making of thought-experiments by means of reason; these have little reliability, so long as the division of the whole has not been able to assign them their determinate place and relation to others. For} this science, by this alone [*breaks off*]

The science of nature (*philosophia naturalis*) consists of two parts, different according to their principles: The first represents the movable in space (matter) under laws of motion, according to concepts *a priori*, and its system was composed under the title *Metaphysical Foundations of Natural Science*. The second part, which proceeds from empirical principles, would, if one wished to undertake it, be called *physics*.

As far as philosophy is concerned, it is my plan – and lies, so to speak, in my natural vocation – to remain within the boundaries of what is knowable *a priori*: to survey, where possible, its field, and to present it as a circle (*orbis*), simple and unitary, that is, as a system prescribed by pure reason, not one conceived arbitrarily. This could not be achieved by the collection of the empirical elements of knowledge, fragmentarily assembled; for this does not allow one to hope for the conviction of completeness. Although physics is the goal to which these preliminary metaphysical notions must aim in their application to objects of experience, it is left here to the work of other hands.

21:525 Since both of these parts of the science of nature are nevertheless related to each other so closely that the former cannot but have regard for the latter, and the latter for the former, the concept of a transition is a concept given *a priori* in the doctrine of elements of the science of nature in general, and requires a special discipline of its own.

Physics contains the natural moving forces and effects of matter, knowable through experience. Regarded objectively, they, and their laws, are merely empirical; but, subjectively, they can (and must) be treated as given *a priori*, for, without reference to them, no experience for physics could be made. The physicist must lay these laws, *as if* given *a priori*, at the foundation of other experiences; otherwise he cannot relate the *Metaphysical Foundations* to the physical. The transition from one territory to the other would be a leap, not a step; whereas he who undertakes a step must first feel that both feet stand firm before he draws one after the other.

[Bottom margin]
•{The original fluid, caloric, is *qualitas occulta, causalitas phaenomenon*, in which inherence is regarded as subsistence, and, in respect to which, inference is always circular. Caloric, the basis of heat, requires heat to become elastic. It is a matter without gravity and not displaceable, but which moves all matter internally, renders matter elastic but also cohesive – nevertheless, it is without gravity. It is extended in the whole of cosmic space: The world, however, has no position from which it might move. Permanent-elastic and yet alterable in its influence on bodies.}•

[Vth fascicle, sheet IV, page 3]
The transition from one science to the other must have certain intermediary concepts, which are given in the one and are applied to the other, and which thus belong to both territories alike. Otherwise this advance is not a lawlike transition but a leap in which one neither knows where one is going, nor, in looking back, understands whence one has come.   21:526

One might think that the transition from the metaphysical foundation of natural science to physics requires no bridge, for the former, as a system constituted by concepts *a priori*, exactly adjoins the ground [*Boden*] of experience onto which it could alone be applied. But this very application creates doubts and contains difficulties which should be embarrassing for physics, as a particular system, separate from the former. For the admixture or insertion of the one into the other, as commonly occurs, is dangerous; not just to its elegance, but even to its thoroughness, because' *a priori* and empirical principles might communicate with or make claims upon one another.

In the metaphysical doctrine of nature, matter was only [dealt with] as the movable in space, as it is determinable *a priori*; in physics the moving forces are [dealt with] as experience reveals them; in the transition from metaphysics to physics, however, the movable with its moving forces is arranged in a system of nature, so far as the form of such a system can be constructed in general from these elements, according to the laws of

---

' Deleted continuation: {physics must needs adopt hypothetical concepts whose reality is uncertain and which, with regard to their possibility, require a deduction from *a priori* principles.}

experience. For the blueprint of a building is far from yielding a full estimate, although the materials for the building, as far as essential requirements are concerned, naturally are taken into account.[29] How much of the expenditure is to be made on what is really necessary, however, and how much on ornament and comfort, depends on the wealth of the owner.

21:527   It is, indeed, a common illusion that one may hope, using nothing but mathematics, to produce a philosophical system of physics, without prior metaphysical foundations; results show, however, that, in this fashion, everything is treated fragmentarily and that a satisfactory whole, or even the plan of one, cannot emerge. It is no less erroneous to suppose that one could undertake to construct physics as a system out of preliminary metaphysical notions and mathematics – even with a rich store of observations and experiments – unless metaphysics has outlined the plan for the whole. Thus it is, if not a particular part, at least a particular obligation of the science of nature (*philosophia naturalis*) to hold itself in preparation for the transition from the metaphysical foundations of natural science to physics; otherwise the guiding thread would be lacking by which to emerge from the multitude of given objects and to present satisfactorily both its divisions and their content.

[. . .]

[IVth fascicle, leaf 6, page 1]³⁰   21:474

Under the name *science of nature* (*scientia naturalis*) is understood the system of the laws of matter (of the movable in space); which, when it contains only their principles *a priori*, constitutes its metaphysical foundations; when it contains the empirical as well, however, it is called *physics*. The latter, as a *doctrine of bodies*, i.e. of matter in a figure determined according to laws, is divided in turn into general (*physica generalis*) and particular (*specialis*); in which either the formative force acts merely mechanically, or else one body forms another of the same species, in propagation of its species, i.e. organically. This latter division of physics is here passed over or relegated to scholia, and the concept of the science of nature [given] a broader scope, namely that of a system of the empirical doctrine of nature in general [*breaks off*]

Merely empirical science of nature can never amount to a system, but, at best, a fragmentary, ever-increasing aggregate. For, however far we may be acquainted with the empirical laws of nature, we do not know to what extent that may suffice for the purpose [*Gebrauch*] of the philosophy of nature; and the gaps make us dubious of our supposed explanations of the laws of nature. The moving forces of nature are not completely known to us.

Metaphysical foundations of natural science yield something that is certain and a complete system; but their purpose [*Gebrauch*] – the only one which can be envisaged for them – is physics, for which they can give us no material. They are divisions for the concept which require to be filled; and mere forms without an underlying material can as little yield a system of experience, as richly distributed material without forms. There must be a transition from the metaphysical foundations of natural science   21:475
to physics if the science of nature is to become a science of reason (**philosophia** *naturalis*).

These two territories (metaphysics of nature and physics) do not immediately come into contact; and, hence, one cannot cross from one to the other simply by putting one foot in front of the other. Rather, there exists a gulf between the two, over which philosophy must build a bridge in order to reach the opposite bank. For, in order for metaphysical foundations to be combined with physical [foundations] (which have heterogeneous principles) mediating concepts are required, which participate in both.

[Top margin, upside down]
Of the mathematical foundations of natural science.

[IVth fascicle, leaf 6, page 2]

[Top margin]
The metaphysical foundations of natural science have their determinate

scope and content. As do those of the transition to physics – because both are given *a priori*.

Physics does not.

[*Main text*]

The moving forces of matter, which can only be known by experience (thus do not belong to the metaphysical foundations), nevertheless belong to *a priori* concepts (and thus to metaphysics) as regards their mutual relations to one another in a whole of matter in general, insofar as one takes moving force simply as motion itself. In that case [the moving force], regarded mathematically, according to its direction and degree, [is] *attraction* and *repulsion* – whether of the parts of matter for one another, or of one matter toward another which is external to it. Density, rarefaction etc. [are concepts] which can be thought voluntarily [*willkührlich*] *a priori*, and for which examples are then sought in nature. Thus they denote logical positions for concepts (*topice*), for which it is possible to determine *a priori* which appearances fit into the one or the other position.

21:476   (a) External attraction (gravity). (b) Internal fluidity and solidity. (c) External repulsion as superficial force and internal (elasticity and the living force of vibration).

The moving forces of *repulsion:* both the internal of matter and its parts, and the external (filling of space).

The moving forces of *attraction:* the external of gravity, or the internal of cohesion.

The moving forces of *impact* and of vibration by external or internal forces (*motus concussionis*).

The moving forces of penetration into bodies or expulsion. Here it is not a case of ascending from experience to the universal, but rather the transition is a descent.

Between metaphysics and physics there still exists a broad gulf (*hiatus in systemato*) across which the transition cannot be a step but requires a bridge of intermediary concepts which form a distinctive construction. A system can never be constructed out of merely empirical concepts.

How matter becomes a (physical) body, in contrast to matter which produces no body because its filling of space (repulsion) is not subsistent but merely inherent? Caloric which is not elastic but only renders other matters elastic. Not relatively ponderable insofar as it is a world-matter.

An *a priori* concept lies at the foundation of all judgments and concepts of experience, under which we subsume appearances, insofar as the object is to be subsumed under a species of things.

Physics is the doctrine of the laws of the *moving forces* of matter. Since the latter, like everything belonging to existence of things, must be known by experience, then [*breaks of*] How does matter produce a body?

However diverse the objects of physics may be (whose properties and classifications must be learned by experience (empirically) in order to make them as far as possible [*kümmerlich*] into a so-called system), they are, nevertheless, merely phenomena. *A priori concepts of moving forces* must always lie at their foundation, and phenomena must be arranged according to them, since these concepts contain the formal element in synthetic representations. Even for the concepts of physics this is necessary, in order to yield knowledge of an object (through the understanding). 21:477

The transition from the metaphysical foundations of natural science consists in the circumstance that the concept of the *moving forces* of matter yields a principle in its possible application to empirical concepts. This concept can be thought *a priori*, according to the relations of the moving forces in space and time, and, as such, can be completely classified. [The task is] to classify the real objects of nature according to a principle, and to bring the empirical study of nature ever closer to a system – although it never attains such completeness, which cannot be expected from experience.

We can classify *a priori* the moving forces according to concepts, and so completely enumerate the properties of matter prior to experience; for the synthetic unity of appearances must lie in the understanding prior to experience – e.g. internal and external repulsion. The transition takes place when I apply these [concepts], not in metaphysical, but in physical-dynamic functions, to real bodies.

[Left margin, next to first paragraph]

N.B. Of the mathematical foundations of physics. Whether this, too, belongs to the Transition?

[IVth fascicle, leaf 3/4, page 1][31]

All droplet-forming fluids become rigid through crystallization (*crystallisatio*) – without intervening time – at a determinate degree of heat whereby the caloric is freed.

Of the conditioned and unconditioned coercibility of matter.

The transition from one science that already exists to another that is only in the idea presupposes *a priori* principles of a possible system of both in combination. So it is with the metaphysical foundations of natural science in relation to physics – which, without the former, would be 21:478 merely an aggregate (*farrago*) of observations of nature that would permit no secure delimitation or outline. The matter of knowledge here is to enumerate the moving forces of nature *a priori*, insofar as they contain *a priori* the principles of possible experience of them. The movable in space insofar as it has moving force. Since then the conditions of motion in general and also the forces lying at the basis of its motion are to be specified *a priori*.

Here, moving forces must be assumed for the laws of motion that are *a priori* given, which [forces] alone serve for the explanation of the latter, although one cannot prove them: e.g. the lever.

The metaphysical foundations have a tendency toward physics as a system of the moving forces of matter. Such a system cannot arise from mere experiences, for that would yield only aggregates which lack the completeness of a whole; nor can it come about solely *a priori*, for that would be metaphysical foundations, which, however, contained no moving forces. Therefore, the transition from metaphysics to physics, from the *a priori* concept of the movable in space (i.e. the concept of a matter in general) to the system of moving forces, can [proceed] only by means of that which is common to both – by means of the moving forces insofar as they act not on matter but rather united or opposed among one another, and thus form a system of the universal doctrine of forces (*physiologia generalis*) which stands between metaphysics and physics. Insofar as it contains for itself a system of the application of *a priori* concepts to experience, i.e. the investigation of nature, it combines metaphysics with physics in a system. The transition is properly a doctrine of the investigation of nature.

[. . .]

[IVth fascicle, leaf 5, page 1]³²   21:481

In the part*f* of the philosophical science of nature (*philosophia naturalis*)   21:482
entitled the metaphysical foundations thereof, there already lies a tendency toward *physics* as the goal to which it is directed – namely, to expound the empirical doctrine of material nature in a system. What are
called the *mathematical* foundations of the science of nature (*philosophiae
naturalis principia mathematica*), as expressed by Newton in his immortal
work, are (as the expression itself indicates) no part of the *philosophy of
nature*. They are only an instrument (albeit a most necessary one) for the
calculation of the magnitude of motions and moving forces (which must
be given by observation of nature) and for the determination of their laws
for physics (so that the quality of the motions and moving forces can be
specified in regard to the central forces of bodies in circular motion, as
well as the motion of light, sound and tone, according to their direction
and degree). Consequently, this doctrine properly forms no part of the
philosophical study of nature. The same can be said of empirical knowledge of nature insofar as this forms only a chance aggregate, not a
system – for which a general classification according to concepts *a priori* is
required.

But this tendency in the transition from metaphysics to physics cannot
be satisfied immediately, by a leap. For those concepts, which lead across
from a system of one sort to another, must be accompanied by empirical
principles as well as principles *a priori*. The former, since they contain
comparative universality, can, like the [wholly] universal, be used for the
system of physics. Thus there is a gap to be filled between the metaphysical foundations of natural science and physics; its filling is called a transition from the one to the other.

1. The moving forces of matter according to the quantity of matter, and
summa according to the categories.

2. The formal conditions of this motion insofar as it rests on principles
a priori.

         attraction   repulsion   21:483
         ponderable – imponderable
         coercible – incoercible
         subsistent in space – or inherent

N.B. The titles in the system of categories here contain only two as
dynamic powers: +a and −a.

1st *part:* Of the doctrinal system of the *a priori* investigation of nature.
2nd *part:* Of the world-system.

---

f   Changed by Kant into "title."

43

[*Left of the foregoing*]
Of the alterability of the heights of barometers – not immediately, by alteration of the weight, but chemically, by a matter which weakens or strengthens the elasticity of air. The former.

To Garve.³³ System of philosophy from a pragmatic point of view, to be developed in one's role as teacher of skill and prudence.

In the *Metaphysical Foundations,* matter was thought of as the movable in space; in physics, matter is thought of as the movable which [has] moving force; and their combination, [as] a relation of matter's own moving forces, according to their own laws of motion, is the object of physics. Insofar as the totality of these forces permits of classification *a priori,* founded on *a priori* concepts, there must exist a *topic* of the moving forces of matter in which each of these forces is assigned its location (*locus communis*) in the system; and a special science will be both possible and necessary, which is solely occupied with these locations in the investigation of nature. Empirical concepts (e.g. gravity), whose moving force can be thought according to *a priori* concepts (e.g. attraction and repulsion) although their existence must be given through experience, belong to this topic of the transition. This class of moving forces could belong to physiology, to wit, the pure, etc.

21:484 For the moving forces can be enumerated *a priori* according to their form; but can be known according to their content [only] by the appearances of their effects.

The investigation of nature, in the absence of any principles of classification, can result in no system of physics; for there would arise from it merely an aggregate (*farrago*) of particular observations, and how far these might extend cannot be anticipated. •This investigation of nature is fragmentary, not systematic.•

[. . .]

[VIIIth fascicle, sheet I, page 1]   22:135

"El. Syst. 1"

OF THE SYSTEM OF THE MOVING
FORCES OF MATTER

First Part
Of the Elementary System of World-Matter

Division

One can ask for no better clue to the division of the moving forces and the laws of motion of matter than the table of categories, regarded according to quantity, quality, relation and modality, and ordering the elementary concepts [namely, of the moving forces and laws of motion of matter] under these headings. For the latter constitute the stages of the transition from the metaphysics of corporeal nature to physics.

{Moving force is of two kinds: either the locomotion of a body (*vis locomotiva*) which forces another to leave its place, or internal motion.}

FIRST SECTION
OF THE QUANTITY OF MATTER

§*1*

Ponderability (*ponderabilitas*) is that property of matter, according to its moving force, whereby alone its quantity can be precisely measured. An intrinsically *imponderable* matter would be such as would allow of no   22:136
measure, •thus can be assumed as = 0.• For even if it could be measured geometrically, in comparison with another of the same type (e.g. pure water in containers of different sizes), the homogeneity of the two could itself be doubted, because their assessment [*breaks off*]

Gravity (*gravitas*), being the penetrative action of the accelerative force of attraction of our earth at equal distances from its midpoint, is measured by the number of the swings of a pendulum; weight (*pondus*), however, as the product of gravity (the moment of motion of a falling body), is measured by the quantity of the matter moved. And, since the former (gravitation) is equal at equal heights, in all measurements of the quantity of matter it is assumed that this is equal to the weight.
[. . .]

45

[VIIIth fascicle, sheet I, page 2]

§2

But the concept of ponderability presupposes an instrument for the measurement of this moving force (of weight) in the form of a lever-arm. One must, however, attribute to this instrument another force which resists flexibility, namely that of the cohesion of its parts among one another; otherwise ponderability would be a concept of what was a mere figment of the imagination [*Gedankending*].

The physical lever-arm always has a certain thickness of diameter, at which the weight appended to it exercises moving force to bend or to break it. Now, the mathematician[34] must, if he wishes to present *a priori* this law of motion, assume the thickness of the lever-arm as infinitesimal – for which, however, he would have to assume an infinite force of attraction between the parts of the lever-arm in the straight line of contact, which is impossible. Thus the ponderability of matter is not a property knowable *a priori* according to the mere concept of the quantity of matter; it is, rather, physically conditioned and requires the presupposition of an *internally* moving matter which results in the immobility of the parts in contact with one another [in the lever-arm], by itself being mobile inside this matter. We know of no other matter to which we have cause to attribute such a property, except caloric. Thus, even ponderability (represented subjectively as the experiment of weighing) will require the assumption of a matter which is not ponderable (*imponderabilis*); for, otherwise, the condition for ponderability would be extended to infinity, and thus lack a foundation.

•Ponderability presupposes the coercibility of the matter in the lever, which resists its bending or breaking, as well as the breaking of the cord by which the weight is suspended. The mechanics of moving forces is thinkable only under the presupposition of dynamics – objective ponderability preceding subjective. A living force of the matter which penetrates the body must be the cause of the dead force of pressure and traction (which produces an infinite series of contacts, in immediate subordination of each to the next, and, hence, the moving superficial force of a mass – i.e. attraction of cohesion). Coercibility, permeability, and perpetuity (or attraction) – thus, the moving force of caloric is required for a lever as an instrument of ponderability.•

§3

An *absolutely* imponderable matter thus cannot be thought, •for that would be a matter without quantity.• But it could be so in a *conditional* manner, namely, merely as part of a matter which is distributed through the whole of cosmic space (the caloric); for then the case would be that bodies do not weigh in their own element.

Note

The moving force of cohesion underlies all mechanism, whether this takes place by *pressure* (as in a lever), or *traction* (as in a pulley), or *shear* (as in the case of an inclined surface, on which a body tends to slide). Machines effect with a lesser *force* (a smaller *moment of motion*) as much as would have been achieved immediately by a greater. •But the possibility of a machine itself presupposes moving forces. The lever must be rigid and neither bend nor break from the weights on the lever-arms. The cord on which the weight is suspended must not break.•

[*Margin* . . .]

[VIIIth fascicle, sheet I, page 3]   22:141

SECOND SECTION
OF THE QUALITY OF MATTER

§4

Matter is either *fluid* or *solid**ᵍ (*aut fluida aut rigida*).

All fluid matter is so by heat, and the state of fluidity precedes all formation of matter into solid bodies (at least, only thus can one explain the origin of this quality).

Heat is something which renders fluid; but can one call it a fluid itself (a substance, not merely the inherence of certain forces)?

Caloric is a matter which cannot be regarded as *coercible* into containers (as, for instance, the air), although it can be prevented from transmitting itself rapidly to bodies in contact. Thus one cannot properly describe it as a fluid (which would be expansive), since all expansibility of matter is derived from heat, and it could, thus, be asked what provides caloric itself with this force of expansion.

Caloric is, hence, *incoercible,* as well as imponderable, and can be coerced (or, as it is called, bound), in whole or in part (dynamically, not mechanically), by no other material – except that which is of its own type (the universally distributed caloric). This property, however, belongs to physics (chemistry) as a system; not to the elementary empirical concepts with which alone we are here dealing. It is a necessary consequence of the relation of the moving forces of matter to one another that a matter which is incoercible is also to be regarded as imponderable (and, as imponderable, as incoercible also).

The transition of matter from fluidity to solidity must, however, also be ascribed to the influence of caloric – but by means of another type of   22:142

ᵍ   There is no corresponding note.

internal motion, namely, that of a *living force* of this matter. This force acts by impact and has an undulatory motion, inwardly attracting and repelling, in rapidly succeeding vibrations. By this motion the space which the matter occupies is expanded.

§5

The moving force of caloric is a *living force* of impact; namely, a concussive motion of the parts of matter by means of its repulsive forces – not a dead force of pressure and counterpressure. Such an *inward*, undulatory (vibrating, oscillatory) motion fills a greater space – by repulsion – than the mere transition of one matter into another, in which case the latter increases in density only.

That the moving force of caloric exerts this force in the state of heat is clear, however, from the fact that, as incoercible, its locomotion can produce no increase of this expansive material (which can penetrate everything). Caloric can expand [something] only by means of its own internal state, by vibration [*hin und her stossen*] in the space which it occupies.

[. . .]

22:146   [VIIIth fascicle, (half-)sheet II, page 1]

"El. Syst.
Beylage zu Syst: 1, S. 4"[35]

THIRD SECTION
OF THE RELATION OF THE MOVING FORCES
OF MATTER
IN THEIR SOLIDITY (*RIGIDITAS*)

§6

I call this active relation the *cohesibility* of matter; by its means the inner parts of a matter resist displacement, as well as forming themselves into solid bodies from the fluid state. Its measure is the weight at which a body (by its gravity) breaks apart at a given section. The degree of cohesion can be specified most easily by the length of a completely uniform prism or cylinder, which breaks apart at a certain length as a result of its own weight.[36] For, however thick it may be, it will break apart at the same length, given that the matter of which it consists is homogeneous, since we can imagine each cylinder as composed of however many individual cylinders it may be *next to* (not after) *one another* – and thus regard each as breaking apart independently.

§7

Now, the cohesibility of a solid body is a mere superficial force, not a force which penetrates matter and immediately attracts the distant parts beyond the surface of contact. Consequently, each segment (plate), however thin one assumes it (hence also the quantity of its matter and attraction) to be, [would be] infinitely small in comparison to the weight of the block. Thus the moment of acceleration required [to resist] the weight with which the body tends to break apart [would be], correspondingly, infinitely large – which is as much as to say, a moment of finite velocity crossing an infinite space in any given time-period – which is impossible. Thus one is com- 22:147 pelled to assume, either that the parts of this block extend their attraction inward beyond the surface of contact of the section, or else that attraction in cohesion is not an accelerative, moving force – of neither alternative can one form a concept.

§8

Hence, one can hardly form a concept of these relatively opposed forces, except by assuming that caloric, which is the cause of all fluidity, is moving *with living force* (as stated above). As the heat escapes, the concussions of caloric bring about a tendency, such as cohesion is, once heat-induced fluidity has ceased. •For, as one of the opposed forces is removed, the other does not also disappear.• A lead ball, rubbed together with another, melts momentarily on its touching surface and immediately solidifies. Hammering and forging always produce an instantaneous but transitory melting.

[*Margin* . . .]

[VIIIth fascicle, (half-)sheet II, page 2]   22:148

§9

Cohesion is either that of a *friable* (*corporis friabilis*) or a stretchable – ductible – body (*ductilis*). Glass or stone, in the former case, metal, in the latter case, are examples of the matter of the universal caloric, penetrating and acting with living force. Caloric produces cohesion by expansion (as heat) and the simultaneous escape (binding) thereof.

Ductility when hammered is malleability (*malleabilitas*), which belongs to all metals, at least when heated somewhat. Each blow amounts to a momentary melting and quickly succeeding solidification. The – as the mineralogists term it – *particular* glow of metal, which appears hardly capable of description, much less explanation, can be explained by this internal crystallization in rays [*Strahlenanschiessung*]. It is to be regarded not just as reflected but as radiating light from the polished surface of the metal. For the beating and polishing of it must be regarded as a momentary melting, [and the metal] is separated into laminae and small rays by caloric on the surface, as can be seen on the wing-cover of many insects (e.g. *Cerambyx moschatus*)[37] which emit the light appropriate to the thickness of these laminae. For without that polish, which is the effect of melting, and thus of crystallization on the surface, metals have their common earth-color.

22:149   *Critical note*

It may seem that in this section we have greatly transgressed the boundary of the *a priori* concepts of the moving forces of matter, which together are to form a system, and have drifted into physics as an empirical science (e.g. into chemistry); but one will surely notice that [*breaks off*]

[. . .]

22:188   [VIIIth fascicle, sheet VII, page 2]

["Elem Syst. 6
Einleitung"]

FOURTH SECTION
OF THE MODALITY OF THE MOVING
FORCES OF MATTER

§

This is comprehended under the category of *necessity,* which, in turn, carries with it the character of universal validity in space and constant continuation in time, and is *necessity in appearance. (Perpetuitas est necessitas phaenomenon).*[38]

Motion resulting from the moving forces of matter cannot cease except because of opposing motions.* Because, however, the totality of all combined matter only forms a dynamic whole by virtue of the internal action and reaction of the moving forces of all its parts, this dynamic whole (be it composed of dead or living forces) can be permanently in a state in which its matters interact with one another. The reason is that, according to the principle of inertia, no matter alters its state of its own accord, and,

---

* *Quantitas motus in mundo summando eos qui fiunt in eadem directione, et subtrahendo qui fiunt in contrarias in universo non mutatur.* This well-known proposition is proved by the fact that otherwise the universe itself would be displaced, which is absurd.[39]

outside this totality, no other material cause will be encountered which could alter it.

[. . .]

In the *Metaphysical Foundation of Natural Science* its object, matter, was represented in a doctrinal system merely as what is *movable in space,* and its motion in time (the latter according to its laws knowable *a priori*).

There is still, however, in these *Foundations of Natural Science,* a tendency toward physics, i.e. to a system of the moving forces of matter which must be taken from experience, and whose investigation (*indagatio, perscrutatio naturae*), as a system of these forces, is called physics. This is a   22:190 doctrine of motion from *empirical* principles which must be [ordered] in a system of perceptions and, hence, formally subordinated to certain *a priori* principles. In it the science of nature represents the concept of matter as the *movable, insofar as it has moving force;* and it contains the empirically given moving forces of matter insofar as they are thought of together in a system (physics), formally and *a priori.* Any physical body can be regarded as a system of the moving forces of matter, and what confers on such a system its *a priori* conceivability can be expressed under the title of the general-physiological foundations of natural science. So, then, the metaphysical, the general-physiological, and, finally, the physical foundations of natural science will, together, represent the system of the moving forces of matter as a transition from the metaphysics of nature to physics.

But yet a fourth concept of the moving forces of matter makes an entry into the system of the science of nature, and lays claim to a particular division of the foundations – namely, certain supposed *mathematical* foundations of natural science, of which Newton's immortal work gives a shining example; although its title (**Philosophiae** *naturalis principia* **mathematica**) is, in fact, self-contradictory. Examples to be found in this work are: the doctrine of the central forces by attraction (gravitation); by repulsion (light and sound); and the doctrine of the wave-motion of fluid surfaces (oscillation).

However, there occurs here an ambiguity in the sense of the term "the moving forces of matter," which can be understood either as primitively or else only derivatively moving. If the motion of a matter must precede, in   22:191 order for the latter to have a moving force (e.g. if a sling-stone must be swung around so that its cord is stretched to breaking point), then the moving force of the stone is derivative, for motion must precede the moving force. But if the cord breaks, solely as a result of the increase of the weight of the stone suspended from it, then the moving force of the stone is primitive.

There exist, therefore, no mathematical foundations of natural science, in respect to the primitive moving forces of matter; rather, the science of nature (*scientia naturalis*) is, as such, wholly philosophy when it subordinates the laws of the moving forces of matter to *a priori* principles.

[*Right margin*]
1. Metaphysical Foundations of Natural Science
2. Physiological, Propaedeutic Foundations of Natural Science
3. Physical-Systematic Foundations of Natural Science

Not as aggregate, but as system; for such is every body. But form [*breaks off*]

[VIIIth fascicle, sheet VII, page 4]
Mathematical foundations for the laws of motion in general, for all possible moving forces of matter (*legum motus principia mathematica*). The division, which here concerns only the formal aspect of motion (and, hence, must lie *a priori* in the concepts themselves) concerns only the direction of the moving forces – attraction, repulsion, and the internal motion of matter, as a result of continual agitation of both (*attractio, repulsio, oscillatio*). Here motion is presupposed, with moving forces as its consequence.

22:192 These foundations are contrasted with the physical foundations of natural science.

The motive forces (*vires motrices*), the moving forces (*vires moventes*), the forces which independently repeat their motion of attraction and repulsion (*vires agitantes*). The force which moves itself in substance is here either locomotion (*vis locomotiva*) (e.g. circular motion) and, thus, external; or it is that of a matter, moved by alternating attraction and repulsion, which agitates it at the same place (*vis agitans interne motiva*), as in oscillation (*motus tremulus, vibratorius*). And this [motion] is either constantly preserved (*perennis*), if it is the internal motion of the totality of matter, or else it is a motion which hinders the reaction of the parts of matter to one another and produces rest in a finite time.

Since empty space is not an object of experience, and, thus, neither the internal nor the external *void* can explain any phenomenon of matter, it is not a hypothesis but a certainty that the totality of all world-matter is a *continuous whole* (*continuum*). That is to say, even attraction in *empty space* is a mere idea insofar as one abstracts from the repulsive force of matter (e.g. in *gravitation*), in that filling of space by repulsion contributes nothing to it – contrary to the opinion of Descartes. Thus all matter, conceived together with its moving forces, forms *one system*. Its manifold parts I regard, on the one hand, *sparsim;* the same matter, however, I regard, on the other hand, as an absolute, *coniunctim,* as belonging to no greater whole. From this the division of the system of the moving forces of matter into the elementary system and the world-system will follow.*†

[*Left margin*]   22:193
Of the atomistic and fluxionary system.
What is force?
The ether is the hypothesis of a matter for which all bodies are permeable, but which is itself expansive.
Of the moving forces of organic matter. Vital force. Reproducing itself according to species. Of existing for itself and for its own sake.

[*Top and left margin*]
The determinability of space and time, *a priori* by the understanding, in respect of the moving forces of matter, is the tendency of the metaphysical foundations of natural science toward physics; and the transition to it is the filling of the void by means of those forms which regard all possible objects of experience in their unity. [The filling of space] is a product of the idea of the whole, in the thoroughgoing, self-determining intuition of oneself. An elementary system which has the potentiality [*Empfänglichkeit*] for a world-system (according to purposes), and contains an objective tendency toward this latter, and without which there would be no physics.

[*Main text, between paragraphs*]
•The mathematical *unity of space and time,* which contains *a priori* the formal conditions of the possibility of experience as a system of perceptions – and hence must be thought of, not *partially (sparsim)*, but as   22:194
combined in *one whole (coniunctim)* – founds the concept of an elementary system of the moving forces of matter. Empty space is no object of possible experience – neither as included, nor as all-inclusive (finite, infinite) empty space. The *filling* of space occupied by matter must be judged by the fluxionary, not the atomistic, principle of the division of matter; in which, firstly, no space is left empty, and, secondly, the matter which fills it is extended to the *minimum quantity of matter* for the same volume – although its expansive force amounts to the *maximum* inasmuch as it is a

---

* Force is the subjective possibility for a thing to be a cause. Thus a category of relation, regarded either as a phenomenon or a noumenon.
† Students of nature have wanted to take offense at the word "force" (as if it were a *qualitas occulta*).
Each physical body is to be regarded as a system of mechanical-moving forces (i.e. as a machine); the matter, however, from which it is composed, presupposes dynamic moving [forces], which do not depend on figure (e.g. in a lever, or wedge).
So a matter must be assumed, the internal mobility of whose parts (which form a continuum) is equivalent for all – i.e. a fluid which, through moving itself purely dynamically, yet moves this matter mechanically.

1

matter which thoroughly penetrates **all** *bodies,* and for which all bodies are permeable – such a matter must unceasingly preserve all the *modes of motion: attraction, repulsion* and *reciprocal agitation.*•

[. . .]

22:199 [VIIIth fascicle, sheet VIII, page 3]

["Element. System 7
Einleitung"]
Fluidity is either an external *locomotive* moving force (*vis locomotiva*) of a continuous matter, insofar as the latter consists of parts which move an object only by means of successive but continual impacts, or else it is an internal moving force, acting uninterruptedly *at the same place.* Only by the latter quality is the former possible; that first definition is only a nominal explanation to which the real explanation belongs as its ground.

Postulate of Dynamics
All the parts of matter distributed in space
stand in mutual relation
22:200 as members of a universal mechanical system
of the forces which originally and constantly
agitate matter*
In the transition from the metaphysical foundations of natural science to physics it is necessary to abstract from everything which rests on empirical principles, for, otherwise, this would amount to a transgression of foreign territory (by μετάβασιν εἰς ἄλλο γένος).[40][h]

[*Right margin*]
The problem is: What is it that first sets the moving forces of matter – taken as a whole – in motion?
Only the forms of combination of the moving forces can be enumerated *a priori* in an elementary system; the forces themselves cannot be developed otherwise than empirically – and, thus, only fragmentarily – for they only indicate the tendency to physics.
The elementary system is that which proceeds from the parts to the entire complex of matter (without *hiatus*); the world-system is that which proceeds from the idea of the whole to the parts.

---

* By the forces *agitating* matter, I understand those which produce real motion in it, in distinction from those which produce only the tendency (*conatus*) toward motion. It will become apparent, however, that even the latter depend on the former as their cause.

[h] The rest of page 3 and page 4 are left empty.

[*Next to* "Postulate of Dynamics"]

The transition from the metaphysics of nature to physics is the tendency of the laws of motion in general toward the principle of the moving forces of nature.

Space and time realized.

The *primum movens* is not locomotive but rather internal, by reciprocal attraction and repulsion of all parts of matter.

The collective idea of all the moving forces of matter precedes *a priori* the distributive idea of all the particular forces, which are only empirical.

The elementary system prior to the world-system.   22:201

That matter whose internal motion makes weighing (therewith, the rigidity of the lever) originally possible, must itself be imponderable. It is expansive, however, because it occupies, by means of internal concussive motion, a greater space than if it were at rest.

[. . .]

[IXth fascicle, sheet IV, page 1(3)]   22:239

["B Übergang"]

All the primitive moving forces of matter are dynamic; the mechanical are only derivative.

The former are penetrative and, in fact, in two possible ways: either in substance (like caloric), by locomotion, or by the immediate action on matter, even at a distance (like gravitational attraction). Combined together in the world-system, however, [they are] attraction and repulsion simultaneously.

Of the difference

between the qualitative *divisibility* (by the species of matter) and the quantitative *divisibility* (by the multitude of the homogeneous parts of the same species). Whether both extend to infinity?

The same in the case of the *composition:* either material composition from elements (mixture) or formal*ⁱ* composition – of a new matter produced by a process of separation.

ⁱ   Changed by Kant from "organic."

THE TRANSITION
FROM THE METAPHYSICAL FOUNDATIONS OF
NATURAL SCIENCE TO PHYSICS

22:240   is the complex of all *a priori* given relations of the moving forces of matter which are required for the empirical system, i.e. for physics.

Thus there are elementary concepts of the science of nature which, however, do not intrude into physics (hence not into the doctrine of experience), and which can be presented – not fragmentarily, but systematically – as an *a priori* whole. How is such a formal elementary system from mere concepts – e.g. intuitions •axiom,• Anticipations •of Perception, Analogies of Experience, systematic unity of the whole of the empirical• – possible?

[*Right and left of* "The Transition"]

22:239   •If [the transition] took place *by means of* experience, it would be physics itself; if it takes place, however, by means of principles of the possibility of
22:240   experience, it precedes physics *a priori* and contains *a priori* principles for its construction. This is, however, a particular part of the science of nature which contains its own principles and founds its own system – although a merely formal one.•

Physics

is an empirical system of the moving forces of nature and a problematic whole thereof. The transition from the metaphysical foundations to the science of nature in general, represented *a priori*, according to the formal principles of mathematics and philosophy, is a transition in which mathematics supplies [*enthält*] only the application of concepts to intuitions *a priori*, by anticipations etc., not fragmentarily, as a mere aggregate, but systematically, according to one principle. Without these premises there can be no science of nature.

This transition is not merely propaedeutic; for such a concept is ambiguous and concerns only the subjective aspect of knowledge. There is a not merely regulative, but also constitutive formal principle, existing *a priori*, of the science of nature, for the purpose of a system.

Axioms of Intuition, Anticipations of Perception, Analogies of Experience, and Postulates of Empirical Thought in general. The first contain
22:241   mathematical principles rather than philosophical ones (by concepts); the second contain the forces, insofar as they are internally moving (through apprehension), as philosophical [principles]; the rest [contain the forces] insofar as they are either mechanically or dynamically moving – or else moving mechanically by means of dynamic forces.

All matter was primordially fluid, and everything fluid was expansible, not attractive. At least, this idea is the fundamental idea.

56

In order to attain physics, as a system of the empirical science of nature, there must previously be completely developed, in the transition to it, *a priori* principles of the synthetic unity of the moving forces of the science of nature, according to their form (Axioms of Intuition, Anticipations of Perception, etc.). These principles contain a propaedeutic of physics as an *a priori* transition to it, which is[j] derived analytically from the mere concept of physics. This propaedeutic is itself a system which contains *a priori* the form of the system of physics. What contains the possibility of physics as a whole cannot be a fragmentary aggregate; for, as a whole given *a priori*, it must necessarily be a system which is capable neither of increase nor of diminution. Regulative principles which are also constitutive.

[*Top margin*]
The first division of the outer objects of sense, as substances, is that into *matter* and *bodies*.

The organized creatures form on earth a whole according to purposes which [can be thought] *a priori*, as sprung from a single seed (like an incubated egg), with mutual need for one another, preserving its species and the species that are born from it.

Also, revolutions of nature which brought forth new species (of which man is one).

[*Right margin*]
The primitive-moving forces of matter are the dynamic forces. The mechanical are only derivative.

The first moving force is that of external attraction, insofar as it is not   22:242
restricted by repulsion – gravitation. The second is that of *internal* repulsion, insofar as it is restricted by attraction. Both are matters which form bodies by their moving forces – which, in turn, determine their own space according to quantity and quality.

The *mechanical ponderability* of matter requires that it be *dynamically imponderable* – for without this internal moving force (not *locomotiva*), weighing would itself be impossible.

Likewise, in order that matter with its moving force be coercible, an incoercible (namely dynamic) matter is required: caloric.

The matter, which *renders* all other matter fluid by penetrating it, is originally fluid; thus it is incoercible.

2. Of the moving force of matter by the coercibility of caloric, as mechanically or dynamically acting force. The one is the phenomenon of the other, or the *means* for *the presentation* of the other.

---

[j] Lehmann changes *wird* into *werden*.

The *objective* principles of the laws of the moving forces of matter are those which are given *a priori*, in their *formal* aspect, by means of the *classification by reason* of all possible such *active relations*.

The *subjective* [principles] are those of mechanics, according to which we set these forces in motion (action), and [are] of empirical origin; hence *suited for physics*. The former for the transition from the metaphysical foundations to physics.

[. . .]

21:181   [IInd fascicle, sheet IV, page 1]

"A Elem. Syst: 1"

OF
THE SYSTEM OF THE MOVING FORCES OF MATTER

First Part
The Elementary System of the Moving Forces
of Matter

Section One
I.
{Definitions}
•*According to their Material Aspect*•

The moving forces are either *locomotive* (*vires locomotivae*), or *internally moving* (*interne motivae*): attraction or repulsion (*attractio, repulsio*) or *continually* changing between the two (*oscillatio, undulatio*). Those impacts which alter in equal time-intervals are called *pulsations* (*pulsus*); otherwise, where they are in indefinitely rapid succession to one another, they are called *vibration* (*concussion*); both presuppose internally moving forces.

The moving force of a matter, insofar as it can only produce *repulsive* motion, is **superficial force** – i.e. one which only acts in *contact;* that which acts also *immediately*, at a distance, is **penetrative force** (not penetrative matter). If matter is penetrative in substance, the body is said to be *permeable* for it.

21:182   If it is penetrative only by activity (*virtualiter*), not by physical presence (*non localiter*), then it is penetrative merely by attraction.

[Left and right of "II," below]
•The moving forces of matter are powers, either purely dynamic or mechanical. The latter are based upon the former. [*Margin: vide* below,

N.B.] What is opposed to a moving force is here understood, not *logically* (as A and non A), but as *real* (as A and −A).•

II.
According to the Formal Aspect of Motion

1. By its **direction:** *Attraction* or repulsion
2. According to its **degree:** *Moment* of the motion, or the latter with *finite speed*
3. By its **relation:** According to the laws of the *external influence* of *bodies* upon one another, or of the internal influence of body-forming matter. *Mechanism*
4. By its **modality:** From the *outset* (of motion) and at all *future* times, i.e. as acting according to necessary laws; for the perpetual is the sensible representation of the necessary (*perpetuitas est necessitas phaenomenon*).   21:183 That, the actuality of which is knowable *a priori.*

All these forms are *a priori* laws, for a system of moving forces; drawn, not from the elements of physics (which always furnish us only with objects of experience), but from *concepts* (to which we subordinate the elements of physics), for the sake of a system of the moving forces; and they have their purpose [*Bestimmung*] only in the *tendency* of the metaphysical foundations of natural science *to* physics.

N.B. Either dead or living force. The moment of motion and acceleration,   21:182 or impact at the commencement of contact, of bodies moved in mass, not in flow. The latter is infinite in relation to the former. Internal, not locomotive motion: undulatory, vibratory, concussive. Internally, not externally moving powers [*Potenzen*] – according to their formal aspect. (1) *Direction:* attracting and repelling, or both continually alternating with each other. (2) Limited or unlimited by *volume,* likewise by time. (3) *Continuous* or interrupted in composition. (4) Homogeneous or heterogeneous in its manifold.

[*Right margin*]   21:183
What, for the sake of an elementary system, can be stated *a priori* about the moving forces of matter, has completeness. The empirical is a fragmentary aggregate, and belongs to physics. Only metaphysics creates the form of the whole.

Finally, the moving forces of matter, insofar as the latter contains the basis of all motion in an original unity. Elementary material.

The concept of final cause is, at first glance, a contradictory concept, namely, that the last shall be first. The cause shall be what precedes – but also the end. This is, nevertheless, an *a priori* concept.

Definitions, axioms, theorems, problems, and postulates.

Imponderable – incoercible – incohesible – inexhaustible.

That all of these moving forces stand under the system of categories, and that one universal [matter] primitively underlies them all.

[Underlying] it, however, a highest – namely, originally independent – understanding.

agitatio.

21:184   [IInd fascicle, sheet IV, page 2]

III.
According to the Completeness of the Division of the System of Forces in General

One can, in fact, also draw on the concept of *organic* (as opposed to *inorganic*) nature, in the consideration of the moving forces of nature, without, [thereby], transgressing the limits, determined *a priori*, of the transition to physics, or mixing into it what belongs to the material part of physics (thus to the doctrine of experience as a part of it). One can, in fact, define the former as follows: Organized beings are those of which, and in which, each part is there *for the sake of the other* (*propter, non per aliam partem eiusdem systematis*).[41]

The *final causes* belong equally to the moving forces of nature, whose *a priori* concept must precede physics, as a clue for the investigation of nature. One must see whether (and how) *they*, too, form a system of nature, and can be attached to metaphysics. In this case, everything is, indeed, only established problematically, but the concept of a *system* of the moving forces of matter requires, nevertheless, the concept of an *animated* matter – which we at least think *a priori* and assign a possible classification (without demanding – or surreptitiously assuming – reality for it).

The word **final cause** (*causa finalis*) literally contains the concept of a causal relationship on the part of something which *precedes* (in the sequence of conditions), but which, nevertheless, is also to succeed its own self (in the sequence of causes and effects) – for which reason it appears to contain a contradiction with itself. For one thing cannot be the beginning and (in just the same sense) the end of the same real relationship.

21:185

Such a relationship may, however, be thought under the moving forces of matter, provided that we restrict our judgment in the following way: We cannot comprehend the system of moving forces except by assuming an understanding, independent of matter, which is architectonic with respect to these forms, and to representing the moving forces of matter according to the mere **analogy** with it. This can occur according to *a priori* concepts, without crossing over (by means of empirical judgments) into physics. For only thus can we render the system of the moving forces of matter comprehensible to ourselves.

The division of the moving forces of matter, insofar as the latter has the tendency to form organic or inorganic bodies, thus also belongs to the form of the combination of these forces in a system. This is, however, only a principle for the *investigation of nature,* which, as an *idea,* precedes empirical [investigation], and may {not} be lacking in the complete division of the transition from the metaphysical foundations of natural science to physics – despite the fact that it is merely problematic and takes [no] notice of the existence or nonexistence of such bodies [and their] forces. •Matter and bodies.•

[*Bottom margin*]

Organism is the form of a body regarded as a machine – i.e. as an instrument (*instrumentum*) of motion for a certain purpose. The internal relationship of the parts of a body, whose purpose is a certain form of movement, is its mechanism. All the laws of motion of matter are mechanical; but only if the internal relationship of the parts is represented as formed for the *purpose* of a certain form of motion, [is] a mechanism   21:186 attributed to the body. Mechanism [*Maschinenwesen*] signifies a particular form of the moving forces (set into a certain matter, by nature) which makes them capable of an artificial [motion] – e.g. the stiffness of a lever which enables a certain load[k] to be intentionally moved, on a fulcrum (*hypomochlium*), by a certain force.

Organic bodies are natural machines, and, like other moving forces of matter, must be assessed according to their mechanical relationships, in the tendency of the metaphysical foundations of natural science; their appearances must be explained in this way, without crossing over into the system of the moving forces of matter according to final causes, which, being of empirical origin, belong to physics.

[. . .]

<hr>

[k]   This sentence is continued in the bottom margin of page 3.

[The ether proofs]

[IInd fascicle, sheet VI, page 1]

"Übergang u[sw.]"

[*Top and right margin*]
Division of the doctrine of nature, by the principles of the transition of its metaphysical foundations to physics. This cannot be derived from objects, for, in that case, it would be empirical and belong to physics. This division, to be founded on principles *a priori*, can [be]: (1) the *method* of treatment [of the doctrine of nature] in general (2) the division of concepts

21:207 in respect to the form of objects – insofar as the former [follows] from concepts (as merely thinkable), but necessarily belongs to the transition from the metaphysical foundations of natural science (organic bodies), in which the science itself is organized (3) the division of movable materials, insofar as their actual motion is knowable *a priori*.

All these sections contain the formal principles of the possibility of an empirical science of the system of the moving forces of matter – i.e. of the transition to physics.

[*Main text*]

INTRODUCTION

I. Of the formal concept of the science of nature

There belong to every science as a system, *a priori* principles concerning its form, to which the matter, as the sum of its objects, is then subordinated; thereby knowledge becomes scientific.*

Thus the scientific principle of the science of nature (*Scientiae naturalis*) as a doctrinal system of the moving forces of matter in general is rational;

---

* A science of knowledge [*Wissenschaftslehre*] in general, in which one abstracts from its matter (the objects of knowledge), is pure logic; and to imagine beyond it another, higher and more general science of knowledge (which, however, can itself contain nothing other than the scientific element of knowledge in general – its form) is, conceptually, to chase one's own tail.[42]

it can be divided into two subjects (*Scientiae naturalis principia mathematica* and *Scientiae naturalis principia philosophica*). Yet how could one (with Newton in his immortal work under the title **Philosophiae** *naturalis principia mathematica*), produce a science which is, in fact, an absurdity (*syderoxylon*)? For one can as little imagine mathematical foundations of philosophy, as philosophical foundations of mathematics. For these sciences (apart from the fact that they both contain *a priori* principles) are specifically different from each other in their necessary procedures; and, with respect to their purpose and the talent required for them, stand as far apart as is possible for products of different origin.

21:208

There exists, therefore, no such hybrid species of science (*scientia hybrida*), for one would destroy the other at the very outset; yet, one may be associated [*vergesellschaftet*] with the other[a] for the sake of making progress in scientific knowledge.

Thus one ought to speak of: (1) *Scientia naturalis* (not *philosophiae*) *principia mathematica;* (2) *Scientia naturalis* (not *philosophiae*) *principia philosophica,* to which latter, then, the metaphysical foundations of natural science will belong – from which the transition to physics is to be made.*

There as little exist mathematical foundations of natural science as there do philosophical of mathematics. Both are located in separate territories, neighboring but not intermingled. Consequently, *mathemateme* do not form such an enclosed *whole* as *philosopheme* – which, regarded objectively, permit the hope of the idea of a system combining them.

21:209

[IInd fascicle, sheet VI, page 2]

Although mathematics is not a canon for the science of nature, it is, nevertheless, a potent instrument (organon), when dealing with motion and its laws, for adapting [*anpassen*], *a priori*, appearances, as intuitions in space and time, to their objects. For philosophy, with its qualitative determinations, would here not achieve scientific evidence without the support of mathematics with its quantitative determinations.

---

* This separation of the *a priori* principles of a science such as the science of nature is (in idea) neither trivial nor vacuous subtlety. Nature, as an object of the senses, is dependent on the forms of pure intuition: space and time. Both are *magnitudes*, however, which cannot exist except insofar as they are parts of an even greater magnitude. For it would be an absurdity, were the forms of space and time taken as properties of things in themselves, and not as mere appearances. One must assume a primary motion of matter, in which the latter is primordially self-moving, and which for precisely this reason continues uniformly to infinity, and is not superficial, but all-penetrative. For what is primary, considered as absolute, is at the same time that whose motion contains necessity.

[a] Reading with Lehmann *mit einander* for *mit einer.*

II. Of the material concept (of the object) of the science of nature

This is either *matter* in general or *body* (namely, physical, not merely mathematical); i.e. a matter which determines its figure and texture by its own forces, and which resists their alteration originally and uniformly. The former can only be a universally distributed matter, occupying cosmic space; this alone makes it an object of experience, for the pure void is no object of possible experience. This totality of matter cannot, for this reason, be *locomotive* (*materia locomotiva*) – i.e. it moves in place but cannot be displaced from it. Its motion, as that of a universally distributed world-material, is internally active and unceasing, and keeps all matter in continual – not progressive – agitation, by attraction and repulsion.

21:210

A
Division of Physical Bodies According to A Priori Concepts. They are Either Organic or Inorganic

The definition of an organic body is that it is a body, every part of which is there *for the sake of the other* (reciprocally as end and, at the same time, means). It is easily seen that this is a mere idea, which is not assured of reality *a priori* (i.e. that such a thing could exist).

One can also present another explanation for this fiction: It is a body in which the inner form of the whole precedes the concept of the composition of all its parts (in figure as well as in texture), in respect to all its moving forces (thus is an end and, at the same time, means).

Because, however, an *immaterial* principle is still mixed in with this definition (namely, a *willing* of the effective cause), and, consequently, the concept would not be purely physical, it can best be formulated as follows: An organic body is such that each of its individual parts contains [*ist*] the absolute unity of the principle of the existence and motion of all others in the whole.

21:211   [*Left margin*]

An organic (articulated) body is one in which each part, with its moving force, necessarily relates to the whole (to each part in its composition).

The productive force in this unity is life.

This vital principle can be applied *a priori*, from consideration of their mutual needs, to plants, to animals, to their relation to one another taken as a whole, and finally, to the totality of our world.

[IInd fascicle, sheet VI, page 3]

A machine is a solid body whose composition is only possible by the concept of a *purpose*, formed according to the analogy of a certain intentional motion. If this form is represented, not as an actual, but merely as a thinkable intention, then such a body is a *natural machine*. Organic bodies are, thus, natural machines.

The division into organic and inorganic cannot be lacking from the division of the moving forces of matter which belongs to the transition from the metaphysical foundations of natural science to physics; and, indeed, it must be thought *a priori* in it, without previously being instructed, by experience, of the existence of such bodies. For the transition from the metaphysical foundations of natural science to physics necessarily leads to this concept [of organic bodies]. The latter, however, appears not to be feasible. For however could one come upon the idea of a production of such bodies (resembling that of the highest form of art), necessary to imagine them even problematically? And how could one think *a priori* of a vegetable or animal kingdom, whose internal and external purposive combination always requires from us further elucidation [*Aufschlüsse*] of its possibility?*

{The principle of the spontaneity of the motion of the parts of our   21:212
own body (as limbs), considering the latter as our own self, is a mechanism.[b] Although this [spontaneity] is an absolute unity of the principle of motion from *desires* (thus not material), nevertheless, reason can do no other than to make general (if only problematically) the concept of a purposive mechanism of matter, under the name of organization, and to contrast it with inorganic matter. It does so in order to present to itself the classification of bodies for the completeness of possible experience in a future (empirical) system of physics; and, thus, is entitled to make the classification *a priori*, not from given empirical propositions and perceptions (for the latter yield no generality of principles), but from concepts.}

[*Margins*]

One must also conceive of a world-organization in a unified body, in which no forms perish without having brought forth other better ones.

---

* One can [imagine] classes of organic bodies, organized for the sake of one another, but specifically different: e.g. the vegetable kingdom for the sake of the animal kingdom, and the latter for mankind (as required for its existence and preservation); thus all of them   21:212
together [can be] classified *a priori* as organic in the first, second, or third degree. The highest level of classification would be that which organized the human species, according to the different levels of its nature, for one another and for the sake of the perfection of the species; something which may, perhaps, have occurred, by revolutions of the earth, many times, and of which we do not know whether another such is in prospect for our globe and its inhabitants.

[b] Undeleted continuation after "mechanism": [It] contains the body's moving forces according to the analogy with a living (hence immaterial) being – causality of motion, original excitability.

21:213 The idea of organic bodies is *indirectly* contained *a priori* in that of a composite of moving forces, in which the concept of a real *whole* necessarily precedes that of its parts – which can only be thought by the concept of a combination according to *purposes*. Regarded *directly*, it is a mechanism which can be known only empirically. For, if experience did not provide us with such bodies, we would not be entitled to assume even their possibility. How can we include such bodies with such moving forces in the general classification, according to *a priori* principles? Because man is conscious of himself as a self-moving machine, without being able to further understand such a possibility, he can, and is entitled to, introduce *a priori* organic-moving forces of bodies into the classification of bodies in general – although only indirectly, according to the analogy with the moving force of a body as a machine. He [must], however, generalize the concept of vital force and of the excitability of matter in his own self by the faculty of desire.

By the same principle, the emergence of the organism of matter and its organization as a system for the needs of different *species*, becomes possible, [stretching] from the vegetable kingdom to the animal kingdom (at which point *desires*, as true *vital* forces of corporeal substances, first arise). One species is made for the other (the goose for the fox, the stag for the wolf), according to the differences between the races – indeed, perhaps, according to different primordial forms, now vanished (but, among them, not men – for the upheavals in the bosom of the earth and its alluvial mountains give no evidence of such, according to Camper).[43] Eventually, our all-producing globe itself (as an organic body which has emerged

21:214 from chaos), completed this purpose in the mechanism of nature. To set a beginning or an end to this process, however, wholly exceeds the bounds of human reason.

The division of bodies into organic and inorganic thus necessarily belongs to the transition from the metaphysical foundations of natural science to physics, as the maximum of progress [in it].

The maximum of the motion of matter in general (considered according to space and time, as a product of the internal moving forces of matter), is the concussive motion of an all-penetrating matter – the minimum of its motion is its weight. Upon its unceasing inner motion rest mechanical motion and the latter's power of movement.

[IInd fascicle, sheet VI, page 4]

{One can take the classification of organic and living beings further. Not only does the vegetable kingdom exist for the sake of the animal kingdom (and its increase and diversification), but men, as rational beings, exist for the sake of others of a different species (race). The latter stand at a higher level of humanity, either simultaneously (as, for instance, Americans and Europeans) or sequentially. For instance, if our globe (having once been dissolved into chaos, but now being organized and regenerating) were to bring forth, by revolutions of the earth, differently organized creatures, which, in turn, gave place to others after their destruction, organic nature 21:215 could be conceived in terms of a sequence of different world-epochs, reproducing themselves in different forms, and our earth as an organically formed body – not one formed merely mechanically.

How many such revolutions (including, certainly, many ancient organic beings, no longer alive on the surface of the earth) preceded the existence of man, and how many (accompanying, perhaps, a more perfect organization) are still in prospect, is hidden from our inquiring gaze – for, according to Camper, not a single example of a human being is to be found in the depth of the earth.}

[IInd fascicle, sheet VII, page 1]

"Übergang 2"

B
{Division of Matter According
to *A Priori* Principles}

The object of the science of nature is either matter in general (formless) or body. A matter which, by its internally and externally moving forces, restricts itself in texture and figure, and resists all alteration of its figure, is called a physical body.

Matter as the subject of this form of the moving forces – material for a body, but without such a combination into a body even in the smallest conceivable parts. Were this to happen, it would suggest the fiction of an atomism of matter. As a continuum (that is, regarded as without empty spaces between its parts), we will call it for now (provisionally) caloric. 21:216 This would be a self-subsistent matter, penetrating all bodies, and unceasingly and uniformly agitating all their parts. The question is whether it is to be regarded, not just as a *hypothetical material*, in order to explain certain appearances, but as a real world-material – given *a priori* by reason and counting as a principle of the possibility of the experience of the system of moving forces. In the former case, its concept does not belong to physics, nor even to the transition from the metaphysical foundations of natural science to physics, but is an insertion in the compilation [*Einschiebsel der Stoppelung*] of a system. The existence of this material, and the necessity of its *a priori* presupposition, I now prove *a priori* in the following manner.

There can be no experience of empty space, nor can it be inferred as an object of experience. In order to be apprised of the existence of a matter, I require the influence of a matter on my senses. Thus the proposition: "There are empty spaces" can be neither a mediate nor an immediate proposition of experience; it is, rather, merely ratiocinative [*vernünftelt*]. The proposition: "There are physical bodies" presupposes the proposition: "There is matter whose moving forces and motion precedes the generation of a body in time." For this latter is only the formation of matter, and occurs of its own accord (*spontaneo*). This formation, however, which is to be initiated by matter itself, must have a first beginning – whose possibility is, indeed, incomprehensible, but whose originality (as self-activity) is not to be doubted. Thus there must exist a matter which, {as internal, penetrates all bodies (as onus), and, at the same time, moves them continually (as *potentia*). It amounts to a whole, which (as a self-subsistent cosmic whole) is internally self-moving and serves as the basis of all other movable matter.} Independently, [it] forms a cosmic whole from a single material (signifying merely the existence of a matter, without its particular forces – thus, in general). In this condition alone, it has moving force and – deprived of all other forces except that of its own agitation – maintains all the other moving forces in their constant and ubiquitous vigorous activity. The ground for this assertion is: Intuitions in space and time are mere forms, and, lacking something which renders them knowable for the senses, furnish no real objects whatsoever to make possible an existence in general (and, above all, that of magnitude). Consequently, space and time would be left completely empty for experience. This material, therefore, which underlies this generally possible experience *a priori*, cannot be regarded as a merely *hypothetical*, but as a given, originally moving, world-material; it cannot be assumed merely problematically, for it first signifies [*bezeichnet*] intuition (which would otherwise be empty and without perception).

[*Right margin*]
Of the moving forces from the *primary* motion.

The prime *mover* appears to presuppose a cause acting through a will; the agitation of matter, however, to preserve itself eternally.

[IInd fascicle, sheet VII, page 2]

Of the primary motion
and the primordially moving matter
(*materia primitiva movens*)

Matter, with its moving forces, can initiate a motion only insofar as it either sets itself in motion externally (*vis locomotiva*), or else sets each of its parts in motion relative to every other – hence internally (*vis interne motiva*). However, any absolute beginning of the motion of a *matter* is inconceivable; if it is conceded, the cessation or diminution of the motion is, then, just as inconceivable – for the hindrance or resistance in the abolition of motion is itself, equally, a moving force (in opposition). To a prime mover (*primus motor*) one would have to attribute spontaneity – i.e. a willing – which wholly contradicts materiality. There follows this *a priori* valid proposition (not derived from physics – and, thus empirical – but belonging to the transition from the metaphysical foundations of natural science to physics):

"There exists a matter, distributed in the whole universe as a continuum, uniformly penetrating all bodies, and filling [all spaces] (thus not subject to displacement). Be it called ether, or caloric, or whatever, it is no *hypothetical material* (for the purpose of explaining certain phenomena, and more or less obviously conjuring up causes for given effects); rather, it can be recognized, and postulated *a priori*, as an element [*Stück*] necessarily belonging to the transition from the metaphysical foundations of natural science to physics."

First proposition

The distinction of matter, insofar as one body in the same space contains more or less of it, cannot be explained *atomistically* (with Epicurus), by composition of the *full* with the *void* between it – for empty space is not an object of possible experience at all (since no perception of the nonbeing of a real object is possible; only the nonperception of its being). Atoms, as dense corpuscles, which are, yet, mathematically indivisible, contain a self-contradictory concept; for what is spatial is infinitely divisible.

Consequently, the universe must be thought of as completely filled with matter (without empty spaces, whether inclusive or included (intermediate spaces)); for neither of these two are objects of possible experience. Nonexistence cannot be perceived.

21:219

[*Top margin*]

We can, thus, conceive of no motion except as in space filled with matter, which forms a continuum. Space which can be sensed (the object of the empirical intuition of space) is the complex of the moving forces of matter – without which, space would be no object of possible experience, and, as empty, no sense-object. Although this primary material with the property which we must ascribe to it of being primordially moving, is merely present in thought, it is not a hypothetical thing. Nor is it an object of experience; for then it would belong to physics. It has reality, however, and its existence can be postulated, because, without the assumption of such a world-material and its moving forces, space would be no sense-object, and experience of it – whether affirmative or negative – would not take place. We consider such a formless primary material, penetrating all spaces (and [whose reality] can only be confirmed by reason) as nothing more than all-penetrating moving forces, distributed in space. Its actuality can be postulated prior to experience (i.e. *a priori*) for the sake of possible experience.

[IInd fascicle, sheet VII, page 3]

2.

No *transition* can be experienced from the full, *via the void*, to the full [again]. For that would amount to a perception of nonbeing as an object present to the senses. Consequently, every space in relation to our outer senses is filled with matter; for which proposition we need no experience

21:220 or inference grounded on experience – thus it can be pronounced completely *a priori*. No effect of the moving forces of matter can reach our senses through empty space. The experience (which should have been made in the connection of one [experience of the full] with the other) suddenly ceases; and matter (for our possible perception) coalesces into a single point, and occupies no space. We cannot be apprised of the existence of what is near or far from us, without presupposing a filling of the space lying between the two points, whether we have a sensation of it or not. The mere possibility of experience already guarantees enough; moreover, it alone guarantees the reality of this material which fills all spaces. For, otherwise, what is intermediary and utterly imperceptible (i.e. nonexistence) would have to be perceptible – which is self-contradictory.

3.

As concerns time, and, thus, the first beginning (the initiation of the motion of matter), this is not comprehensible, for an empty time before it and a subsequent duration of it would have to be assumed. Since, however, the spontaneity of this beginning permits one to presuppose no cause, other than an immaterial one, the motion of matter which signifies [*bezeichnet*] time can be thought of only as a uniform and permanent *continuation*. For the possibility of experience permits no change [in the latter], neither cessation nor increase, for that would be as if time could be stopped or accelerated; an empty time is, however, no object of possible experience.

21:221

Note

There is something strange about this method of proving the existence of a special world-material which penetrates all bodies and constantly agitates them internally, by attraction and repulsion. For the ground of proof is *subjective*, and derived from the conditions of possible experience, which presupposes moving forces and excludes the void, in order to fill space with an always active matter which may be called *caloric*, •or ether, etc.• And to ground this proposition *a priori* and *nonhypothetically* on concepts [is strange]. Not only our entitlement to do so, but also the necessity of postulating such universally distributed material is grounded in the concept of this material as space thought *hypostatically*. Space (like time) is a magnitude which cannot exist save as part of a greater whole. The whole must be given first in order that the manifold be thought in it as a part, the reason being that it is inconsistent that a thing in itself should exist as part merely; for parts are necessarily grounds of the possibility of a whole [*breaks off*]

[*Margin*]

We must not ask when motion commences but when I begin the motion; not where the limit of matter begins, but by what and how far it is limited.

Note   21:222

There is something peculiar about this method of proving the existence of a particular world-material, which penetrates all bodies in substance and moves them internally, but which is itself also a self-unifying whole. The ground of proof is subjective and derived from the conditions of possible experience; the latter, as effect of the moving forces of matter, stands under one principle.

The spontaneity of the primary beginning of motion reveals both a sphere of elementary material and a permanent continuation of motion.

Of caloric as the means of lifting [*Hebemittel*] in machines with respect to their rigidity, tenacity or slipperiness.

[IInd fascicle, sheet VII, page 4]

OF AN ALL-PENETRATING MATTER,
WHICH FILLS THE WHOLE OF COSMIC SPACE,
AS A NONHYPOTHETICAL,
BUT *A PRIORI* GIVEN, MATERIAL
FOR A WORLD-SYSTEM.

§

The concept of a primary beginning of motion is itself incomprehensible, and a spontaneous motion of matter is incompatible with [the concept] of matter; nevertheless, a *primordial* motion of matter and the existence of its moving forces must inevitably be postulated, simply because there is mo-

71

tion in cosmic space. For to assume that this motion has existed forever and will always continue, is to assume a necessity for it which can in no way be accepted. The prime mover (*primus motor*) would, however, base his motion on an act of free will [*Willkür*]; yet this latter would be an immaterial principle, of which there is here no question.

21:223

Theorem

"Primordially moving matters presuppose a material, penetrating and filling the whole of cosmic space, as the condition of the possibility of experience of the moving forces in this space. This primary material is not conceived hypothetically, for the explanation of phenomena; it is, rather, identically contained for reason, as a categorically and *a priori* demonstrable material, in the transition from the metaphysical foundations of natural science to physics."

Proof

The motion of matter in empty space is not an object of possible experience; so neither is the transition from what is full, *via the void*, to the full [again]. There can thus be no motion for the senses, and hence no forces moving them, save in a *space filled* with matter; for of this alone is it *possible* to have experience. Among the greater or lesser degrees of world-material (given the same volume of matter) there can be only one which is the medium for the locomotion of bodies. For motion through empty space is not in any way an object of possible experience, and, in full space, no locomotion (*facultas locomotiva*) takes place. The matter which fills space can, at any one place, only be internally in motion. And yet it can be an object of possible experience – a material space, as it were; a material not^c penetrable by any other; a principle of possible experience. It is to be acknowledged as a primordially moving material – not hypothetically invented, but one whose forces give it reality and which underlies all motion

21:224 of matter; a continuum which, taken in its own right, forms a whole of moving forces, whose existence is known *a priori*.

[*Top margin*]

There is only one space, one time, and one matter, in which all motion is to be found. The real and objective principle of experience which, in its form, amounts to a unified whole, leaves no space (inside or outside itself) unfilled. It contains all moving forces. This composite is not locomotive; nor is it a body. The beginning of its motion is its own eternity.

^{c} Kant's original version of this sentence reads: "penetrable (*permeabilis*) by any other."

72

[Left margin]
Caloric is the basis for the unified whole of all moving forces of matter (the hypostatized space itself, as it were, in which everything moves); the principle of the possibility of the unity of the whole of possible experience.

Caloric is perceptible space, stripped, in thought at least, of all other properties. As the principle of possible experience of all the dimensions of space, it is the opposite of empty space. Since, in space, everything can change position, except for space itself, and no space, as empty, is an object of experience, it follows that this matter is extended through the entire cosmos and that its existence is necessary – necessary, that is to say, relative to objects of the senses.

Matter, which moves originally (and thus also permanently) in all its parts and is incoercible except by itself.

Matter, which can begin its own (internal) motion and preserve itself in it, [can] be neither solid, nor fluid, nor coercible. It must, rather, be permanently moving, by its own attraction and repulsion alone [*breaks off*]

A matter whose function (as possessing moving force) is just this: to make space in general an object of experience in general. Attracting and repelling itself internally, it displaces no other [matter] but wholly penetrates it. It naturally moves primordially in order to be an object of experience.

Understanding and experience form, indeed, the sum of all our knowl-   21:225
edge: both the *a priori* and the *a posteriori*. But what do we *understand* by "the understanding"? [To say that] it is an ability, derived from experience, to use the understanding in accordance with its laws, is an explanation in a circle. It is the faculty of connecting representations with consciousness of their rule. Separate from the objects of sense, it is the pure understanding; in combination with them, the applied. The latter is the faculty of experience. Pure understanding is the faculty of *a priori* knowledge – but unreason and deliberate deception are Herder's trademark.[44]

[IInd fascicle, (half-)sheet VIII, page 1]

"Übergang 3"

The basis of all possible perceptions of the moving forces of matter in space and time is the concept of an elementary material, distributed everywhere in cosmic space, attracting and repelling only in its own parts, and which is continuously internally self-moving. Its concept is made into the sole principle for the possibility of experience of an absolute whole of all internally moving forces of matter, and is known as such according to the rule of identity.

This form of a universally distributed, all-penetrating world-material, which is in continuous motion in its own location, characterizes the originally moving matter as a real, existing material, according to the principle of the possibility of experience itself. It thereby furnishes objective reality to this concept. This *material* is thus not a merely *hypothetical* one, feigned so as to explain certain phenomena according to given laws of experience.

21:226

Note

To carry out this indirect mode of proof – which is not objective, from experience (empirical), but from the principle of the possibility of experience in general (*a priori*), and consequently *subjective* – appears strange; for such a mode of inference does not seem at all consistent or possible. One wishes to know whether something like this all-penetrating material distributed throughout the universe (call it caloric or ether or whatever) *exists,* and the answer one receives is that, if it does not exist, then even the *possibility* of experience of it (which, as *a priori* certain, cannot be doubted) would not be permissible. This difficulty is resolved in the following manner.

Emptiness in space or time is in no way an object of possible experience, since it is not an object of outer or inner sense. Nonetheless, it is not an absurdity (*nihil negativum*). The nonbeing of the object is not self-contradictory, therefore.

That a material in cosmic space exists, which forms the basis for all moving forces of matter, may be inferred *a priori*, according to the principle of identity, from the fact that the actuality of empty space (without limitation by full space) would not be an object of possible experience.

[*Right margin*]
Matter causes [*wirkt*]. Will acts [*Willkühr handelt*]. He who acts [*handelt*] according to purposes (*artificialiter*) operates [*operirt*].
agere, facere, operari.

[IInd fascicle, (half-)sheet VIII, page 2]
Empirical proposition: Matter, with its moving forces, exists. These are either primitive (with respect to time, primordially moving), or derivative, in community in one space. This reciprocity, however, presupposes a continuum of forces, in the form of the unity and the homogeneity of the material. Concordance of the whole as principle of the possibility of experience in general. Since there is only one space and one time, if both are, as it were, hypostatized (made into actual objects of experience), then, underlying them, is a matter which underpins the moving forces which belong merely to experience in general. The latter are nothing other than attraction and repulsion in actual motion, contained in the concept of matter in general.

21:227

The movable, insofar as it moves only through the motion of something other, is mechanically moved; insofar as it moves primordially, through its own force, however, it is dynamically moved.

Mechanically produced motion is not primordial, and moved material would require another moving matter to bring it into excitation. In order to initiate a motion, a spontaneity would have to be attributed to matter, and this contradicts the concept of the moving forces of *matter*. To derive a motion from a preceding one, however, presupposes a regress of causes to infinity. For these reasons, the dynamical principle of motion can be effective in no other way than as a postulate of a matter in space and time, which moves and is moved without beginning or end, and which, infinitely divided, conserves all matter [in] motion.

•What exists in space, insofar as it has repulsive moving force with respect to its parts, is matter. Something existing in space has moving force at all times and is mobile.•

Empty space is not an object of possible experience. For that it would have to be occupied by matter in all its parts. That which occupies space, and whose existence [is considered] apart from all properties except that of being an object of possible experience, is a matter which fills the whole of 21:228 cosmic space with moving forces. Its existence is sufficiently grounded by the principle of identity. For empty space is not an object of possible experience, given that the latter is the effect of the moving forces of matter, which have as their basis a self-subsistent material whose motion is not mechanical but purely dynamical. Because for the former motion [*breaks off*]

The whole of cosmic space as an object of possible experience is not empty in any of its parts, but is a full space, for empty space is not an object of possible experience. The material which must be attributed to it in this regard, is, with its properties (filling [space], presence – in the form of the occupation and penetration (permeability) of all spaces), not a hypothetical material, but one that emerges from *a priori* concepts, according to the law of identity. For, in virtue of this all-penetration, the unity of this material (as of space itself) is the highest principle for the possibility of experience of outer sensible beings, and, since matter in this space independently resists all other matter of the same kind, this material is the elementary material. In virtue of the fact that it must be presupposed in order to determine the location in space for each matter, it is not a mere thought-object but, movable and in motion, is everywhere homogeneous and unique [of] its kind. Nowhere can it be either increased or diminished. If one speaks of attraction through empty space, then this is merely an idea.

[*Left margin*]
Space itself, represented as object of possible experience, is the elemen-

75

tary material. It makes space sensible. Is called caloric although the function of its activity is not warmth. Primitive idea of moving forces.

Although world-attraction (gravitation) attracts through empty space, this signifies no more than that it attracts bodies without the mediation of an intermediary matter (*actio immediata in distans*); thus the intermediary matter adds nothing to it and, in this respect, space is regarded as empty.

21:229 The transition from one object of the senses to another cannot be an experience if there is an intervening void; the two objects can be combined with each other within one experience only by means of the intermediary object of perception, which is a moving force and real material.

Thus a real material (caloric) lies at the basis of the possibility of the moving forces and their combination into one experience.

[IInd fascicle, sheet IX, page 1]

"Übergang 4"

2.

Empty but perceptible intermediary space is, thus, really a matter which, in degree, is imperceptible relative to our sense; it is an object of possible but mediate experience, e.g. light-matter which occupies the space between the eye and the object, and [which] can become an object of experience only by its excitation.

That by means of which space becomes an object of possible experience in general (of measure, direction etc.) is a universally distributed, all-penetrating world-material, possessing moving forces; its actuality rests solely on the principle of the possibility of outer experience and is thus known and confirmed *a priori*, according to the principle of identity. For, without presupposing this material, I could not have any outer experience at all: Empty space is not an object of possible experience.

This material, which is commonly called caloric (notwithstanding that heat may only be one particular effect of its moving forces) is not a *hypothetical material*, feigned for the explanation of certain appearances, but is *postulated* as a principle of the possibility of experience of those forces. The concept of this material is the *basis* for the *a priori* connection of all the moving forces of matter, without which no unity in the relation of this manifold of forces in a single whole of matter could be
21:230 thought. For this would not otherwise be proper except by establishing from the principle of the agreement of these forces into the possibility of experience (that is, from a subjective principle) that which can be self-subsistent – [avoiding] the dubious confusion [of it with] what [is] an

object of experience or [with] what may [simply] be noncontradictory in itself.[d]

Note I

It must strike anyone as strange that an empirical judgment should be given the prerogative of an *a priori* valid proposition, for in this there appears to lie a contradiction. However, there are only two different forms of relation, namely, the relation of the representation to the object, and the relation to the possibility of knowledge which the subject can have of it. If I proceed by the former principle, the judgment is *direct* and the said matter is a merely hypothetical material, which I ratiocinate on the basis of all my representation. In the second case, in which I direct myself solely toward the principle of the possibility of experience of the forces of matter, my judgment is *indirect*, derived from principles – which, nevertheless, gives the desired result. For the necessary (unique possible) agreement with the conditions of possible experience, also brings about the agreement of the representation with the object. That there is space and time agrees very well with the conditions of the possibility of experience, insofar as they both belong to the real determinations of existing things. That, however, there should be an empty space or an empty time, does not agree with them at all, since that would require experience of that which is not. The *hypothesis* of a matter, distributed through the whole of cosmic space, filling the latter[e] by attraction and repulsion of its homogeneous parts, and which penetrates all bodies, is only a thought-object (*ens rationis*), but not, for that reason, a merely *hypothetical* material, as one is accustomed to say of the universally distributed caloric. Its assumption as a principle of the possibility of experience [is] an inevitable and necessary assumption, not in order to explain phenomena, but *a priori*, for the sake of the unity of the moving forces in a system, and to bring about the agreement of the principles for the possibility of experience.

21:231

[*Margin:* •. . .•]

[IInd fascicle, sheet IX, page 2]

Note II

The properties of this world-material are (1) that it is *imponderable* (*imponderabilis*). For ponderability presupposes the capacity of a machine – that is, the moving forces of a body as instrument of motion; this itself presupposes, in turn, the internally moving force of a penetrating material, able to produce, by means of the inner motion of the constituent parts of

21:232

---

[d] This rendering is speculative: Kant's sentence is corrupt.   [e] Reading *diesen* for *diese*.

the lifting device, the capacity to move. (2) *incoercible* (*incoercibilis*). For any body coercing this matter (a container) could have such a force only in virtue of a property which must be presupposed in order to resist the expansion of the material. This material can only restrict itself; for all other it is penetrative. (3) *incohesible* (*incohaesibilis*) in regard to all its parts, neither fluid nor solid matter, but repulsive. [4] *inexhaustible* (*inexhaustibilis*) with respect to even the smallest quantity.

All this regarded as a whole.

Note III

As far as a first beginning of all motion is concerned, such a thing would be the limitation of motion by a preceding empty time, an effect without cause, a consequence without precedent.

But that an epoch of world-historical change should follow as effect upon a cause, is an object of possible experience.

Space of which no perception is possible (*spatium insensibile*) would be nothing outside me, but only the form of pure intuition of outer objects, and so, as neither positively empty nor positively full, not an object existing outside myself at all. To exist somewhere and at some time in empty^f space is a relation of matter which carries no correlative with it – a relation to nothingness; and just that is the existence of the included and inclusive void, in external combination with the full. A material which is assumed to be composed in the former or latter way (from two heterogeneous principles), cannot even be regarded as a hypothetical material; for a hypothesis of this [sort] (of the combination of the void with the full) is not an object of possible experience at all, since perception of nothingness is a contradictory concept.

21:233

The permanent appearance of matter with its moving forces in a space which fills everything, and limits itself by alternating attraction and repulsion, may be called the universally distributed caloric (although the feeling of warmth must not play any role here). It is the basis for the system of moving forces which emerges analytically, from concepts – that is, according to the rule of identity – from the principle of agreement with the possibility of experience in general; hence, this material is a categorical, not a hypothetical one (which would remain only problematic). It becomes a matter of experience in relation to the possibility of experience.

[...]

^f Lehmann's reading is uncertain between *In diesem Raum* and *Im leeren Raum*.

[IInd fascicle, (half-)sheet X, page 2]

["Übergang 5"]
The unity of the object of all possible outer experience in general. (1)
Analytical, according to quality (identity). (2) synthetic, according to quantity (according to the moving force of matter in one space, and of motion
in relation to time). Supplies the material for a space which is nowhere
empty – caloric – as the basis for the unification of all outer experience in
one object. This is the object and condition of the agreement of matter
into the unity of possible experience in general, according to the modal
principle of reason (possibility, actuality and necessity) for an *a priori*
thinkable system of matter.

[*Left margin* (rest of page empty)]
This proof by *a priori* concepts of the existence of a matter is unique of
its kind in proofs from concepts alone – just as the matter itself [is unique]
in concerning the absolute unity of a whole; it is not applicable to any
other object. The logical unity which is directed toward the *universal*, is
here identified with real unity, which is directed toward the totality of
matter.

[. . .]

[Vth fascicle, sheet VII, page 3]

["Übergang 8"]
The existence of an elementary material with the attributes: (a) occupation of space (*occupatio spatii*); and (b) filling of space (*repletio spatii*), as
caloric, cannot be *directly* proved; for that would have to be done by
experience. Experience, however, offers only phenomena whose grounds
of explanation themselves can only count as hypotheses. Its existence can
be proved (insofar as that is in any way possible) only *indirectly*: on the
basis of the **subjective** principle of the *possibility* of experience, instead of   21:549
the objective principle of experience itself. More precisely, this amounts
to making the capacity to have experience of this object in general into the
ground of proof; to derive from this ground of proof its concept of **object**;
and to present *a priori*, through reason, the conditions of the possibility of
knowledge of the object, as well as its actuality (under those determinations). [The proof] is not synthetic, through an ampliative judgment, but
analytical, through an explicative one – that is, according to the principle
of identity. [Such a proof] is appropriate to the subject, with respect to its
mode of investigation of the object and of determining the latter for itself;
it is not appropriate to the object and its inner constitution. The object

(caloric) is in this case not hypothetical; but the hypothesis along with its principles constitutes the object.

The latter material can in this way be regarded as the real basis of the moving forces of matter.

§

Empty space, and likewise empty time, is not an object of possible experience. The nonbeing of an object of perception cannot be perceived.

The proof of the existence of an all-penetrating and all-moving elementary material in a system of matter, must, if it is to emerge *a priori* from principles, think all experience as contained in a single experience which embraces all of its objects. And, if one speaks of experiences, then these are nothing further than parts and aggregates of a synthetic-universal experience; and, whatever conflicts with the condition of being an object of possible experience, is not an existing object.

21:550 Hence, empty space (be it enclosed by the full or enclosing it) is not an object of possible experience. For the nonbeing of an object of perception cannot itself, in representation, be a perceptible object. Empty space, thus, does not *exist* as *object*, but, rather, space is merely a mode of representation, pertaining to the *subject* for it to represent to itself an outer object in a certain form (of pure outer intuition, not thought) – not as it is, but as it necessarily appears to the subject, and thus is given *a priori*, insofar as the latter[g] is affected by the object.

Hence no negative experience of a sense-object can be made; nevertheless, the thoroughgoing determination, which the existence of any thing carries in its concept, requires that negative characteristics [*Verneinungsmerkmale*] – although they do not belong to the conditions of possible experience as elements and material for the subject's power of representation – must nevertheless be counted among the conditions in the object of a possible experience.

[*Right margin*]

1. The occupation of space (*occupatio spatii*) concerns only the existence of something spatial.

2. The filling of space (*repletio spatii*) [concerns] the moving force of attraction and repulsion of matter in space for the prevention of the void.

The difference between empirically given space and that which is given *a priori* (in pure intuition): The latter, however, is not an object given externally to me, because it is not an object of the senses, but rather of sensibility.

[g] Reading *es* for *er.*

Space in itself is a mere form of intuition and not an object of it. Empty space is *contradictio in adiecto.*

There must first be a matter filling space, ceaselessly self-moving by agitating forces (attraction and repulsion), before the location in space of every particle can be determined. This is the basis for any matter as object of possible experience. For the latter is what first makes experience possi- 21:551
ble. This space cannot be filled with bodies, unless matter has previously filled a sensible space by self-activity. For space must first be an object of experience; otherwise no position can be assigned to them.[h] The all-penetrating caloric is the first condition of the possibility of all outer experience. Empty space does not *exist.*

[Vth fascicle, sheet VII, page 4]

[. . .]

Note

This proof is indirect, such that, if one assumes the contrary, one is led 21:552
into self-contradiction. A whole of simultaneously existing outer sense-objects is given (unless one wishes to adopt idealism – the assertion of which belongs to another branch of philosophy, with which we are not here concerned). The principle for the agreement of all perceptions with the conditions of the possibility of experience excludes any void, since this is not an object of possible experience. Experience of external things, however, can, as regards its material element, only be thought of as the effect of sense-objects on the intuiting subject. In view of the universality of this proposition, experience itself cannot (objectively) prove it, but, rather, it must be by the condition of the possibility of experience in general (that is, subjectively for the cognitive faculty). Thus the existence of such a universally distributed world-material can only be proved indi-rectly, that is, according to *a priori* principles. Hence, this proof is unique in its kind, since the idea of the distributive unity of all possible experience in general here coincides with its collective unity in a concept.

The thought of an elementary system of the moving forces of matter (*cogitatio*) necessarily precedes the perception of them (*perceptio*), and, as a subjective principle of the combination of these elementary parts in a whole, is given *a priori* by reason in the subject (*forma dat esse rei*).[45] Hence, the whole, as object of possible experience, does not emerge atomistically, from the composition of the empty with the full – that is, not *mechanically;* it must, rather, emerge *dynamically,* as the combination of externally and reciprocally mutually agitating forces (thus initiating and infinitely and

[h] Reading *ihnen* for *ihm.* (Lehmann's reading is uncertain; Reicke reads *in ihm.*)

uniformly continuing all motion, by means of the primordial attraction and repulsion of the elementary material, which is thoroughly and homo-
21:553 geneously distributed in space). This proposition still belongs to the meta-physical foundations of natural science in relation to the whole of one possible experience; for *experiences* can only be thought of together as parts of a total experience, unified according to one principle.

This principle is subjective, for the world-observer (*cosmotheoros*):[46] a *basis* in idea for all the unified forces which set the matter of the whole of cosmic space in motion. [It] does not prove the existence of such a mate-rial, however, (for example, that which is called the all-penetrating and permanently moving caloric); to this extent, [it] is a hypothetical material. The idea of this material, however, is what first represents (albeit indi-rectly) space itself as something perceptible and as an unconditional whole (internally moved and externally, universally moving); this matter is, hence, to be assumed as the prime mover (*primum mobile et movens*), subjectively – as the basis for the theory of the primary moving forces of matter, for the sake of a system of experience.

[*Margin: . . .*]

22:543 [XIIth fascicle, sheet I, pages 1–4]

INTRODUCTION[47]

Of the transition, founded on a priori *principles, from the metaphysical foundations of natural science to physics*

FIRST SECTION
FORMAL DIVISION OF THE METHOD OF THE TRANSITION

Newton, in his immortal work, entitled: *Philosophiae naturalis principia mathematica,* must necessarily have had in his thoughts another science of nature as its counterpart. The latter, however, could not have been titled: *philosophiae naturalis principia philosophica,* for then he would have fallen into a tautology. It was necessary for him to proceed from a higher concept of the science of nature, namely, that of *scientiae naturalis,* which can, then, be either *mathematica* or *philosophica.* Thereby, however, he steered into another cliff, namely, self-contradiction.

There as little exist mathematical foundations of natural science, as there do philosophical of mathematics. The two are divided from each other by an unbridgeable gulf; and, although both sciences proceed from *a priori* principles, the difference is that the former does so from *intuitions,* the latter from *a priori concepts* – a difference so great that it is as if, in the transition from one to the other, *reason* itself (for that is what *a priori* knowledge means) were to displace one into quite different worlds. It is, furthermore, just as fruitless and inconsistent, to philosophize* in the sphere of the objects of mathematics, as it is to want to make progress in $\quad$ 22:544 the sphere of philosophy by means of mathematics – both as regards their *purpose*, and the *talent* required for them.† Both are founded on reason (for $\quad$ 22:545

---

* It could well happen that one were to ratiocinate about (geometrical) objects of $\quad$ 22:544 mathematics – but, of course, in vain; at best, it can be undertaken with the intention of placing in a clear light the difference between philosopheme and mathemateme. E.g. to require from *a priori* concepts alone an answer to the question: Why a *curved* line (line of which no part is straight) on a plane of equal curvature throughout (i.e. equal parts of which are congruent), when continued in this manner, returns to itself and encloses a surface in the form of a circle?[48] Or else: Why, on a surface with such a curve, there exists one point which is equidistant from all points on the same circumference? Or, indeed, the problem whether a straight line could be given *a priori*, standing in the same ratio to a curved line, as one straight line to another?, etc. This could be called "philosophizing about mathematical objects" – but it yields no net profit for the latter science.

†D'Alembert, in the *Discours* preceding his *Encyclopédie*, is (the mathematician's justifiably high claim in comparison with the philosopher notwithstanding) of an opinion which considerably deflates the former's arrogant tone: [He believes] that the interest, now accruing to mathematics, will soon (not without cause) diminish – for, although mathematics is [still] making progress, it is, nevertheless, fast approaching its point of completion; which (because the human mind cannot remain unoccupied) will make more room for philosophy. [It is his opinion], namely, that *astronomy* will bring this about: Its conquest [comes to an end] as its instruments gradually become inadequate for observation in immeasurable space; and, when mathematical analysis, too, will have reached its completion (which it appears to have attained already), restless reason must turn itself – without prejudice to mathematics – from that which was always but an instrument for the *skillful employment* of reason, to another branch of rational science – to the doctrine of wisdom, as the *science of the final end*.[49]

Herr Kästner,[50] apparently, can conclude from experience of the way in which self-styled $\quad$ 22:545 philosophers have behaved until now that this epoch will never come about – and this because of two species of ratiocination on their part:[51] *Firstly*, because these philosophers must always start *afresh* in constructing their systems, science (which is always [thus] compelled to retreat) can hope for no true progress or to achieve its goal. *Secondly*, because, to the objections of their opponents, they are always ready with the excuse that the latter "do not understand them" – which, naturally, justifies the suspicion that they may well not understand themselves. This is the vexation of a philosophy (that of Wolff) which, lacking a critique of reason itself, was given a multivolume popularization according to the *mathematical method* in this mathematician's earlier years.[52] Let it remain so, now that he has grown old in it! More especially because it affords him the opportunity to entertain himself in poetic temper, filled with genuine caustic wit, and to play the philosopher on the side – a game which makes its own contribution to his aging.

Hereby may be judged the absolute value of mathematics, in comparison with philosophy, with respect to the practical. The former is that of *technical-practical* reason (skill in the discovery of *means* for whatever ends), the latter is *moral-practical* reason and is directed to the *final end*, which is absolutely (categorically) obligatory, namely to create men of improved character [*Gesinnung*].

Now the cultivation of one's talent by mathematics, makes not the least contribution to the latter: One can be great in that subject, yet, at the same time spiteful, envious and malevolent – it does not follow that one is a *good man* in all respects. To which philosophy, which cultivates the subject's original disposition [to goodness], gives direct guidance. So the that is what *a priori* knowledge means), but, as such, differ from each other not by degree, but according to species. The heterogeneity of these spheres is to be observed (not without astonishment) in the *individuals* who treat of them, and in their different natural dispositions toward one another; in the way in which they depreciate or treat one another with hostility, regarding their importance and the value of the particular activity of each.

22:546

SECOND SECTION
MATERIAL DIVISION
OF THE NATURAL BODIES WHICH PRESUPPOSE
THESE MOVING FORCES

§

Natural bodies are either organic or inorganic.

Matter (natural material) can be termed neither organic nor inorganic. Such a concept is in contradiction with itself (*sideroxylon*). For, in this concept, one abstracts from all form (figure and texture) and thinks in it only a *material* (*materia ex qua*), which is capable of various forms. Thus, it is only to a **body** (*corpus physicum*) that one can attribute one of these predicates. And this division [into organic and inorganic] necessarily belongs to the transition from the metaphysical foundations of natural science to physics, as a system of the empirical science of nature, which can never become a completed whole. There are internally moving forces among the parts of a body, which lead to a certain *construction* [*Bau*] of matter, determined according to laws.

22:547

Definition

§ An organic natural body may be thought of as a natural *machine* (that is to say, as a system of externally moving forces, inwardly united into a whole, founded upon an idea) in the following way: The organic body is thought of as a *solid body* and (in virtue of the inner principle of its combination, according to form) as rigid. The moving forces of matter in

22:546

latter stands beyond the former in the ordering of the incontestable inward advantages of human character (in the *mode of thought*). Nevertheless, the [mathematician's] talent far outshines [the philosopher's] in the *mode of sense:* in part, because it is an instrument of such great utility (for whatever final purpose one may have), and, in part, because (since it is able to give its results with the most complete evidence) it is an object of respect, and inspires a friendly attitude (an analogy of benevolence) toward [its] speculation. Benevolence, however, is not an essential ingredient in the makeup of his scholarly talents. Nor is it often [to be found]; rather, envy and mockery can coexist peacefully with them[i] in the same subject.

[i] Reading *jenen* for *jener*.

such a body are either merely *vegetative* or else *vital forces*. For the generation of the latter,

[XIIth fascicle, sheet II, pages 1–4]
an *immaterial* principle, possessing an indivisible unity in its power of
representation, is necessarily required. For the manifold, whose combination into unity depends on an idea of a purposively (artificially) acting
subject, cannot emerge from moving forces of matter (which lack the *unity*
of the principle). That these bodies, however, possess the ability to preserve their *species* from the available matter (by propagation), does not
necessarily belong to the concept of an organism. It is, rather, an empirical
adjunct, for the purpose of assigning other properties to organic bodies
(e.g. that of producing their own kind by means of two sexes) – properties
which one can abstract from in their *concept*.

§ *Further determination of the concept of an*   22:548
organic body
and of its internal possibility

One may define it, **firstly**, as follows: *"Such that each of its parts, within a
whole, is there for the sake of the other,"* and, in this case, the explanation
clearly indicates *purposes* (*causae finales*). **Secondly,** however, one can also
give as its definition: *"An organic body is that, in which the idea of the whole
precedes the possibility of its parts, with respect to its unified moving forces"*
(*causae efficientes*).

An organic natural body is thus thought of as a *machine* (a body arranged **intentionally** as to its form). Under no circumstances can it be a
property of matter to have an *intention* (since it is the absolute unity of a
subject which *connects* the manifold of representation in one consciousness); for all matter (and every part of it) is composite. Thus, such a body
cannot derive its organization merely from the moving forces of *matter*. A
single (thus, immaterial) being must be assumed as the *mover* outside or
within this body – whether as part of the world of sense, or as a being
distinct from it. For matter cannot organize itself and act according to
purposes. Whether this being (a world-soul, as it were)[53] possesses understanding, or whether merely a capacity which is analogous to the understanding in its effects, is a judgment which lies beyond the limits of one's
insight. Nevertheless, the title *"organized body"* belongs in the classification of concepts which cannot be overlooked in the transition from the
metaphysical foundations of natural science to physics – be its object com-   22:549
prehensible to us, or not.*

* Nature organizes matter in manifold fashion – not just by kind, but also by stages. Not to
be comprehended: That there are to be discovered, in the strata of the earth and in

{SECOND DIVISION
OF THE SPECIFIC DIFFERENCE OF MATTER
IN BODIES IN GENERAL

If, regarding the existence of a certain matter with a particular quality, the question is raised, whether it is demonstrable *a priori*, or only to be established empirically (*probabilis*), we can only expect *subjective* conditions of the possibility of knowledge of it – i.e. of the possibility of *experience* of such an object. For existence is not a particular predicate of a thing, but the absolute position of it, with all its predicates. Hence, there exists only one experience; and, if one is to speak of *experiences*, this signifies only the *distributive* unity of manifold perceptions, not the *collective* unity of its object itself in its thoroughgoing determination. From which it follows that, if we wish to judge *a priori*, concerning objects of 22:550 experience, we can only require and expect principles of the agreement of the representation of objects with the conditions of *possibility* of experience of them.

There is, however, in the transition from the metaphysical foundations of natural science to physics an unavoidable problem: Whether, indeed, there exists a *material*, thoroughly distributed throughout cosmic space (and thus also penetrating all bodies), which one might perhaps call **caloric** (without thereby having regard for a particular feeling of warmth, for the latter concerns only what is subjective in a representation, as perception) – whether, as I say, such a material *is* present or *not*, as the **basis** of all the moving forces of matter, or whether its existence be only dubitable; in other words: Whether it is to be assumed by the physicists as a merely *hypothetical material* solely for the explanation of certain appearances, or whether it is to be set up *categorically* as a postulate. This question is of the greatest importance for the science of nature as a system, especially since it leads from the elementary system of this science to the world-system.

If it can be proved that the unity of the *whole* of possible experience rests upon the existence of such a material (with its stated properties), then its actuality is also proved, not, indeed, **through** experience, but *a priori*, merely from conditions of *possibility*, for the sake of the possibility

mountains, examples of former kinds of animals and plants (now extinct) – proofs of previous (now alien) products of our living, fertile globe. That its organizing force has so arranged for one another the totality of the species of plants and animals, that they, together, as members of a chain, form a circle (man not excepted). That they require each other for their existence, not merely in respect of their nominal character (similarity), but their real character (causality) – which points in the direction of a world organization (to unknown ends) of the galaxy itself. This, however, will not be treated at this point; since we here have occasion to deal only with the elementary system (not yet the world-system).

of experience. For the moving forces of matter can only come together into a *collectively universal* unity of perceptions in a possible experience insofar as the subject, [affected] by them, unites them externally and internally in one concept, [and] affects itself by means of its perceptions. Now the concept of the whole of outer experience also presupposes all possible moving forces of matter as combined in collective unity; to wit, in full space (for empty space, be it space enclosed within bodies or sur-   22:551
rounding them externally, is not an object of possible experience).* It further presupposes, however, a constant *motion* of all matter, by which the *subject,* as an object of sense, is affected. For without this motion, that is, without the stimulation of the sense organs, which is its effect, no perception of any object of the senses, and hence no experience, takes place – the latter containing only the form belonging to the perception. Hence there exists as an object of experience in space (although without empirical consciousness of its principle) a particular material which is continuously and boundlessly distributed and constantly self-agitating. That is, **caloric** is *actual;* it is not a material feigned for the sake of the explanation of certain phenomena, but rather, a material demonstrable from a universal principle of experience (not from experience) according to the principle of *identity* (analytically) and which is given *a priori* in the concepts themselves.

NOTE
ON THE CONCEPT
OF CALORIC}

To assume the existence of a matter which is *universally distributed, all-penetrating* and *all-moving* (one can add, in relation to time, *which initiates all motion*), and which fills cosmic space, is a hypothesis which, indeed, is neither sustained, nor can be sustained by experience. Hence, if it is   22:552
justified, it would have had to emerge *a priori* from reason as an idea; be it in order to *explain* certain phenomena (in which case this matter would be *thought* as a merely *hypothetical material*); {or be it to *postulate* it, for the reason that there must be some motion by which the moving forces of matter *begin* to agitate. Nevertheless, it is to be regarded altogether as an object of experience (*given*).

It is easily seen that the existence of such a material, although not demonstrable as an object of experience, and hence as *derived* from experience (that is, empirically demonstrable), must, nevertheless, be postulated

---

* Space represented merely as *subjective* form of outer intuition is no external object, and, as such, neither *full* nor *empty* (predicates which belong to determinations of the object, from which we here abstract). Space, however, as *object* of outer intuition, is either the one or the other. Since the nonbeing of an object of perception cannot be perceived, empty space is thus not an object of possible experience. [Note undeleted]

as an object of *possible* experience. This can very well take place *indirectly a priori*, but only [as] the sense object in general, [to exclude]ʲ what is no object of *possible* experience – just as *empty space* (whether inclusive or included) would be, or again an *empty time*, either preceding the motion of matter, or inserted as an intervening absolute standstill (which is likewise nothing at all).

Objectively, there is only one experience, and if one speaks of *experiences*, then these are to be regarded only as representations of the existence of things, which are subjectively connected in a continuous series of possible perceptions. For, were there a gap between them, a gulf (*hiatus*) would [prevent] the transition from one act of existence to another, and the unity of the guiding thread of experience would be torn apart. Which circumstance, in order to be represented to oneself, would, in turn, have to belong to experience – which is impossible, for nonbeing can be no object of experience.

Subjectively, outer *perceptions*, as material for possible experience (which lack only their form of connection), are nothing other than the effect on the perceiving *subject* of the agitating forces of matter, which are given *a priori*. The latter are postulated even before the question arises *which* objects of the senses may or may not be objects of experience; provided, however, that it is a matter only of the form of their connection, that is, of the *formal* element of **possible** experience. The question is whether or not this formal element be in conformity with possible experience (*forma dat esse rei*), regarded as the collective unity of experience and its conditions. The unity of experience in the thoroughgoing determination of the object is likewise the latter's actuality.

22:553

If a certain material, although initially assumed only hypothetically, is thought as an object of possible experience, and if the concept of this material contains at the same time its thoroughgoing determination according to the principle of identity (the concordance of its properties [*Requisite*]), then this is likewise a proof of its actuality (*existentia est omnimodo determinatio*).⁵⁴ And, since this determination addresses the totality of the mutually combined forces, it is also a proof of the material's singularity (*unicitas*). That is, any such whole, which is in a spatial relationship to other systems, forms with them an absolute whole, relative to the moving forces of matter; and this amounts to the absolute unity of all possible objects of experience, consequently also to the existence of such a whole. It follows that the whole is knowable, hence that the possibility of the existence of such a whole can be demonstrated *a priori* (as necessary).

ʲ Based on the earlier version (see AK 21: 576.36, not included), from which Kant deleted "to exclude" and added "the sense object in general," leaving an ungrammatical sentence.

The object of an all-embracing experience contains within it all the subjectively moving forces of matter (that is to say, those affecting the senses and producing perceptions). Their whole is called caloric and is the basis of this universal stimulation of forces, which affects all (physical) bodies and hence also the subject itself. From synthetic consciousness (which cannot be empirical) of these forces which move the senses, their formal conditions are developed in attraction and repulsion.*

Now what is at issue in the question whether there is an all-penetrating etc. *elementary material* is the subjective element of receptivity to the sense-object, [which is required] for this material to be the object of a synthetic-universal experience; it is not whether the material exists *in itself* with those attributes. It is a matter of whether the empirical intuition of the elementary material, as belonging to the whole of a possible experience, already contains these attributes in its concept (according to the principle of identity) – an issue which relates solely to the cognitive faculty, insofar as this faculty contains in idea the whole of possible experience in one total representation (and so must think of it as given *a priori*). Hence, the material must be valid both subjectively, as the basis of the representation [of] the whole of an experience, and objectively, as a principle for the unification of the moving forces of matter. Caloric is actual, because the concept of it (with the attributes we ascribed to it) makes possible the whole of experience; it is given by reason, not as a hypothesis for perceived objects, for the purpose of *explaining* their phenomena, but rather, immediately, in order to found the possibility of experience itself.†

22:554

No explanation of the difference in the specific densities of bodies can be given from *full* (*atomi*) and *empty* (*inane*) space, as atomism would have it; the reason being that, on the one hand, *atoms* do not exist (for every part of a body is always further divisible to infinity) and that, on the other hand, empty space is not an object of possible experience – thus, the concept of a whole of moving forces from such constituents is an untenable concept of experience.

22:555

* Only by means of what the understanding itself *makes* does the subject understand its object, that is to say, by the formal element of the whole of perceptions in a possible experience. Empty space is not an object of possible experience; only space which is thoroughly occupied by matter, as substance. Empty time – that is, the existence of the movable as such insofar as it is *without motion*, and which consequently (as regards coexistence and succession) is not a sense-object – is likewise not an object of possible experience.

22:554

† This indirect mode of proof of the existence of a thing is *unique* in its kind and therefore also strange, but it will appear less so if one considers that its object is also *unique* and not a concept which several [things] have in common. For just as there is only one space and only one time (as objects of pure intuition), there is likewise only one object of possible outer experience in the field of the causality of perception of outer things. For all so-called *experiences* are always only parts of *one* experience, in virtue of the universally distributed, unbounded caloric which connects all celestial bodies in one system and sets them into a community of reciprocity.

The object of collectively universal experience (of the synthetic unity of perceptions) is therefore *given;* the object of distributively universal experience, of which the subject forms a concept for itself (of the analytical unity of possible experience) is merely *thought,* for it belongs merely to the form of possible experience.}[k]

[. . .]

21:581   [Vth fascicle, sheet XI, page 1]

"Übergang 12"

{What is at issue in the solution to this problem – namely, the question concerning the existence of a caloric, as matter possessing moving forces – if it is to be decided *a priori,* is not to determine how the object (*quaestionis*), but, rather, how the experience of the object is possible as a comprehensive concept [*Gesamtbegriff*] of it in its collective unity (that is, as one experience – hence subjectively). For, if this concept agrees with the conditions of the possibility of one experience (of its unity), then the object is subjectively actual. The question here is not that of the object given, but only of our knowledge of the object; and this is sufficient for the solution of our problem, which does not derive concepts from experience, but experience from concepts.

Note

This proof is indirect; it proves the proposition by representing the impossibility of its contrary – but not by the logical opposition of concepts (which is analytic), but by representing the real opposition of mutually opposing forces (thus, synthetically, as belonging to the possibility of experience). In this are opposed not *a* and *non a,* but *a* and $-a$.}

21:582

Propaedeutic

The *transition* from the metaphysical foundations of natural science to physics – [which is] not a leap into fresh territory – originates with the subjective principle of the combination of the manifold of moving forces of matter in one experience. And the object of this collective unity (*omnitudo collectiva*) – the idea of the whole of moving forces – is the basis of the distributive [*teilweise durchgängig*] determination (*omnitudo distributiva*) of the object of all possible empirical concepts of this object – namely, matter. For physics is the science of the coordination of all *empirical* representations (all perceptions) into a system of the whole, for which

---

[k] End of amanuensis's copy.

nothing further is given *a priori*, through the understanding, than the form of this thoroughgoing connection.

The empty space between two wholes of matter and the empty time between two moments (as limitations) are not objects of possible experience, for nonbeing cannot be perceived. Thus the following propositions emerge:

There exists outer experience as a collective whole of all perceptions; that is, as *one* all-embracing possible experience. There exists outside us a sense-object, for whose *perception* externally moving forces of matter are required; the empirical representation of these forces, combined in a   21:583 subject, is the *basis* of all the appearances, which together form the unity of experience.

The agitation of the senses of the subject by some matter, is what alone renders outer perceptions possible. And these moving forces must be thought *a priori*, as combined in one experience without gap (that is, without an intervening *void* – for that is not an object of possible experience). They must be thought as combined in an absolute *whole*, which, nevertheless, as such, is not an object of possible experience either. Thus the principle of this synthetic unity of the whole of the object of possible experience is merely *subjective* (a principle of *composition* – not of the possibility of what is *composite*, outside the representation of the object). Consequently, the objective reality of the material (its existence in space as object of outer and all-embracing experience, and as containing the whole of the moving forces) is grounded *logically*, according to the principle of identity – not *physically*, by hypothesis, in order to explain certain phenomena. For what belongs to the unity of *possible* experience, formally, is also contained really in experience; that is, the whole of this material is actual and an object of *physics.**

[*Right margin*]   21:584
Caloric is not a subsidiary hypothesis but an original one; thus not a hypothetically – that is, conditionally – but a categorically given material.

That there is no caloric in bodies that are completely dense and impenetrable to all other matter; but, equally, no cold which could resist heat.

---

* The material principles of possible experience (perceptions) furnish empirical judgments, which only partially yield judgments of experience. But, in the very transition from metaphysics to physics, the principle of its composition must be given in form (hence, *a priori*), [in order to] postulate materially, in the representation of the subject, an object of physics as the basis of all combination of the moving forces into one experience. For to be an object of the absolute unity of the whole of possible experience, is itself experience of the object of experience; and, as the whole of the determinations of this object (*omnimoda determinatio*), its existence.

For what occupies the absolute *whole* of space, has no room outside into which it could transpose itself.

Transition from the metaphysical foundations of natural science to phys-ics, as a system of empirical natural knowledge, whose form is given *a priori* (system of the moving forces of matter). The terrain of this science is empirical.

The first problem is the concept of caloric, as we are advancing from the whole of the object of possible experience to that of the condition of possible experience.

The agitating force of matter: (1) in the totality (synthetic universality) of the material in space. Self-limiting by attraction. (2) Initially commenc-ing. (3) Permanently continuing. Since experience cannot cease and empty time is not an object of possible experience.

The existence of caloric is the basis of the possibility of a single experience.

[Vth fascicle, sheet XI, page 2]

§

The attributes of this [material] (since it is all-embracing, *individual* (*unica*) and the basis of all [forces] for the unity[1] of the object of the one experience) are given according to the principle of identity: namely, that it is *universally distributed, all-penetrating,* and *all-moving* (not that it is itself movable (*locomotiva,* that is, displaceable)). And, as such, it is necessary, that is, *permanent.* For *sempiternitas est necessitas phaenomenon.*[55]

21:585   This material is called caloric; not, because it distributes *heat.* For that – for all of this material's energy in relation to the bodies in which it acts – can be entirely lacking, since it is an effect which only relates subjectively, to *feeling,* not to the object of *representation.* It is called caloric because to bring about the state of heat is but one of this matter's activi-ties; a better way of characterizing it with complete generality would be in terms of its capacity to expand those bodies which it penetrates. That is why it is thought *a priori* that, in a heated space, no part of that space can remain cold[56] and that this matter must necessarily communicate its activ-ity externally, if there is outside itself something with which it has a common border. The word "*contact*" is out of place here (since that con-tains moving force in its very concept); in that case it would have to be conceived like the *angulus contactus*[57] in geometry – as being a merely spatial determination, not a natural determination, of some matter. Calo-ric is given another name when it is called *light-material,* of which it is also true that it penetrates certain bodies, and, that it produces community in the moving forces of the matter of celestial bodies. The goal of all these concepts, however, is to have a material principle of the unity of possible experience; one which combines all experiences into a single experience.

---

[1]   In the manuscript *Einheit;* Lehmann reads falsely *Einsicht.*

Without this combination (and its form) there would be no coherent whole of experience; it would, in that case, only be an *aggregate* of perceptions, not experience as a system.

Thus caloric exists (regardless of the subjective property of heat). That is, we can only achieve the subjective unity of experience through the moving forces of matter in us, which produce sensible representations of their objects. It is not possible except by the existence of the moving forces, which activate the material for their combination in a single possible experience. This connection does not just establish the *hypothesis* of   21:586
the existence of caloric, but its actuality; which latter is contained in the concept of experience as the unity of moving forces (by the principle of identity).

Note

This *indirect* proof is **unique** of its kind – a fact that should not appear strange, since what it concerns is an **individual** object, which carries with it real (not logical) *universality*. There is to be found here a *collective unity* (*omnitudo collectiva*) of the objects of a *single* experience instead of *distributive* unity (*omnitudo distributiva*), which is merely logical and abstracts from the existence of the object. Whatever agrees with collective unity is *actual* (*existentia est omnimoda determinatio,* as ontology has it); but to achieve this thoroughgoing determination *empirically* (as is envisaged in the transition from the metaphysical foundations to physics) is utterly impossible. It is possible, however, in relation to the absolute unity of possible experience in general, insofar as the object of this concept contains the One and All[58] of outer sense-objects. The deduction of caloric, as the basis of the system of moving forces, has an *a priori* principle at its foundation: namely, that of necessary unity in the comprehensive concept of the possibility of one experience. This unity likewise carries with it identically (that is, not synthetically, but analytically, following *a priori* from a principle) the actuality of its object [namely, caloric].

[*Left margin*]
It is not a matter of establishing which objects are given to us for experience, but what experiences must be like so as to give these objects.

The object of one universal outer experience must be a natural material,   21:587
spread out in cosmic space and all-moving; and the ground of this is the sense-organ, insofar as it is suited to it.

Experience depends on the forces which agitate the subject.

[. . .]

[Vth fascicle, sheet XII, page 1]

"Übergang 12
Bogen a) S.2"

PHYSICAL-COSMOLOGICAL
PRINCIPLE[59]
OF THE ELEMENTARY SYSTEM
OF ALL WORLD-MATTER

§

One cannot begin with the object – matter in space – as the object of *empirical intuition,* and as the complex of an infinite magnitude of possible perceptions in a single empirical intuition. For that would already be a step into physics as a system of experience. Rather, one must begin from the concept of the understanding in the subject, insofar as the latter *thinks* for itself a whole of the moving forces of matter. For, when it is a question of *a priori* principles of synthetic knowledge, the *formal element* of the systematic presentation of the manifold of perceptions in an object must underlie its arrangement (*coordinatio*) into a whole.

21:590   Herein space itself must be represented as an object of experience (*spatium perceptibile*), albeit only indirectly, by means of an intermediary concept: that is, by tactile awareness [*Betastung*] of one's own body, as to its three dimensions; or again, by drawing lines by moving one's hands, limiting those lines with points, and thus representing surfaces as limits (and, finally, corporeal space itself) empirically for oneself. In this way one can say something spatial exists, and is, as the whole of perceptions necessarily combined into unity, an object of possible experience.

An absolutely empty space – in which matter, as outer sense-object, is not simply abstracted from, but is completely excluded, be it *enclosed* or *surrounded* by matter, is not an object of possible experience, and cannot feature in the system of the moving forces of matter. Thus, atomism – that is, the doctrine of the possibility of bodily composition of the full with the void, according to differing quantitative relations of matter in the same volume (corpuscular philosophy) – contains no principle of the possibility of bodies. For, on the one hand, no body (and no part of a body) is indivisible; on the other hand, the void, as spatially existing, is something which is not an object of perception (for nonbeing cannot be perceived).

[. . .]

94

[Vth fascicle, sheet XIII, page 3]   21:601

[. . .]

§
Proof of the existence of caloric

•Just as there is only one space, so• there is only one experience •possible
of objects in space•; and, if one speaks of *experiences,* these are nothing
other than *perceptions* whose connection under a formal, *a priori* given
principle, if made fragmentarily, will •indeed• yield an aggregate for physics; but this can never be complete, and, because the data are empirical,
no end can be expected in the progression from the metaphysical foundations of natural science to physics as a system of perceptions.

Nevertheless, the idea of this [system] is unavoidably given *subjectively* –
as a necessary problem, namely, that of the connection of perceptions as
effects of the moving forces upon the subject in a *single* experience. What,
however, belongs to experience (which can only be single) as its ground of
determination, is likewise *objectively* given – that is, *actual.* So there *exists,*
as an absolute whole, a matter with those attributes, as the *basis* of its
moving forces, insofar as they are moving.

Now those perceptions, *regarded subjectively* (namely, as empirical representations), are effects of the moving forces of matter and belong as such
to the collective unity of *possible* experience. The collective unity of the
moving forces, however, is, objectively, the effect of the absolute whole of   21:602
the elementary material^m – that is, a matter which uniformly occupies
cosmic space according to the aforementioned (§   )^n attributes (for empty
enclosed or enclosing space is not an object of possible experience). The
influence of this matter on the subject's faculty of representation is the
efficient cause of its representation (which, combined with consciousness,
is called *perception*). Thus, the subjective element of the effects of those
forces which agitate according to the attributes mentioned above (that is,
the whole of perceptions) is, at the same time, the *presentation* of the
aforesaid matter – hence, identical with the objective element. That is to
say, this elementary material, as a given whole, is the *basis* for the unification of all the forces of matter into the unity of [experience]. Now, whatever belongs to the absolute unity of possible experience is actual. Hence,

^{m} This sentence originally continued: "which forms the *basis* of these combined forces.
Thus, also objectively regarded, caloric belongs to the unity of the whole of all possible
experience. The concept of that which belongs to such a whole is itself a concept of
experience, i.e. such an object (as caloric) *exists* and is actual." The new version given
above is added in the bottom margin of the previous page to which Kant here refers by
"*vide* page 2, bottom."
^{n} Sheet XI, page 2.

95

such a material is actual as a not merely distributively universal, but also collectively universal world-material.

This material is called caloric; not because it pertains specifically to the production of heat, but only for the sake of analogy with one of its effects; which is that it (this heating) is incoercible, and communicates itself in contact to other [things] as mere motion.

21:603

Note I

This mode of proving the existence of an outer sense-object must strike one as *unique* of its kind (without example); nevertheless, this should not appear strange, since its object also has the peculiarity, that it is *individual* and (unlike other representations from *a priori* concepts) contains in itself *collective*, not merely *distributive* universality. *Existentia est omnimoda determinatio*, Christian Wolff says, •and so also conversely: *omnimoda determinatio est existentia*,⁶⁰ as a relationship of equivalent concepts.• But the thoroughgoing determination which is here *thought* cannot be *given;* for it extends to an infinity of empirical determinations. Only in the concept of a single object of *possible experience* – which is not derived from any experience, but rather, itself makes it possible – is objective reality (this *omnimoda determinatio*) necessarily granted to the [outer sense-object], not synthetically, but analytically, according to the principle of identity; since that which is individual in itself, and also unique, is not determinable in more than one way, but is determined *for* experience.

[Vth fascicle, sheet XIII, page 4]

Note II

Whoever finds the direct (demonstrative) mode of proof insufficiently illuminating, can here use the indirect (apagogical) mode.

For, if we take caloric to be merely a hypothetical material (assumed for the explanation of certain appearances) and, if nature did not exercise (through its influence on the sensible subject and the latter's consciousness of moving forces) an influence which can serve as the foundation for
21:604 a system, then we would have sensations (and the perceptions which correspond to them) only as they [arise] from outer forces – that is, without form (tumultuously); this latter we ourselves, indeed, must provide for their combination. [We would] have a fragmentary aggregate, but no principle of form in the connection of empirical representations (perceptions) into one experience; and the rule, [which is required] for a concept of their whole, would be entirely absent. Not only would this be a deficiency for the establishment of a system, but the unity of experience itself would be self-contradictory and impossible. What is empirically manifold, but

whose coordination does not qualify for the unity of possible experience, is not an existing object: It is nothing.

Empty space is not an object of possible experience (nonbeing cannot be perceived). And if, under the heading of the moving forces, mention is also made of *attraction* of bodies at a distance, *through empty space* (as when gravitation is discussed), then this signifies nothing further than that bodies, distant from one another, can act upon one another by attraction – that is, immediately, without contact – *without the mediation* of an intermediary matter (notwithstanding that such a matter really lies between them). It does not, however, signify that empty space (which is in no way an object of possible experience) belongs to the composition of outer sense-objects, and is among the objects of one possible experience.

The concept of a caloric derives from the concept of an empirically determinable space in general, and is to that extent an *a priori* concept. Its aforementioned attributes, as attributes of a substance in space, are only thought as moving forces (powers) according to the different functions of active motion, and may be completely enumerated [*qualificiren*] *a priori.* To this extent they amount to a mere thought-object. The step from possibility to actuality occurs with certainty, however, for the reason that caloric is   21:605
the object of a single possible experience; it is an object of experience in virtue of the totality of determinations which belong to the concept of an individual, which amounts to the same thing as to say that its assertion is an empirical proposition.

One can also term *caloric* the *basis* (first cause) of all the moving forces of matter, for it is thought as the immediately moving *primary material* (*materia primaria*). All other materials (e.g. oxygen, hydrogen etc.), in contrast, which must first themselves be moved by this material, move as *secondary material* (*materia secundaria*), and are only modes of the latter (e.g. light). And the formation of bodies by specifically differentiated elements produces composite forms, which, however, must be subordinated to the principle of the possibility of a single experience, not placed beside it.

[. . .]

[XIIth fascicle, (half-)sheet X, page 1]   22:609

Definition

By the concept of caloric, I understand a universally distributed, all-penetrating matter, internally uniformly moving in all its parts, and remain-   22:610
ing permanently in this state of internal motion (agitation). It forms an absolute, self-subsistent whole, which, as elementary material, both occupies (*occupans*) and fills (*replens*) cosmic space. The parts of it, continu-

ously agitating one another in their place (hence not locomotively, [but] concussively – not progressively) and ceaselessly agitating other bodies, preserve the system in constant motion, and contain the moving forces as an outer sense-object.

This matter is also, as a consequence of the aforementioned attributes, negatively characterized: as imponderable, incoercible, incohesible and inexhaustible; for the contrary characterization [*Beschaffenheit*] would conflict with those attributes. Ponderability, coercibility, cohesion and exhaustibility, presuppose moving forces which act in opposition to the latter and cancel their effect.

Axiom

Regarded subjectively, there is only a single outer experience, since there is only one space.

The moving forces of matter which occupy (*occupant*) or fill (*replent*) space, stand in a universal active combination with one another, and, objectively, form a system. The system emerges *a priori* (not empirically, from experience) from the concept of the possibility of *one* experience, and contains the existence of one absolute whole of moving forces in its very concept.

22:611

Note

There is only one experience, and, if experiences are spoken of (as if there were many of them), then this is simply a misunderstanding; for what are meant thereby are merely *perceptions* (empirical representation of an object, with consciousness), of which there are, indeed, many. The **universality** of the concept of experience is, however, here not to be taken *distributively* (by which many characteristics are ascribed to one and the same object), but *collectively*, as the *collective unity* which is required for the unity of possible experience. The latter must be thought of as emerging not fragmentarily (by a compilation of perception), but, as necessarily synthetic, from the understanding. For a whole of possible perceptions •which, at the same time, as laws, carry universality (hence also necessity) with them in their concept,• is in contradiction with itself; since empirical propositions are always attached to other empirical conditions (*circumstantiae*), and so stand as part of a progress to infinity from one characteristic to the next. •The object of a single, all-embracing experience is, at the same time, an individual (*individuum*).• It is the formal element of the unity of possible experience which is required to be given *a priori*.

Now, what cannot be an object of experience – space empty of things and time empty of activity – does not belong subjectively to the one possible experience. And atomism, which, for the sake of possible experience, furnishes an elementary system of it from these constituents (*atomi et inane*), is contradictory in itself; for, on the one hand, there is no completely indivisible matter, and, on the other hand, empty space is not an object of possible perception (and thus not an object of experience).

Theorem

22:612

There exists an absolute and unique whole of matter with the aforementioned attributes; this is not a hypothetical material, in order to explain properly certain phenomena, but an *a priori* demonstrable one. Under the name of *caloric* (but without being bound to the feeling called warmth) it forms a self-subsistent whole (continuously agitated internally by its moving forces).

[. . .]

[How is physics possible? How is the transition to physics possible?]

[Xth fascicle, sheet I, page 2]⁶¹

["Einleitung"]

[. . .]

[Left margin]
The transition to physics cannot lie in the metaphysical foundations (attraction and repulsion, etc.). For these furnish no specifically determined, empirical properties, and one can imagine no specific [forces] of which one could know whether they exist in nature, or whether their existence be demonstrable; rather, they can only be feigned to explain phenomena empirically or hypothetically, in a certain respect. However, there are nevertheless also concepts (e.g. of organic bodies, of what is specifically divisible to infinity) which, although invented, still belong to physics. Caloric – the divisibility of the decomposition of a matter into different species. The *continuum formarum*.

[Xth fascicle, sheet I, page 3]
In this transition from the metaphysical foundations of natural science to physics there is [also] that from matter to the formation of bodies. A physical body is a self-limiting whole, by the united attraction of the parts of a quantity of matter. A mere aggregate of matter (in regard to which one abstracts from these unifying forces) is, if it both fills and occupies a space, a mathematical body – e.g. a cubic foot of water, in a vessel, because it does not limit itself by its own forces.

The first division of physical bodies is, thus, that into organic and inorganic. A physically organic body (in contrast to a mechanically organic body) is one, each of whose parts is by nature there in it for the sake of the other; in which, conversely, the concept of the *whole* also determines the form of the parts – externally as well as internally (in figure and texture). Such a formation indicates a natural cause, acting according to *purposes*. That such a body must be a solid body is already contained in its concept. Likewise, one can seek the productive force of this inner form nowhere

100

else than in a formative understanding – that is, seek it solely in a non-material cause (for understanding is the faculty of synthetic unity of representations with consciousness). And a being which can make a purpose into the determining ground of its forces must [be] solid [*breaks off*]

The concept of an organic matter contains a contradiction in itself, since the material for organization is taken for the organized subject.

[*Rest of page empty, except right margin*]

The matter which remains when organization is destroyed is not organic.

Vegetative and animal life, or the division into vegetative and life-force.

Living corporeal being (animals and men) can also [be] organized in relation to one another: (1) by sex, then, further, tribes and peoples [*breaks off*]

Whether the specific differentiation of matter extends to infinity or only to ponderable matter, and to caloric as imponderable, incoercible etc. matter. The division of concepts can be completed; the division of bodies extends to infinity.

[. . .]⁶²

[Xth fascicle, sheet I, page 13]   22:291

Objects must all fit into the topic of the principles, without which they could not be objects of experience (e.g. *caput de finibus*). Thus we find in our own body and in nature characteristics by reason of which we must regard them as organized – that is, as formed for purposes – since we would not otherwise understand them as such. These concepts always precede the confirmation of their objects by experience; they are *a priori* principles by which experiences are made.

That objects must be in conformity with the concepts which we ourselves form *a priori* in our reason can easily be seen; for by means of them, and of the principles of the synthetic unity of their appearances (which are not of empirical origin), it first becomes possible for us to think of objects according to these forms. To this extent, we know   22:292
nothing except as under rules, and we have no rules but those which we (not arbitrarily, but necessarily, according to principles of thought) have prescribed for ourselves.

The *transition* from the metaphysical foundations of natural science to physics according to its subjective *a priori* principles of form, is (or contains) a principle of the possibility of physics as a system of empirical concepts and laws; it is the outline of the elementary system of the moving forces of matter for [*als*] a special science of nature, which is always in the process of progressing, observing and aggregating, but is never completed. It is, thus, a scientific investigation of nature, whose *a priori* principles in the doctrine of motion are partly mathematical, partly dynamic.

101

Axioms of intuition, anticipations of perception, analogies of experience, postulates of empirical thought (coordination) in general.

[. . .]

22:294   [Xth fascicle, sheet I, page 14]

[. . .]

[Bottom margin]

In the metaphysical foundations matter is regarded as *mobile;* in the progression to natural science as *movens,* according to its moving forces

22:295 (mathematical and physiological), in relation to the system of the latter in physics in general. It is regarded, indeed, *a priori,* according to the form of an elementary system of the moving forces, [in order to] present, by the investigation of nature, its tendency toward a system (not fragmentarily).

Unity of the active principle must belong to the possibility of a natural organic body, since the latter's principle must be regarded not merely subjectively, but as objective in itself – namely, a purpose as its inner ground of determination.

N.B. Of the amphiboly of the concepts of reflection: to take that which is only subjectively conditioned as objectively valid and demonstrable as such – e.g. to assume mechanical principles as sufficient for moving forces (in the lever) without the required dynamical principles.

An organic body presupposes an organizing principle, whether inner or outer. The latter must be simple, for otherwise it would itself require an organization. As simple, it cannot be a part of matter (for each part of matter is always itself composite). So the organizing principle of an organic body must be outside space in general. It can, however, be internally active in one respect, while being external in another: that is, in another substance, the world-spirit.

[. . .]

22:298   [Xth fascicle, (half-) sheet II, page 2][63]

[A]

PRINCIPLE OF THE TRANSITION FROM THE METAPHYSICAL FOUNDATIONS TO PHYSICS

Physics is the systematic investigation of nature as to [*durch*] empirically given forces of matter, insofar as they are combined among one another in one system.

Physics is the empirical science of the complex of the moving forces of matter. These forces also affect the subject – man – and his organs, since man is also a corporeal being. The inner alterations thereby produced in him, with consciousness, are perceptions; his reaction on, and outer alteration of, matter is motion.

Physics is a system of the empirical investigation of nature which [can] only take place by observation and*a* experiment. In the first case, the project moves the physicist; in the second, the physicist moves the object and sets it in another state for perception. 22:299

Physics is a system; but we cannot know [*erkennen*] a system as such, except insofar as we ourselves compose the manifold of an aggregate according to *a priori* principles (insert them ourselves) – which takes place by means of the concept of motion. Consequently, the division of the study of nature within physics, as far as its highest division, the topic of the moving forces, is concerned, will be analytically investigated [*aufsuchen*] and synthetically presented, according to the following system.

The first [division] is into that of matter and bodies, according to their moving forces. For to think of *matters* is absurd, and, although there can be as many differences in the basis of its forces as there are materials, yet there can be no more than one universally moving force. For in the relation of the unification of motion, unity of the combining forces is contained in the same synthetic concept with the unity of space.

The second division is that of the formal element of the moving forces. Mechanical or dynamic, namely by means of other bodies as machines or immediate.

The third is that of organized and organizing matter, [based] on an objective principle of purposes, and thus made to propagate itself in living nature and to perpetuate its species in the demise of individuals.

The fourth is that which rests on willpower, and assigns the creature, as intelligence, to the moving forces of nature.

These belong all together in the field of physics, in which there are no laws of freedom, but [which] contains all forces which initiate the motion of matter – not just those which continue motion. The skillful initiator [*Kunsturheber*] of motions for the preservation of vital force is called a *physician* (town or country doctor), and his branch of the study of nature is called zoonomy[64] and rests on the employment of four animal powers [*animalische Potenzen*]: (1) on nervous power as a principle of excitability (*incitabilitas Brownii*);[65] (2) on muscular power (*irritabilitas Halleri*);[66] (3) on a force which preserves all the organic forces of nature as a constant alteration of the former two, of which *one* phenomenon is heat; (4) on the organization of a whole of organic beings of different species, for each other, serving for the species' preservation. 22:300

The first principle of representation of the moving forces of matter

---

a Lehmann's reading uncertain between *oder* and *und.*

[is] to regard them not as things in themselves but as phenomena, according to the relation which they have to the subject – as they[b] affect our sense, or as we affect our sense ourselves. [It involves] inserting the formal element of sensible representation into the subject in order to progress from the Axioms of Intuition, the Anticipations of Perception, etc. to experience – that is, *for* experience as a system, not as derived from experience. Consequently, [it amounts to] oneself founding such a system *a priori* – composing it synthetically, not deriving it analytically from the material element of empirical representation. Hence, it is this principle of form – not the *material* which moves the senses – which provides *a priori* the basis for the possibility of experience (by the rule, *forma dat esse rei*).

[Left margin]
The transition, by the subjective principle of the aggregation of perceptions – as a formal principle *for* (and not *through*) experience, whose consciousness is not empirical – to the objective unity of their connection into experience as a system (according to laws of motion which lead *a priori* to the whole of acting and reacting forces); this is the formal unity of experience as a system of perceptions. The material unity of experience is the idea of a whole of moving forces as the absolute (unconditioned) unity of the world-system, in which the moving forces contain and initiate nothing outside this *complexus*.

22:301   The transition to physics is, in the natural system, also directed toward the world-system, and this, too, can be regarded as organic in a certain respect. The surfaces now contain only the strata – are the discarded husks.

The system of organization is directed to the planetary system [*den Weltkörper*] itself, in which one organic whole is there for the sake of another (vegetation for the sake of animals, etc.) and, for example, the moon is there for the sake of the earth, and all *nexus effectivus* is at the same time *finalis*.

Zoonomy contains three vital powers [*Lebenspotenzen*]: *nervous power*, as a principle of excitability (*incitabilitas*); *muscular power* (*irritabilitas Halleri*); and a *third one* which brings both forces into active and reactive, constantly alternating, play: one all-penetrating, all-moving etc. material, of which heat is one phenomenon. (4) The force of organization in space and time, which contains a *nonmaterial* higher principle, namely an effectivity according to purposes.

[. . .]

---

[b] In the text, singular: *es afficirt*.

C

The aggregate of the moving forces of matter is itself only appearance, and their aggregation in empirical knowledge contains a formal element, which is *a priori* a principle of possible experience. Experience is itself a relation of phenomena in appearance, because motions are, in turn, also appearances of the moving forces; which forces (as principles of principles) are, in comparison to their appearances, the sense-objects themselves. That the forces are, in empirical knowledge, only appearances, is   22:318 clear from the fact that they are always only represented as aggregates of a higher system. We can have knowledge of the object of the senses only through a concept of reason (not through experience), namely, the concept of a system of moving forces [that is to say, through] a system of empirical representations, represented *a priori*, through that which we insert into sensible representation for the sake of empirical representation (and which we *must* insert for the sake of possible experience). And both observation and experiment are only methods to extract from sensible representation what we have tentatively [*versuchsweise*] inserted.

Problem

(1) How is physics possible? (2) How is the transition from the metaphysical foundations of natural science to physics possible? (3) How is the estimation of the scope of objects belonging to physics possible?

Physics is knowledge of sense-objects in experience. The latter, however, contains the representation of objects as appearances (*phaenomena*) which does not present (*exhibit*) what objects are in themselves but how they affect sense. [Physics] makes into its principle the moving forces, according to the constitution of the subject as affected (internally – not externally, that is, as the forces are empirically given (*dabile*)); which is to say [that its principle is] the connection of the manifold of sensible representation as it is thought *a priori* (*cogitabile*), according to the form of composition. And so it contains experience, as a system of empirical knowledge, which has absolute unity as its consequence, and whose form already contains objectively in its[c] concept the thing [*Sache*] itself as phenomenon (according to the rule: *forma dat esse rei*).

Physics is, thus, the doctrine of the connection of what is empirically represented into the unity of experience, and, hence, of progressing subjectively within a system. The individuality (*singularitas*) of possible experience, which [is presented] through the synthetic unity of adjacent and successive representations of space and time, given in pure intuition (*plu-*   22:319

[c] Reading *ihrem* for *seinem*.

ralis), [grounds] the absolute unity of experience. Hence one must say: "There is only one experience, and, if one hears mention of *experiences*, this must always be understood thereby only as an aggregate of perceptions, which belong to a single experience."

Because the concept of sense-objects as mere appearances, nevertheless, always, through reason, refers back to the thing [*Sache*] in itself (of which, however, no intuition can be expected), physics – which has to do with outer representations of the senses, their system for the sake of experience, and the principle of the possibility of experience – will have to occupy itself with nothing other than the systematic inner connection of these representations of the moving forces of matter.

Progression toward physics.

•Physics is the doctrinal system of the moving forces of matter, insofar as they are objectively contained in a natural system of them. It contains as a science an absolute whole of empirical knowledge of outer sense-objects. The enterprise of attaining it is called the investigation of nature, whose material (empirical) principle rests upon observation and experiment; its formal one, however – how and what one must investigate – rests on *a priori* principles. The latter contain the ground of the possibility of experience as a system of the study of nature, although they are not derived *from* experience.•

[*Right margin*]

We can extract nothing from the sensible representations which form the matter of cognition, except when we ourselves have inserted (according to the formal principle of the composition of what is empirical in the moving forces). Appearances are here to be regarded as things [*Sachen*] in themselves.

22:320   Physics has to do here with appearances of appearances, and the former's principles must be capable of being classified *a priori* by division, both in regard to objects (e.g. organic ones) as also in regard to the moving subject.

The objects of the senses, regarded metaphysically, are appearances; for physics, however, these objects are things [*Sachen*] in themselves, which affect sense, or as the subject affects itself (represent *a priori*).

The sole means to absolute unity for the sake of experience is to turn the nominal system of sensible representations into their real system.

Of direct and indirect appearances in comparison with things in themselves.

Since the moving forces by which we are affected are themselves, in turn, appearances, with respect to the system of forces affecting the senses, we can (and may) view them as things in themselves only in regard to the system.

[Xth fascicle, (half-)sheet IV, page 2]

There are two ways of distinguishing appearance from the thing [*Sache*] itself [and] the subjective element of a mode of representation from the objective. The first is metaphysical, the other physiological; and both consist in representing, as to its form, the mode in which the subject is affected (by the object). In which, however, the deception occurs that what belongs to the subject (which is affected) is attributed to the represented object – a deception which belongs to the error of subreption in *concepts*. The second deception consists (as concerns the existence of a sense-object) in immediately taking empirical consciousness of the object (perception) as a principle of the connection of perceptions for the possibility of experience – and to do so, indeed, directly, despite the fact that this can only take place mediately (indirectly) and that the existence of the object is not [derived] *from* experience but must precede it *for* experience (that is, for the sake of the possibility of experience in physics). For experience does not come of its own accord as influence of the moving forces on sense, but must be made. The *sensible element* in the representation of experience (*sensibile*) is the material for physics from which empirical knowledge must first of all be formed, by observation and experimental investigation of nature (*observatio et experimentum*), according to a formal principle. The *thinkable element* in the representation of experience (*cogitabile*) does not, however, absolutely (*absolute tale*), but only conditionally (*hypothetice tale*) provide physics with a guiding thread in the investigation of nature. The latter, without outlining *a priori* a whole of its object (according to the laws of the connection of these sensible representations) can, as regards scope and content, establish no system [worthy of] the name of physics. A subject of moving forces, however, which can have a concept of its objects in a system of the moving forces (as lawlike determinations of nature) only through the understanding, has a constitution which already contains identically in itself (through an analytic principle) the concept of such a whole of outer sense-objects. For, without this rule and order, we would know nothing of the latter's existence.

Knowledge of moving force in appearance in space, against moving force in itself. Appearance of appearance, insofar as the subject is affected by the object, and affects itself, and is a motion in appearance for itself.[d] The indirect moving force of outer sense in the investigation of nature – since the subject itself makes and causes the motion through which it[e] is affected, inserts *a priori* into the subject what it receives from without, and is self-moving.

Empirical representation combined with consciousness is perception. Consciousness of the combination of perceptions into a whole (not as a

22:321

---

[d] Reading with Adickes *ihm* for *ihr.*   [e] Reading with Adickes *es* for *sie.*

107

fragmentary aggregate but as a system) is not, in turn, itself empirical, but *a priori* knowledge as to its form – that is, experience. This agreement is not derived *out* of (or *from*) experience, but is a synthesis of appearances in the subject *for* experience, and for the sake of its possibility. Here there occurs an amphiboly of the concepts of reflection: [One] takes what nature produces (*appearances* in the subject) for one and the same as what this subject does. That is to say, [one] misinterprets the connection of empirical representations, taken into a whole, and takes it as a thing *in itself*. Thus [one] takes the formal element of appearance for the material element of the object itself, and what the subject inserts for the sake of the possibility of experience (the form) as what is encountered in the sense-object itself (the matter). The transition from the metaphysical foundations of natural science to physics.

22:322

To take hold of the moving forces of matter empirically, and to collect them fragmentarily, cannot ground a physics as a system. Rather, it must be capable of being erected as a whole – not as an aggregate (*sparsim*) but as a system (*coniunctim*) – according to an *a priori* principle which determines the number and order of the moving forces. This cannot occur otherwise than by [taking as its principle] what we insert for the sake of a possible experience (consequently according to a formal principle), not what we extract from the aggregate of perceptions. In this way, a science is brought about in which the investigation of nature (by observation and experiment) proceeds from the appearance of appearances (and so according to an *a priori* principle); science is thus, indeed, made possible indirectly, not as an indeterminately digressing compilation (*cognitio vaga*) but according to principles of the division of the manifold according to concepts. Because, not intuition but the understanding, not the sensible (*sensibile*) but the thinkable (*cogitabile*), according to the principle of all coordination (*forma dat esse rei*), prior to all [*breaks off*]

The amphiboly of concepts: to make a leap from that which comes to us empirically, and is merely appearance, to experience – since the latter would be an appearance of an appearance, and experience cannot be received as a representation which comes to us, but must be made.

[*Margin . . .*]⁶⁷

22:324

[Xth fascicle, (half-)sheet V, page 1]

D

Just as the physical *division* of all bodies extends to infinity, and no simple part of matter – hence no atomism – can be found, so it is with the logical *division* of the concept of body in general (that is, the principle of the species of matter). Bodies can be classified in an infinite number of ways:

according to their material (mixture); their fabric (texture); their shape (figure); and, as solid, purposively self-forming bodies, according to their preservation (nature); and so to infinity, such that in the division of any system there can never be a final member.

(1) The apperception of objective composition (*a priori*). (2) The apprehension of the subjectively composite (empirical). (3) The synthetic unity of appearances, under one concept, in a whole of space. (4) The principle of the investigation of nature in regard to objects. 22:325

We have *a priori* intuition, with consciousness of outer objects; also empirical representations with consciousness, that is, perception. (The actuality of objects is assumed, because, otherwise, the passive consciousness [would have] no ground for the lawfulness [of empirical representations], and for outer communication [*breaks off*]

(1) Appearance in its metaphysical significance, as sense is affected. (2) Appearance in its physical significance, as the subject itself affects sense, by means of moving forces, according to form. (3) How the latter significance is subordinated to the former. (4) How the moving forces of the whole (determinable and determining – not [in regard to relation] of the aggregate to its parts but [in regard to] the system) form a system called physics – that is, experience which has as its basis absolute unity in its concept: progressing from the empirical (which is not a system, but fragmentary) to the rational idea of the whole of the objects of sense (ponderable, coercible, cohesible, exhaustible,*f* and their opposites). And how an elementary system of the moving forces is constituted *a priori* by the understanding (according to the absolute synthetic unity of space) by means of a universally distributed, all-penetrating, etc. matter, which forms a self-subsistent whole. •(The appearance of appearance, thought in the connection of the manifold, is the concept of the object itself.)•

Thus physics is constituted, not *out* of and from experience, but, [by means of] the concept of the unity of moving forces, *for* the possibility of experience (by means of observation and experiment) according to the principles of the investigation of nature. It is constituted according to the aforementioned universal principles for the coordination of whatever phenomena may ever be presented to the outer senses, •insofar as outer forces act upon them and their organs.• These principles found an *a priori* classification which outlines a system of nature as a schema, and in which a place is developed for each natural object. 22:326

The appearance of appearances (that is, how the subject is mediately affected) is metaphysically [the same] as how the subject makes itself into an object (is conscious of itself as determinable in intuition). It contains the principle of the combination of the moving forces in space, in order to realize space through empirical representation, according to its form –

---

f Above the last four words: •Categories: quantity, quality, relation, modality.•

not through experience, but for the sake of the possibility of experience as a system of the subject's empirical representations. (Axioms of Intuition, Anticipations of Perception, Analogies of Experience, and coordination of empirical representations in a system in general (thus not fragmentarily).)

The amphiboly of reflective judgment is the self-deception of taking empirical apperception as intellectual apperception in composition (which takes place *a priori* according to principles). It is a conjunction, not by a stepwise progression from metaphysics to physics, [but] by a leap; because a middle term – namely, the consciousness of synthetic unity in the progress of the investigation of nature – is lacking.

This composition (or, rather, the composite of phenomena in a system) is not itself a phenomenon, but a connection of the moving forces by a concept of the understanding. By its means we systematically establish, according to a principle, the manifold (which has been fragmentarily composed by us, through observation and experiment) into a whole of empirical knowledge for the sake of the investigation of nature.

Division of the moving forces in relation to the five senses; then to bodily forms in general.

The moving forces of matter are what the moving subject itself does with its body to [other] bodies. The reactions corresponding to these 22:327 forces are contained in the simple acts by which we perceive the bodies themselves. Mechanics and dynamics are the two principles.

[. . .]

22:340 [Xth fascicle, (half-)sheet VIII, page 1]

G

Thus, in physics, concepts are founded on that which is furnished by the empirical investigation of nature – and, hence, on a subjective *a priori* principle of this investigation in the elementary system of the moving forces. So the subjective principle presupposes a principle of the division of the system as to its material element, that is, its primary materials (*bases*).

The appearance of things in space (and time), however, is twofold: (1) that of objects which we ourselves insert in space (*a priori*), and which is metaphysical; (2) that which is empirically given to us (*a posteriori*), and which is physical. The latter is direct appearance, the former indirect – that is, appearance of an appearance.

The object of an indirect appearance is the thing [*Sache*] itself – that is, 22:341 one which we only extract from intuition, insofar as we ourselves have inserted the appearance, that is, insofar as it is our own cognitive product.

For we would have no consciousness of a hard or soft, warm or cold, etc. body, *as such*, had we not previously formed for ourselves the concept of these moving forces of matter (of attraction and repulsion, or of extension and cohesion, which we subordinate to them) and thus can say that one or the other of these [properties] falls under such a concept. Hence, there are given for empirical knowledge concepts which are •not, for that reason, empirical, but• *a priori;* they are given for the sake of experience – •to have natural things subjectively, [as] given objects according to an *a priori* principle.• [This latter is only possible,] because we made the object of empirical intuition (of perception) ourselves; produced it ourselves for the instrument of sensation (by composition); and thus presented a sense-object for experience in accordance with the latter's universal principles; and thereby produced in sensible intuition, for the subject, the individual (of sense-representation) in what is universal as to its form.

Thus, for example, rock crystal is a species of the genus "stone" in the classification of minerals – that is, a hard, brittle, once fluid now transparent body, formed regularly into a certain figure and texture, whose production we think of as originating from a particular kind of matter. Now, by means of the *description (descriptio)* – which, however, is not *explanation (definitio)*, since it has not emerged from *a priori* concepts – the understanding forms from this empirical material (*basis*) the concept of a transparent body, combined by attraction, and, by repulsion, forcefully resisting alteration in its figure. And, thus, the understanding adds the formal element of 22:342 experience to the material element of empirical intuition.

The moving forces of matter, however, in virtue of the unity of space and its thoroughgoing fullness (since empty space would be no object of experience), form an *elementary system,* which is, indeed, the object of physics. The latter is a *doctrinal system* of the moving forces, and, by means of the investigation of nature, is always progressing as regards logical specification.

[Right margin]

Physics is the empirical science of the moving forces of matter, insofar as it (matter) forms a system; the latter is founded in nature itself, and, hence, can be said to be a natural system (*naturale*) – not an artificial one (*artificiale*). But how can we demand *a priori* a system of empirical knowledge which, itself, neither is, nor can be, empirical?

Discursive universality (unity in multiplicity) is to be distinguished from intuitive universality (many in one). The latter is an act of composition, and collective; the former of apprehension [*Auffassen*], and distributive. Axioms of Intuition precede the Anticipation which forms the *basis* of perception.

The vacuum, in regard to the moving forces as sensible representations, is not an object of possible experience. *Atomi et inane* are no objects of experience.

111

The aggregate of empirical representation cannot precede, but the form of the system, which contains a principle.

Spatium cogitabile is the form of the whole in the system – in form, a thought-object (*ens rationis*). The insensible is vacuum.
Spatium dabile and *spatio cogitabile* as system – not noumenon. Contradiction.
The elementary concepts of the moving forces of matter are:

1. [Those] which move others without themselves being locomotive – ponderable, coercible, etc.
2. These stand under categories
22:343   3. The forces, under the categories, under the universal moving principle of an all-penetrating, etc. matter.

In the amphiboly of the concepts of reflection, indirect appearance is apparentness [*Apparentz*], that is, illusion [*Schein*].
Appearance gives *a priori* principles of the whole of moving forces only formally. The material element remains undetermined. Only the system is the thing [*Sache*] itself.

[Xth fascicle, (half-)sheet VIII, page 2]
We can extract nothing other from our sense-representations than that which we have inserted (with consciousness of its presentation) for the empirical representation of ourselves – that is, by the understanding (*intellectus exhibit phaenomena sensuum*). This presentation produces a system out of an aggregate of perceptions, according to the formal conditions of intuition and the coexistence of these perceptions in the subject. It produces a •cognition of the outer• sense-object, as *appearance*, by composition of manifold of the moving forces of matter in appearance, for the sake of the possibility of *experience* { – that is, for the investigation of nature. The presentation is the schema of a concept which, as mere appearance, makes *a priori* possible the form of the composite in the object and the ground of experience for knowledge of it. For only appearance permits *a priori* knowledge.
The five outer senses, to which belongs further an inward one (sensation of warmth).}
Now, this complex of empirical representations in one consciousness is not thought as an aggregate, compiled fragmentarily from perceptions; from that no experience arises, for to •the possibility of• experience there
22:344   belongs synthetic unity *a priori*, •according to a principle of connected perceptions.• Thus all empirical data of outer sense-representation will have to be thought of in no other way than as necessarily combined in one system, in order to be thought as belonging to experience. Hence there is, with respect to these objects, only one experience (as language itself

conveys, which does not speak of experiences, but only of experience). It is this experience, as a *system*, which the empirical investigation of nature aims at, not empirically, however, but according to a principle (the formal element of knowledge), based *a priori*, in order to represent the appearances of natural things appropriately to experience.

Now, as regards the synthesis of appearances (that is, how the objects of empirical representations and their spatial relations must necessarily appear to us, and, consequently, also, what experience will offer us if we pursue it, by observation and experiment, in the investigation of nature) we can, indeed, very well determine *a priori* what they are for our senses; not, however, what they are for every human being (that is, in themselves). Thus we cannot, as it seems, even with all our means of having experience, discern *a priori* – with universal validity – which (and how many) objects of perception (which, taken together, constitute *matter*) and moving forces (in kind and number) there are which could be taken by us as underlying our possible experience. Rather, [it seems,] that we could, at best, by random groping among outer sense-objects, merely compile an enumeration of certain forces – e.g. hardness, softness, heaviness, lightness, and so on – which together do not amount to a complete system of forces (and thus also to the materials which they contain). The reason is that we cannot come to knowledge of them by the investigation of nature, according to an *a priori* principle – that is to say, we cannot specify the primary materials of the moving forces and develop an elementary system of them.

[. . .]

[Xth fascicle, (half-)sheet X, page 1]   22:353

[1]

[. . .]

[Right margin]
Difference between natural system and doctrinal system of the objects of experience. The latter is science of nature. Transition from the metaphysical foundations to physics, according to *a priori* principles.

Galileo, Kepler, Huygens and Newton.

Huygens's transition from the metaphysical foundations of natural science to the mathematical ones, and that of Newton to physics – merely by means of the concept of gravitational attraction, which did not occur to Kepler.

Of the doctrinal system of nature which is preceded by the zetetic system.

(1) The object in intuition (2) in appearance, subjective and thus *a priori* (3) in perception, empirical consciousness (4) in experience, whereby it is self-made through composition. Given object, through observation and experiment – the formal element of apprehension, apperception, reflection of judgment in which the amphiboly (4) the elementary system, subjective – as natural system, objective.

That we have insight into nothing except what we can make ourselves. First, however, we must make ourselves. Beck's original representing.[68]

Experience (that which is to be experience), which is compiled fragmentarily, from nothing but individual facts, is not an experience, but only the ground to expect experience.

22:354

[Xth fascicle, (half-)sheet X, page 2]

That the objects of sense must allow of being specified and divided by genus and species, prior to experience and for the sake of it, does not, thus, take place by fragmentary groping around, but according to an objective principle of combination in a system of empirically given natural forces. The latter have influence on the senses, and yet, at the same time, must be thought of as united *a priori* by the understanding into an absolute whole, as regards quantity and quality; and, hence, represented as united specifically into a system of physics. This amounts to the transition from the metaphysical foundations of natural science to physics, in which the manifold [is] united according to the form of a system (*non sparsim sed conjunctim*) and, [likewise,] the whole of all objects of perception for the sake of the possibility of experience – not through that which the understanding merely extracts from the manifold, but only insofar as it has itself previously inserted [the form of] the system. In this way, the investigation of nature may hope to achieve a natural system – [that is,] a system out of the elements of these [natural] forces.

It is impossible to specify *a priori* the empirical manifold of the moving forces of matter (for the latter are matters which act upon our sense-organs, and so [produce] sensations, by which we acquire perceptions) unless it is itself posited in the very problem (and in representation as a problem). Of this kind is: All matter is either ponderable or imponderable. . . . For it is the influence on the senses of the affected subject which amounts to the representation of the object, insofar as it is apprehended.

The inner and outer objects of the senses in appearance (*obiecta phaenomena*) (which are, for this reason, not [to be regarded] as immediate – as the thing [*Sache*] in itself – but only subjective and mediate, according to

22:355 what they are in relation to the subject and the form in which the latter makes the moving forces of matter for the sake of experience) are the basis of the unification which the understanding *thinks a priori* into this manifold – the formal element of composition in one concept – which amounts to the essence of the object. [The understanding does this] by connection of the given manifold according to laws (*forma dat esse rei*), whose complex (*complexus*), as empirical representations for the sake of the possibility of experience (by specification of perceptions in the apprehension of appearances and their coordination according to a law) forms a doctrinal system called physics. The transition to physics (which [lies] in the natural tendency of the metaphysical foundations of natural science as a universal doctrine of experience) can develop for itself a **topic** of concepts, according to a law of the connection of perceptions in the investigation of nature (by observation and experiment). In this topic, ever-progressing physics is led to *classify* and specify, according to a single principle, the objects of experience (as appearances, to which the investigation of nature leads), not by *random groping* among perceptions as an aggregate, but [in] an *elementary system*.

The moving force of matter is now classified, according to its reciprocity, into the force of free matter (*materia soluta*) and into that of matter which is bound by itself (*ligata*) – that is, matter which forms bodies and which limits its own space by attraction of its parts among each other. Bodies are, in turn, either organic or inorganic. The former are such that their inner and outer form (in texture and figure) is not comprehensible *a priori*, as belonging to a natural system, without a principle of reciprocally moving forces (according to purposes). [The latter,] on the other hand, require no such principle (*materia bruta*). Finally, organized matters are either *animate* or merely *vegetative beings*. The possibility of organized bodies cannot be known *a priori;* hence their concept can only enter physics through *experience.* For who would think that there would be, in *nature,* bodies which, like works of art, are formed inwardly and outwardly, and which, furthermore, preserve their species despite the destruction of individuals, if experience were not to supply examples of such in rich measure? Hence the latter must not be lacking in the elementary system of the moving forces in the transition from the metaphysical foundations of natural science to physics.

22:356

[*Margin* . . .]

[Xth fascicle, (half-)sheet XI, page 1]

K

The topic of the moving forces of matter (which, combined with consciousness, awaken perceptions, as empirical representations of objects of the senses) does not yet, on its own, found an experience – that is, empirical knowledge of these objects. Rather, it founds the objects only [as] they

22:357

are initially [given] in *appearance,* according to the subjective characteristic of their intuition, insofar as they affect the intuiting subject.

Now the form of intuition (as appearance) is, however, the only thing which can be given *a priori* for the sake of the possibility of experience (hence, in the transition from the metaphysical foundations of natural science to physics) and its complex forms the elementary system of physics. Hence empirical representations (as perceptions of the objects of sense) will allow of being established and classified, in relation to one's own bodily subject in appearance, as a system which can be specified *a priori* as to kind and number. The latter furnishes a transition from the metaphysics of nature to physics – as a whole, outside the subject, which is appearance for its own self. The subject, as the appearance of an appearance in a system of empirical knowledge (which is called experience) presents *a priori* the first transition from the metaphysics of natural science to physics in an elementary system of the moving forces of matter. It presents this transition in the form of an object of experience in the relation to the subject's body, according to all the functions of the fragmentary aggregations of the manifold.

The division of the moving forces – if it is to be drawn up systematically, not fragmentarily (in which case it would be lawless) – can be drawn up according to no other logical form but that of disjunctive judgments (for which reason, the forces remain problematic). Thus, in a doctrinal system of the moving forces, it must be said, as far as the formal element of their coordination (*coordinatio aut subordinatio*) is concerned: All matter is either ponderable or imponderable as to its moving forces, and so on.

22:358 Consequently, the moving forces can and must [be enumerated] in an elementary system, which belongs to physics; and these forces, when thought together with the form of their combination into the system, according to principles, constitute the doctrinal system of physics itself. These forces, as objects of empirical intuition with consciousness (perceptions) may be called *materials (bases materiale),* that is, movable substances, which may be either locomotive (*locomotivae*), or else repercussively moving their place (in motion at the same location) (*interne motivae*) [*breaks off*]

[Bottom margin]

In order to attain *a priori* empirical cognitions and their system (that is, experience) the subject must first apprehend subjectively the relation of the moving forces to itself in the representation of inner sense; apprehend them, fragmentarily, in the aggregate of the perceptions of inner sense; and combine them in one consciousness. This cannot take place by random groping among perceptions, but systematically, [according to] the formal elment of the appearance of the manifold of the intuition of itself. Through this act of composition (*synthetice*), the subject makes itself, according to a principle, into an object as it appears to itself – [that is,] as it affects itself and appears to itself, and extracts nothing more from intuition (the empirical) than it has inserted into it.

[Right margin]

The materials (*bases*) in given matter in general do not permit of being specified and classified *a priori*. But the moving forces of these materials do very well permit enumeration in a division of the manifold modes of motion.

Consciousness of one's own organs in the use of one's moving forces, as appearance of a body in general – as subjective transition to physics, as regards perception, insofar as the latter contain *a priori* unity of the object: 22:359
appearance of the whole of appearances.

The subject in appearance, which collects the inner moving forces for possible experience (for the completeness of possible perceptions) in conformity with a formal law; therein it affects itself according to a principle, hence appears to itself as compositive (by inner moving forces).

Only appearances are intuitions such as can be given *a priori*. Empirical intuitions with consciousness (that is, perceptions) depend on forces which move the senses and form an elementary system of matter. The latter, however, [is] only present in appearance; in physics, however, it is raised up into experience.

[. . .]

[Xth fascicle, (half-)sheet XIII, page 1]   22:367

M

Empirical intuition (as the subjective element of perception of the moving forces of the matter of the outer object which affects [the senses]) represents space itself into an object of experience, as a synthetic cognition of the sense-object, by means of the *a priori* composition of the manifold in appearance; •and this, indeed, in empirical intuition.•

The pure intuition of the manifold in •space contains *a priori* the form of the object in the• appearance of the first order, •that is, direct appearance.• The composition of perceptions (appearance •in the subject•) for the sake of experience is, •in its turn,• appearance •of the subject thus affected as it represents itself (hence, indirect appearance) and is• of the second order: appearance of the appearance of perceptions in one consciousness; that is, appearance •of the self-affecting subject (hence, indirect)• •and• of the synthesis of perceptions of the possibility of experience (which is single). •Mediate appearance is• the subjective element of the connection of presentations in the subject, according to principles of the consciousness of their composition into a cognition of these phenomena,

22:368

in the consciousness of the synthetic unity of experience. In consequence, [in] the coordination of perceptions into the unity of experience, [there arises] a system of those inner perceptions which allow of being classified and specified *a priori,* with the effect that the composing subject appears to itself in the composition according to principles, and so, in a system of perceptions •(as forces of matter affecting the senses),• progresses *a priori* toward the possibility of physics.

[. . .]

22:372

[Xth fascicle, (half-)sheet XIII, page 2]

[. . .]⁶⁹

[Bottom margin]

22:373

The objective element in appearance presupposes the subjective in the moving forces; or, conversely, the empirical element in perception presupposes the form of composition of the moving forces with respect to what is mechanical. The doctrinal element in the investigation of nature in general presupposes in the subject an organic principle of the moving forces in [the form of] universal principles of the possibility of experience. Axiom of Intuition. Anticipation of Perception, etc. Since [*breaks off*]

The transition from metaphysics to physics as a *doctrinal system* requires principles of *a priori division* according to concepts; in which the question is whether this division, like the (mathematical) *division* of matter, extends to infinity, or is atomistic. First division of matter into *materials* and *bodies.* The former are represented as elements, albeit formless; the latter as formative, and the molecules as formed. Bodies whose inner form can be thought as intentional (that is to say, as possible only according to a principle of purpose) are organic; and, hence, must also be thought as rigid. They are machines – either *lifeless* (merely vegetative) or living, *animal* – for which indivisible unity of the moving principle (soul) is required; for an aggregate of substances cannot by itself found a purposive unity. Such a natural characteristic cannot belong *a priori* to the principle of the division; for even the possibility of an organic body cannot be appreciated [*a priori*]. We experience organic forces in our own body; and we come, by means of the analogy with them (with a part of their principle), to the concept of a vegetative body, leaving out the animal part of its principle. In both cases, the [characteristic] phenomenon of a species which preserves itself in space and time is the continuation of the genus and the alternating death and life of its individuals: Sickness forms the constant transition between the two. The original moving forces, however, presuppose a certain number of those forces which act subjectively upon the empirical power of representation and determine it into perception.

Subjectively indirect appearance – since the subject is an object of empirical knowledge for itself, and, yet, at the same time, makes itself an object of experience, insofar as, in affecting itself, it is the phenomenon of a phenomenon.

[. . .]

[Xth fascicle, (half-)sheet XIV, page 2]   22:377

[N]

Now, there must be an *a priori* principle, in order to apprehend perceptions as effects of the moving forces of matter on the subject for the sake of experience, and to coordinate them into a physics (not to be extracted from physics); since, otherwise, that science would turn in a circle. Hence there must be a system of the moving forces which are thought *a priori*, that is, according to the modifications of motion in general. The motions [yield] a schema for the combination of the moving forces according to the latter's rule, and are thought of as systematically combined in conformity with the schema of the Analogies of Experience. This takes place insofar as the understanding presents its own acts – being its effects on the subject – in the concepts of attraction or repulsion, etc., in a whole of experience produced formally thereby.

1. *What is physics?* It is the doctrine of the complex (*complexus*) of empirical •representations with consciousness• (perceptions) insofar as they contain an aggregate of appearances •(of the subject, as affected by moving forces)• for a system (according to a principle of their combination) – that is, subjectively, the ground of the possibility of experience.

So physics is not yet itself the system of empirical knowledge, but the tendency of the metaphysical foundations of natural science toward the doctrine of experience [as an unconditional whole]. •Since there is only a single experience, the synthetic unity of perceptions, thought *a priori* in the unconditional whole of perceptions (*cogitabile*), is, at the same time, given (*dabile*).•

Since all perceptions are effects of the moving forces of matter on the   22:378 subject which contains their representation, the moving forces are contained by the transition to physics, according to their quality, etc., as objects of experience dissolved into their elements.

{Appearance as the form of representation – how the subject is affected by an object – can be given *a priori;* thus the moving forces of matter can effect empirical representations in the subject, but not yet experience.}

First, the subjective element of appearances, as pure *a priori* intuitions. Then, the objective element of empirical intuitions from moving forces which inwardly determine the subject – that is, of perceptions as empirical intuitions with consciousness. Third, the relationship of perceptions to experience as a system (not as a mere *aggregate*) of the moving forces affecting the subject; simply according to their form *a priori* (disjunctively) •for the sake of the possibility of experience.• According to the rules of composition of the forces – •hence, only• problematically: ponderable or imponderable, coercible, etc., according to the categories of quantity, etc., of the elementary system of the moving forces as *materials;* that is, as substances which, as independently movable, *form bodies* •both inwardly and outwardly,• •in• texture (inwardly) and figure. One all-embracing, all-penetrating material of the manifold (by crystallization, etc.) lies at the basis of these materials (without being hypothetical) in a whole of the elementary system; it is this which dynamically forms the subject of the moving forces in a single system.

[. . .]

22:383   [Xth fascicle, (half-)sheet XV, page 2]

[O]

Physics has as its object things whose cognition is only possible through experience; that is to say, such objects – whose concept, idea, or even fiction, as being without any reality (albeit without internal contradiction either) contains no guarantee of their possibility – as can have such a guarantee only from experience. The concept of such an object would, for instance, be that of an organized body – e.g. in the vegetable or animal kingdom. Were experience not to furnish examples of them, the possibility of such bodies would be dismissed by everyone as fantasies of the Prince of Palagonia.[70]

Nevertheless, since man [has] not just a feeling of his own body, but also a sensible representation (combined with understanding) of it ([of] his own form) [which he] can abstract from his body as object, and so present in a universal concept, he can recognize himself by experience in something which, were this not so, he would have to reject from his concepts as an empty fantasy. Thus there are sense-objects (even) whose possibility is only thinkable through actuality.

Physics is the doctrine of the aggregation of appearances (that is, of the subject of empirical representations as possible perceptions, •which affects its senses itself•) into a doctrinal system, called experience. Hence the manifold of appearances is coordinated within it, not *from* experience, but (automatically) *for* experience, according to a principle of the connection of perceptions as effects of the forces which move the subject •itself.•

22:384   Physics is thus not an *empirical system* (for that would be a contradictory concept) but a doctrinal system of all empirical representations. The latter, as regards their form, are initially *given a priori* in appearance [through] the relation of the moving forces; then, however, *thought* through the understanding as in combination under a principle – not apprehended, but inserted *a priori* into empirical intuition (into sensible representation) by the subject itself, according to principles of the possibility of experience.

In this way, it can be understood how it is possible that that which can only be •represented as• empirically given (immediate sensible representation – *intuitus*) may yet, as made by the subject itself (hence mediately – *per conceptus*), and thought *a priori*, be counted among the objects of experience. The reason is, namely, that sensation (which is the perceiving subject's own effect) is, in fact, nothing other than the moving force which determines itself to composition, and the perception of outer objects is only the appearance of the automacy of the conjunction of the moving forces affecting the subject themselves.

What thus belong first of all to physics are the formal differences of the active relations of the moving forces of matter, which make their object into an object of experience. Attraction, repulsion – pressure, impact, etc. Second, however, there belong to physics the material relations in a whole of possible experience (as absolute unity), a system of empirical knowledge of these forces; consequently, to think the division of whatever can only derive its concept from experience: e.g., of the difference between organic and inorganic bodies; or else of a matter (as elementary material) which can form no body but is inwardly present in all bodies, in substance (caloric). These differences, as a whole, belong to physics (architectonically).

[. . .]

[Xth fascicle, sheet XVIII, page 4][71]   22:405

[R]

It is not in the fact that the subject is affected empirically by the object (*per receptivitatem*), but that it affects itself (*per spontaneitatem*), that the possibility of the transition from the metaphysical foundations of natural science to physics consists. Physics must make its object itself, according to a principle of the possibility of experience as a system of perceptions. It transforms thereby the discursive universality of the aggregate of perceptions into intuitive universality; not partially (*sparsim*) but as unifying appearances (*contiunctim*), not through experience but *for* it. Thus the subject is an object of empirical intuition – that is, appearance – for itself; for only as such can it [serve] *a priori*, in conformity with the formal conditions of the possibility of experience, for the sake of physics (and the latter be introduced as a possible science). For experience cannot be given but must be made; and it is the principle of the unity of experience in the subject which makes it possible that even empirical data (as materials by

22:406 which the subject affects itself) enter into a system of experience and, as moving forces, can be enumerated and classified in a natural system.

One must proceed from the system of the empirical (physics) to perceptions (which contain the moving forces of matter in experience) and to the functions of these forces with respect to the determination of sense-objects – that is, the principle of the possibility of experience – in order to be able to expound these forces *a priori*, as materials in a division.

Experience does not emerge in collective universality, from perceptions, but is made in distributive universality – as synthetic unity of the empirical manifold of perceptions (by the moving forces affecting the subject) for the sake of experience, as a system of those forces which affect sense – that is, for physics. The latter system is not empirical (for that would be a self-contradiction) but progresses to a complex of empirical determination, according to a principle.

That we are conscious of ourselves *a priori*, in a system of empirical representations, which is itself, therefore, not empirical. In this system, the moving forces of matter exercise the functions of progress for the possibility of experience. They contain the form of the synthesis of perceptions (Quality, Quantity, Relation and Modality) [in] the relation of these forces to the subject (hence as appearances of the object in the composition of the material element of experience); thus, they give physics an *a priori* foundation. Experience is not given but is made objectively by[g] the subject. Not through experience, but for the sake of its possibility, and of perception, and of the system of perceptions of physics.

In physics, however, there must be included thought-entities (*entia rationis*), as problematic, for the division of possible moving forces of matter; these are thought as so constituted that they *cannot* be thought *otherwise* than through experience. Of this kind are organic bodies, every part of which is there for the sake of the other, and whose existence can *only* be thought in a

22:407 system of purposes (which must have an immaterial cause); of which the perception by man of his own organs furnishes the example. (Darwin's *Zoonomia*,[72] Cullen,[73] Brown,[74] who are called physicians (town or country doctors) although they only treat one branch of physics.) Now that which acts mediately on the senses in empirical intuition, as perception, is the real element (of perception) in physics; it is the material of representations which are not given *a priori;* and, yet, it is required in order to enumerate *a priori* such effects of the moving forces of the subject. One must first resolve them into relations (active), of which there exist a certain number.

---

[g] Reading *vom* for *zum*.

[Left margin]

What is physics? It is the scientific doctrine of the knowledge of sense-objects (of outer as well as inner) in experience. It is not an empirical science (for that would be a self-contradiction, since all knowledge, insofar as it is to be scientific, must be founded on formal principles of the combination of the manifold of its representations). It can, nevertheless, be a complex (*complexus*) of empirical cognitions which are combined into one experience; for experience must be *made*, and cannot, like mere perception (empirical representation with consciousness), be *given*.

Physics is, thus, not a mere aggregate of perceptions (which, composed fragmentarily, will not amount to a science) but presupposes a principle of the composition of empirical representations; the latter founds knowledge, not *from* experience but *for* it (and for its sake), as the principle of its possibility. Consequently, there is only one experience (just as there is only one matter) which furnishes a great manifold of appearances. Experience, proceeding from the moving forces of matter, furnishes an absolute whole of empirical representations, which supply *a priori* – not partially (*sparsim*) but [systematically] unified (*coniunctim*) – the material for experience.

Question.   22:408

How is *a priori* knowledge of the system of the moving forces of matter, as an aggregate of empirical representations for the sake of experience, possible?

Answer: not according to a synthetic, but to a merely analytical principle, namely, the rule of identity; since experience does not emerge immediately from an aggregate of perceptions (thus not empirically) but only as the consequence of a formal principle of the coordination (*coordinatio*) of the manifold of empirical representations in a system, called experience – not from experience (empirically) but for experience (for its sake). In which the object is represented in appearance (that is, in relation to the form of intuition in the subject), not as immediately related to the object. From this, it can thus be seen, how the strange (paradoxical) element of the *transition* from the metaphysical foundations of natural science to *physics* can and must proceed in constant relation (not through a leap, but by a natural tendency) from the merely empirical to the rational. To which must be counted not merely that which can be an object of experience (to which belong those forces of matter which immediately affect the senses) but also that "*which cannot* be thought as a possible sense-object *other than by experience*"; whose own possibility is otherwise problematic (e.g. organized bodies) [and] which may be apprehended and classified, not *from* experience but systematically *for* experience (in a scientific doctrine, called physics).

Whatever is an object of perception (*empirice dabile*) is not, for that very reason, at once an object of experience – for the latter, as a system of perceptions, must be *made*. Now, all outer perceptions are effects of the

22:409 influence of the moving forces of matter and of the outer object affecting the subject, and, to that extent, merely appearances; thus, they can be given *a priori* as to their formal element. Thus forces can also be thought in matter which are *materials* (that is, substances which belong to the motion of matter and which form the basis of these forces); and physics is a doctrinal system of them. These materials, regarded in their capacity as moving forces, permit of being enumerated *a priori*, according to principles: as founded on *attraction and repulsion* (both, however, on penetrating or superficial [force], acting from whole to parts, etc.), coercible, etc. May be enumerated and classified *a priori*, according to principles. *Basis* and matter, which is guiding.

22:453 [XIth fascicle, sheet III, page 1]

S

Perception (empirical representation with consciousness) is merely a relation of the object to the subject as the latter is affected by it: hence, an action or reaction of the moving forces which the subject exercises on itself in apprehension for the sake of sensation, and there are *given* to its objects as the material element of experience. These objects can never be anything other than empirically affecting moving forces, even if the effects are inner, and, as appearance, presuppose pure intuition *a priori*. In accordance with the latter, [there occurs,] formally, the connection of given empirical representations into a principle of the possibility of experience; which (as with matter itself) can only be one – namely, a systematic, absolute whole.

This possibility of the connection of perceptions in a system, according to a principle of the possibility of experience, contains the answer to the question: "How is physics, as a doctrinal system conformable to the elementary system of nature, and so the transition from the metaphysical foundations of natural science to physics, possible?" That is, what are (according to their kind, number, and composition) those moving forces of matter which can be objects of experience? Or, how can one acquire experience of their existence?

Empirical intuition with consciousness (perception) in a system of perceptions – that is, thought in experience – is given *a priori* through the understanding. The subjective is likewise objective, according to the principle of identity. The moving forces of matter which, accompanied by consciousness, affect the sense in perception (as empirical representa-
22:454 tion), stand *a priori*, through self-consciousness, under a principle of composition by the *understanding* – and, thus, also of the possibility of experience. Conversely, what makes possible the systematic coordination of perceptions (as empirical material of matter) for the sake of *experience*

[is] that which (affecting sense) leads, as object in *appearance,* toward systematic combination [*breaks off*]

We cannot, by means of *sense,* extract the moving forces of matter, unless, by the understanding, we have previously inserted them, *a priori,* •according to the order of categories (the impulse as a complex).• We do this insofar as we unite the empirical representations, as appearances, to a whole of experience in general. This combination to a system is first *thought,* not as empirical intuition of the object, but as coordination of sensible representations in the subject, according to the formal principle of their combination (as[h] the elementary system) before it is given *for* experience. The subject does not collect fragmentarily (as an aggregate) empirical representations with consciousness into a single experience – for that is in advance of the formal principle (which is to say, without principle); rather, it founds the relation of the representations toward one another, and founds a physics (which, thereby, first becomes possible). It represents •the form of possible experience• subjectively, •as *a priori* condition• in the transition of the metaphysical principles of natural science to the science of nature (as a tendency of progress to the latter) – •hence,• as necessary.

Physics in general has two kinds of objects: (1) Those whose assumed or inferred possibility can only be sustained by experience – and of this sort are organic bodies, as also gravitation. The latter is, indeed, drawn from experience, but that it should be attraction – as Newton first maintained – was problematic. It required that a leap be made, namely, to assume something for the sake of the system. [(2)] Second, a primitive and immediate (both belong together) universally moving material (*primitive movens*): caloric or light-material.   22:455

[Right margin]

So the question is: How is physics possible? Not by perceptions, as receptivity of empirical representations flowing into the subject; for that gives only appearance.

Physics is the science of the principles of the possibility of knowledge of the objects of experience – either of immediate experience or of experience of experience. It is the latter which contains the subjective principles. That is, *first,* in an aggregate, second, in a *system* of perceptions, in which objects are only investigated in appearance (as the object is affected). In the second, as a complex of empirical knowledge itself (tendency toward physics).

If, instead of matter (material) I take the moving forces of matter, and, instead of the object which is movable, the moving subject, then that becomes possible which previously seemed impossible: namely, to repre-

---

[h] Reading *als* for *aus.* (Lehmann's reading uncertain.)

sent *a priori* empirical representations, which the subject makes itself, as given according to the formal principle of combination. The subject has no perceptions except for empirical representations, which it combines autonomously, corresponding to appearance, in a single consciousness; by this, the subject is, likewise, principle of the possibility of experience.

[. . .]

22:456   [XIth fascicle, sheet III, page 2]
The perception of the object is consciousness of the moving forces of the subject itself; not insofar as it is affected, but as it affects itself – that is, through the understanding, brings the manifold of appearance under a principle of its own composition; which principle is the ground of the possibility of experience – that is, of the systematic combination of perceptions. Sense contains the receptivity of the object in regard to appearance; the understanding adds the conditioned spontaneity of the connection of perceptions (according to a law for the possibility of experience); and the latter's principle (subjectively regarded, as a doctrinal system) forms the transition to physics.

I.
WHAT IS PHYSICS?

2.
WHAT IS THE TRANSITION FROM THE METAPHYSICAL FOUNDATIONS OF NATURAL SCIENCE TO PHYSICS?

22:457   ## 3.
HOW IS SUCH TRANSITION POSSIBLE?

A. A fragmentary aggregate of perceptions is not yet experience; rather, the latter takes place only in a system of perceptions which is founded *a priori* on a certain form (of their connection). Experience is the absolute unity of this system, and one cannot speak of experiences (although one can well do so of perceptions, as empirical-sensible representations with consciousness) but only of experiences as absolute unity. Likewise, one cannot speak of *matters*, but only of matter in general, which belongs to this or that perception.

B. Sense-objects in perception are of two kinds. (1) Those that can be given in experience. (2) Such objects as can *only* – if they actually do exist – be given by means of experience; that is, one would not even be able to assume them as possible, were experience not to prove their actuality. And of this kind are organic bodies, in contrast to inorganic: •the two are different in species.•

Third, there can also [be assumed], furthermore, a primitively moving material, which, in substance, limitlessly fills space – that is, such a material, as principle of the possibility of experience, does not leave any *void* in time or in space. Without assuming moving matter as a continuum, experience would permit a leap – a gulf in nature; which, according to the law *natura non agit per saltum,*[75] means nothing other than that the void cannot be an object of perception (nor, hence, of experience). Because this occupation of space in substance must be thoroughly movable (thus, also, universally moving) in order to bring the moving forces into agreement [*Consens*], understanding, too, must be assumed for the sake of universal organism, which [*breaks off*]

Physics is the doctrinal system of knowledge of the objects of the senses   22:458
(outer or inner) in experience. *Experience* presupposes *appearances (phaenomena)* which are given, that is, a mode in which the subject is affected by the sense-object – be that regarded as taking place by means of an outer object, or as inner self-affection. The representation of the object, insofar as action takes place on sense immediately, is *empirical* (sensible representation). The composition of perceptions, according to a principle of form, must proceed not *directly*, in relation to the object, but *indirectly*, in relation to the subject given to the senses and to perceptions for the sake of the possibility of experience.

•Summa

Physics is a system of perceptions from the forces of matter which affect the senses, insofar as they modify the subject according to a principle of the possibility of experience (outer as well as inner). This experience is a work of the understanding, which gives it its form *a priori*, according to an *a priori* law. That these are either directly *moving* forces (outer), or forces acting on sensation (of inner sense in sensation) rests on the difference between outer and inner sense in the apprehension of appearances – which has its form a priori.•

[*Top margin*]
The transition to physics consists, first, in transforming what is subjective in perception into what is objective in the appearance of the object of the senses; second, in presenting *a priori* the form of empirical intuition, in relation to the system of perceptions, for the sake of experience in general, according to laws of the moving forces.

127

22:459 *[Left margin]*
How is physics as a system of perceptions for the sake of experience possible?

Experience presupposes unity of the system of empirical representations with consciousness – hence of the moving forces (both subjective and objective); not, however, as a mere empirical aggregate, but as a synthetic *a priori* principle of the manifold of representations, for the sake of the possibility of experience (according to its form).

But the data which form the moving forces – the material (matter *in abstracto*, regarded metaphysically) – must be capable of being enumerated systematically, *a priori*. How is it possible, however, to establish *a priori*, for experience, the moving forces of matter, which belong to physics and presuppose experience – and, yet, without this, no physics can be possible?

There exist not merely outwardly moving forces of matter, but also inwardly moving, sense-affecting ones (first division); the latter, however, are accompanied by outer appearances (of motion) – sensations. Second, in general – that is, the totality of inwardly moving forces, which neither commence nor cease (caloric) and are all-penetrating (*incoercibilis*), a non-hypothetical material. Third, organic (purposively formative matter – for itself, or for others (in propagation)), which can be thought *a priori*, and yet belongs to physics. Healthy or sick – in the vegetable or animal kingdoms, insofar as these are automatic; and mechanical or dynamic powers can be divided *a priori*, according to the order of the categories (or the quantity [etc.], of attraction and repulsion). As imponderable, incoercible, incohesible and inexhaustible – or the contrary (here modality contains the category of necessity).

[XIth fascicle, sheet III, page 3]
Physics is a *doctrinal system* (*systema doctrinale*) of sensible representations, insofar as they are combined through the subject's understanding to
22:460 a principle of experience. It is not a fragmentary aggregate of perceptions •(empirical representations with consciousness)• but a system of perceptions in the concept of the subject, according to a principle of their combination to the synthetic unity (in experience) of the manifold which is given in intuition. {Physics is a doctrinal system of the connection of the perception of sense-objects to the formal unity of experience in the subject. To the doctrinal system there corresponds, as regards the aggregate of objects given to the senses, the natural system – as a whole of the coordination of natural things, according to principles of the division of objects of experience into classes, genera, species, etc., in an elementary system of objects.} The **system** of empirical representations (in a single experience) is, however, not itself empirical, but is founded on a formal principle, which emerges from a synthetic *a priori* principle (hence from a transcendental principle).

The formal element of the principle of the connection of perceptions, for the sake of the possibility of experiences, in which the subject is its own object of inner intuition (appearance), must precede physics *a priori;* it is not a part of physics (as empirical) but only amounts to the transition to it. It is the condition of the possibility of making *empirical* representations (as the *material* element of empirical knowledge) into an object of experience, according to a *formal* principle (thus, *a priori*) which makes physics possible, as a doctrine of experience of sense-objects, insofar as it •(or its knowledge)• is a system. What is required for this, however, is that matter, as sense-object (as efficient cause of perceptions, which are *given* (fragmentarily), and thought as •inwardly and outwardly• moving forces) [be made] into a system of representations, according to the order of the categories in the composition of the empirical representation produced by the moving forces; that is, composition for the possibility of experience – without being derived from experience.

Perception is empirical representation, by means of which the subject affects itself *a priori* in intuition, and makes itself into an object, according to a principle of synthetic representation *a priori* (of transcendental knowledge) in conformity with the system of categories. The subject progresses to physics, composes its perceptions into a system, for the sake of experience and its possibility, and classifies its perceptions as appearances of empirical knowledge. Hence, it is not from experience but for it (*thought* [as] a systematic whole, as to its form) that the understanding [carries out] the transition from the metaphysical foundations of natural science to physics. 22:461

•(What is physics? How is it possible? What is the Transition? How is the Transition possible? How can the material element be completely enumerated as an elementary system? How its form [is possible]: consequently, *a priori, for* experience. Objects are of two kinds: (a) those [given] through experience, (b) those that can *only* be given through experience. *Organic bodies,* and matter which never [forms] a body but is, nevertheless, thought as active in all bodies. Caloric. From the whole to all its parts.)•

[Right margin]

If the question is: How can objects, to be represented empirically, yield a system of possible experience as synthetic *a priori* knowledge – that is, as an aggregate of perceptions? then the answer is that the conditions of the possibility of an experience in general are identical to the concept of the connection of perceptions, according to an *a priori* principle, since experience is a subjective system of perceptions.

Therefore, having to start from the subjective system of perceptions, we can and must make the transition from it [to] perceptions (as the mediate or immediate influences of the moving forces on the subject of empirical representations) according to the principle of experience as a system – hence, according to *a priori* principles.

[. . .]

[XIth fascicle, sheet III, page 4]

1. The appearances of the object of empirical representation, as an *a priori* intuition in space and time, namely, as the subject is affected by the object.

2. How the subject affects itself in apprehension (in perception as empirical representation with consciousness) into an aggregate of the manifold of sensible representation.

3. The synthetic unity of the empirical manifold (*complexus*), as moving forces of the subject, combined in a system.

4. Physics itself, as science according to the principle of the possibility of experience (which is only one). Answer to the question: How is physics possible?

Experience is synthetic unity of empirical representations with consciousness, insofar as they are combined by the understanding to unity •under a principle.• Experience – the object of perceptions combined in a system of thought – is (just like matter) only one. Not (as in atomism's account of the object) [put together] •in space• from the full and the void; nor [one experience] separated from another by blind chance (*casus purus*) in an empty time; for, in that case, nothingness would be an object of possible experience.

The *subjective element of empirical intuition*, as *appearance*, is first given. The *composition* of its •empirically given• manifold is thought *a priori*, as to its form – that is, the *understanding* combines the manifold, according to a principle, into the synthetic unity of the consciousness of the manifold in the object. It does so for the sake of the possibility of *experience*, as the synthetic unity of perceptions (for the sake of the unity of the system of perceptions – which, thought *a priori*, is thus *made* by the understanding).

Empirical representations with consciousness are merely subjective – that is, they are not yet representations referred to •an• object. When, however, as impressions, they yield cognitions [*Erkenntnisstücke*], they are perceptions of an object – be this an outer object or an inner one. Empirical representation, thought as the effect of the moving forces, is a concept of the understanding, and not empirical; rather, it is postulated *a priori*, by physics. Objective.

[*Additions above the main text* (*which occupies the lower third of the page*)]

Physics is the principle for representing what is subjective in perceptions (as appearances) as objective – by means of the understanding.

This subjective element is the appearance of the sense-affecting manifold, by whose means the understanding progresses from perception to
experience.

Experience is an aggregation of perceptions, insofar as, subjectively,
they form a system of knowledge. This system is founded *a priori* by the
understanding, and contains a principle of synthetic *a priori* knowledge of
the manifold of appearances (whose form precedes [experience]).

This system of perceptions is not a system *from* experience (empirical)
but is *a priori* (*for* experience); and, for the sake of the possibility of
experience, it founds a doctrinal system, called physics. For which the
Transition (in virtue of the tendency of the metaphysical foundations)
already contains subjective necessity, by the principle of identity.

The concept of a physics in general, and the possibility of a transition to
it, require principles of the division of the elementary system of physics,
which must be given *a priori*. And the first of them can be none other than
this (as a dichotomy): Its objects can be given in experience; and some of
them, further, cannot be given otherwise than *through* experience (from
it). Of the latter kind are organic *bodies;* for the very possibility of such
concepts founded on purposes would be only chimerical, were experience   22:465
not to teach it [to us].

The problem (*quaestio problematis*) is one and the same as (*identica*) the
solution (*resolutio*). The synthetically expressed proposition of the possibility of experience, analytic. For experience is the connection of perceptions – not merely as an aggregate, but as the synthetic *a priori* unity of a
system of perceptions, given by the understanding. In physics, the understanding progresses from appearance, etc. It neither continues in progress on the same territory (physics), nor makes a leap, as over a gulf
(empty space), but proceeds from the object in appearance to the connection of the moving forces in experience (that is, physics) as in an elementary system of the moving forces of matter.

Perception (empirical representation with consciousness) is *receptivity*
for the moving forces of matter, as spontaneity of the understanding [in]
self-determination, according to an *a priori* principle – that is, of the object in appearance: The subject, *which affects itself,* recognizes itself as
phenomenon, and, likewise, necessarily determines its existence in experience, through apprehension in space and time.

In this fashion, empirical representations, which are perceptions belonging to physics, are *produced, as object,* by the *subject* itself. And the *influence*
of the subject *on its own self* makes possible synthetic *a priori* progress to
empirical knowledge, as in the transition to physics (μετάβασις εἰς ἄλλο
γένος, *indirectly,* •by being a mediate cause•); and that objects of the
subject's sensation (e.g. pressure, or traction, or tearing) are displayed *a
priori*, as *a priori* moving forces, in a system – e.g. caloric (not merely
matter), even health, etc.

131

22:466 *[Top margin]*
The concept of *organized bodies* also belongs to physics, and, with them, their subjective relations, as *health* and sickness.

Bodies as systems whose parts relate to one another as *ends* and *means* – namely, appear as such (for *matter* cannot have such a property).

[Left margin]
Understanding is required in order to connect objectively the manifold of empirical representations (as subjective appearance in an aggregate of perceptions) into the unity of experience, according to a principle. It makes a system out of the aggregate of perceptions, and composes *a priori* (according to a principle of the possibility of experience) the moving forces which affect sense – not from experience, but for the sake of it.

Positing and perception, spontaneity and receptivity, the objective and subjective relation, are simultaneous; because they are identical as to time, as appearances of how the subject is *affected* – thus are given in the same *actus* and are in progression toward experience (as a system of perceptions). Yet *for* physics, as a system of thought and as a theory, in two ways: (1) for the object of possible experience (or the possibility of experience in general); (2) for objects which can be given *only* in (and through) experience, *heteronomously* or *autonomously*.

Hence, first, problematically – through division into organic and inorganic beings (not organic matter), for which the division is given *a priori;* and physics receives a second subject.

A. Physics from a subjective point of view: as a doctrinal system of empirical representations (perceptions) for the sake of the possibility of experience, in which case appearances make up the matter, whose form is given *a priori* (not made);

B. from an objective point of view: the aggregate of perceptions as moving forces which affect the subject; as dynamic powers outside the subject, they present the correlate of the moving forces – a matter,
22:467 which, thus, contains the latter. *Experience* in physics, as a system of perceptions – that is, of the active forces on the object (by *attraction*, repulsion); the *aggregation* of partial representations into a whole and the resolution of the whole into its parts. The difference of *materials*, given the similarity *[Gleichartigkeit]* of motions. •Modality of physical *powers*, according to their inner necessity or contingency. Their *mechanical* and *dynamic* unity.• The absolute whole of these materials and their primitive motion in time.

[. . .]

[T]

Definition

What is physics? It is the science of objects of the senses, insofar as this science is possible in experience.

•*Note.* Not *through* and *from* experience, but what is possible *for* it (for its sake). There are no *experiences*, however (for those are merely perceptions). The first problem here is: How is experience possible (as unity of the empirical)? From the subject's point of view, through *observation* and *experiment*. But, according to its principle, physics belongs to metaphysics.   22:474 Directly (immediately) or indirectly (mediately). Not the *material* element, but the *formal*. How are synthetic *a priori* propositions possible? A problem for transcendental philosophy.•

What is experience? It is the combination of empirical representations with consciousness (that is, of perceptions), insofar as they stand under a rule, •according to the system of categories.• Thus not a complex (*complexus*), as a mere aggregate (*farrago*), but [*breaks off*]

Axiom

1. There are no experiences; and, if one refers to such, then these are only perceptions (of which there can be many). Observation and experiment, by whose means one can well attain experience, do not constitute the latter; and experience is unity of the combination of sensible representation.

2. There can be no experience of the void in space and time – at most, inferences from experience (mediate experience). •There is no experience of what is indivisible.•

3. Matter cannot be thought of as consisting •of• elements (as atoms). •There is no experience of the unlimited.•

4. Matter can, however, be thought of as being composed of elements which, as to their quality, are not further divisible (qualitative elements). •There is no experience of the merely metaphysical properties of matter, since these consist solely in *a priori* knowledge – knowledge from concepts, indeed, not construction.•

Theorem

All matter contains a complex of moving forces; and the subject which is affected by them (and his experience of this complex) itself determines these forces which provide the material for experience.

133

22:475 •The object of experience and the latter's efficient cause. Not merely receptivity – but spontaneity, too. Caloric is postulated, insofar as it is *universally distributed*, etc.•

The universal basis of the moving forces of matter affecting the senses is a universally and uniformly distributed world-material; without whose presupposition an outer object of the senses [cannot] have an empirically possible object. In that case, space [would] be only an idea – not an actual whole of objects of possible perception, given (with its dimensions) for the sake of knowledge of sense-objects, but a mere form, according to which things can be ordered alongside one another, by *a priori* principles. This

22:476 radical world-material is not problematic and merely assertoric, but apodictically certain. Its existence belongs to the transition from the metaphysical foundations of natural science to physics; and its recognition (according to *a priori* concepts of objects in appearance in general (regarded not *sparsim* but *coniunctim*)) makes physics initially possible, according to the principle of the possibility of experience, which is itself only single, and, objectively, forms a system.

•Not *out of* and *by means* of experience; but *for* it and its possibility.

What are the *a priori* principles by which a doctrine of experience is possible?

The conditions of the possibility of a system of empirical cognitions (perceptions) insofar as it is an object of experience.•

[*Margin* . . .]

22:477 [XIth fascicle, sheet IV, page 4]

Doctrinal system – natural system. Subjectively and objectively an object of experience. The primitive, force-arousing principle of all motion. *Heat.* We cannot proceed from experience as a beginning; for experience does not, *simpliciter,* produce universality, but only *secundum quid* – and yet, universality is *postulated.* The latter can,[i] however, be given for experience – and for its subjective possibility.

The principle of the ideality of the objects of the senses as appearances: by which we ourselves make the empirical representation, by which the subject affects itself and perceives that which it has itself inserted into empirical intuition (perception), and is the author of its own representation.

Only *appearances* can be *given a priori.* The principle of the possibility of experience is *thought* – but as *given* and as necessary, with respect to the form of the composition of the manifold.

What comes *first* (intellectually) is consciousness of oneself – an act of thought which is foundational and *a priori* – as the subject [is] an object

22:478 for itself. The *second* is, as object of sense, to be self-*affecting* – not merely

---

[i] Reading *kann* for *können.*

to be represented as object of pure intuition, but also to *appear* in a particular form. This is the metaphysical foundations of natural science, insofar as it contains the transition to the possibility of experience in general. The transition consists, namely, in progressing, by means of the understanding, from an aggregate of perceptions of oneself, to a system of perceptions in one experience in general (that is, to physics as a doctrinal system) – hence, according to a principle of the *a priori* combination of empirical representation; herein, the elementary system of sense-objects exists only in idea.

1. The agreement of sensible representation for the possibility of experience is physics; and this agreement of the empirical with the construction of concepts (mathematics) is thus thought *a priori* in the apperception of appearances. The concept of a physics did not arise empirically, as an aggregate of perceptions, but *a priori* – for the possibility of experience and the transition to a system of empirical representations (thought in one system). Preceding it, according to the scale of the categories, is the doctrinal system of the moving forces affecting the subject.

(a) The principles which the subject carries with it (by means of its understanding) for the production of experience, are different from those which relate to the conditions of the *possibility* of experience. (b) Those which concern the possibility of their objects. Of this kind: the concepts of a self-organizing matter, and of the organic body produced thereby (whose possibility cannot be given *a priori*, but can only be thought in the system). (c) The principle of experience [*Erfahrungsprinzip*] of the actuality of a certain species of matter (material) – one which is *universally distributed*, etc.; is of a species which contains the basis for other species (e.g. muriatic acid); or contains the universal basis of all *primitively moving* forces (called *caloric*).

The primitive forces are attraction and repulsion, which – 22:479 united, to be precise – both *occupy* cosmic space (by attraction) and fill it (by repulsion); without which no matter would exist. A matter, however (insofar as it is regarded only according to its attractive property), because it does not act merely *superficially*, but, immediately, on all its parts (gravitational attraction), is said to *act at a distance* – that is, through empty space. It was *Newton* who first introduced this concept; not as an empirical proposition (for how can one experience an effect which does not occur on the senses, but only on the object of pure intuition?) (Galileo, Kepler, Huygens, Newton). Or else [the matter may be called] penetrating – in substance (like caloric), or, like gravitational attraction, dynamically, through empty space (although there is no such thing).

Empirical representation with consciousness (*perception*) – as the subject affects itself or is affected by the outer object, is just the subjective element of *sensation*. It is followed by the objective element of intuition (outer and inner) in space and time – the object in *appearance*. First of all, however, what must precede the object *a priori* is the form under which the subject intuits, insofar as it is affected. Thereafter, the aggregate of perceptions, according to a subjective principle of the systematic unity of perceptions, for the sake of experience. Herein lies the *punctum flexus contrarii*[76] – the transition to physics, in which the possibility of experience is taught subjectively, and the complex of its objects objectively.

[*Left margin*]
    1. What is physics?
It is the aggregate of empirical knowledge of the moving forces of matter in experience.
    2. What is experience?

22:480   It is the unification of perceptions, under the principle of their connection, •according to concepts,• to a doctrinal system (a systematic whole of the aggregate of perceptions).
    3. What is the transition from the metaphysical foundations of natural science to physics? •It is the doctrinal system of experience in general, applied to the natural system.•
    4. How is the transition from the metaphysical foundations to physics *possible:* (1) in respect of the material element of the object; (2) of the formal element of the subject?
    The *material element* – insofar as it [is] only thought •*problematically,*• •and contains a tendency for one• to represent it •to oneself• assertorically, as given (*organic, inorganic*).
    As to motion: imponderable, incoercible, incohesible • – not a *rigid* cohesion which resists the displacement of touching surfaces – •, inexhaustible.
    There are two kinds of sense-object, for whose perception a transition to physics is made: (1) that which can be known through experience; (2) that which *cannot* be known *otherwise* than through experience – e.g. organic bodies – and whose possibility is *problematic;* (3) what cannot *immediately* be an object of experience, e.g. matter whose motion is *primordial,* and, hence, endures *eternally.*

The formal element of pure (not empirical) intuition is in representation *a priori* (in appearance); that is, represents the self-determination, how the subject affects itself.

Experience is the self-determination of empirical intuition with consciousness (or perceptions) under a principle of apprehension of its appearances into a system of the understanding in general:
    What is required for the possibility of experience, does not come *from* experience, but is *a priori.*

22:481   Whether life (as according to Hildebrandt)[77] is a property of matter itself. (Life is the activity of a simple being, since it acts through the *representation of purpose* – an immaterial principle – which acts only as the absolute unity of the subject of moving forces.) Living matter is a *contradictio in adjecto:* The guiding principle is immaterial. The *operation of life* (operation of the will [*Willkühr*]).

[*Bottom margin*]
  Rational knowledge is mathematics, physics and metaphysics.
  The possibility of an organic body cannot be proved or postulated; it is, however, a fact. To know oneself in experience as an organic body. •N.B. *The concept of an immediately and primitively moving material* (**caloric**).•
  The concept of organic bodies (which contain a vital principle) already presupposes experience: For, without the latter, the very idea of organic bodies would be an empty concept (without example). But man has in his own self an example of an understanding which contains moving forces, which determine a body according to laws.

Atomism does not occur in matter (as object of outer sense). Corpuscular philosophy is concealed atomism. N.B. There can be living *bodies* (not matter). The *vital* principle is *immaterial*.
  Causa – *agit, facit, operatur.* Acts, does, *operates* (animal).

[. . .]

[XIth fascicle, sheet V, page 3]   22:487

[U]

What is physics?

Physics is science and nature (*scientia naturae*) insofar as its principles are given in experience •and contains the progression from the metaphysical   22:488
foundations of natural science [to physics].• It is not necessary that the principles are thought of as drawn *from* experience and derived *from* it, rather it is sufficient for the concept (of a physics) •to think of this science as being one• which is assumed *for* experience (for the sake of the latter) •as an aggregate of empirical representations under a principle of their connection.•
  Note I. To refer to this science by the Latin expression *scientia* **naturalis** could, •however,• produce misunderstandings, for one might thus be tempted to oppose it to either *artificial* (*artificialis*) or revealed (*revelata*) science. Hence the expression *science of nature* •(*scientia naturae*)• – instead of *natural* science, as the literal translation would be – is the most appropriate one for physics as the •univeral• doctrine of experience •of the

137

objects of both outer and inner sense• (insofar as it forms a doctrinal system).

Note II. Physics belongs to *philosophy;* •it is a philosophical, not merely empirical, not mathematical [discipline] (although to use mathematics in physics is philosophical).• It is a special subject or area (*territorium*) of philosophy •in contrast with *mathematics,* both having their *a priori* principles; both have their fixed limits and, though they lie adjacent to each other,• must not transgress •these latter.• So if physics should be termed *philosophia naturalis,* this term would become self-contradictory if one does as *Newton* does in his immortal work **philosophiae** *naturalis principia* **mathematica,** •and thus, as it were, creates a bastard (*conceptus hybridus*) which is neither purely one nor the other. Science of nature, according to its formal element as a system for experience, is distinguished from the *systema naturae,* which in its content relates to objects.•

22:489

For as little as there can be *philosophical* foundations of *mathematics* can there be *mathematical* foundations of *philosophy* (as Newton would have it). A crossing is made here to a different terrain (*Styx interfusa coërcet*);[78] even the •greatest of• mathematicians must, •as mathematician,• observe defined boundaries [*abgeschnittene Grenzen*] •both as regards the object of his activity and his talent.*• Otherwise, •in a delusion of superiority,• the mathematician casts scornful sideway glances at the philosopher, for the latter is unable to advance with such a sure trend as the mathematician himself does •in his own subject,• and so he would (by a gross amphiboly of the concepts of reflection) wish to make philosophy and one of its branches (namely, metaphysics) into a department of mathematics.[79] It must be called *Matheseos applicatae principia philosophica.*[80]

It is important, too, to distinguish philosophical knowledge, including its principles, from philosophy itself (the formal from the material aspect of philosophy). The philosophizer cannot be recast as a philosopher; the former is a mere underlaborer (as a versifier is in comparison with a poet – the latter must have originality).

Even if, as is proper, one takes account in the word "philosophy" of its concept as a doctrine of wisdom, the science of the *final end* of human reason – that is, of what is not just technical-practical but of that which is moral-practical, the keystone of the edifice – philosophy with its principles will still be subject to the concerns of human reason, even where the latter's aim is scholastic (mere knowledge). It must set metaphysical foundations prior to mathematical ones (although both are given *a priori*) for the former have in view the unconditional employment [of reason] – •that is, the object in itself• – the latter, however, only its conditional employment as a tool for a particular purpose.

22:490

For mathematics is the finest *instrument* for physics and the knowledge

---

* [not written].

138

which falls therein (for that mode of sense) but it is still always only an instrument for another purpose.

The proper title would have to be **scientiae** *naturalis principia vel philosophica vel mathematica,*[81] for the form can be philosophical even if its matter (the content) is mathematical.

Using mathematics in physics as an instrument for science is *philosophy,* but *mathematics* is not itself a principle of philosophy, nor does it contain the latter in its concepts.

There are both mathematical and metaphysical foundations of natural science – but not mathematical foundations of *philosophy,* for they are incompatible. *Scientia naturalis* can indeed be so divided but not a *philosophia naturalis* – that would be *gryphes iungere equis,*[82] an imposture by the mathematician in a field in which he lacks that element on which he would have to base himself. It can well be united with poetry (for mathematics is pure invention [*Dichtung*]): namely, subjectively.

A philosophy exists (and this is metaphysics) which employs mathematics merely as an instrument in order to organize the *empirical* representations of sense according to an *a priori* principle (hence, not empirically) and which classifies *a priori* the pure intuitions according to their form in order to present the schematism of the concepts of reflection in a system. Physics (the study of nature) can be regarded with respect to its formal element, the laws of nature, but also by its material (the objects of nature) as a *realm of nature* and by this classification it belongs to philosophical knowledge of nature. *Physiologia specialis de regnis naturae.*[83]   22:491

[*Top margin*]

(1) What is physics? (2) What is transition from the metaphysical foundations of natural science to physics (for natural science is not yet physics)? (3) How is this transition from one science to another possible? (By the schematism of judgment.) By the principles of subsumption of appearances under the law of perceptions.

[*Right margin*]

It is the science of the laws of nature insofar as they are an object of experience. (*Naturae scientia*)

It is divided (a) into the science of the *things of nature* (*rerum naturae*) whose coordination in a system is empirical and is thereupon called (according to Linnaeus)[84] "system of nature"; (b) the *laws* of nature, insofar as they are given *in* experience and *for* experience (for the latter's sake) through the understanding and from concepts (that is, *a priori*); thus they are not borrowed *out of* or *from* experience.

There cannot be mathematical foundations of philosophy (to which latter, nevertheless, physics belongs) any more than there can be philosophical foundations of mathematics. Nevertheless, Newton has given his immortal work this title. The title should be *scientiae naturalis principia mathematica* (not *philosophiae*). •and a contradiction due to presumption.•

The terrain of physics contains a great gulf which cannot be overleaped (*Styx interfusa coërcet*). The capacity to progress in one or the other [region] is specifically different in each case, even as regards talent. The two can, indeed, be *united* for the purpose of a science of nature, but must not in any way be *mixed*.

No science can spring from experience. The experienced man (*expertus*), if he is no more than that, is an ignoramus, someone who proceeds by a guide-rope, following in the footsteps made for him by another (or which he has made for himself in earlier practice).

22:492   Experience is perception, known (or thought) in its thoroughgoing determination, so that one has grounds for assuming that it will prove to be thus in all cases.

Of the great leap in proceeding from the class of those materials, of matter in general, containing salt, oil and earth, to *metals*.[85]

Seeming *metals* and mineral (cat-gold, cat-silver).[86] Animal. Insects whose wing-covers show metallic color. Bodies, however, which are fluid in fire and polished to shine when cold give off the same colors, as if by their own light, but only reflecting it – and their weight is very different. Compared to other mineral bodies, if one compares the lightest of these with the lightest of the mineral kingdom; to be hammered when hot [*breaks off*]

Of the shimmering of the wing-cases, or of the underside, of insects, like tarnished blue.[87]

[XIth fascicle, sheet V, page 4]

HOW DOES THE TRANSITION FROM THE METAPHYSICAL FOUNDATIONS OF NATURAL SCIENCE TO PHYSICS TAKE PLACE?

[*Around the heading*]
•First, according to its matter; second, according to its form. System of nature and description [of nature].

Materials (*bases* of motion) which are not themselves *locomotive*, but move in their own place. Physical bodies which dynamically limit their space themselves. How can one completely enumerate *a priori* the moving forces *for* experience?

Light – repulsive; caloric – *cohesively penetrating;* magnetism – *permeably penetrating.*

The happy audacity of Newton in making the mathematical principles
of motion into dynamical principles of the moving forces. Universal gravitational attraction through empty space. Centrifugal force is derivative.
The dynamic principles in full space originally [amount to] the existence
[of a matter] which necessarily *makes* space an *object* of experience at all
points, and is repulsive (*light*)• [*breaks off*]

22:493

[*Main text*]

It is strange – it even appears to be impossible, to wish to present *a
priori* that which depends on perceptions (empirical representations with
consciousness of them): E.g. sound, light, heat, etc., which, all together,
amount to the subjective element in perception •(empirical representation
with consciousness)• and, hence, carries with it no knowledge of an object.
Yet this act of the faculty of representation is necessary. For, were a
counteract of the object not to correspond to this act, the subject would
receive no perception of the object by means of the latter's moving force
(which is here presupposed).

The receptivity of having sensible representations thus presupposes a
relative spontaneity of producing perceptions in oneself indirectly (and [is]
the *a priori* possibility [of perception]). Experience is not the means but
the end of knowledge of sense-objects in their moving forces.

What is physics?

Physics •(the study of nature)• is the doctrinal system (*systema doctrinale*) of
the moving forces of matter which affect sense (externally or internally)
insofar as they are an object of experience.

Note. It is a science of nature which, subjectively, depends on empirical
grounds of knowledge, but, as regards its objective element, forms a
system of sensible representations which is an object of experience; the
latter is itself not a mere empirical aggregate of perceptions (by observation and experiment) but is an object of experience in virtue of being a
principle of the thoroughgoing determination of the object.

22:494

For, •in the first place,• experience is absolute unity of the complex of
appearances •of the object.• One *makes* experience – it is not a mere
influence on the senses.

Second, experiences do not exist (that is, they are only scattered perceptions) but the unity of the system of the manifold is founded on a
schematism and [*breaks off*]

The influence of the subject on the outer object, and the latter's reaction on the subject, make it possible to know the moving forces of matter
(and, hence, matter itself, in substance) and to develop them for physics.
So much for *motion* as the *outer phenomena* of reaction. It is just the same

141

as regards the inner moving forces of *sensation* and the *reaction* of the subject upon itself.

The schematism of the concepts of the understanding, according to the form of a syllogism: (1) the major premise; (2) the subsumption of the minor premise; (3) the inference or conclusion, for the sake of experience in general – that is, the requirements for the possibility of experience, which presents *a priori* the system of perceptions, according to its form, and contains the empirical element of representation in its thoroughgoing determination from intuition, through the Anticipations of Perception, to the Analogies of Experience.

Vital force in excitability. Motion of the brain (the nerve root), the heart, the lung. Decomposition of air and absorption [*Absetzung*] of oxygen by cold-water fish.

(1) The object in pure *a priori* intuition; (2) in appearance (of oneself); (3) in perception – empirical intuition; (4) in experience (*omnimoda determinatio, existentia*). *Consciousness of one's own self* precedes *a priori* all determination of the subject as object. The *schematism* of the faculty of judgment formally prepares the transition of physics. •(4) The aggregate of empirical thought in general.•

22:495

Organic creatures have not just a life but also a vital feeling which is eroded [*aufreibt*] through intercourse (and, in insects, through exhaustion). Remarkable that no organic being procreates without two sexes.[88]

Outer perceptions are effects of the moving forces of matter on the subject, [which occasion] it to affect itself inwardly. Inner perceptions are empirical representations with consciousness, as the subject voluntarily or involuntarily affects itself. Space and time in general are pure sensible representations, both of which are single. There is only one space and one time.

[*Margin . . .*]

22:496

[XIth fascicle, sheet VI, page 1]

X

The doctrine of the transition from the metaphysical foundations of natural science to **physics** contains two progressions (*passus*) of which each, in turn, includes two divisions as subjects: *one*, the aggregation (*complexus, sparsim*) of empirical representations with consciousness – that is, of perceptions – according to a schema of the association of empirical intuition; the *second* [*breaks off*]

I

A. What is physics?
B. What is a transition?
From the metaphysical foundations of natural science to physics?

II

a. How is physics possible
(as a doctrinal system)?
b. How is the transition from the
metaphysical foundations of natural science to physics possible?

{The **study of nature** in general (*physica*) can concern itself either merely with the *formal element* of physics – [what it is] to be an object of sensible representations, and the division of physics according to concepts (that is, *a priori*) – or else with the *material element* of the objects of experience, as existing things, and their *classification* through experience – the methodical (but empirical) coordination of which is called *system* of nature (e.g. according to Linnaeus). The latter is an enterprise of physics which can never be wholly completed, while the former, which concerns the formal principles of natural science, can (and should) be presented completely.}

Definition   22:497

Physics is the doctrinal system of the laws of the moving forces of matter, insofar as they are given in experience.

•[Physics is] the scientific *study of nature*, insofar as it is an object of experience. It is either investigation of nature or doctrine of nature, and its principles are either given rationally *a priori*, or empirically. The transition from metaphysics to physics, as a part of philosophy, is the systematic foundation [of physics].•

   1. *Note.* One cannot *have* •(receive)• *experience* without *making* it. Consequently, there belongs to its possibility an *a priori* principle of the presentation of sense-objects, •which predetermines what kind• *perceptions* (empirical representations with consciousness) the *thoroughgoing determination* of the object of perception •(that is, the latter's existence)• will require •in the production of experience.• Conversely, one cannot *make* perception but only *receive* it as given. •The faculty of making experience is the understanding. With the principles according to which the subject makes (or produces) experience, this faculty is called reason. Experience does *not* belong to *physics* as a doctrinal system.•
   2. *Note. Experience* is absolute *unity* of the knowledge of the sense-objects,

143

and it is inconsistent to speak of *experiences* (which are merely misjudged perceptions). There is something empirical (as material – or the material element of sensible intuition) which is necessarily contained in every experience. Further, however, there is required the **thoroughgoing** *determination* of the concept of this material, in all the relations in which it affects the senses •(as the formal element of the connection of the manifold of empirical intuition)• in order for an aggregate of perceptions of an object to count as •an• object which is founded in experience. Since the *thoroughgoing* determination of an object of perception (its complete apprehension and presentation) is a mere *idea* •(problematic concept)• which is, indeed, suitable for approximation (*approximatio*) •but not for the totality of perception,• experience can never provide a certain proof of the existence •of the object• of these or those •sense-objects, as• moving forces of matter. It is the collected grounds of determination – united partially •(*sparsim*)• but never completely (*omnimode coniunctim*) – which suffices as the testimony of an experience. For only thoroughly determined [perception] (that is, existence) grounds experience.

22:498

[*Top margin*]
Physics is [regarded], first, according to concepts of the formal element of *its* principle – its possibility of being a study of nature; 2nd, according to the material element, i.e. the actual outer *objects* of experience. *Systema naturale* and *systema naturae*.

The first is *systema physices naturale*, as opposed to the [*systema physices*] *artificiali*, which is called *systema naturae*. The first has formal principles *a priori*, the second merely methodically aggregated objects of experience.
Experience is not a merely *natural*, but *artificial* aggregation of perceptions. Experience is not *given* through the senses but is *made* for the purpose of empirical knowledge.

[*Right margin*]
If the reacting moving forces are to be established *a priori*, then they must themselves form a system for physics.

22:499

Experience has as its basis (1) *perception* – which always requires moving forces affecting the subject (be they outer or inner) (2) [that] the perceived be elevated to *experience*. For which an inner principle of the subject is required, to think the perceived object in its thoroughgoing determination. For whatever we have experience of there is required a formal principle of thoroughgoing determination.

[XIth fascicle, sheet VI, page 2]
3. Note. The influence of the moving forces of matter on the subject in respect of its inner sense (in action and reaction) has, in consequence,

certain phenomena for outer sense as their effects (sensations); it forms a particular field of appearances which, as object of experience, belongs to physics and (since the moving forces are directed toward ends) [has] as its basis (directly or indirectly) an immaterial cause [*breaks off*]

A matter whose form is possible only by purposive determination [*Zweckbestimmung*] (that is, an organized body) can only be thought as moved and as moving, by a principle which [carries with it] the absolute unity of its combined forces – hence, as constructed by a nonmaterial being. In which, the body is thought of as *animated* and matter as animating. The possibility of an organic body cannot be assumed, without knowledge of its actuality in experience. Thus an organic body is such as is not thinkable otherwise *than through experience alone.* A living body thus contains a principle of vegetative or animal life: a healthy, sick or dying state and regeneration – not, indeed, of the same individual but of a body which preserves the species, from similar materials, through intercourse of two sexes.

Physics (study of nature) is a complex of outer as well as inner representa-   22:500
tions of sense in a system {i.e. of outer and inner empirical intuitions as well as inner perceptions of the subject, i.e. sensations (called feelings if they contain pleasure or displeasure).}

Physics is this in a twofold sense: first, •*subjectively,* as a logical, [i.e.]• *doctrinal system* according to concepts of the •subordination of the manifold of• empirical representations, under one principle of the possibility of experience. Secondly: objectively, as an aggregate of objects of experience, given in experience, insofar as they, *coordinated* with one another, form a whole according to principles of the possibility of experience – a system of nature. In the first, the division takes place according to concepts of comparison; in the second, through the coordination of •objects of nature as substances,• according to their genera, species and classes as found in experience (just as Linnaeus ordered them in his natural history collection).

[Top and left margins]

Perception can be outer or inner (that is, sensation). The latter (in relation to the object) can be a feeling of pleasure or displeasure – that is, which strives to eliminate the sensation or to unite it with itself, and issues in desire or repugnance. Both belong to outer or inner experience – hence to the subject of physics.

As a science of experience, however, physics is naturally divided into two subjects. The one is the subject of the forms in action and reaction of   22:501
forces in space and time. The other is the complex of the substances which fill space.

The one could be called the *systematics* of nature, the other is called (following Linnaeus) the system of nature.

In the first, knowledge of nature depends on formal principles of moving force; in the second, it depends on the presentation of objects as they appear alongside one another, in a place which must never be represented as empty.

In the latter part of physics, the highest division of *bodies* (not just matter) is [into organic] and inorganic. The division can emerge *a priori* from concepts. For, the possibility of an organic body (that is, a body each of whose parts is there for the sake of the other, or which is so formed that the possibility of the parts and the form of their inner relations emerge only from its concept – a body which is thus only possible through purposes, which presuppose an immaterial principle which forms this substance either mediately or immediately) produces a teleological principle of the continuation of kinds and individuals [which] can be thought as all-governing and everlasting with respect to species [*breaks off*]

One cannot even think the possibility of such a body, and only experience can prove it.

[*Bottom margin*]

Empirical representations with consciousness (that is, perceptions) are given through the forces which affect the subject (of whatever kind and origin they may be); for otherwise there would be no physics (doctrine of experience of nature). But the aggregate of the forces in a system (that is, with consciousness of their completeness – not *sparsim* but *stricte coniunctim*) cannot be given as a whole otherwise than *a priori,* through a principle, which carries with it the concept of necessity: which and how many forces form the aggregate of forces in a system.

22:502

In regard to matter and those of its forces which affect the subject •externally• (hence, are *moving* forces), perceptions are themselves moving forces combined with reaction (*reactio*), and the understanding *anticipates* perception according to the uniquely possible forms of motion: attraction, repulsion, enclosure (surrounding) and penetration. Thus the possibility of establishing *a priori* a system of empirical representations (which otherwise appeared impossible) and of *anticipating* experience *quoad materiale,* is illuminated.

[XIth fascicle, sheet VI, page 3]

The material element of sensible representation lies in perception – that is, in the act through which the subject affects itself and becomes appearance of an object for itself. The formal element is the act of connection of perceptions for the possibility of experience in general, according to the table of categories (Axiom of Intuition, Anticipation of Perception, Analogy of Experience, and the composition of these principles to a system of empirical knowledge in general). Perception, through which the [subject as] object is affected by the object (as the subject affects itself according to the categories), makes a system of the moving forces of matter out of the aggregate of perceptions. The system contains, objectively and *a priori*, the conditions of the possibility of experience, in those actions and reactions which, altogether and unified, contain the dynamic functions (both outwardly in the intuition of space and inwardly in sensation). Such functions amount to the moments required for cognition of objects for physics, which are, nevertheless, contained *a priori* (according to the rule of identity) in the empirical aggregate as a system.   22:503

•The *systematics* of nature and the *system of nature*. The former, according to concepts of the connection of the empirical in one system for the sake of experience, the latter from experience.•

In the transition from the metaphysical foundations of natural science to physics, the understanding progresses from the axioms of pure *a priori* intuition of the object to perception (that is, empirical representation with consciousness in the subject) [and] to the possibility of experience – which is itself nothing other than an aggregate of perceptions under a principle of their coordination (*complexus*) in a single concept. Not, however, *from* experience but for its sake, as a systematic combination of the manifold of empirical representations.

The understanding has the faculty for making an empirical representation of a sense-object for itself, and so, too, the perception of an object (by means of the fact that it stimulates *a priori* the moving forces of the object on which it acts to reciprocity). Now the understanding can enumerate *a priori* these actions (with their reactions) which, since they are merely relations of differing quality, only belong to perception.

These organizations (referred to below) cannot be subsumed under experiences or perceptions – of which it can be required that their principles and the grounds of the possibility of their empirical connection (e.g. cohesion or repulsion) be enumerated *a priori;* and yet it is necessarily part of physics to present such organizations as anticipations (hence, according to *a priori* principles). How is this possible?

A substance, which cannot act otherwise in the distribution of force than as absolute unity (and, consequently, cannot be an aggregate of atoms) is an immaterial principle.   22:504

Matter, heat, light cannot be referred to in the plural – perhaps because in their inner constitution they permit absolutely no limitation, and this, indeed, lies already in their concept. But some of them permit of degree (e.g. illumination and heat) although not of spatial magnitudes and bounds.

Organized bodies (which are not just matter) indicate an immaterial principle, and, insofar as organization extends through all parts of the world (transforming bodies and replacing dead ones with new formations in their place) indicate an *anima mundi*. The latter, however, may not be represented as a thinking being (*spiritus*), but, at most, as *anima bruta*;[89] for, without this, purposive generation cannot, I will not say be explained, but be thought at all. Of an organized world-body: even in respect of its inorganic parts, or else of organic bodies determined for the use of certain other organic bodies.

[*Right and top margins*]

It is strange – it even appears impossible – to present perceptions *a priori* for the sake of experience; •yet, nevertheless, without this, no physics, as a system of experience, would emerge. One must be able to enumerate these reactive forces. This is what matters, in regard to the problem of the principles of the *investigation of nature*. Only those forces which we insert into phenomena can we extract from what is empirical, for the sake of experience. Not observation but experimentation is the means to the discovery of nature and its forces.• Axioms of Intuition can and must be grounded *a priori*. But, in this case, it is anticipations of empirical concepts which are elevated to principles [*Grundsätze*] – that is, to principles

22:505 [*Prinzipien*] of *a priori* knowledge. The matter is as follows: Perception is empirical representation with consciousness that it is such (and not merely pure intuition of space). Now the effect of the subject on the outer sense-object represents this object in appearance, and does so, indeed, with the moving forces directed toward the subject (which are the cause of perception). So one can determine *a priori* those forces which effect perception, as anticipations of sensible representations in empirical intuition, inasmuch as one only presents *a priori* (specifies) the action and reaction of moving forces (including, perhaps, understanding and desire) according to principles of motion in general (which the understanding specifies and classifies, as dynamic powers, according to the categories). The representation of these forces is identical with the representation of perception.

[*Margin . . .*]

22:506 [XIth fascicle, sheet VI, page 4]

Only because the subject [is conscious] to itself of its moving forces (of agitating them) and – because in the relationship of this motion, everything is reciprocal – [is conscious] of perceiving a reaction of equal strength (a relation which is known *a priori*, independently of experience) are the counteracting moving forces of matter anticipated and its properties established.

A natural thing which, as the movable in space, is an object of the outer senses (outer perception), that is, *matter*, cannot be self-*organizing* through its own forces and form organic bodies. For, since this requires a composition of the material according to purposes, matter would have to contain a principle of the absolute unity of the efficient cause – which, as present in space, would be an atom. Now all matter is divisible to infinity, and atomism, as a ground of explanation for the composition of bodies from smallest parts, is false. Hence only an immaterial substance can contain the ground of the possibility of organic bodies; that is, matter does not organize itself but is organized by what is immaterial. One is not, however, for that reason, entitled to assume this efficient cause to be a soul inherent in the body or a world-soul belonging to the aggregate of matter in general; it is, rather, only an efficient cause on the analogy with an intelligence: that is, a cause which we can represent to ourselves in no other way, since there may be quite other kinds of forces (and laws by which those forces act) than those of our thought. All organized bodies are systems; and we (the school) in turn organize the natural system.

22:507

The first act takes place through the understanding, through which the subject determines itself as an object with respect to objects in space and time, and apprehends in perception both outer and inner intuition (the *dabile*, as phenomenon, with the *cogitabile*) in empirical intuition in space and time. (Space and time become sense-objects hereby: are, thus, not mere forms of intuition.)

Before the investigator of nature establishes for physics the moving forces of matter, which are the cause of perceptions, he must consider how he is to interrogate nature, which he cannot undertake otherwise than according to *a priori* principles, which furnish the conditions under which a sense-object can become an object of experience (or, rather, of perception as apprehension). The formal element of apprehension must take precedence in the investigation of nature.

(a) A complex (*complexus*) of empirical representations of the object, with consciousness, as an *aggregate* – then, united to a single representation of the object (as effect of the moving forces on the subject). (b) To a *system* of these perceptions. The representation of space as sense-object (that is, in perception) is given *a priori*, namely, as in a system of action and reaction.

The four mechanical powers are the moving forces of apprehension and reciprocal reaction.

22:508

There are four acts by which the subject affects itself as object and thinks itself an object in appearance into a system of empirical representations, by means of perceptions of action, and the reaction corresponding to it.

It is only because space becomes an object of the senses (hence knowledge of it is empirical) that phenomena of matter are possible in it. Light appears to be the means with respect to what is outer, heat with respect to what is inner.

Space, as object of empirical intuition, is matter in appearance, which is distributed to infinity; for space is limitless.

Matter is what makes space into an object of the senses – hence, the substrate of all possible empirical intuitions, which form a limitless whole. Matter is thus, in comparison with empty space, absolute physical unity.

There are, however, *in matter* (that is, the space which forms the object of perceptions of space as an infinite object of the senses, in which there is no void) materials which require special kinds of sense, and specific moving forces which have their own particular basis (e.g. the basis of muriatic acid, etc.). In this regard, one must not speak of bases (in the plural) but only of one basis; for [the latter] is merely a relational concept, to the extent that we do not know the object itself but only the phenomena from their effects. The separation of two matters from each other, as in the case of hydrogen from water (in which the remaining part, as oxygen, unites with iron,[90]

22:509 while, at the same time, relinquishing the all-penetrating caloric) does not thereby establish a light-material etc., except as merely problematic. There is only one basis (*materia substrata*).

That one cannot say "*matters*" but only "matter," and, similarly, not "*experiences,*" but "experience," indicates that both concepts stem from a single principle or are analogous to each other; that the *a priori* principle lies in the knowing *subject,* not in the object of sensible representation; and that the understanding anticipates the influence on the senses. One does, however, also speak of *materials* – which one only terms *basis,* of whose activities, however, there can be several kinds – [that is] of different specific *elementary substances.* As, for instance, caloric, carbon, etc. and their moving forces.

It is not by compilation, but according to a principle of connection of the moving forces of matter in a system (that is, in relation to the possibility of the object for the sake of experience) that the moving forces of matter – empirical intuitions (perceptions) – can yield an *a priori* cognition of the object. The *understanding* is thus, subjectively, the principle of the possibility of making sense-objects into one experience, as an aggregate of empirical representations. The axioms of pure intuition, as the principle of form, are followed by the anticipations of appearance.

[*Margin* . . .][91]

22:511   [XIth fascicle, sheet VII, page 1]

Y

The doctrine of the transition from the metaphysical foundations of natural science to physics (study of nature, *philosophia naturalis*) contains two questions: (1) *What is physics?* (2) *What is a transition from the metaphysical foundations of natural science to physics?*

A
WHAT IS PHYSICS?

Physics is the doctrinal system of the moving forces of matter, insofar as it can be presented (*exhiberi*) in experience.

1. *Note.* What is at issue in this definition is not, objectively, the system of moving forces itself, but deals, merely subjectively, with the *doctrine* of the moving forces (*systema doctrinale*) of the science of nature. The designation of the *science of nature* as *scientia* or even *philosophia naturalis* is thereby subjected to a certain ambiguity, in that it could also be understood in contrast to supernatural [science].

2. *Note.* In a certain work with the title: *Metaphysical Foundations of Natural Science*, philosophical principles of the latter were developed. For metaphysics is a part of *philosophy*, and nothing but metaphysics could be at issue in the transition from philosophy to the science of nature, if it is a matter of knowledge from concepts. But there is an opponent [*Nebenbuhler*] of this view: no less a man, indeed, than Newton himself in his immortal work **Philosophiae** *naturalis principia* **mathematica.**

But there is a self-contradiction in the very title of his book: For, just as little as there can be *philosophical principles of mathematics*, can there be *mathematical principles of philosophy* (such as physics is supposed to contain). It should have been called: **Scientiae** *naturalis principia mathematica;* the [above] principles cannot be subordinated to each other but must be placed side by side. One can, •indeed,• also make philosophical use of mathematics, •but only indirectly,• as an *instrument;* remaining on the track laid down by the transition from the metaphysical foundations of natural science, without trespassing onto mathematics' own field and taking a leap (*salto mortale*) into physics. [This is possible] if the laws of motion for the given moving forces of matter, consisting in attraction and repulsion, are given *a priori* in relations of space and time whose determination is subject to mathematical principles.[j]

If it is the case that motions must precede in order for moving forces to take place, then the principles are mathematical; if, on the other hand, it is the case that the moving forces must precede in order for motions to take place, then the forces are appropriate to physics, which is an empirical science. Both are philosophical sciences: the one directly and immediately related to the science of nature; the other indirectly, by means of the use which mathematics, as an instrument, can make of the concepts of the moving forces.

22:512

22:513

[Bottom margin]
Although mathematics does [not] have to establish philosophical princi-

[j] Connected with sheet VII, page 3, by "θ θ θ *verte* page 3."

ples of mathematics *directly*, it nevertheless acts indirectly, establishing problems which point in the direction of physics and the moving forces of matter (and hence, also, toward philosophy). *Kepler's* three famous analogies led to a coup on Newton's part, in which he declared gravitational attraction by a bold but inevitable hypothesis for physics; in this way mathematics was endowed, for the sake of the science of nature, with the ability to prescribe laws to nature *a priori*, laws which it could by no means have made use of for philosophy in the absence of such a capacity [*Organ*]. Yet this transition was a step [*breaks off*]

Although it is not possible to philosophize by means of mathematics, yet one can philosophize about it and the connection to it.

{Newton made his most important conquest by means of philosophy, not mathematics.}

[*Bottom part of main text*]

B
HOW IS PHYSICS POSSIBLE?

22:514
In the *Metaphysical Foundations of Natural Science*, matter in general was explained thus: It is the *movable in space*.⁹² Another explanation, however, can be given as follows: It is that *which makes space an object of the senses*, •namely,• the substrate of all outer empirical intuition with consciousness; that is, of all perceptions •(*sparsim*), insofar as the latter (*coniunctim*) are• thought as an object of possible experience.

[Right margin]
The moving forces belonging to physics must first be given through experience, which itself must be based on principles, namely, as to its possibility – [hence they] must be given *a priori*.

One can say: It is matter which makes space into an object of experience (perception); that is, the moving forces outwardly in space and internally in sensation. For sensation and feelings also belong to physics.

Attraction, as cause of gravity, is conditionally given *a priori*, as a moving force; for, without attraction and repulsion, infinite space would remain empty.

[XIth fascicle, sheet VII, page 2]
Now the concepts of *matter* and of *experience* in general are of such a kind that they contain an *absolute unity* in the thoroughgoing determination of the sense-object, as do space and time (as forms of outer and inner appearances). There is one space and one time. One cannot speak of *matters (in plurali materiae, materiarum)* or of *experiences (experientiae experientiarum)*; if one intends to refer to them, as the first parts of a whole,

one must speak, rather, of *materials* (that is, elementary substances (στοιχεῖα)) insofar as the subject's outer sense-objects are concerned, or of *moments,* with respect to time in inner relation – whether the latter be moments of motion (external) or of sensation in perception (internal), increasing or decreasing in *degree.** 22:515

3rd Note. Although there can thus be no mathematical principles of philosophy in the field of the science of nature, yet there can be a *philosophical* **use** of mathematics, insofar as the latter serves as a mere instrument of philosophical physics and is, hence, an *indirect* principle of the science of nature; not, indeed, in an objective, but in a subjective respect, which can, however, lay claim to a certainty which is not empirical but rather apodictic, analogous to that of mathematics.

Motion can be treated entirely mathematically, for it is nothing but concepts of space and time, which can be presented *a priori* in pure intuition; the understanding *makes* them. Moving forces, however, as effi- 22:516 cient *causes* of these motions, such as are required by physics and its laws, need philosophical principles. All mathematics, then, brings one not the least bit nearer to philosophical knowledge unless a causal combination, such as that of the attraction or repulsion of matter by its moving forces, is first brought onto the scene and postulated for the sake of appearances. As soon as the latter occurs, the transition to physics has taken place, and there can be *philosophiae naturalis principia mathematica.* This step was taken by Newton in the role of a philosopher who brings new forces onto the scene; not, indeed, as forces derived from presupposed motions (centripetal and centifugal) which would contain only mathematical principles, but original forces (*vires primariae*) in which mathematics is only used as an instrument for the moving forces (whereas philosophy is required to ground them primordially).

This occurs because, once Kepler's three analogies had grounded all the mathematically determined laws of the rotation of the planets by sufficient observation, there yet remained the question for physics regard-

---

* The ground for these restrictions in thought lies therein that the object is not represented according to intuitions of objects, which are subject to restriction, but according to concepts – which are thought as a mere relation of the represented objects, which is boundless (*indefinitum*). Matter is that which makes space empirically intuitable – that is, sensible. Since the latter, however, pertains to the subject merely [as] what is formal in [*als*] appearance, the totality of this object of intuition is *entirely* one, but yet, at the same time, all-embracing; and one cannot speak of *matters,* but only of *matter,* which is given to physics as its object. Such grammatical unity in designation can also be observed elsewhere in different languages (e.g. German and Latin). There is no singular for "weapon," but only "*arma.*" One cannot say, "*the* knowledge" [*das Erkenntnis*] (as if there were several of them) but only "knowledge" [*die Erkenntnis*]. Why cannot we do without the word "*body*" [*Körper*] in physics and not instead replace it with "human body" [*Leib (sollte gesagt werden Laib)*]? Presumably because, for theological reasons, there has to be a living body which, nonetheless, has mass.[93]

ing the efficient cause of this appearance; Newton, in order to find a way out of this difficulty, built a bridge from mathematics to physics, namely, the principle of an attractive force, penetrating all bodies through empty space, according to the law of the inverse square of the distance. He did not, thus, rest content with appearances, but brought into play a primordially moving force, which, on the one hand, presented universal reciprocal gravitation [as] merely forces striving toward one another according to Kepler's law; and in the end, however, it presented these forces as a 22:517 universal attraction in infinite space of bodies and of the matter in general which fills the universe. As hypothesis [*breaks off*]

In this way, the principles of natural science (*scientiae naturalis s. naturae scientia*) were established in a necessary manner as belonging to philosophy, in which the mathematical [principles] are incorporated, not as components belonging immediately (directly) to the system, but only as a means (indirectly) and as a tool for its production.

As regards, *firstly*, the relations of the moving forces (in space) Newton made use of the concept of the *attraction* of all cosmic bodies in infinite space, and their motions by means of those forces in time. **Secondly,** [he made use of the concept of] the *repulsion* of parts of matter, which [extends] itself in cosmic space, according to the same law, by means of light and its laws of motion in colors (imponderable, incoercible, incohesible, inexhaustible); all of which is thoroughly mathematical. Then, however, also [the concept] of fluidity and solidity [*breaks off*]

[*Margin . . .*]

[XIth fascicle, sheet VII, page 3]

Space, regarded subjectively, in formal intuition, as an object of the senses, as object in appearance, is *sensible* space – in contrast to intelligible space, which is merely subjective. It is the substrate of all possible perceptions, which forms a system of the moving forces of matter, and, hence, 22:518 according to the rule of identity, as an absolute unity, makes space an object of experience, which is an absolute whole of the thoroughgoing determination of sense-objects.

The moving forces of matter are the causes of the possibility of perception in it.

The first of the moving forces, which constitutes the existence of sensible space, is intuition extensively – giving empirically what is external in the object, in the possibility of perception; the second is intensive in sensation, in sensible time, as a matter of degree. Both are subjective, that is, in appearance, according to the form in which the subject is affected. Attraction and repulsion are the acts of the agitating forces of matter, which contain *a priori* a principle of the possibility of experience and the transition to physics. It is part of the metaphysical foundations of natural science – and, hence, of philosophy – to make use of the mathematical principles with regard to the relations of the given forces of matter, as an instrument for the sake of philosophy; to [proceed] from Kepler's forms (his three analogies) to the moving forces which act in conformity with them; [to develop] the system of universal gravitation from original attraction or motion from repulsion (in [the form of] which light and sound [are given] for optics and acoustics); and thus to found physics, in conjunction with other relations of force. It is noteworthy that Newton's propositions in his *Principia philosophiae mathematica* are not developed systematically, from a principle, but had to be compiled empirically and rhapsodically. Consequently, they led to the expectation of ever new additions, and, hence, his book could not contain a philosophical system.

The universe, as object of the senses, is a system of the forces of a matter which affect one another outwardly (objectively) in space, by motion, and inwardly (subjectively) by sensation, with consciousness, of substances – that is, as objects of perception. Their elements, regarded mathematically,   22:519 as substance, would, as atoms (in such an amount that they fill space, or else dynamically, as moments of motion, according to the degree of magnitude of their forces) form sense-objects should we wish to regard the latter as constituted by composition. Yet mathematical division allows of no last part. For the latter would be a point, which is only the limit of a line, not a part of it; force, however, as *moment* (of gravity and attraction) does not [allow of] smallest moments of motion [*breaks off*]

•There can be mathematical principles of philosophy, if mathematics, proceeding from Kepler's laws, establishes originally moving forces in space; mathematics is thereby, mediately, an instrument for philosophy.•

[. . .]

[XIth fascicle, sheet VIII, page 1]   22:524

Z

Space is, in fact, merely the form of outer intuition and the subjective element of the mode of being outwardly affected. But it is, nevertheless, considered as something outwardly given – as real relation insofar as it must be thought as a principle of the possibility of perceptions; yet it must precede experience.

In this respect we *must* represent matter (the movable in space) to ourselves and in this also a moving force of their masses which represents an action of them through empty space (*actio in distans*), extended to infinity. It is unlimited, but it limits any whole of matter (body) and, in fact, through

155

two original forces of attraction and repulsion. Without their combined effect there would be absolutely no matter and space as such would be empty and yet, at the same time, known – which is contradictory.

It is not a proposition based on physics (empirical doctrine of moving forces) but a proposition that originally grounds physics, that there must be an attraction – even without opposing repulsion – among bodies which move around a common center of motion. In virtue of this attraction and their circular motions they (the celestial bodies) [are] moved in circles around midpoints of motion, and so must finally move in all of space around an unmoved [midpoint].

All bodies strive to approach one another through motion in empty space – and, in fact, in direct proportion to the quantity of their masses and in inverse proportion to the squares of the distances, in virtue of an impulse (*impulsus*) of attraction. (But how are the distances to be perceived if the moving forces should be effective in empty space?) In order to determine the distances through perception space must be perceptible, hence it cannot be empty. There are, therefore, mathematical foundations of natural science which at the same time belong [*anheimfallen*] to philosophy; for they concern the quality of the moving forces according to their *causality*, and mathematics acts here as instrument.

Materials – complementa virium moventium materiae.[94] The quantity of matter cannot be thought as grounded atomistically but must be thought as grounded dynamically. This grounding is the original attraction of bodies through empty space which therefore can be no object of perception but can merely be thought. Intelligible space is the formal representation of the subject insofar as it is affected by outer things.

From the unity of matter it follows that there is a common principle of its forces (*basis*). It contains the forces moving in particular modes (*basis specifica*) and makes unlimited space into an object of the senses (*originaria basis et communis*). As the latter, it is represented as occupying space everywhere; [it is] represented *a priori* for itself, as substance having no particular properties except merely that of occupying space. This sensible space is assumed to be limiting itself through moving forces.

Matter is the outer object of the senses in general insofar as it can be only one and unlimited – in contrast to empty space. Its moving forces as specifically different types of matter are called *materials* (*materies, materiei*): parts of matter to which thus also belong specifically different forces and [which] are movable substances (as nitrogen, carbon). One of these so-called materials, which, as assumed to be present everywhere and all-penetrating (the *guiding* material) is merely hypothetical: Namely, it is the caloric which is suited for the motion and distribution of all materials and [which] may also be mere quality of motion.

[. . .]

[XIth fascicle, sheet VIII, page 2]   22:528

The *laws* of motion were sufficiently established by Kepler's three analogies. They were entirely mechanical. Huygens knew also of composite yet derivative motion, forces fleeing the midpoint or constantly driving toward it (*vis centrifuga et centripeta*). But no matter how close they both [came to postulating universal gravitation] – for Galileo had long before that given the law of the gravity of falling bodies at heights which led to an approximately equal moment in their fall – all that which had been achieved remained empiricism in the doctrine of motion, and there was as yet no universal principle properly so-called, that is, a concept of reason, from which it would be possible to infer *a priori* to a law for the determination of forces, as from a cause to its effect. This solution was given by   22:529
Newton, inasmuch as he gave the moving force the name of *attraction*, by which he made apparent that this cause was effected by the body itself immediately, not by communication of the motion to other bodies – thus, not mechanically, but purely dynamically.

By what means, however, is this force which governs the whole of cosmic space made manifest – since this cannot be empirically, for it contains an *a priori* law? How shall we know the places at which this universal attraction [acts], and which, in comparison with other [forces], is of a greater or lesser moment of acceleration, in order [to determine] the distances at which the attraction acts? For of this we must previously have been informed before we can apply the law of gravitation to any particular part of matter, and *actio immediata in distans* can produce no perception for the intuiting subject, since space is empty and not at all sensible.

Hence matter in contact must be given in order that matter at a distance be acknowledged as such – that is, not as a locomotion [*Fortrücken*] through space void of contents (for the latter cannot be perceived). Rather, what is to be understood by matter in contact is only that a body can exercise force on others, even without the mediation of an intermediate matter, and that this takes place through attraction (which, in itself, is not perceptible). Yet, this attraction, without occupying space in the form of substance, initiates motion by its force, and makes empty space indirectly sensible. •Such [a motion] can only be the motion of a matter which acts in a straight line and acts at a distance within a certain time.•

To this Newtonian principle of universal attraction through empty space there corresponds a similar principle of repulsion (*virium repel-*   22:530
lentium), which, likewise, cannot be an object of experience in itself, but is only necessary in order to present space as an object of the senses. It is the characteristic of matter to act on the senses at a distance; thereby the object, by its means, is presented immediately to sensation and empirical *intuition*, rather than the intermediate matter affecting the subject. Light and sound (with their colors and tones) are such transitions, which make an action at a distance (*actio in distans*) representable as immediately

157

possible. We see or hear light and sound, not as immediately in contact with our eye or our ear, but regard it as an influence of sense-objects on our organ, as distant from us.

The merely subjective modifications in the stimulation of our perceptions (called feeling), which impel us either to preserve the state of inner perception or to free ourselves from it, do not belong to the present (merely theoretical) investigation. We are here concerned only with the problem of transcendental philosophy: How is synthetic knowledge *a priori* possible?

[*Margin . . .*]

22:535   [XIth fascicle, sheet VIII, page 3]

[. . .]

[*Right margin*]
The receptivity of appearances depends upon the spontaneity of composition in the intuition of oneself.

Matter is what makes space into an object of the senses. (Object of possible perception.) (The definition that it is the movable in space is the consequence thereof.) The parts of matter, specifically different with respect to their moving forces, are materials (*stoicheia*) which, mutually penetrating, are in the same space.

Supposing that only a single cosmic body is present: The question now is whether there are, in that case, forces of attraction everywhere in infinite space (albeit inoperative for this space) or whether there is really nothing external to this body, but that, as soon as a second body is posited, these forces manifest themselves in relation to the latter.

One must first have an intuitive representation of the size of [a] space – its
22:536 position and situation, as well as its shape – in order to be able to determine what exists in it. For there is only one space and only one time. Sense-objects within them are posited in them.

Of attractions according to the inverse ratio of the square of the distance, insofar as that is a rule given *a priori*, whose ground lies in [the nature of] space – as it were, an experimental positing.[k]

[. . .]

---

[k] Lehmann's reading of last three words uncertain.

[AA]

Space is not an object of intuition, •neither pure nor empirical intuition (of perception)• – not a self-subsisting thing – but rather is •itself a mode of intuition• (intuition itself). That it should be something external and different to the subject signifies nothing more than that this intuition is   22:434 original, and not derived from perception; it signifies only the subjective element of the synthetic unity of the manifold, which precedes *a priori* the latter's formal relation in appearance. Hence motion and moving forces in space can, according to transcendental principles, precede *a priori* the principle of the possibility of a system of perceptions for the sake of experience.

The medium by which we perceive things as external to us at a distance, is *light* and *sound.* They are mediate perceptions. Heat is an immediate one.

Space and time are not *objects* of intuition. For were they objects of intuition, they would be real things and require, in turn, another intuition in order to be represented to one as objects, and so on to infinity. Intuitions are not perceptions (that is, empirical) if they are **pure,** for that requires forces which determine the senses. How is it possible, however, that pure intuitions yield, at the same time, principles of perception – e.g. the attraction of cosmic bodies?

[Space and time are not *objects* of intuition] but, rather, subjective forms of intuition itself, insofar as they contain a principle of synthetic *a priori* propositions and of the possibility of a transcendental philosophy; [they contain] appearances prior to all perceptions. Space in three dimensions, time in *one.* The formal element of sense-intuition in the subject is here [represented] as object, and moving forces in space (in which there is nothing in substance) as something sensible (*sensibile*), which contains moving forces (hence objects of perception). Attraction of *bodies* at a distance, and repulsion (in virtue of which they are bodies, that is, self-limiting matter) already lie *a priori* in the concept of the possibility of experience, as unity of space and time. *Light* and *sound,* action at a distance.

(Everything here stands under the principle of identity.)

What comes first is the consciousness of composition (*complexus*) of the   22:435 manifold in appearances in space and time, as a continuous whole (the totality, which contains the position, the locations, and the moving forces for outer and inner perceptions – that is, for the possibility of experience. For space itself is not an object of perception. It is the system of the active relations of the moving forces, given *a priori*, according to its form, in three dimensions of intuition. Space itself is not an object of perception.

Space and time are not objects of a given (empirical) intuition, *for, in that case, they would be something existent which affected our sense;* they are, rather, intuitions themselves – *not a dabile but a cogitabile* – the mere form in which something can be object of empirical intuition for our sense. They are not •objects of• perceptions (empirical representations with consciousness) for in that case they would themselves presuppose appearances as *a priori* intuitions. They are not objects of perception – that is, space is not given in perception – but *subjective forms of intuition.*

Space is not something existing, as an object of intuition (just as little as time is) but the mere form of the coordination of the manifold *alongside* and *successively.* That it should be posited *alongside* and *successively* (*iuxta et post*), however, already presupposes space and time in the subject; not as something which is given in itself for sensible representation but which is thought as its formal element. It is not an object of perception, but a formal *a priori* condition for *perceiving* what is given to the senses as a whole. The moving forces, attraction and repulsion are in it [*breaks off*]

22:436　Space and time, the one like the other, as forms of outer and inner intuition, are not objects of perception (empirical representation with consciousness) but only receptivity for sense-objects, to be affected (outwardly and inwardly) by them – that is, to represent objects of ourselves in the manner in which they *appear* to us. They are just for that reason appropriate as *a priori* principles for the possibility of synthetic *a priori* knowledge ([principles] of transcendental philosophy) and are merely subjective, not objective – not, according to what objects are in themselves, but what they are *for sense.* Hence space and time are not themselves objects of intuition, a *given* manifold for perception, but only the formal element of the composition (*complexus*) of possible objects of the perceptions of outer and inner sense.

If, however, one posits the moving forces, affecting the subject outwardly in spatial intuition and inwardly in sensation, the concept of these forces must precede the concept of the spatial and temporal relations in which they are posited; for, without this, space and time would not be an *empirical* intuition, without which, in turn, the existence of these forces is not *given* but only thought. Space itself, as *sensible* (*spatium sensibile*), as object of perception, [can] become an object of the senses through those forces which affect the subject, or be thought as such.

It is a *contradictio in adiecto* that the apodictic certainty of a proposition should emerge *from* experience; however, *for* experience – that is, for its sake, to produce it, indeed (by observation and experiment) – principles of it can be given, and these belong entirely to physics. Under the title of physicist, however, one also understands the expert on and controller of organic bodies, primarily living ones. •Extensive or intensive magnitude

160

(degree) of the moving forces of attraction and repulsion in space and time, as objects of possible perception.•

[*Margin* . . .]

[XIth fascicle, sheet II, page 1]   22:439

BB

Space and time, as intuitions, and the unity of consciousness – the necessary unity in the connection of the manifold of them – is the necessary (original) sense-object.

Space and time are not objects of intuition but pure intuition itself; and the formal element in the synthetic unity of the manifold of them as appearances, under the principle of their composition, is spontaneity, not receptivity.

The understanding cannot proceed from perception (empirical knowledge with consciousness) [in order to] determine the intuiting subject into a complex of representation, as knowledge of the object. [It] contains *a priori* the formal element of a system of perceptions, prior to these empirical cognitions; for perception is itself the effect of an act of the moving force of the subject, which determines itself *a priori* into a representation.

Space and time •are not things, but mere modes of representation of things in appearance,• and objective intuition [is] contained *a priori* in subjective intuition as appearance. The positing of both as united •does• not •contain something• *given* but •something which• is *made.* The formal element of intuition prior to the material. The possibility of transcendental philosophy (that is, synthetic *a priori* propositions): not by groping, as toward an aggregate, but according to principles in a system; in which it is not perceptions, •*sparsim*• (for they are empirical) but the principle of the possibility of experience, •*coniunctim*• (as unity of the thoroughgoing determination of the object) which takes precedence; and the transition from the metaphysical foundations [of natural science] to physics founds a system of knowledge, by anticipations of[1] the internally and externally moving forces, in sensation and in the construction of concepts – philosophically and mathematically.   22:440

The movable in space, matter as a continuum, not aggregated through *vacuum interspersum,* •or• atomistically, but (since there are no atoms) dynamically forming bodies (through the attraction and repulsion of the matter of bounded masses in empty space) and mutually *attracting,* but nevertheless thoroughly distributed in full and sensible space as mere matter for the communication of forces: These are mere thought-objects, which (like caloric) are not so much hypothetical entities as principles of

---

[1] Reading *der* for *die.*

the understanding, without which experience itself is not possible. Space is a continuum for sensible knowledge, and, were it not to be apperceived, it would be merely an empty imagining. One may, however, also represent it to oneself merely idealistically, so [*breaks off*]

Space, time, and that which combines both •intuitions – the outer and the inner – • in one, *motion* (•that is, the act of• description •of space in• a certain time) are not •given• things, as objects of perception (empirical representation with consciousness) given independently, outside the subject; they are mere forms of sensible representation which belong to the subject *a priori,* and contain the general problem of transcendental philosophy: How are synthetic propositions *a priori* possible? These objects are here given only in appearance, as subjective forms of intuition, on which the possibility of synthetic *a priori* knowledge is also founded.

{*Space* and *time* are *subjective* forms of outer and inner sensible intuition as appearance, and they are the principle of the possibility of the combination of the manifold of intuition into the systematic unity of perceptions in experience, with the consciousness of the absolute totality of the combination of the manifold in one object.}

22:441

Space, time and •the absolute unity of the two in the connection of sensible intuition• in space and •[in] the pure sense of• time.

{Space and time, the intuition of the object (according to its form). The consciousness of unity in the composition within the subject, according to the absolute totality of this intuition. There is one space and one time. The absolute unity, which embraces everything, is likewise the infinity of this object, which is really subject, and which is intuiting and, at the same time, intuited.}

Space, time, and the determination •or determinability• of existence in space and time. Where, how, and when something is. Space and time are not themselves indirect (mediate) •and derivative,• but direct (immediate) and •primitive• intuitions, •through• which the object affects itself as appearance, and •thus• they represent their object as infinite (limitless). The complex (*complexus*) of representations which are contained in this intuition are a progress to infinity. The object is given neither idealistically nor realistically; it is not *given* at all, but merely thought (*non dari, sed intelligi potest*). Composition – not the composite, but the positing.

[*Top margin*]

Matter (as generic concept) can be thought of as consisting in specifically different elements, which are then known as *materials* (*partes elementares*), and which *entirely* occupy the same space, without driving one another from their places – e.g. caloric, light-material, magnetic material, *electricity.* Are they materials or mere forces – that is, otherwise modified materials?

[*Right margin*]

True locomotion can only be grounded on dynamical principles, e.g.   22:442
attraction, but, even then it is not, with respect to space in general [*breaks
off*]

Alteration of place A is not always motion of the body A. For, if B is
moved, the place of A is also *altered*, but A does not *move* (does not alter its
place).

It is one and the same in transcendental philosophy whether I make
sensible representations idealistically or realistically into a principle. For
what matters is only the relation – not of the objects to the subject, but
among one another.

Self-intuition (making oneself into an object of the senses) belongs to
transcendental philosophy, and is synthetic but, at the same time, analytic.

Space, time (as intuitions), motion: synthetic unity in the *relation* of
intuitions as appearances, and the *cause* of motion – moving force; [they]
are together the conditions of the sense-object. •Principles of possible
experience.•

That there is a space cannot be perceived. I *posit* a space (likewise time);
and yet it is not something existent which has three dimensions, etc.
There is only one space.

Space is an *intuition;* not something which *is intuited.*

An empty space can have forces in its locations – e.g. attractive
forces – but not, however, without some body, namely at a distance; and
these forces, if this body ceases, are themselves likewise nothing.

Organic bodies propagated by two sexes, by germs and eggs.

Even idealism can coexist with the subjective reality of the concepts of
space and time as intuitions. For everything synthetic is combined in the   22:443
unity of intuition, according to the principle of identity.

For the subject is an object of the senses for itself, according to these
forms. The subject which *makes* the *sensible* representation of space and
time for itself, is likewise an object to itself in this act. Self-intuition. For,
without this, there would be no self-consciousness of a substance.

[XIth fascicle, sheet II, page 2]

The quantity of matter in a cosmic body is determined by the distance of
a planet in motion around it, by the former's attraction, and by the moving
force which operates at every distance in empty space – hence the forces in
all these places. If the attracting body disappears, together with the attracted, then there is a void – in regard to which the question is, whether
space itself be something which is yet positive, and an object of intuition.

The understanding does not start from the object, but from its own subject, in order to construct the sensible intuition, according to its form; that is, to present the manifold of sensible intuition synthetically *a priori*, in the unity of the manifold, according to a principle – which is a mathematical operation of the understanding, and an act of transcendental philosophy: How are synthetic representations *a priori* possible? The representation of *space* and *time*, and their synthetic unity in one space and one time, and the principle of thoroughgoing combination for the sake of the possibility of experience in space and time.

The extraposition is combined with the intusposition of the manifold of intuition as appearance, through a principle of the synthetic unity of *a priori* knowledge – consequently, by transcendental principles. The subject makes itself into an object.

The unconditioned unity of the manifold in intuition is not *given* to the subject by another object, but is *thought* through itself. Space and time are not anticipations of perception, as concepts of the understanding, but forms of the objects in appearance.

22:444

Matter does not consist of atoms; for what is encountered as a simple element in one place is not a part but a point. Only forces can act – spherically, indeed.

The objects of intuition are thought as composite, for space is only the formal element of appearance – that is, the subjective element of the self-determination of intuition in three dimensions, for the sake of the composition of perceptions. I cannot say I *have* this or that experience; rather, I *make* it for myself, and this system of perceptions is valid for everybody. *Observation* and *experiment* •are ingredients• [and] presuppose a principle in order to *make* experience (not experiences). The mathematical foundations of natural science precede *a priori*, as intuitions; the philosophical [foundations] apply appearances to them; the mathematical principles of the philosophical doctrine of nature, however, fully ground the *doctrinal system* of the science of nature as physics. However, the transition from the former science to the latter progresses from the partial representations (the empirical data – perceptions) to the whole (physics) and contains the *conditions of the possibility of experience.* Perception belongs to the moving forces, as operating within the subject in sensation. But, as such, it is not to be counted to experience, according to a *general* rule.

Space, time, and the thoroughgoing determination (existence) of things in space and time – principle of the possibility of experience.

Space is not a sensible object, and, to that extent, has no reality – that is, nothing existent – but, rather, contains merely the formal element of intuition which our own principle of thought posits synthetically. It is nothing outside my representation, but something merely subjective – a mere intuition, without [being] an object different from my representation. The ideality of space, as the mere form of an intuition, also makes it the case that we can attribute *a priori* certain properties which carry with them synthetic *a priori* propositions – e.g. three dimensions to an object which, in itself, is nothing. Space is not intuited but is an intuition. Thus it is (like time) limitless (not infinite). Not *progressus in infinitum,* as a composite whole, but *in indefinitum* – something limitless, self-restricting. *Thaeatetus.*95 22:445

The subjective principle of consciousness of oneself in the synthetic *a priori* unity of the composition (synthesis) of an object of self-intuition, as appearance of an object in general *outside myself* – that is, space – or of myself *in me* – time, as the *formal* element of intuition, lies at the foundation of *perception* (empirical representation with consciousness) as the material element both outside and inside myself. The understanding makes the progress to the possibility of experience. Experience, as the transition from the metaphysical foundations of natural science to physics, is an unconditional unity – that is, *experiences* do not exist, but only perceptions. Experience, as the synthetic unity of that manifold of empirical representations in a system, is, as a thoroughgoing determination, only one. For the sake of physics.

[. . .]

[Left margin] 22:446
How is experience possible?
The principle of the possibility of the aggregate of perceptions for the sake of the possibility of experience: (1) Intuition (2) Perception (3) 22:447
Experience – which latter also has *a priori* principles of its possibility.

The material out of which experience is originally woven is not the perception (empirical representation with consciousness) of some object – that is, not that which sense *receives* as material – but that which the understanding *makes* out of •the formal element of• sensible intuition. So it is not from receptivity but from the spontaneity of the subject (thus, from the (formal) principle of composition, that is, from that which the understanding makes out of this simple material – hence autonomously, not heteronomously) that the aggregate of perceptions becomes a system, which, according to the principle of identity, is only one – that is, contains absolute (unconditional) unity in itself. Experience is already a system of perceptions, and contains a principle of the possibility of experience (which can only be one). For [to speak of] making experiences is a *hysteron proteron*96 of the knowledge of the understanding, •which,• in the place of perceptions, must first have observation and experiment given as the principle of the possibility of experience.

Space, time, and the absolute synthetic unity of the manifold of appearance in general in space and time, by which the whole of the objects of sense is given for the sake of a single possible experience.

Not even a Thaeatetus can dispute the actuality of these objects, and it is superior to the doubting of idealism. For this mode of representation of the objects of intuition as such is decided according to the principle of identity – that is, according to logical principles. We cannot think sense-objects in the whole of intuition, as possible experience, for ourselves, if we do not connect them, according to this rule, in one concept – no Thaeatetus.

22:448   The subjective element of •inner• space- and time-intuition, as appearance, is, at the same time, the objective element of the synthetic *a priori* unity of their relation, for the sake of the possibility of experience, as a system, according to its form, of perceptions in composition.

[Bottom margin]
Space is not intuited as object, and is not a sense-object for an aggregate of perception for the sake of the possibility of experience. For the formal unity in the synthesis of the manifold of intuition, in which the manifold is not *given* in combination, but *made* by the understanding, is the principle of the possibility of empirical representations with consciousness for a system of representations in the unity of experience. All experience is problematic; it becomes assertoric through perception as an aggregate. It is never apodictic, however.

[XIth fascicle, sheet II, page 3]

BB²

The consciousness of myself does not commence with what is material – that is, not with sensible representation as perception – but with what is formal in the synthesis of the manifold of pure *a priori* intuition; not with the object of knowledge, but with the coordination (*coordinatio*) of possible sensible representations in the subject which is affected by objects – that is, knowledge of the object as appearance.

Space and time are the unique forms of the intuition of the manifold as appearance, and each of these intuitions is, each independently, given *a priori* as an unconditional whole: "There is one space and one time" and the whole of possible perceptions (empirical representations with consciousness) regarded *a priori* in one system, is experience – that is, thoroughgoing determination of the object of sensible intuition.

In conformity with this, in regard to physics as a system of all empirical knowledge (not an empirical system – for that would be a *contradictio in adjecto*), one never speaks of *experiences,* but only of **experience,** since 22:449 perception in its thoroughgoing determination is an absolute cognitive whole of the object.

But a principle of progressive approximation toward experience, through an indeterminate number of accumulated perceptions (by means of observation and experiment) in an aggregate, does not entitle one to the expression: "Experience *teaches* this or that"; for an empirical judgment as such can never be represented as apodictic. •They are not concepts of consequence [*Folgerung*] but of association [*Beigesellung*] and of progression in the aggregation of empirical representations, which, no matter by which and by how many determinations, progress to the whole of the thoroughgoing determination, as existence.• Although, for example, given ten different compounds, which constitute the precipitation of a solution, as given by chemical rules, one may imagine that the experiment has thereby advanced into a demonstration (thus making further experiments superfluous), yet one cannot guarantee success in the eleventh – in which, for example, there is the unnoticed influence of atmospheric electricity affecting the instruments. Nor can a physician predict from his Hippocratic armchair the intended success for (apparently) similar individuals and cases without, from time to time, being deceived in his expectations.

Space and time, as objects of intuition, regarded as unity – the one of outer intuition, the other of inner – are given *a priori* with their determinations in three dimensions (of magnitude): body, plane, and point. They are not concepts.

The consciousness of myself in the formula: I am, is identical with the proposition: I am an object to myself; an object, indeed, of inner intuition (*dabile*) and of the thought of the determination of that which I ascribe to myself (*cogitabile*). The proposition: I am to myself an object of the intuition and thought of the manifold of the intuition of myself, is a synthetic *a priori* proposition, into whose possibility I may not inquire. It [is] the 22:450 principle of transcendental philosophy, which answers the problem: How are synthetic propositions *a priori* possible?

Intuition is twofold, however, in the representation of space and time, which [contains] the formal element of the combination of the manifold, only in appearance, indeed – that is, how I affect myself [and] can constitute myself *a priori* into an empirical cognition, for example, into cognition of the sensible representation of a matter and of the bodies which are composed of it.

We know the object through the manner in which the subject is affected by it; this, however, is given *a priori* in appearance.

[*Margin . . .*]

IMMANUEL KANT

[XIth fascicle, sheet II, page 4]

Space and time, as subjective forms, not as objects of the intuition of the *a priori* given manifold in appearance, are not derivative cognitions (*repraesentatio derivata*) but given originally in representation (*repraesentatio primaria*); they are thought as the unconditional synthetic unity of the manifold, and their complex as an infinite whole, in which perceptions (empirical representations with consciousness) are thought of as in a system – that is *coordinated* and *subordinated* according to the principle of the possibility of experience.

Intuition of an object without limits – space and time – and thoroughgoing determination of oneself as subject in thoroughgoing determination in space and time; as principle of the possibility of (outer and inner) experience, as knowledge of a doctrinal system called physics – toward which, by this act, a transition in doctrine from the metaphysical foundations of natural science to physics takes place.

In this there is no ideality of a given object, but, rather, the reality of the synthesis of the *a priori* self-constituting principle of the combination of the manifold in intuition in general, as appearance; insofar, that is, as this synthesis, according to the formal aspect of its unity (there is one space and one time) is, at the same time, an infinite progression, in which empirical representations with consciousness (perceptions) progress [to] the unity of possible experience – to a system – which is thought, rather than given.

Thus, space, time, and the principle of the thoroughgoing determination of the appearance of the object of intuition in space and time, constitute something which is not merely an aggregate •of the manifold• of perception, through observation and experiment, but a system, called experience, which is single, and to which the understanding progresses.

The first act of the faculty of representation, through which the subject posits the manifold of its intuition and makes itself an object of the senses, is a synthetic *a priori* cognition of the *given* (*dabile*): space and time as [the] formal element of intuition, and of what is *thought* in the composition of this manifold (*cogitabile*), insofar as, as appearance, the latter is representable *a priori*, according to what is formal in intuition. Hence, space and time are not themselves objects, but forms of the representation of the intuition of objects. Which latter, as empirical representations with consciousness (that is, as perceptions) are – inasmuch as they are combined *a priori* into a whole in the form of a system – experience; and, insofar as they are an object of experience, they are, as such, an object of physics (that is, of the science of nature).

A great deal is required, however, in order to establish whether an empirical cognition can be held to be a principle of knowledge and an empirical proposition. For this requires *thoroughgoing* determination, which alone can establish the existence of what is thought. Experience is

168

the absolute unity and completeness of perception, not in an undetermined aggregate but in a system; and the completeness of empirical knowledge cannot be constituted from the system, but only for it – hence there is only progression toward empirical knowledge, but not [a] physical doctrine of experience, properly so called.

[. . .]

[The Selbstsetzungslehre*]*

[VIIth fascicle, sheet I, page 4]

[Insertion]

The first thought from which the power of representation proceeds is the intuition of oneself and the category of the synthetic unity of the manifold in appearance – that is, of pure (not empirical) representation, which precedes all perception, under the *a priori* principle: How are synthetic propositions *a priori* possible? Its answer is: They are contained identically in the unconditional unity of space and time, as pure intuitions, whose quality consists therein that the subject posits itself as given (*dabile*); their quantity, however, in that the act of composition (as infinite in progression (*cogitabile*)) contains the intuition of an infinite whole, as thinkable (subjectively). What is thought *in indefinitum* is here represented as given *in infinitum*. Space and time are infinite quanta.

That which is in infinite progression is represented as something infinite, which is given (space and time) according to mathematical predicates of intuition (the three dimensions of space and one of time), just as if they were real positions in which things [are] and alterations in them occur. Hence, attraction according to the inverse ratio of distances. These forms lie *a priori* in the power of representation, and are actually the real [*das Reale*] in the subject, from which alone knowledge of the object can emerge (*forma dat esse rei*). The possibility of a system of perceptions, as belonging to the unity of experience, is, at the same time, the ground of their coexistence and of the succession of the appearances which they can produce (and which already have their place *a priori* in the understanding). It is an analytic proposition, according to the principle of identity, that the forms in the synthesis of intuition and the principles of their unity contain, at the same time, as in mathematics, the *construction* of these concepts. No Thaeatetus or skeptic can take issue with this.

22:12   Space is not an existing object of sensible intuition, nor – as little as time – is it something existing outside me, in which the manifold of perceptions is determinable as to its position (*iuxta et post se invicem ponendo*);[97] rather [space and time are] themselves intuitions given *a priori*, which contain in themselves, *synthetically a priori*, the formal principle of the composition of the manifold in appearance. As limitless with regard to their extensive magnitude, they hence contain unconditional unity (and thus, infinity); there is only one space and one time. Through this representation, all objects of empirical representation are connected into an absolute whole – all are representations through which the subject constitutes itself according to its possibility (by synthetic *a priori* propositions).

Space and time are not objects of intuition (for, in that case, there would have to be something previously given which grounded the subjective knowledge of the manifold of representations). They are, rather, pure intuition itself, as the subjective element of form (that is, the receptivity of being affected by an object of the senses) of objects as they appear to me, and are an infinite given whole of the manifold, as the basis of all perceptions – not as an aggregate, but in a system for the sake of the possibility of experience (Axioms of Intuition, Anticipations of Perception, etc.). The understanding constitutes itself to this philosophy, through concepts, and mathematically, through the construction of concepts.

Space and time are not *concepts* (*conceptus*) but pure sensible intuition (*intuitus*), each of which contains absolute unity in the composition of the manifold of representations, and, as the formal element of the manifold of this intuition, extends to infinity. It is not space as object which is intuited; space is, rather, the synthesis of the manifold in the representing subject itself. In this mode of representation, through which the subject constitutes itself [*breaks off*]

[*Top margin*]   22:13
Space is a quantum, which must always be represented as part of a greater quantum – hence, as infinite, and *given* as such. Progress in this quantum is not to be regarded as given; the progression, however, is.

[. . .]

[VIIth fascicle, sheet III, page 1]   22:28

Insertion

III

The unity of the manifold of intuition, in the manifold's composition (synthesis) *a priori* in the sensible representation of the object in space and time, together with the unconditional unity of space and time as a whole (there is only one space and one time) contain *axioms* of intuition in the latter's formal aspect. In conformity with which, the subject posits itself as object (*dabile*) and the supreme problem of transcendental philosophy arises: "How are synthetic propositions *a priori* possible?" [through] which the thinkable (*cogitabile*), as principle, is necessarily brought into focus.

Now this inquiry would be unanswerable, however, and the problem raised in it irresolvable, if a concept were to present its object directly (immediately); for that could only take place analytically, by the resolution of concepts, according to the principle of identity – which would yield no ampliative propositions, such as should form the desired synthetic judgment.

Now synthetic *a priori* judgments do exist, for example, those of mathematics: e.g. space contains three dimensions.*

Pure *a priori* intuition contains, in the subject as thing *in itself,* the acts of spontaneity and receptivity, and (through their combination to unity) the act of reciprocity – through the subjective determination of intuition, as object in appearance. Herein this = x is only a concept of absolute position: not itself a self-subsisting object, but only an idea of relations, to posit an object corresponding to the form of intuition; the object [is] made, in thoroughgoing determination, into an object of possible experi-
22:29 ence (its concept, as principle, [is] not derived from experience).[a] As in the Axioms of Intuition, the Anticipations of Perception etc., according to the system of the categories which lie at the foundation of knowledge of the given object.

Space and time are only subjective forms of sensible intuition, which contain the axioms: There is only one space and one time, in which an infinite aggregate of perceptions can be coordinated with one another into a system. They are both subject to the principle: Space and time are intuitions of a whole, which must always be thought of only as part of a greater whole – that is, they are infinite magnitudes. One sees from this that the manifold in space and time does not contain things in themselves, but only appearances, which are given synthetically *a priori,* and the[b] supreme problem of transcendental philosophy is: How are synthetic propositions *a priori* possible? Answer: They are possible only insofar as their object is restricted merely to appearance.

[*Margin* . . .]

22:30   [VIIth fascicle, sheet III, page 2]
Our knowledge contains synthetic propositions (of arithmetic and geometry) and, indeed, synthetic *a priori* propositions; how are such propositions possible? A question (the fundamental problem of transcendental philosophy).

---

*   *vide* 2nd Insertion.[98]

[a] There is no closing bracket in Kant's text. Lehmann places the bracket at the end of the next sentence, after *the given object.*
[b] Reading *die* for *deren.*

Only insofar as we regard the objects of knowledge as appearances, not as things in themselves, for otherwise we would express more in our judgment about these objects than is contained in their concept; on the other hand, if the intuition through which this object is given is repre- 22:31 sented merely as appearance, a synthetic judgment is framed by the understanding according to a principle of synthesis. The thing in itself (*objectum noumenon*) is here only a thought-entity without actuality (*ens rationis*), in order to designate a place for the representation of the subject. [There is] a different relation of intuition to the subject, according to the extent to which the subject is affected immediately by the object (and thus the object is represented as appearance in a specific form) or whether the power of representation is immediately aroused.

The representation of apperception which makes itself into an object of intuition contains a twofold act: first, that of positing itself (the act of spontaneity); and [second], that of being affected by objects and combining the manifold in representation to *a priori* unity (the act of receptivity). In the first case, the subject is an object for itself only in appearance which is *given a priori* as the formal element; in the second case, it is an aggregate of the material of perception insofar as that is *thought a priori* in space and time in the synthetic unity of the manifold of intuition.

Space and time are not objects of intuition, but are themselves intuition; they are, as such, not objects of sensible representations, valid in themselves, but only appearances, that is, subjective – but only as the appearance $= a$ or *non a* of positing or negating. The object of intuition as appearance is given only mediately (inasmuch as the subject is affected) as a sensible representation. To this there corresponds the idea of the object represented, and the ideality of the given representation as appearance contains the ground of the possibility of representing the object *a priori* in space and time.

The thing *in itself* is not an object given outside representation, but merely the position of a thought-entity which is thought of as corresponding to the object. So space and time are not *perceptible* objects but mere forms of intuition, which nevertheless make up a manifold contained *a priori* in the subject, and which supply synthetic *a priori* propositions to 22:32 geometry. Just this in philosophy.

{What I posit as in appearance, myself, or as thing in itself, or as [*breaks off*]}

Synthetic knowledge *a priori* from concepts, or from the substrate of concepts, space and time, as outside me in appearance. I posit myself as an object of intuition according to the formal principle of the determination of the subject of self-consciousness, and of combination to the unity of the object (space and time) – but, in virtue of this, as something *existing* in relation to myself, consequently as *appearance* (object of sensible intuition). I am the *cogitabile* according to a principle and likewise the *dabile* as object of my concept: the representation of the thing in itself and then in appearance.

Only the object in appearance can be determinable synthetically *a priori*, and form one of the subjects [*Fach*] of transcendental philosophy. N.B.: The thoroughgoing determination by perceptions, as a system of perceptions, is experience and can permit only approximation, not, however, apodictic certainty.

Not empirical intuition with consciousness (*perception*) but the pure intuition of the formal element of combination (composition) of the manifold according to a principle (law), is the thought-entity (*ens rationis*) which precedes everything material in the object, and subjectively, as appearance, forms a foundation.

The object = x (the *dabile*) presupposes the unity of the composition of the manifold according to its form (the *cogitabile*), that is, as a principle of the form of the object in appearance which underlies it *a priori*. The *thing in itself* is *ens rationis*.

That light be no discharging motion (*ejaculatio*) of a matter but an undulating motion (*undulatio*).⁹⁹

[Top margin]

22:33 We must, with respect to the intuition of an object in space or in time, at all times make the distinction between the representation of the thing *in itself* and that of the same thing as *appearance* – although we can attribute to the former no predicates, but, as = x, can regard it only as a correlate for the pure understanding (as *cogitabile*, not *dabile*) in which concepts, not things, are contrasted with one another. The proposition: All sense-objects are things in appearance (*objecta phaenomena*) to which a noumenon corresponds as the ground of their coordination; but no particular intuition (no *noumenon aspectabile*) corresponds to the latter, for that would be a contradiction with respect to the subjective element of the principle.

[Left margin]

All synthetic *a priori* judgments are determinations of the object in general with respect to its relations in space and in time. The latter are mere appearances, that is, representations which relate to the object of intuition insofar as [the subject] is affected by it, and are the subjective element of the subject's self-affection (formally). Judgments through concepts are analytic (by the principle of identity), those through predicates of intuition are synthetic. Intuition itself is either pure intuition *a priori* or empirical. The intuition contains the representation of the object either as appearance or as it is *in itself* (*objectum vel phaenomenon vel noumenon*).

The difference between an *ens per se* and the *ens a se*. The former is an object in appearance, which is affected by another; the latter an object which posits itself and which is a principle for its own determination (in space and time). The thing in itself $= x$ is not an object given to the senses, but only the principle of synthetic *a priori* knowledge of the manifold of sensible intuition in general, and of the law of its coordination. Space and time are only subjective forms of intuition, given *a priori*, and are thus only the object of the senses in appearance. The understanding combines this object according to the categories into an unconditional whole. The subject is not a particular thing but an idea. The principle of the ideality of space and time is the key to transcendental philosophy, by which alone knowledge can be increased synthetically and *a priori*, insofar as the objects of sense are represented merely as appearances. In which the thing *in itself* is not an existing being but $= x$, merely a principle.

22:34

A demiurge (creator of the world), author of matter.[100] If one goes by experience, and wishes to judge from it the character of the author, it appears that he has taken no account of happiness, but acts as a *despot*.

[. . .]

[VIIth fascicle, sheet III, page 4]

22:36

First, the representation of the object in intuition. Second, [the representation] of the intuition as appearance, of how the subject is affected by the sense-object (outwardly or inwardly). The affecting object is $= X$. The formal element of appearance is the position of the object in space and time; not of space itself as a thing in itself, as an apprehensible thing. Only through the representation of the object as appearance, not as thing in itself, are synthetic propositions *a priori* possible according to the formulae of transcendental philosophy, and it is likewise necessary for the knowledge of the science of nature as a doctrine of experience. Space and time are *a priori* intuitions but not given objects of intuition.

Without laws no experience can take place and, without a principle of the combination of the manifold in *a priori* intuition, no law. For knowledge [*Wissen*] exceeds judgment and only makes the latter capable of thoroughgoing determination; the receptivity of certainty in synthetic *a priori* judgments only takes place if the objects of intuition first qualify for this, merely as appearance in my consciousness of myself. For this constitutes the formal element which, merely in the understanding, free from everything empirical, posits [*aufstellt*] rather than apprehends a manifold of intuition inasmuch as it emerges from the subject's activity. Hence space is not an act of apprehension •of the object of intuition• for it is in itself not a thing or object [*Sache*] and positions in it, as points, cannot be accumulated – they all coalesce into one point.

22:37

175

Someone said that the most beautiful statues are already present in the block of marble; it is only necessary to remove parts of it, etc.[101] – that is, one can represent through imagination the statue within and the sculptor [really] inserts it. It is only the appearance of a body. Space and time are products (but primitive products) of our own imagination, hence self-created intuitions, inasmuch as the subject affects itself and is thereby appearance, not thing [*Sache*] in itself. The material element – the thing in itself – is = X, the mere representation of one's own activity.

Space and time are sensible objects in appearance, not representation of an object *in itself.* It is the coordination of the manifold of intuition under one concept of empirical representation, insofar as both are made by the subject, rather than given to it, and the latter presents itself and constitutes an absolute whole. Hereupon is grounded the problem of transcendental philosophy: "How are synthetic propositions *a priori* possible?" The solution is: through the representation of objects of intuition in appearance, not according to what they might be in themselves, but what they are for the subject by which they are affected – that is, formally, not according to what the object might be in itself, for such a question contains a contradiction. Space and time are not apprehensible objects, but mere modifications of the power of representation in which the concept of a thing in itself is merely a thought-object (*ens rationis*) and serves as an object = x in order to represent the object of intuition in contrast to appearance. The thing in itself is not something given (*dabile*) but what is thought merely as corresponding (notwithstanding that it remains absent), belonging to the division. It stands only like a cipher [*Ziffer*].

22:38   [*Left margin*]

That propositions concerning space and time present objects only as appearances and, for that reason, *a priori*. In themselves, they are not objects but determinations of the subject in respect to synthetic *a priori* knowledge as transcendental philosophy.

One cannot have a surfeit with respect to science, but one can well do so with respect to ethics as worldly wisdom.

The different functions of the determination of the objects of intuitions make the rules for nature and the basis of the possibility of experience. Space as an object of the senses is subject to the transcendental philosophical principle of the laws of the square ratio, and it is necessitated so to intuit.[*f*]

[*f*]   Reading of last word uncertain.

Wisdom is the highest principle of reason. One cannot become yet wiser. Only the supreme being is wise. The smartness [*Naseweisheit*] of children. *Sciolus*, a sciolist, or who knows something about everything.

Spontaneity and receptivity with reaction at the same time.

(Not organized matter, for that is a contradiction, but organic body.)

Of the necessity of spiritual forces for the sake of organic bodies and even organic systems; because one must attribute an understanding to their cause in which the subject is thought as a simple being (of the sort which matter or an element of matter cannot be).

Demiurge, universal world-spirit.

No phenomenon under laws can be given as demonstrable by experience unless the phenomenon has been previously determined *a priori* thereto, for experience is *omnitudo determinationis*, which is never demonstrable through the completeness of perceptions (which must be infinitely manifold). So an *a priori* principle for the possibility of experience is required.

That which is given originally in pure intuition (*dabile*); next, that which is in the composition of the manifold, the thinkable (*cogitabile*) for sense-perceptions (*apprehensibile*), or the complex of the manifold in *a priori* appearance.

According to Meiners,[102] ethics is the *metaphysics* of *morals;* not yet worldly wisdom but the theory which leads to it.   22:39

Wisdom, unwisdom (*mechanism*) and folly belong to ethics.

That concerns *purposes*. Prudence is directed only to means (*nullum numen[d] abest si sit prudentia*)[103] and [is] no part of ethics.

[VIIth fascicle, sheet IV, page 1]

Insertion IV

[. . .]

Every proposition (*propositio*) presupposes a judgment (*iudicium*),   22:40 which, undetermined as to what should become its subject or predicate, precedes it. The proposition was problematic, becomes assertoric through the determination of the subject (the judgment becomes a proposition), and, as a proposition given *a priori*, apodictic – that is, combined with the consciousness of its necessity (which can also be called universal validity).

All analytic judgments, that is, those which are valid according to the principle of identity, are also called discursive judgments, because they contain nothing further in the predicate than that which was already

---

[d]   Reading with Reicke *numen*. Lehmann reads *nomen*.

thought in the concept of the subject; those, on the other hand, which go beyond the concept of the subject and predicate of it something which was not contained identically in the concept of the object, are synthetic, and, if they are also valid *a priori*, the question arises: "How are synthetic propositions *a priori* possible?"

Pure mathematics with its nonempirical intuitions can, in any case, already make clear that such propositions do exist and, if it is a matter of explaining the ground of possibility of these propositions (which although not nonsensible are yet independent of experience), [then] this takes place in relation to the pure intuitive representations, space and time, which make such objects representable as contained in appearance, not as things in themselves.

That space and time are not apprehensible objects – that they are not objects of perception whose systematic connection could be termed experience – is independently clear; that, however, synthetic *a priori* judgments must lie at the foundation, and that, for this purpose, sensible representations must not be thought otherwise but *indirectly* (that is, not as knowledge of objects in themselves, but only their intuition as appearance, which alone can be given *a priori*) is clear from the fact that, without taking such a mode of representation for its foundation, even experience itself would not be possible.

22:41 The object of the senses, represented as what it is *in itself* in comparison with the same object *in appearance*, founds the possibility of synthetic *a priori* judgments.

[*Top margin*]
Space with its manifold cannot be apprehended, but is apperceived as the original consciousness of oneself, as positing such a manifold. So it is only appearance of the object = X.

[. . .]

22:43 [VII fascicle, sheet IV, page 3]
The first act of the faculty of representation (*facultas repraesentativa*) is the representation of oneself (*apperceptio*) through which the subject makes itself into an object (*apperceptio simplex*); and its representation is intuition (*intuitus*), not yet concept (*conceptus*): that is, representation of an individual (*repraesentatio singularis*), not yet that which is common to many (*nota, i.e. repraesentatio pluribus communis*), that is, a generally valid representation, which is to be encountered in many [things], in contrast to the [representation of the] individual.

Space and time are two relations of the objects of pure intuition which contain *a priori* principles of their coordination as alongside one another and successive (*iuxta et post se invicem positorum*) – hence, merely their formal element; and they exist only in the intuiting subject, as conditions of the composition of this manifold, each represented as unconditional unity – hence also as infinite magnitudes – whose parts, however, are not objects of perception (empirical representation with consciousness) but are in themselves nothing (existing) but pure formal intuition, that is, *appearance.*

What is an object in appearance, however, in contrast to the same object but as *thing in itself?*

This difference does not lie in the objects, but merely in the difference of the relation in which the subject apprehending the sense-object is affected for the production of the representation in itself.

That space and time, in the manifold which these representations contain (for they are not apprehensible things, but nothing other than representations themselves) must be thought in twofold relations to the subject: first, insofar as they are intuitions (and sensible ones, indeed); second, in the way in which their manifold makes synthetic propositions *a priori* possible in general, and so founds a principle of synthetic *a priori* propositions (but, hereby, also a transcendental philosophy) without which this necessary science would not take place. 22:44

Now the latter is only possible for the reason that these objects are regarded in dual rational relations.

Space and time are intuitions with the dynamic function of positing a manifold of intuition as appearance (*dabile*); thus also an *aspectabile,* as appearance, which precedes all apprehensive representation (perception as empirical representation with consciousness) and is thought synthetically *a priori,* according to a principle as thoroughly determining (*intuitus quem sequitur conceptus*) in which the subject posits itself in the collective unity of the manifold of intuition.

The latter is, *a priori,* as unconditional unity, the formal element of *appearance,* in contrast with the *thing in itself* = x, which is not itself a separate [*absonderliches*] object, but is only a particular *relation* (*respectus*) in order to constitute oneself as object – from which the problem of transcendental philosophy: "How are synthetic propositions in relations of space and time possible?" emerges.

Both combined together, yield to absolute (unlimited) whole of intuition, which, yet, is always possible only as part of a yet greater whole – hence it is not an object (*dabile*): a *cogitabile* which yet is not, as a whole, *dabile.*

[. . .]

[Xth fascicle, sheet XIX, page 2] 22:413

[Insertion V]

The first act of knowledge is the verb: I am, – self-consciousness, for I, [as] subject, am an object to myself. In this, however, there lies a relation which precedes all determination of the subject, namely, the relation of intuition to the concept, in which the I is taken doubly (that is, in a double meaning) insofar as I posit myself: that is, on the one hand, as thing in itself (*ens per se*), and, secondly, as object of intuition; to be precise, either objectively as appearance, or as constituting myself *a priori* into a thing (that is, as thing [*Sache*] in itself).

Consciousness of itself (*apperceptio*) is an act through which the subject makes itself in general into an object. It is not yet a *perception* (*apprehensio simplex*), that is, not a sensible representation, for which it is required that the subject is affected by some object and that intuition becomes empirical; it is, rather, pure intuition, which, under the designations of space and time, contain merely the formal element of the composition (*coordinatio et subordinatio*) of the manifold of intuition, and which, thereby [contain] an *a priori* principle of the synthetic knowledge of the manifold – which, for this reason, represents the object in appearance.

The difference of the manifold of intuition – whether it represents the object in appearance, or according to that which it is *in itself* – signifies nothing other than whether the formal element is thought as merely subjectively valid (that is, for the subject) or objectively, valid for everybody; which amounts to the question whether the position should express a noun or a verb.

The intuition of space, with its three dimensions, and that of time with its single one, furnish synthetic *a priori* propositions, as principles – but not for sense-objects; for they are not apprehensible things which present themselves to intuition (empirically) and their representation with consciousness is not perception. Just as little [is] the system of the aggregate of such presumed perceptions experience; rather, it is a whole of intuition which, objectively, is merely appearance, to which the object as thing in itself is thought as corresponding merely in the idea.

That space and time are nothing existing *outside* the subject, much less still *inner* determinations of things, but merely thought-objects (*entia rationis*).

What comes first is that space and time (and the object in them) is given (*dabile*) in indeterminate but determinable intuition (that is, in appearance), and so is thought as a possible whole (*cogitabile*). Both together, however, found a principle for synthetic *a priori* propositions, which is called transcendental philosophy, and which [forms] the transition from the metaphysical foundations of natural science, through which the subject constitutes itself into an object of experience for physics; the latter does not introduce thoroughgoing determination from experience, but for it, as a system of perceptions. The subjective element of intuition, as the latter's formal element, is the object in appearance as it emerges *a priori* from synthetic representation, according to this principle. The thing in itself is a thought-object (*ens rationis*) of the connection of this manifold whole into the unity to which the subject constitutes itself. The object in itself = x is the sense-object *in itself,* but as another mode of representation, not as another object.

One cannot, in the synthesis of intuition, commence from empirical intuition with consciousness (from perception), for in that case the form would be missing. So one begins from an *a priori* principle of what is formal in intuition, and proceeds to the principle of the possibility of experience: does not draw anything *from* experience, and posits oneself.

All existence of consciousness in space and time is mere appearance of inner and outer sense, and, as such, a synthetic principle of intuition takes place *a priori,* and affects itself as a thing existing in space and time. The subject is here the thing in itself because it contains spontaneity. Appearance is receptivity. The thing in itself is not another object, but another mode of making oneself into an object. The intelligible object is not an *objectum noumenon,* but the *act* of the understanding which *makes* the object of sensible intuition into a mere phenomenon. 22:415

It [namely, space] is something given *a priori* (*dabile*), that is, not a mere object of intuition but intuition itself and not merely a thinkable object. It is not an *ens* (something existing) nor either a *non ens* (something unthinkable) but a principle of possibility.

What is to be known through sense (that is, perceived) must affect our sense, and the intuition of the object which arises from it is appearance (thing in itself).

Space is not something apprehensible (not an object of perception, that is, of empirical representation with consciousness). Neither is it something given outside the thinking subject, but only an aggregate of representations which are in us; not something in whose concept there is a contradiction, but which, however, is also not nothing, and, where there is only space for things, but not something which fills it, nothing [*breaks off*]

Universalitas – universality
Universitas – totality
The thing in itself, which corresponds to a thing in appearance, is a mere thought-object, but yet not a nonentity [*Unding*].

[Xth fascicle, sheet XIX, page 3]
All our knowledge consists of two components: intuition and concept, which lie *a priori* at the foundation of knowledge; and the understanding is that form of the connection of both into the unity of their manifold in the subject, through which that which was thought subjectively is represented objectively, as given (*cogitabile quatenus est dabile*).

The first act, proceeding from the representation of an object of intuition to the concept, and so [to progress] through reciprocal relation, is the

22:416 constitution of the relation of these representations into synthetic unity (not logical unity, according to the principle of identity, but metaphysical, according to the principle of transcendental philosophy – •the possibility• of synthetic cognitions *a priori*); it is not the act of apprehension of the manifold given in intuition •(*apprehensio simplex*)• but the principle of the autonomy of making oneself into an object, as given in appearance •(*objectum phaenomenon*)•. In this, the thing [*Sache*] in itself = x (*objectum noumenon*) is only a thought in order to represent the object merely as appearance (thus as indirectly knowable) and to present in intuition its[^e] existence in space and time (which are not real relations but mere forms thereof).

Space and time are, indeed, not things in themselves (*entia per se*), but mere forms of the complex of representations in the coordination of the manifold of intuition, as sensible representation; and each of them contains unconditional unity. There is only one space and one time, each of which, as limitless (negatively infinite) [contains] a sensible intuition in a manifold not of perception (empirical representation with consciousness) but merely the complex of all relations in sensible representation [*breaks off*]

Intuition and concept are the two modes of representation •of a thing in general,• whose manifold is given to sense *a priori* (that is, as pure intuition) prior to all perception (empirical knowledge with consciousness) as the formal element of the composition of the manifold according to the principle of its synthetic unity, and which is thought through the understanding. •Both can be either pure or empirical. The pure concepts are principles, which precede *a priori* all intuition. Pure intuition (outer as well as inner) is a principle, corresponding to the discursive principle, of *a*
22:417 *priori* knowledge insofar as it is synthetic. These two principles belong to transcendental philosophy and space and time are their objects.• Their object in this representation is not given as an existing thing (not a *dabile* but *cogitabile*) which inheres in the subject, and is represented merely as the formal element of appearance in an absolute whole of the manifold of intuition – hence, as infinite. There is one space and one time.

The objects of representation in intuition are not apprehensible objects outside this object, but the relation of objects to the subject – not as things in themselves = x but as appearances.

[*Margin*]
22:418 [. . .] By the word "soul" is understood not merely a living or animated substance, but something which animates another substance (matter). Every animal has a soul (as an immaterial principle) and parts of animals still appear to demonstrate a *vita propria*[104] when they are separated. Plants

[^e]: ᵉ Reading *die* for *von der*.

permit grafts, and hence aggregates without a system. The organ in an organic body which one calls "nerve" is the seat of sensation and is called "soul," of which there is always only one, so that, when the body is divided, another atom, in its turn, carries out the task of the soul.

First, that we posit a manifold of the intuition of ourself. Second, insofar as we posit something outside ourselves, by which we are affected (that is, as appearance in space and time). Third, that the understanding posits synthetically, according to a principle, the manifold of intuition (that is, connects it together to the unity of the intuition of the manifold in a whole) and progresses to thoroughgoing determination. The determinable is the thing in itself; it is what is given through the understanding and posited (*dabile*) synthetically, *a priori*, according to its form; the manifold of intuition is the assignable. The principle of the possibility of experience (progress to physics).

[Xth fascicle, sheet XIX, page 4]

(1) The consciousness of myself as subject (according to the rule of identity). (2) Knowledge of oneself through intuition and concept. (3) The positing of oneself: in space and time. This positing takes place according to *a priori* principles and contains merely the formal element of the coexistence and succession of the manifold of intuition. (4) Intuition is either pure or empirical intuition; the former alone contains synthetic *a priori* judgments for sense-objects, and thus the theme of transcendental philosophy, which contains the problem: "How are synthetic judgments *a priori* possible?" (5) The solution is: They are only possible insofar as the objects of the senses are represented only as appearances, not as things in themselves. The existence of the manifold in space and time (*dabile*) stands under the condition of the formal element of the coordination of the manifold as appearance – that is, as subjective mode of representation of the way in which the subject is affected, not according to what it is in itself; for it is this formal element alone of which a synthetic *a priori* principle is possible. Empirical synthesis through perceptions can yield no *a priori* principle •(nothing universal)• of the kind which the principle of relations in space and time must have. 22:419

All of our faculty of knowledge consists in two acts: intuition and concepts; both, as pure (that is, not empirical) representations (for the latter already require an influence on the senses – that is, perceptions, which already presuppose the former representations) emerge from the faculty of representation, from formation [*Gestaltung*] (*species*) and thought; and the places in which we posit the objects of these representations are space and time, which, independently, have no reality (existence) but are mere forms which inhere in the subject (*entia rationis*). Though limitless as to their quantitative relation, they contain, with respect to the qualitative, however, an inner infinite manifold. 22:420

All my faculty of representation (*facultas repraesentativa*), which consists of intuition and concept, commences from consciousness of oneself, which, first, is called logical (explicative, according to the rule of identity), then, however, is also a metaphysical principle of synthetic *a priori* knowledge – that is, it is ampliative, and goes beyond the given concept thereby that the subject *posits* itself in space- and time-relations, as pure (not empirical) intuitions, which, however, are only objects in appearance. Hence merely subjectively, not objectively, determining – not that which is itself object, but only the form of •the intuition of• the object. The transcendental mode of representation is that of intuition as appearance; the transcendent, that of the object as *thing in itself,* which is only an *ens rationis* (that is, only thought-object) and, determining, not objectively but only subjectively, is a *conceptus infinitus* (*indefinitus*).

Our sensible intuition is, initially, not perception (empirical representation with consciousness), for a principle of positing oneself and of becoming conscious of this position precedes it; and the form[s] of this positing of the manifold, as thoroughly combined, are the pure intuitions, which are called space and time (outer and inner intuition) and which, as unlimited according to concepts (*indefinita*), are represented in appearance as infinitely positive (*infinita*).

Consciousness of oneself is (1) logical, according to the analytical principle, (2) metaphysical, in the coordination (*complexus*) of the manifold given in self-intuition – (a) through concepts, (b) through construction of concepts which form the intuition of the subject and a mathematical representation.

22:421 N.B. Transcendental philosophy does not contain merely the complex of synthetic *a priori* propositions in a complete system, but contains such propositions from concepts, not through the latter's construction; for then it is mathematics. The concept of an all-filling, all-penetrating, moving matter lies already in the fact that, otherwise, space would not be perceived – and, hence, not be an object.

[*Left margin*]

Life, however, stems from a distinct substance, from an *archeus*[105] (animated matter is contradictory), and organic bodies stand, through the ether, in the relation of a higher organ toward one another.

We have to do only with synthetic *a priori* knowledge, with the composition of the manifold of intuition in space and time, and with an object which we make ourselves, as spectators and, at the same time, originators.

That our representations are not produced by the objects, but that the latter conform to the faculty of representation and its synthesis.
•The thing in itself = x is a mere thought-object (*ens rationis ratiocinantis*).•

Of the mechanical powers which are only possible by means of the dynamic powers (primarily attraction) and are indirectly machines.

•The subjective element of intuition as appearance is the *a priori* form, the thing in itself is = x. *Transcendental* philosophy.•

1. To posit oneself.
2. To posit for oneself an object of intuition, not of empirical sense-intuition, but *a priori*, according to the formal element, space and time.
3. Subjectively as appearance prior to all perception.
4. Synthetic *a priori* propositions (transcendental philosophy) which contain the possibility of experience under a principle.

Note. The difference between the representation of a thing in itself = x and that in the mode of which the thing in itself appears to the subject – *dabile* and *cogitabile*. Both together *repraesentabile*. Unity (logical), according to the principle of identity, and metaphysical (not opposed as *a* and *non a*, but as *a* and -*a*, *oppositio s. correlatio realis*) in the subject.

[. . .]

[VIIth fascicle, sheet VII, page 1]   22:76

Insertion VII

The pure intuitions of space and time prove that we must present a manifold of representations synthetically and formally into a whole (that is, into the unity of composition in consciousness). [And this we must do] *a priori;* prior, that is, to all empirical representation with consciousness (i.e. prior to perception). These pure intuitions have as their object nothing perceptible (existing) or real, but merely a form, a form which we ourselves must make in order to become conscious of this object. We must present [the manifold of representations] both as an infinite complex (*complexus*) of representations in a whole and as a formal ideality of relations, preceding all material reality of perceptions (*aspectabile ceu dabile*).

Space and time are, •in fact,• not objects of intuition but •merely its subjective• forms which do not exist outside our representations. They are only given in the subject, •that is,• their representation is an act of the subject itself and a product of its imagination. •For the subject's sense, however, the cause of perception is the object in appearance (*phaenomenon*)• which is not derived (*repraesentatio derivativa*) but original (*originaria*). The principle [of this original appearance] does not found metaphysics but transcendental philosophy and leads to a twofold task: (1) How are synthetic *a priori* principles possible from intuitions? (2) How are synthetic *a priori* principles possible from concepts?

Thus transcendental philosophy likewise founds mathematics by its use

22:77

of the latter as instrument. •But it does not do so directly, for it would be a contradiction to make directly into a concept that which is merely knowledge from the constitution of concepts.•

The first act of the faculty of representation is the consciousness of myself •which is a merely logical act underlying all further representation,• through which the subject makes itself into an object. The second act is to determine this object as pure *a priori intuition* and also as *concept;* that is, [to progress] to knowledge, as the complex (*complexus*) of representations, completely determined according to a principle of the categories: the system of the categories of quality, quantity, etc., and thus to represent the manifold in appearance as belonging to the unity of experience (as existing).*

22:78

What is given first to the power of representation is space and time, and the existence of things in space and in time as the complex (*complexus*) of a manifold of intuition, infinitely extended in two directions. The objects of this representation are not existing things (*non sunt entia*), yet nor are they nonentities (*nonentia*). For they are not •objects of perception,• objectively •outside the representing subject, but are our representation itself,• that is, are only subjectively given in •the subject's• representation. Their unlimited magnitude is not universality (*universalitas conceptus*) but totality (*omnitudo •complexus universitas•*); not a merely thinkable whole •according to concepts• (*cogitabile*) but given as an object (*dabile*). Progress to the knowledge of it is the transition from metaphysics to transcendental philosophy, which does not advance analytically from concepts to intuitions, but only constitutes itself synthetically and *a priori* from intuition into a system according to a principle.

[The subject's] consciousness of itself (*apperceptio*), insofar as it is affected, is the representation of the object in appearance. However, insofar as it is the subject which affects itself, it is equally to be regarded as the object in itself $= x$.

[*Right margin*]

There is no spontaneity in the organization of matter but only receptivity from an immaterial principle of the formation of matter into bodies, which indicates [*geht auf*] the universe, and contains a thoroughgoing relation of means to ends. An understanding (which, however, is not a world-soul) [is] the principle of the system, not a principle of aggregation.

Mathematics is indirectly founded by philosophy.

Even the organism is contained in the consciousness of oneself. The subject makes its own form in accordance with *a priori* purposes.

---

*   *Omnimoda determinatio est existentia.*

Instinct is an autonomous instance of the dynamical principle which produces [*hinwirkt auf*] a mechanism of self-preservation. •Unity of purpose.
Spontaneity. Vegetative life.•

Metaphysics and transcendental philosophy differ from each other in the   22:79
respect that the *former* contains already given *a priori* principles of natural
science, the latter, on the other hand, such as hold within themselves the
very possibility of metaphysics and of its synthetic *a priori* principles.

[In transcendental philosophy] one does not begin from objects, but
rather from the system of the possibility of constituting one's own thinking
subject, and one is oneself the originator of one's power of thought.

Space and time are forms of the receptivity of our representations.

[VIIth fascicle, sheet VII, page 2]

The faculty of representation proceeds from the *consciousness* of myself
(*apperceptio*), and this is a merely logical act, an act of thought, through
which no object is yet given by me. {For knowledge, what is thinkable
(*cogitabile*) requires an object (*dabile*), namely, something which corresponds as *intuition* to a concept. If the intuition is *pure*, that is, as yet not
mingled with *perception* (empirical representation with consciousness) then
the act by which the subject makes itself into an object, is metaphysical.

The act: I think myself, is merely subjective; I am an object of apprehension for myself.}

In the proposition: I am thinking, because it is completely identical,
no progress, no synthetic judgment is given to me; for it is tautological
and the alleged inference: I think, *therefore* I am, is no inference. The
first act of knowledge, rather, is: I am an object of thought (*cogitabile*)
and intuition (*dabile*) for myself, initially as *pure* (not empirical) representation, which knowledge is called *a priori*. This act contains as the *formal*
element of this unity a principle of the connection of the manifold of
these representations, independent of all perception •(the material element of the representations).•

Space and time are pure intuitions. Each carries with it the absolute   22:80
unity of its representation, that is, unlimitedness. There is one space and
one time, and if we speak of spaces and times, we mean thereby parts of
the unlimited magnitude of a thought-object (*ens rationis*). But it is not
therefore a nonentity (*non ens*), something impossible, to which no representation corresponds. Its science emerges from metaphysics if it carries
discursive universality in its concept, but from transcendental philosophy,
if it carries intuitive universality (totality). The latter must emerge synthetically from pure intuition, not analytically, that is, by the principle of the
identity of concepts.

Transcendental philosophy, however, is the science of a system of *synthetic
a priori* knowledge from concepts; for it is philosophy, whose principle lies

in the general problem: "How are synthetic *a priori* propositions *from concepts* possible, •how are they possible from pure intuition•?"

Synthetic *a priori* propositions are given in intuition, namely, in pure *mathematics*. The latter consists entirely in such propositions; and, if one attempted to progress in this science by proceeding analytically from

22:81 concepts, one would breach its principles, •that is, its formal element as a science within philosophy,•* although not demonstrating falsely.

[*Bottom margin*]

Transcendental *philosophy* contains the principles of synthetic *a priori* judgments from concepts. That which contains synthetic *a priori* judgments from pure intuitions alone is not philosophy, but pure mathematics. Nevertheless, a philosophical *use* of mathematics is possible, as Newton has established in his immortal work: *Philosophiae naturalis principia mathematica*. Mathematics thereby becomes an *instrument* of philosophy, without itself being philosophy; and the principles of this instrumental doctrine belong to transcendental philosophy also. The key to this problem lies in the principle of the determination of objects (their intuition) in space and time, which [contain] identically in themselves the existence of their objects in *thoroughgoing determination*. For *omnimoda determinatio est existentia*, even if that is only an idea. The phenomena of affection by light and heat (objective and subjective representation) provide *a priori*, not matter, but twofold motion.

[*Left margin*]

Analytic universality (*universalitas*). Synthetic universality, totality (*universitas rerum*).

Entia sunt vel res vel intelligentiae.[107] The latter are either pure intelligences or things which stand in reciprocity with them (*inhabitantes*), *animantia. Omnitudo conceptus est universalitas – omnitudo complexus est universitas.*[108]*ʄ* Totality and universality.

I, the subject, am an object to myself, that is, [the] object of my self. The

22:82 manifold of representations by which I determine myself stands under an *a priori* principle of self-determination, which is a principle not of apprehension but of apperception, for the purpose of the synthetic unity of space and time. The *consciousness* of myself is logical merely and leads to no object; it is, rather, a mere determination of the subject in accordance with the rule of identity. Only a synthetic *a priori* knowledge which progresses from metaphysics to transcendental philosophy opens the way to

* Euclid's proposition regarding two parallel lines which are intersected by a third can be proved quite rigorously by a philosophical treatment.[106]

ʄ In the text: *omnitudo complexus est universalitas.*

transcendental philosophy. But the manifold of intuition in space and time, being a pure, not empirical, intuition, gives objects in appearance which = x. The representation of space and time is a propaedeutic to transcendental philosophy, not yet transcendental philosophy itself. For that, the question: How are synthetic *a priori* propositions possible? is required. There are synthetic *a priori* principles of the determination of the object in space and time, that is, from intuitions. But there are also such principles from concepts. The latter belong to transcendental philosophy, and this in turn to the possibility of experience as *omnimoda determinatio.*

I am an object of myself and of my representations. That there is something else outside me is my own product. I make myself. Space cannot be perceived. (But neither can the moving force in space be perceived, insofar as it is represented as actual without a body which exercises it.) We make everything ourselves.

[VIIth fascicle, sheet VII, page 3]

The understanding begins with the consciousness of itself (*apperceptio*) and performs thereby a logical act. To this the manifold of outer and inner intuition attaches itself serially, and the subject makes itself into an object in a limitless sequence.

This intuition is not empirical. It is not perception, that is, not derived from a sense-object, but determines the object by the subject's *a priori* act, [through which] it is the owner and originator of its own representations. With its power of representation [the subject] then advances from the metaphysical foundations to transcendental philosophy which establishes a system of synthetic knowledge from intuitions, not merely from concepts. The system [yields] philosophical knowledge for the sake of mathematics (not a philosophical mathematics – for that would be a self-contradiction). The quantitative unity of the manifold and its relations are therein united with the qualitative unity in one principle, and mathematics becomes available as a tool for philosophy. 22:83

Synthetic *a priori* propositions are only indirectly possible in philosophy, namely, in relation to objects of pure intuition in space and time, and to those objects' *existence* in space and time as their thoroughgoing determination (*omnimoda determinatio est existentia*). But the objects of sense are given in space and time only as things in appearance (*phaenomena*); that is, they are, by their form, not objects given purely and simply, but only subjectively, under the limitation of their principle.

First, the consciousness of myself (*sum*), which is logical (*cogito*) – not an inference (*ergo sum*), but by the rule of identity (*sum cogitans*). In this act of representation (of thought) no synthesis of the manifold of intuition is yet met with; it merely contains an analytic judgment. The first progress of the faculty of representation (*facultas repraesentativa*) is that from pure thought in general to pure intuition: space and time, which contain synthetic *a priori* knowledge. They are not objects (*entia*), but mere forms of *a priori* intuition.

Space and time are not objects of the perception of given things, nor are they *concepts* of the composition of the (thought-) manifold in them; they are, rather, pure outer and inner intuitions, as *individual* (not general) representations, and each of them is *infinite*. From this there follows the existence of things in space and time, as existence in *appearance* only (that is, as merely subjective, not directly and objectively given as something outside representation). The infinity of both [i.e. space and time] (*unitas quantitativa*) is combined with the *qualitativa* in a single concept.

On the Newtonian concept: *Philosophiae naturalis principia mathematica.* Transcendental philosophy renders such a [*philosophia*] possible without μετάβασις εἰς ἄλλο γένος; because one determines space for the forces – that space in which they act, and the laws according to which they do so. The forces already lie in the representation of space.

One may also postulate *a priori*, although only conditionally, the existence of a light-matter, spread through the entire universe; for otherwise we would not perceive objects in space at all distances. According to the rule of identity. In the case of heat, it is not necessary that such a matter should exist, for heat is something merely subjective, and the expansion of bodies through heat exists only for the eye, that is, for light (consequently, is only inferred as the effect of a cause).

Discursive and intuitive universality. The former in concepts, the latter in intuition. Logical, metaphysical, transcendental – cosmological universality (not totality, *universalitas*, but *universitatis*).

Of natural science from dynamical and, subsequently, physical-mechanical principles – because one begins from the universe and its production. Matter which makes space an object of sense, that is, first makes it perceptible. The existence of things in space. That which precedes all physics. Ether repulsive. Ponderable material.

Light-centers (suns); eccentric planets (comets) and their appearance by their tails which, like the zodiacal light, render visible the scattered particles, these atoms, in the sky.

[*Right margin*]

The metaphysical foundations of natural science contain the principles of progression to physics.

Mathematical principles of philosophy are a contradiction in the subclause of the judgment. A philosophical use of mathematics can, however, be made *indirectly* if the qualitative relation is combined with the quantitative, the dynamical with the mechanical; for example, central forces by circular motion (which, however, require attraction by the thread). [One may] postulate original attractive forces, belonging to matter in space, and only activated through motion.

The logical consciousness of myself (*sum*) contains no determination but the real consciousness of intuition (*apperceptio*).

"I am" is the logical act which precedes all representation of the object; it is a *verbum* by which I posit myself. I exist in space and time and thoroughly determine my existence in space and time (*omnimoda determinatio est existentia*) as appearance according to the formal conditions for the connection of the manifold of intuition; I am both an outer and inner object for myself. What is subjective in the determination of myself is, equally, objective by the rule of identity, according to a principle of synthetic *a priori* knowledge. There is only one space and one time, each of which is represented in intuition [as] an unconditional intuitive whole, that is, as infinite. My synthetic *a priori* knowledge as transcendental philosophy is a transition from the metaphysical foundations of natural science to physics, that is, to the possibility of *experience.*

[Main text, between the lines]
The first synthetic act of consciousness is that through which the subject makes itself an object of intuition; not logically (analytically) according to the rule of identity, but metaphysically (synthetically).

[Top margin]
Intuition and concept: The first is for representation of the senses, the second for the understanding, which combines the manifold of intuition according to a principle. Appearance is the subjective and formal element of intuition, as the subject affects itself or is affected by the object. Space and time, united together, make up pure intuition; both [are] infinite, but only subjective. Only what is formal in appearance can be counted as   22:86 knowledge *a priori.* The object (*materiale*) = x is only the ideal element of composition. Not apprehensible. *Cogitabile – dabile.*

Note. Of the autonomy of the concept of the organization of matter, without which we ourselves would have no organs.

[VIIth fascicle, sheet VII, page 4]
The representations of sense-objects do not enter the subject; rather, they and the principles of their mutual connection emerge from the subject [*wirken hinaus*] for the purpose of knowledge of the subject, and to think objects as appearances.

The transition from the metaphysical foundations of natural science to transcendental philosophy and from it to physics.

Unity of *space,* unity of *time,* and the unity of both in *thoroughgoing determination. Existence* of objects in space and time. The function of the *categories* to constitute oneself (the subject) as an object. These forms of synthesis in appearance are original, not derivative. They are not objective things, but relations of the subject to the power of thought, or vice versa. How are synthetic cognitions *a priori* possible from *concepts,* how from *intuitions,* and how from both together?

Existence in space and time, which stems solely from the subject's power of representation (is made by itself), is contained in a system according to the principle of *transcendental philosophy* as absolute synthetic unity. It is contained not as an aggregate of empirical representations, but as belonging to the unity of experience and to the possibility of the transition from metaphysics to physics. The latter determines itself in its form according to the system of categories. Problem: How are synthetic cognitions *a priori* possible?

22:87 Space and time are pure intuitions, not perceptions (empirical representations with consciousness); that is, contained *a priori* as intuition in representation, but are not existing things connected with each other in relations of coexistence and succession. The subject makes this manifold of representations, namely its complex as an object in appearance, be it inner or outer, according to the principle of transcendental philosophy.

The consciousness of myself is not yet an act of self-determination for the knowledge of an object, but is only the modality of knowledge in general by which a subject makes itself into an object in general; it is what is formal in intuition in general. Space and time, each of which is an absolute whole, together with the undetermined manifold, are what is given (*dabile*); to which something else is juxtaposed as what is thinkable (*cogitabile*). The representation as an act of knowledge is then called appearance, which contains a coordination (*complexus*) according to the principles of positing oneself.

The transition from the metaphysical foundations of natural science to physics lies between the two limit-points of a doctrinal system. This relation [contains] the connection of the one with the other according to a principle of synthetic *a priori* knowledge. It founds the transition from one science (*metaphysics*) to the other (namely, *transcendental philosophy*), not analytically (that is, merely logically and *explicatively* from the principle of identity) but *ampliatively,* in real relationship.

By transcendental philosophy we mean the principle of *synthetic a priori* knowledge from *concepts;* thus a principle of *philosophical* knowledge, not of mathematical knowledge by the construction of concepts. Transcendental philosophy indeed belongs to metaphysics insofar as it proceeds from the latter; it is, however, no part of metaphysics but an independent science, containing the conditions of progress to the possibility of physics (as a doctrine of experience).

[Bottom margin]   22:88

Space and time are objects in appearance; the categories, because we ourselves posit them through the understanding, objects in themselves. *Experience* as *appearance*. Both direct and indirect, but *a priori*. (1) for experience, (2) from it.

Transcendental philosophy is the science of synthetic, not analytic, *a priori* [knowledge] from concepts, not from their construction. In the presentation of space and time as *a priori* intuition [there is] absolute unity, and thus something infinite. By *complexus*, unconditional unity; by the appearance of the subjective, determination as appearance according to its form. (1) Metaphysical; (2) Newton's *mathematical* •foundations of natural science,• or *philosophical* [foundations]; [3] and, finally, the philosophical presentation by First. (a) *Mathematical* foundations of natural science, not *philosophical* foundations of *mathematics*, as *only* mediate (indirect).

[Bottom left margin]

How do *conceptus, notio, idea* differ?

[Top margin]

The sense-intuition contains the manifold; thought produces its unity. By the former, the manifold is the object in appearance = x and the *dabile;* by the latter, the understanding comes into operation and produces the *cogitabile.* Both [are] *a priori* because [the subject] posits itself. The pure (not empirical) original (not derivative) representation, determining directly or indirectly . . . Space and time in intuition are not things but the *acts* of the power of representation positing itself, through which the subject makes itself into an object.

[Left margin]

N.B. Of the predicables and their complete enumeration, which belong after the predicaments (categories) in the complete system of metaphysics.

What comes first is that . . . the subject determines its self-consciousness, makes itself into an object and is appearance of itself. Synthetic and analytic.

Unity of space and time and of the possibility of experience (that is, of   22:89 the thoroughgoing determination in space and time) for *omnimoda determinatio est existentia.*

On this, and on the principle of the possibility of experience, is founded the idea of the existence of a universally distributed, all-penetrating etc. material which forms the basis of the possibility of there being *one single* experience, and whose existence can thus be comprehended *a priori*. For it is the attractive, repulsive and centrifugal forces which make experience as a system possible at all, and, without this absolute and *real unity*, even the negative principle of the void is impossible.

To frame the world according to the principle of atomism or corpuscular philosophy is to make space into something which is yet nothing.
Atomi ac inane.

[. . .]

[VIIth fascicle, sheet VIII, page 3]

[Insertion VIII]

To have something, or to claim to know it, *from* experience is more than
any understanding is capable of; for who can enumerate all perceptions
which can present themselves to his senses? They are extended to infinity
(*indefinitum*). But [to do this] *for* experience, for the possibility of producing it subjectively and of progressing toward it, that is the task which
(although only according to its form, not its content (*qualitative non quantitative*)) can be met with in the subject and required of it.

The investigation of nature can thus be regarded as a *philosophy* which
is meant to have two subjects – metaphysics and physics – from which
there yet stands open a perspective onto another subject, namely that of
transcendental philosophy, which deals particularly with the principle of
synthetic *a priori* propositions.

The logical act, I *think* (*apperception*), is a judgment (*iudicium*), but not yet
a proposition (*propositio*), not yet an act of the faculty of knowledge (*facultas
cognoscendi*) through which an object is given; rather, it is only thought in
general. It is, according to its form, a logical act, without content (*cogitans
sum, me ipsum nondum cognosco*),[109] even less is it a rational inference: I think
therefore I am (*ratiocinium*). I, the subject, makes itself into an object
according to the rule of identity. Two elements belong to knowledge
(*cognitio*), intuition and concept, a representation through which an object is
given and another by which it is thought. I, the subject, am an object to
myself. This, however, expresses more than self-consciousness.

•The principle of the ideality of intuition lies at the foundation of all our
knowledge of things outside us: That is, we do not apprehend objects as
given in themselves (*apprehensio simplex*), but, rather, the subject produces
(*fingit*) for itself the manifold of the sense-object according to its form,
and does so, indeed, according to a principle (*iudicium*), prior to all empirical representation with consciousness (perception) – that is, [it does so] *a
priori*, by means of the faculty of judgment (*iudicium*), through a syllogism,
into a complex (*complexus*), not of a ruleless aggregate but of a system.•

The object of pure intuition, by means of which the subject posits itself,
is infinite – namely, space and time.

Intuition and concept belong to knowledge: that I am given to myself
and thought by myself as object. Something exists (*apprehensio simplex*); I

am not merely logical subject and predicate, but also object of *perception* (*dabile non solum cogitabile*).

We can only commence from the totality of things as absolute synthetic unity (whose phenomenon is space and time). Thoroughgoing determination is possible in it *a priori* and this is the existence of the world. If one speaks of worlds, the latter are only different systems of one world in an absolute whole which is yet unlimited; for empty space is not a sense-object, not a thing (*non est ens*) – although not a nonentity (*non ens*), that is, something self-contradictory. Atomism (corpuscular philosophy) is an aggregate of points.

The "I am" is not yet a proposition (*propositio*), but merely the copula to a proposition; not yet a judgment. "I am existing" contains apprehension, that is, it is not merely a subjective judgment but makes myself into an object of intuition in space and time. Logical consciousness to what is real, and progresses from apperception to apprehension and its synthesis of the manifold. I cannot say: I think *therefore* I am; rather, such a judgment (of *apprehensio simplex*) would be tautological. The 22:97 whole of the objects of intuition – the world is only in me (transcendental *idealism*).

[*Right margin*]
The word "*intuition*" (*intuitus*) points toward vision. The *concept* (*conceptus*) toward the coordination of touch. All subjective determinations of the faculty of knowledge. The third [element] is the *foundation* of appearances as if established in immovable solid ground. A justified [*fundiert*] possession.

Progress from metaphysics to transcendental philosophy, and, eventually, from the latter to physics.

Apart from (logical) consciousness of myself, I have to do objectively with nothing other than my faculty of representation. I am an object to myself. The position of something outside me, itself first commences from me, in the forms of space and time, in which I myself posit the objects of outer and inner sense, and which, therefore, are infinite positings.

The existence of things in space and time is nothing but *omnimoda determinatio*, which is also only subjective (that is, in representation) and whose possibility in experience also rests only on concepts. We can know only what is formal, thinkable *a priori*.

An immaterial moving principle in an organic body is its soul, and, if one wishes to think of the latter as a world-soul, one can assume of it that it builds its own body and even that body's dwelling-place [*Gehäuse*] (the world).

[VIIth fascicle, sheet VIII, page 4]

Experience is absolute subjective unity of the manifold of sensible representation. One does not speak of experiences, but of experience as such, and it is easily seen that, since the understanding is here occupied with
22:98   mere relations, something which is pure intuition, not something perceptible, must lie at its foundation, in which these relations can be given *a priori;* and these are space and time, which are not things in themselves but forms of intuition, and do not just contain *appearances* in themselves, but, as objects *in appearance* – as absolute synthetic unity (singularity) of intuition [*breaks off*]

Space and time are forms of outer and inner intuition, given *a priori* in one synthetic representation; that is, they are inseparable, mutually dependent representations, such that their concepts of composition stand in mutual dependence to each other.

The representation of objects in space and time, as the principle for the possibility of experience, is the progression from the metaphysical foundations of natural science to physics.

I am the object of my own representation; that is, I am conscious of myself. This logical act is not yet a proposition, for it lacks a predicate. It is supplemented by the real act: I *exist* (*sum*), thinking (*cogitans*), through which something (me myself) is not merely *thought* but also *given* (*cogitabile ut dabile*). This act, however, is not an inference (*cogito ergo sum*) but only the subject thought in its *thoroughgoing determination;* thus represented not analytically (according to the principle of identity) nor merely explicatively, but synthetically, as ampliative, [it] yields the proposition of the existence of an object (*omnimoda determinatio est existentia*).

The empirical cognition of the object of intuitions in its thoroughgoing determination is experience. Since this thoroughgoing determination with consciousness, however, requires an infinite manifold of intuition, the
22:99   complex of experience can only be founded *for* experience (for its sake) in knowledge – not *from* experience.

The complex of all outer sense-objects, according to its formal principle, is space as one intuition, which is merely subjective (appearance); that of inner sense-objects and of thought, is time: whereby both qualitative and quantitative relations and the unity of space and time are encountered.

Space and time are not *entia per se* but mere forms of sensible representation.

[*Bottom margin*]

The principle of the ideality of all representations as pure *a priori* intuition: I make myself into a sense-object outside myself. (*Aenesidemus.*)

What is formal in this intuition is the One and All, coordinated; [it] is the representation of space and time, which represents an infinity (unlimited magnitude), not analytically through concepts, but synthetically through the construction of concepts. There is one space and one time, and unity of experience in space and time: both reciprocally determining each other in one consciousness. Matter and bodies. Not *matters* but materials for *bodies*.

Asymptota of thoroughgoing determination, as knowledge in experience, for the latter's sake: not *from* it but *for* it.

•All organic beings (not mere matter, but bodies) are beings in which there is life (immaterial principle, inner final cause).•

The principles of the progression to physics are transitions, if they merely deal with appearances, in which the object in itself is = x.

[*Top margin*]

(One feels the state of being sick, although the sickness could be quite hidden. Health itself is not felt, but only its hindrance – *agilitas*. Discomfort is itself not a sickness but often only the desire to increase one's well-being – not the negative but the *contrarie oppositum*. We only feel symptoms. Organic beings are those in which there is life, in souls.)

[*Left margin*]   22:100

One can think of *health* and *sickness* with regard to organic bodies (not organic matter), since they possess a vital force, be it vegetative or animal, and for this reason also death or decay. This does not apply to minerals, except insofar as they are the materials that make up organic bodies (combined in chaotic or in lawlike fashion). The latter preserve their species through sexual relationships.

The principle of the possibility of such bodies must be immaterial, since it is possible only through *purposes*. It remains undetermined whether this encompasses the entire universe and hence underlies [everything] in cosmic space – as a world-soul, as a unifying principle of all life (which thus must not be called *spirit*) – or whether several be arranged hierarchically.

Whether a system of the world, or merely of the earth, is required to generate organic formations, including their sexual principles?

Thinking and intuiting: The consciousness of oneself (*apperceptio*) and the apprehension of the manifold of the intuition of the object (*apprehensio*), combined, are acts of the cognitive faculty (*facultas cognoscitiva*).

I am an object to myself, that is, I am, (1) conscious of myself (*sum*) is a logical act; (2) [*breaks off*]

Space and time are pure sensible intuitions (not perception, that is, not empirical representation with consciousness), and in them [there is] an infinite progression of manifold determination. There is one space and one time, and if one speaks of spaces and times then these are parts of space and time.

22:101 *Light, sound* – with their modifications, *color* and *tones* – as external forces making space sensible, and heat as inner feeling of life, are perceptions of objects in the distance, in opposition of the inner [perceptions] by contact (touching what is hot and cold).

actio in distans. Perception without contact.

[. . .]

22:104 [VIIth fascicle, sheet IX, page 2]

Experience is the whole of the sequence of empirical consciousness in continuous approximation. As a whole, it is absolute unity; and one cannot speak of experiences, although one can do so of perceptions – and present the latter piecemeal (*sparsim*) through observation and experiment, but not in a full complex (*coniunctim*).

There is an all-comprehending nature (in space and time) in which reason coordinates all physical relations into unity. There is a universally ruling operative cause with freedom in rational beings, and, [given] with the latter, a categorical imperative which connects them all, and, with that, in turn, an all-embracing, morally commanding, original being – a God.

The phenomena from the moving forces of moral-practical reason, insofar as they are *a priori* with respect to men in relation to one another, are the ideas of right – •moral-practical reason. Categorical imperative which our reason expresses through the divine. Freedom under laws, duties *as* divine commands. There is a God.•

Metaphysics has to do with sense-objects and their system, insofar as the latter is knowable *a priori*, analytically (*cogitabile, cognoscibile*). •*Aenesi-demus*[110] inwardly determining.• Thence the transition to the synthetic *a priori* principles takes place through concepts (not through representations of intuition) which contain *a priori* the formal element of the connection of the manifold (ampliatively) and coordinate a whole of sensible representations in one system (not empirically, through experience, but according to rational principles for the sake of the possibility of experience) which, subjectively, amounts to only that which can be thought [through] reason. [The latter also] contains ideas of right [which lead] toward the concept of a highest moral being under which all world-beings stand – God. Which cannot be the *dabile* (intuition) but only the *cogitabile*
22:105 (thinkable) – the moral-practical. There is a God: for there is in moral-practical reason a categorical imperative, which extends to all rational world-beings and through which all world-beings are united. •*Eleutherology*,[111] which contains freedom under laws (moral-practical reason) according to *maxims*.•

The concept of God is the idea which man, as a moral being, forms of the highest moral being in relation according to principles of right, insofar as he, according to the categorical imperative, regards all duties as commands of this being. •*Concept of freedom. Moral-practical reason is one of the moving forces of nature* and of all sense-objects. These form a particular field: for *ideas.*•

I am an object to myself through the *concept* of myself – that is, I am *conscious* of myself: a *logical* judgment (*sum, cogito*) without yet proceeding further through an inference (*cogito ergo sum*), for such a proposition would be identical (merely analytical), hence an empty judgment which does not found knowledge.

(1) I am (2) to myself both an object of *thought* and an object of inner intuition, a *sense-object;* an object of intuition, that is, although not yet of *empirical* intuition (perception) but of pure intuition. Space and time as appearance of something which is merely form of the composition of the manifold.

Progression from logic to metaphysics, and from the latter to transcendental philosophy, and to the connection with mathematics as one of the instruments of philosophy.

Synthetic *a priori* propositions are only possible in pure *a priori* intuition – space and time.

Amphiboly of the *concepts of reflection* (of *medius terminus* of subsumption), *conceptus, iudicium, ratiocinium.*

[. . .]

[Practical self-positing and the idea of God]

22:115

[VIIth fascicle, sheet X, page 1]

I am

This act of consciousness (*apperceptio*) does not arise as a consciousness of something preceding (as, for instance, if I say to myself: I think *therefore* I am) for otherwise I should presuppose my existence in order to demonstrate this existence – which would be a mere tautology.

There is one world as my sense-object; for space and time constitute the whole complex of sense-objects. These forms of sensible intuition

22:116 represent objects, however, only as *appearances* (because we must be affected by them in order to intuit them), not as things in themselves, because they contain merely the formal element of the relation of things to the affecting subject.

There is, however, apart from sensible representation, yet another faculty of knowledge, which contains not merely receptivity but also spontaneity (as highest faculty of knowledge): namely, understanding, judgment and reason. The latter can be either technical, •intuition-constructing• reason or moral-practical reason, •both combining *a priori* the manifold of representations to knowledge under a principle.• Moral-practical reason, if it contains laws of duty (rules of conduct in conformity with the categorical imperative), leads to the concept of God.

A being, who is capable of and entitled to command all rational beings according to laws of duty (the categorical imperative) of moral-practical reason, is *God (ens summum, summa intelligentia, summum bonum)*.[112]

•The world is the whole of all sense-objects, thought not in an aggregate but in a system, and there is one world and one God (*contra pluralitas mundorum*); and, if God is assumed, then there is a single God.•

The existence of such a being, however, can only be *postulated* in a practical respect: Namely, the necessity of acting in such a way as if I stood under such a fearsome – but yet, at the same time, salutary – guidance and also guarantee, in the knowledge of all my duties as divine commmands (*tanquam non ceu*); hence the *existence* of such a being is not postulated in this formula, which would be self-contradictory.

A being, which has unrestricted power over nature and freedom under
22:117 laws of reason, is **God**. Hence God is, according to his concept, not merely a natural being but also a moral being. Regarded in the former

200

respect *alone*, he is the *creator* (*demiurgus*) and *omnipotent;* in the second, *holy* (*adorabilis*) and all human duties are, at the same time, his commands. He is *ens summum, summa intelligentia, summum bonum.*

However, there still seems to be the question as to whether this idea, the product of our own reason, has reality or whether it is a mere thought-object (*ens rationis*), and there remains to us nothing but the moral relation-ship to this object [namely, God] – which is merely problematic, and which leaves only the formula of the knowledge of all human duties as (*tanquam*) divine commands, whenever the iron voice of the categorical *imperative of duty* resounds between all siren temptations of the senses and threatening deterrents.

[*Top margin*]

The unity of the world of bodies, through the principle of the attraction of all matter in the universe, and also of repulsion – for otherwise space would be empty and hence not an object of perception (that is, not a sense-object).

God and the world are not coordinated beings, but the latter is subordi-nate to the former.

If the feeling of *pleasure* precedes the *law*, it is pathological; in the reverse case, the pleasure is moral.

[*Right margin*]

The totality of beings, the highest being, the being of all beings in their unconditional unity (*ens summum, summa intelligentia, summum bonum*).

There are two ways in which men postulate the existence of God; they say sometimes: There exists a divine *judge* and *avenger,* for wickedness and *crime* require the extinction of this loathsome race. On the other hand, reason thinks of an *achievement* [*Verdienst*] of which man is 22:118 capable – to be able to place himself in a higher *class*, namely that of autonomous (through moral-practical reason) beings, and to raise him-self above all merely sensuous beings (and he has a *vocation* so to do); he is such a being, not merely *hypothetically*, but has a destination to enter that state, to be the originator of his own rank – that is, obligated and yet thereby self-obligating.

There is no feeling of duty although there is, indeed, a feeling from the representation of our duty, for the latter is a necessitation through the categorical moral imperative. Duty of compulsion not duty of love.

In it, that is, the idea of God as a moral being, we live, move and have our being;[113] motivated through the knowledge of our duties *as* divine commands.

The concept of God is the idea of a moral being, which, as such, is judging [and] universally commanding. The latter is not a hypothetical

201

thing but pure practical reason itself in its personality, with reason's moving forces in respect to world-beings and their forces.

Freedom under laws of *compulsion* of *pure* reason.

Freedom under pure laws of reason.

    There is a concept of right in the relation of men among one another, as principle of moral-practical reason, according to the categorical imperative, with regard to *duties of right* (not duties of love [*breaks off*]

[*Bottom margin*]
    Formally, nature and freedom under laws which, if [we] judge them not merely according to their receptivity but also according to their spontaneity – that is, not merely according to rules but according to principles, and as appearances, not as things in themselves. Difference between metaphysics and transcendental philosophy. The former grounded on analytic, the latter on synthetic *a priori* principles.

22:119

    Understanding, judgment and reason, according to their *a priori* principles. Reason (1) technical (2) moral-practical.[114]

[VIIth fascicle, sheet X, page 2]

[*Top margin*]
    (1) Transition from metaphysics to transcendental philosophy. (2) From transcendental philosophy to physics through mathematics in pure intuition of space and time.
    I am conscious of myself (*apperceptio*). I think, that is, I am an object of *understanding* to myself. But I am also an object of the *senses* to myself and of empirical intuition (*apprehensio*); the thinkable I (*cogitabile*) posits itself as the sensible (*dabile*), and this *a priori* in space and time – which are given *a priori* in intuition and are mere forms of appearance.

[*Main text*]
    It is by no means required for the categorical imperative that a substance exists whose duties are also its commands, but only that the holiness and inviolability of the latter be understood. The property of being a person is personality.
    A moral-practical rational being is a *person* for whom all *human duties* are likewise *this person's commands* – is **God**.

22:120

    To prescribe all human duties as divine commands is already contained in every categorical imperative.

    The categorical imperative is the expression of a *principle of reason* over oneself as a *dictamen rationis practicae*[115] and thinks itself as law giver and judge over one, according to the categorical imperative of duty (for thoughts accuse or exonerate one another),[116] hence, in the quality of a person. Now *a being which has only rights and no duties is* **God.** Consequently, the moral being thinks all duties, formally, also as divine commands; not as if he thereby wished to certify the existence of such a being: For the supersensible is not an object of possible experience (*non dabile sed mere cogitabile*) but merely a judgment by analogy – that is, to the relational concept of a synthetic judgment, namely, to think all human duties *as if* divine commands and in relation to a person.

Every human being is, in virtue of *his freedom* and of the law which *restricts* it, made subject to necessitation through his moral-practical reason, stands under command and prohibition, and, as a man, under the imperative of duty. A being which has the authority and power to command over all beings is God, and only one God can be thought. There is a God in the soul of man. The question is whether he is also in nature.

An *ens rationis* and *ens rationabile* are different from each other; the latter is *dabile*, the former merely *cogitabile*. The categorical imperative of the command of duty has at its basis the idea of an *imperantis*, who is capable of everything and commands everything (*formale*). Is the idea of God. The idea of a universally commanding and omnipotent moral being is that of the *ens summum*.

22:121

Existence and actuality (*existentia* and *actualitas* from *agere*). The thing is there when and where it acts. Substance is the thing in itself; the independent, the *cogitabile* and the *dabile*. The independent and accidental or attributive. All are modes of existence. A thing, *res;* a substance which is conscious of its freedom is a *person* and has *rights*.

One cannot directly prove the *existence* of any thing *a priori*, neither by an analytic nor by a synthetic •principle of• judgment. To assume it, however, as a hypothetical thing for the sake of possible appearances, is to feign, not to demonstrate, •*cogitabile non dabile*.• The concept of God is, however, the concept of a being that can *obligate all moral beings* without itself [being] obligated, and, hence, has rightful power over them all. To wish to prove the *existence* of such a being *directly*, however, contains a contradiction, for *a posse ad esse non valet consequentia*.[117] Thus only an *indirect* proof remains, •inasmuch as it is assumed that something else be possible,• namely, that the knowledge of our duties *as* (*tanquam*) divine commands is certified and authorized – not in a theoretical but in a pure practical respect – as a principle of practical reason, in which there is a valid inference from *ought* to *can*.

There is, •indeed,• in the mind of man, a principle of moral-practical reason, a command of duty, which he sees himself as unconditionally necessitated to honor •and obey (*obtemperantia*),• and which corresponds to a categorical imperative, whose formulation is expressed either affirma-

22:122 tively or negatively (Honor thy father and mother. Thou shalt not kill.)[118] [and] *expresses* [itself] *unconditionally* with regard to all matters of well-being (happiness): to make freedom under the law into the ground of the determination of one's action. The idea of such a being, before whom all knees bow, etc.,[119] emerges from this imperative and not the reverse, and a God is thought necessarily, subjectively, in human practical reason, although not given objectively: Hereupon is founded the proposition of the knowledge of all human duties *as* divine *commands.*

There is in man a principle of technical-practical reason, a relation of will toward purposes, which, with regard to himself, are unconditionally necessitating (*necessitantia*); if he intends to bring about this or that, then he must use this or that procedure: The imperative is conditional. There is, however, in man as a free being also a principle of moral-practical reason, unconditionally commanding, that is, in the imperative of *duty* which is categorical.

[*Between 7th and 8th paragraph of main text*]
A rational being (*ens rationale*). A rational being insofar as it personifies itself for the sake of a purpose is a moral person.
A thought-being (*ens rationis*).
A theorem of transcendental philosophy.

[*Left margin*]
A universal, morally law-giving being, which, thus, has all power, is God.
There exists a God, that is, one principle which, as substance, is morally law-giving.
For morally law-giving reason gives expression through the categorical imperative to duties, which, as being at the same time substance, are law-giving over nature and law-abiding.

22:123 It is not a *substance* outside myself, whose existence I postulate as a hypothetical being for the explanation of certain phenomena in the world; but the concept of duty (of a universal practical principle) is contained identically in the concept of a divine being as an ideal of human reason for the sake of the latter's law-giving [*breaks off*]

There is contained in man, as a *subordinate* moral being, a concept of duty, namely, that of the relation of right; to stand under a law of the determination of his will, which he imposes upon himself, and to which he subordinates himself – which, however, he also treats imperatively, and •asserts• independent of all empirical grounds of determination (and [which] is determining merely as a formal principle of willing).

The *originator* of a certain effect, according to laws which the subject prescribes to itself, is also called a principle, insofar as it is thought as substance (the good or evil principle).

The evil principle would be a subjective practical principle [*Grundsatz*] without a principle – to act against all principle, indeed; so it is a *contradictio in adjecto*. Hence merely *inclination* (instinct), that is, well-being (*in diem dicere: vixi*), to live for the day.

[VIIth fascicle, sheet X, page 3]

The categorical imperative is the expression of a moral and holy, unconditionally commanding will, which is also omnipotent, and, without requiring or even permitting incentives, is independent – freedom and law united in it. The idea of it is that of a substance which is unique in its concept, and is not subordinated to a classification of human reason. *Ens summum, summa intelligentia, summum bonum* is an *ens rationis* and, thought (or, rather, feigned) as a natural being, [is] an all-embracing substance – inscrutable;   22:124
as ethical being, however, a principle of the practical [*breaks off*]

The formal element of the synthesis of representations of the object in transcendental philosophy (which forms the progress from the metaphysical foundations to physics) not the material element of knowledge of the represented object, is that from which the thoroughly self-determining subject proceeds: the categorical imperative of the knowledge of duty. God and the world contain the *totality* of existence.

Forces in empty space (attraction, Newton) presuppose bodies, not mere matter (*actio in distans*) – ether, repulsion through which space can become a sense-object; and, [as such,] space does not contain bodies but merely matter.

Furthermore, bodies can be organic or inorganic (animal, plants). The latter cannot be explained through atomism, merely mechanically, but must be explained dynamically, from concepts of purposes.

What leads reason to the idea of God, not as a natural being but as a moral being, and his unity, freedom and law, whose capacity constitutes personality, through which man distinguishes himself as a moral being from all natural beings? Herein lies a dignity: He can forgive himself nothing (categorical imperative) and, through this, he makes himself responsible to himself.

A moral being who would be thought as *obligating*, but as *obligated* by no other, would be **God**. If such exists, then he is a *single* God; for to think of several of them is a self-contradiction, since they would be thought in a relation of obligation to one another.

Equally, the thesis of the plurality of worlds contains in itself a contradiction, for the totality of the whole of existing things – that is, the concept of the world – already contains the concept of singularity.

The question, *de pluralitate mundorum*, is self-contradictory, and it is as   22:125
little the case that there are many Gods as that there are many worlds; but

205

there still remains the general question: *Is there* (does there exist) a being whom we wish to think as *God* at all? Or is it a merely hypothetical thing (*ens rationis*) which (as, for instance, the universally distributed and all-penetrating ether) is assumed only in order to explain certain phenomena?

But moral-practical reason yet contains in itself laws of compulsion (that is, commands of pure reason (*obligationes strictae*)) which the categorical imperative carries with it (the imperative of pure reason, as it were (*vetita ac praecepta*)). Before the inner seat of judgment (*in foro conscientiae*) and regardless of any actual pronouncement issued by God, the knowledge of all human duties **as** divine commands (*tanquam, non ceu*) is of the same force as if a real world-judge were assumed. Freedom under the pure law of reason.

The unity of the sensible in space. Correspondingly, that of the intelligible (*omnipraesentia*) – *virtualis* not *localis*.

One can also, by analogy, posit virtual attraction in empty space as *actio in distans* – *locomotiva* – *interne motiva*.

The *cogitabile* which is *incomprehensibile*. To which no aggregate [is] adequate, but can only be given as one.

The first question is: whether there is a moral-practical reason, and, with this, concepts of duty as principles of freedom under laws; then: whether there is a substance which judges according to these laws (by exonerating or condemning men), declares men worthy or unworthy of happiness, and makes them partake of it in consequence. Such a personal substance would be God, and, since it represents the totality synthetically, as an individual, not as belonging to a class of rational beings, the single God. Only as 22:126 hypothetical, however, can such an *ens* constitute a principle – not as given, but only as thought (thought-object, *ens rationis*) – but only for the sake of the recognition of our duties as divine commands.

[*Top margin*]

God regarded as a natural being is a hypothetical being, assumed for the explanation of appearances – as, for instance, the ether, in order to make space into a sense-object.

There is a philosophical use of mathematics – is, however, a mathematical use of philosophy possible?

[*Right margin*]

The most important of all the concepts of reason, because it is directed toward the final end (for the concepts of the understanding are only there for the sake of form), is the concept of duty and the legislation relating to it, as a concept of practical reason.

The categorical imperative, expressed affirmatively or negatively (in command and prohibition) yet with greater rigor in the latter than in the former (*dictamen rationis moralis*): Thou shalt not steal. (Thou shalt not lie, is not in the Decalogue.) Honor thy father and mother. The last are not an expression of proper duties of compulsion.

There must also, however, be – or at least be thought – a legislative force (*potestas legislatoria*) which gives these laws emphasis (effect) although only in idea; and this is none other than that of the *highest* being, morally and physically superior to all and omnipotent, and his holy will – which justifies the statement: There is a God.

There is in practical reason a concept of duty, that is, of a compulsion or necessitation according to a principle of the laws of freedom – that is, according to a law which the subject prescribes to itself (*dictamen rationis practicae*) through the categorical imperative, indeed.

A command, to which everyone must absolutely give obedience, is to be 22:127 regarded by everyone as from a being which rules and governs over all. Such a being, as moral, however, is called God. So there is a God.

[Bottom margin]
A being which is never obligated, but would be obligating for every other rational being, is the highest being in a moral sense. The rational being which, with respect to nature, is capable of everything is the highest being in the physical respect. In both respects. All-sufficient (*omnisufficiens*): Is God he who, because he is totality in all relation, can only be one; the single God (of whom there cannot be different genera and species)?

There is only one practically sufficient argument for faith in one God, which[a] is theoretically insufficient – knowledge of all human duties *as* (*tanquam*) divine commands.

[VIIth fascicle, sheet X, page 4]

Under the concepts of practical reason (*dictamen rationis practicae*) the *concept of duty* is a principle of the unconditionally commanding (categorical) imperative; it does not prescribe the means to arbitrary ends, but prescribes actions, which are to be made one's own ends, apodictically, as well as a certain commission and omission, merely according to the principle of freedom under laws, and it contains a command to which the subject sees himself unconditionally subordinated through pure reason.

Now the idea of an omnipotent moral being, whose willing is a categorical imperative for all rational beings, and is both all-powerful with regard to nature as well as unconditionally, universally commanding for freedom, is the idea of *God* – not a generic concept, but that of an individual (a 22:128 thoroughly determined being); for the *totality* is only one, thus there can

---

[a] Reading *das* for *der.*

207

be no question of gods. {The existence as substance of such a being allows itself to be assumed only as a hypothetical being (as, for instance, caloric) in order to explain the phenomena of its sphere of activity as experience may supply it; however, its unity – like that of space and time – certifies the totality of its presence, and the only possible question is: Is there one God or not?

•Of the law of continuity (*lex continui*) from a physical and moral point of view. From a transcendental point of view.•

There is only one experience and all perceptions only form an aggregate for the sake of the possibility of a whole of experience, through observation and experiment.} This ideal being governs [*exercirt über*] the principle of all human duties, as commands issuing from himself, that is, as God: Hence the (moral) law of duty, in virtue of the categorical imperative, is a principle of the recognition of all human duties *as* divine commands, even though one leaves undecided the existence of such a powerful being. The formal element of the law here amounts to the essence of the thing [*Sache*] itself, and the categorical imperative is a command of God; this dictum is no mere phrase.

The idea of the absolute authority of a moral being's unconditionally dictating command of duty is the divinity •of the person who commands• (*divinitas formalis*). A substance which possesses this authority would be God. That such a substance exists cannot be proved; for neither experience nor pure reason from mere concepts can found such a proposition, for it is neither an analytic nor a synthetic proposition.

22:129 . In moral-practical reason there is not only a principle of benevolence, that is, of the advancement of the *happiness* of others (the duty of love) which sets limits to egotism (*officium late determinans*) •but also a principle of *rejection*.•

The *dictamen rationis practicae* is a reason other than theoretical; it does not determine but is determined through another, not analytically self-[determining], but synthetically [through a] divine command. Thoughts which mutually accuse or excuse one another. Just as [there is] only one space and one time. Ether.

•To be worthy or unworthy of happiness.•

Not the relation of things, but of the representations of things to one another. The *a priori* relation of right as moral compulsion. Spontaneity and receptivity.

In moral-practical reason, there is contained the principle of the knowledge of my duties as commands (*praecepta*), that is, not according to the rule which makes the subject into an [object], but that which emerges from freedom and which [the subject] prescribes to itself, and yet as if another and higher person had made it a rule for him (*dictamen rationis practicae*). The subject feels himself necessitated through his own reason (not analytically, according to the principle of identity, but synthetically, as a transition from metaphysics to transcendental philosophy) to obey these duties. •*What* God may be can be developed from concepts, by means of metaphysics; but *that* there is a God belongs to transcendental philosophy and can only be proved hypothetically (caloric).•

Officia humanitatis et institiae late et stricte posita (proprie determinantia).[120]

[*Bottom margin*]

The subject of the categorical imperative in me is an object which deserves to be obeyed: an object of adoration. This is an identical proposition. The characteristic of a moral being which can command categorically over the nature of man is its divinity. His laws must be obeyed as divine commands. Whether religion is possible without the presupposition of the existence of God. •*Est deus in nobis.*•[121]   22:130

[*Top margin*]

Metaphysics analyzes given concepts; transcendental philosophy contains the principles of *synthetic a priori* judgments and their possibility.

Homo agit, facit, operatur. Sense, understanding, reason, – meritum, demeritum.

Consciousness of positing something (*spontaneitas*), of receiving (*receptivitas*).

[*Left margin*]

The idea of a being which would be its own originator, would be the original being, and a product (not educt) of pure practical reason. The concept of it (the subject) is identical with it (the object) and transcendent without being contradictory.

Among rational world-beings is the class of those which are endowed with moral-practical reason, hence with freedom under laws which they prescribe to themselves (*dictamen rationis practicae*) and necessarily recognize the concept of duty, hence, the categorical imperative; yet also the class of those who must admit the corruption and weakness of human nature that, as a world-being, permits itself transgressions.

One can, however, represent in man the dictate of reason, in respect to the concept of duty in general: the knowledge of his duties *as* (*tanquam, non ceu*) divine commands; because that imperative is represented as governing and absolutely commanding, hence as pertaining to a ruler (befitting a person). The ideal, which we create for ourselves, of a substance.

I am a principle of synthetic self-determination to myself, not merely according to a law of the *receptivity of nature,* but also according to a principle of the *spontaneity of freedom.*   22:131

A cause operating in the world according to purely moral principles, thought as substance (*ens extramundanum*) which, insofar as it embraces the *totality* of sense-objects under its power, is single.

22:48 [VIIth fascicle, sheet V, page 1]

Insertion V[122]

Man, insofar as he is conscious of himself (object to himself) *thinks.*

One thinks for oneself under the concept of God a substance which [is] adequate to all conscious purposes – that is, a person; whereby the tautologically reinforced expression "the living God" only serves to designate the personality of this being: as omnipotent being (*ens summum*), as omniscient (*summa intelligentia*) and omnibenevolent (*summum bonum*). Its activity is on the analogy with technical-practical reason [*breaks off*]

World-beings can be obligating, and obligating to others. But a being which, although obligating of others, can never itself be obligated, is God.

A human being can be a person, that is, a being which is capable of rights; but personality cannot be attributed to the Deity.

There are persons in the world. But God as pure intelligence can only be one; for several of them would have rights against one another.

22:49 World is the *whole* of sense-objects – thus also including the forces acting on the senses – insofar as it amounts to a unity (that is, combined synthetically according to a principle). "*Totality* of sense-objects," [since it represents merely] logical unity, does not express the concept of "world." Thus [the concept of "world"] does not just belong to metaphysics but to transcendental philosophy – in which latter, knowledge is given *a priori* in intuition, through concepts (not through their construction, for that would be mathematics) and forms the transition from the metaphysical foundations of natural science.

There is one world, one space, one time; and, if one speaks of spaces and times, these are only thinkable as parts of one space and time. This whole is infinite – that is, there are no limits of the manifold possible in it as *real* limitations, for otherwise the void would be an object of the senses. It is not a mechanically but a dynamically given concept – a transcendental idealism. Only one *experience,* not experiences.

One must progress from subjective principles of appearance to what is objective in experience. One must progress from technical-practical to moral-practical reason, and from the subject as natural being to the subject as person – that is, as pure being of the understanding – God.

God is a being who contains in his concept only rights and no duties. World is the opposite.

Person is a being who has *rights* and is conscious of them. If he has *rights and no duties,* then he is *God.* To have duties and no rights is the characteristic of the *criminal.* Categorical imperative of the highest being.

The *world* is the complex of all sensible beings: *God is the rational being.* Each of the two is single in its *species.*

What man *does* (*agit*), what he makes (*facit*). What he produces through action in a certain time (*operatur*).

God and the world are correlates, without which the idea of God as a   22:50
practical being would not occur. In the world, however, nature and freedom are two active powers [*Vermögen*] of different kinds, of which one
(*quae agit, facit, operatur*) [*breaks off*]

Of organic *bodies,* which already contain the concept of purposes in themselves according to the principle of identity; an immaterial principle must
be thought in them, which, however, can therefore not be spirit (*mens*).

Experience contains the whole of possible perceptions (all possible
observation and experiment).

Division. (1) A being who has only rights and no duties (moral-practical
reason according to its laws and principles), *God.* (2) Who has rights and
duties: *man.* (3) Beings which have neither rights nor duties, which have
no desires at all (mere matter). (4) Those which have desires, but no will.

The formula of an unconditional command of duty (*dictamen rationis
stricte obligantis*) is the categorical imperative of right – *late obligantis* is that
of benevolence (*benevolentiae*) of which kind gratitude is the strongest.

[VIIth fascicle, sheet V, page 2]   22:51
The categorical imperative does not presuppose a supremely commanding substance which would be outside me, but is, rather, a command or
prohibition of my own reason. Notwithstanding this, it is nevertheless to
be regarded as proceeding from a being who has irresistible power over
all.

(1) What does the concept of God express? (2) Is there a God? (3) Is the
existence of God given *a priori,* that is, as unconditionally necessary (not
merely thought, that is, a thought-object (*ens rationis*) in order to found
certain consequential concepts, in the way that, for instance, caloric [is] a
hypothetical being)? (4) Is God and the world an active relation of two
relations determining the totality of things into a heterogeneous whole,
namely, the one as intellectual principle of the pure understanding, that is,
as a person, the other as complex of sensible beings, insofar as they are at
least conscious of themselves.

Person is a being who has rights of which he can become conscious.

The categorical imperative represents all human duties *as* divine commands; not historically, as if [God] had ever issued certain orders to man,
but as reason [presents] them through the supreme power of the categori-   22:52

211

cal imperative, in the same manner as a divine person can rigorously command submission to himself.

So it is not technical-practical reason (which prescribes means for the purposes of sense-objects) but the moral-practical (which prescribes right to man, as pure rational object, and makes subjective grounds of determination into objective ones – in which the bold idea of intuiting all objects in God, at least in transcendental idealism, etc. [*breaks off*]

Among all the good deeds (*facta obligatoria*) it is not benevolence toward men but the right of men which is the act of the highest authority, and the ideal person who exercises it is God. Not as a substance different from man.

God is not the originator of the world (*demiurgus*), from whom all evil (as mere sense-objects) proceeded. God as person, that is, regarded as a being who has rights.

The complex of all sensible beings is the world, to which man also belongs, but who is yet at the same time an intellectual being.

Mechanism of nature and freedom of rational beings.

Freedom and transcendental idealism and moral-practical reason. The former is postulated. The concept of duty precedes even freedom and proves the reality of freedom.

That there is also in man, alongside his *nature, freedom* and practical reason as the counterpart of mechanism (technical-practical).

22:53 Whether there is a God (in substance) or not, cannot be a point of controversy, for it is not an *object* of dispute (*objectum litis*). It is not existing beings *outside* the judging subject, about whose characteristics it would be possible to dispute, but a mere idea of pure reason which examines its own principles.

The concept of God is not a technical-practical but a moral-practical concept: That is, it contains a categorical imperative [and] is the complex (*complexus*) of all human duties *as* divine commands, according to the principle of identity.

It is an individual concept (*conceptus singularis*): There are no gods, just as little as there are worlds, but God and the world. He is a person, that is, a being who has rights, but not a sensible being; so [there are] not *gods*.

The categorical imperative, which founds the incomprehensible system of human freedom, does not begin from freedom but ends and completes with it. There is a certain *sublime wistfulness* [*Wemuth*] in the feelings which accompany the sublimity of the ideas of pure practical reason, and, at the same time, a *humility* which leads one to subordinate oneself to this object. But also an elevation of the honest man [*des Wackeren*] in his decision.

God and the world, represented in the idea of pure reason.

212

technical-practical. pragmatic-moral

The possibility of freedom cannot be directly proved, but only indirectly, through the possibility of the categorical imperative of duty, which requires no incentives of nature.

Wrong (*curvum* opposed to *recto*, crooked *obliq.* to the straight) can also be called *pravitas* (e.g. *usuravia*). Opposed to what is round and returns upon itself, similar from all sides.

[VIIth fascicle, sheet V, page 3]

The subject determines itself (1) by technical-practical reason, (2) by moral-practical reason, and is itself an object of both. The world and God. The first is appearance in space and time. The second according to concepts of reason, that is, a principle of the categorical imperative. *Ens summum, summa intelligentia, summum bonum: thing* [*Sache*] *and person. Apperceptio, apprehensio et comprehensio phaenomenologica, cognitio et recognitio.* 22:54

The knowledge of oneself as a person who constitutes himself as a principle and is his own originator.

God and the world are both a maximum. The transcendental ideality of the subject thinking itself makes itself into a person. Its divinity. I am in the highest being. According to Spinoza, I see myself in God •who is legislative within *me.*•[123]

All commands which bind man through the categorical imperative and make pure practical laws absolute duty (implacable internal obligation) independent of any account of internal or external advantages, are holy duties; that is, they are to be regarded as commands of an unconditionally demanding being, independent of nature. Now the idea of a being commanding according to moral-practical laws contains the idea of a *person* having all *power* [in] relation to nature as a sense object. [It also contains] an expression of the categorical imperative of all commands of duty, by the principle of pure reason, not by empirical incentives of world-determination. There are, however, only two active principles which can be thought of as causes of these appearances: *God* and the **world**. Thus the idea of moral practical reason in the categorical imperative is the ideal of God.

What has here been sufficiently (from a practical viewpoint) demonstrated as belonging to transcendental philosophy, is not, indeed, the existence of God as a particular existing substance, but the relation to such a concept. *Vide* Lichtenberg's Spinoza,[124] a system of the intuition of 22:55
all things in God. Transcendental idealism [of positing] oneself synthetically and *a priori.*

•The cause of the world regarded as a *person*, is the author of the world. Not as a demiurge of matter which is passive, but [*breaks off*]•

The subject of the categorical imperative (not of technical-practical but of moral-practical reason), a transcendental ideal which emerges from transcendental philosophy as from a synthetic *a priori* proposition from a pure concept, not from sensible intuition, is God. It cannot be denied that such a being exists; yet it cannot be asserted that it exists outside rationally thinking man. In him – the man who thinks morally according to our own commands of duty – we live (*sentimus*), move (*agimus*) and have our being (*existimus*).

From this there follows the necessity of the division of the complex of all beings (of everything that exists): *God and the world.*

In man there dwells an active principle, arousable by no sensible representation, accompanying him not as soul (for this presupposes body) but as spirit, which, like a particular substance, commands him irresistibly according to the law of moral-practical reason, [and which], by its own actions, pardons or condemns man's commissions and omissions. In virtue of this property of his, the moral man is a *person;* that is, a being capable of rights, who can encounter wrong or can consciously do it, and who stands under the categorical imperative; free indeed, but yet under laws to which he submits himself (*dictamen rationis purae*) and who carries out divine commands according to transcendental idealism. Knowledge of all human duties as divine commands,[b] [*breaks off*]

22:56

[*Between lines of main text*]

Conflict with the right of humanity in my own person, and with the right of men.

A person is a rational being who has rights.

Man is not an animal with internal purposes or *senses,* etc. (e.g. organs, *understanding*) but a *person* who has *rights,* and against whom all other persons have rights. Not merely is he animated by a soul (thus *animans*) but there dwells in him a spirit (*spiritus intus alit. Mens*).

Organic bodies have an *immaterial* principle as their basis because they are founded on purposes.

[*Top margin*]

According to Spinoza's transcendental idealism, we intuit ourselves in God. The categorical imperative does not presuppose a highest commanding substance as outside me, but lies within my own reason.

[*Right margin*]

How are laws for the united space- and time-determinations of moving forces possible *a priori*? Newton's work. Immediate *actio in distans* (through empty space).

Of the reciprocally acting motion of light in full space, but without

---

[b] Through *I* verte connected with beginning of page 4.

diffusion – for the divergence of the beams and Römer's time-condition of their motion act against one another.[125] Of the magnet.

Heat, an internally moving force of bodies, is a hypothetical material, because it expands and disperses matter, and may well be the mere effect   22:57 of the repulsion of a matter set in oscillation.

The fear of God is the beginning of wisdom;[126] this, however, is nothing other than *horror vacui*, abhorrence for everything which conflicts with the right. For this interruption which contradicts moral-practical reason [*breaks off*]

Man: *logical, metaphysical, mathematical, aesthetic,* transcendental. The consciousness determining itself contains spontaneity, also personality, has rights.

A body for whose possibility one must think of an organizing force, that is, a force which only acts through internal purposes. Next, not an indwelling soul, empirically, but a spirit as a spirit.

Homo est animal rationale.[127]

There is a difference in saying: I believe in *God,* or: I believe in *a* God (of which there might be several).

The knowledge of all human duties toward one another as divine commands (not as a particular duty toward God, for that would presuppose God).

[VIIth fascicle, sheet V, page 4]

[Man is a person, that is, a being capable of rights, who can encounter wrong or can consciously do it,][f] and to whom both can be done by others, which is not the case in animals or even lower organic beings. That being, in relation to whom all human duties are likewise necessarily his *commands,* is called *God,* and the categorical imperative which imposes them on man, contains the knowledge that all duties of right are to be regarded *as* divine commands (in him).

Human reason does not attain what kind of being God is in himself; only relation (the moral relation) indicates him, so that his nature is inscrutable and all-perfect for us. *Ens summum, summa intelligentia,*   22:58 *summum bonum:* all moral [determinations], but which leave his nature unattainable.

God is a *spirit,* that is, not the world-soul, for example, since this determination would make him dependent upon empirical determinations, as a sense-object. The transcendent concept of him is always only negative, and so [we] can only [know] him thereby that knowledge of him

---

f   See preceding note.

215

is not knowledge of the world, but the knowledge of all human duties *as divine commands* (hence not as if one had actually received such a command or prohibition) [*breaks off*]

So knowledge of this being is ampliative, not for the theoretical but only for the practical. He is inscrutable (*imperscrutabilis*).

The first act of the faculty of representation is that through which the subject makes itself into an object of its representations (*conscientia sui ipsius*) and belongs to *logic*. [It is a] representation through *concepts* or the *thought* of the given object, and is analytic. The second [act] contains the manifold given in intuition, insofar as that is represented under a principle of its aggregation; this [act] is thought synthetically *a priori* and belongs to *transcendental philosophy* (which contains synthetic knowledge *a priori* from concepts). Such knowledge is here not opposed to knowledge through the construction of concepts (for that would be mathematics) but, since it is here a question of philosophical knowledge (*metaphysics*), belongs to transcendental philosophy. That, however (as in Newton's *Philosophiae naturalis principia mathematica*), at least the ratio of the moving forces of bodies *in empty spaces* can be given *a priori*, belongs neither to metaphysics nor to transcendental philosophy – and thus *not to philosophy at all* but to pure *mathematics* insofar as it is applicable to physics.

The concept, or rather, the idea of *God* is the thought of a being before whom all human duties at the same time count as his commands.

22:59   God is the supreme power which is all-obligating, a being who is all-obligating but is not obligated in any relation.

God and the world. •Nature and freedom. Spinozism and naturalism. Transcendental idealism and personality.• The real, which cannot be a sense-object, and the real which must necessarily be such, if it is to be a given object – as space and time are each only one.

The totality of beings regarded as a whole or *sparsim* as multitude.

First division: *God* and the *world.* Second, in the world: nature and freedom of world-beings. Both contain absolute unity (there is only one God and one world). The world, insofar as it is not a whole combined *sparsim*, but an organic whole – e.g. of plants for animals and even for man.

An organic body is one which is possible in itself through purposes; hence, it is grounded through an immaterial being, or must at least be thought accordingly. The *continuum formarum* from plants, not as far as God (for there is no continuity in between).

Just as the species of organized bodies progresses from mosses to animals and [from] these to men as animals (a *continuum formarum*). N.B. Not that we intuit in the deity, as Spinoza imagines, but the reverse: that we carry our concept of God into the objects of pure intuition in our concept of transcendental philosophy.

Ideas of moral-practical reason, too, have moving forces on human nature. That means: to fear the Deity indirectly.

216

Of the indirect proof of God's existence, insofar as his necessary conse-   22:60
quences (the categorical imperative) precede.

It is not the concept of freedom which founds the categorical imperative
but the latter first founds the concept of freedom. Not technical-practical
but moral-practical reason contains the principle of God. Likewise, nature in the world does not lead to God (e.g. through its beautiful order)
but the reverse.

The holy Ghost judges, punishes and absolves through the categorical
imperative of duty, by means of moral-practical reason. Not as a substance
which belongs to nature. God and world are not empirical correlates.

The concept of God and of the personality of the thought of such a being
has reality.

There is a God in moral-practical reason, that is, in the idea of the
relation of man to right and duty. But not as a being outside man. God and
man is the totality of things.

The complex of all natural beings (the world), that is, all existence in
space and time – but not, therefore, of all beings, for pure moral beings
are not, in fact, also understood thereby.

Distributive ⎫
           ⎬ unity
Or collective ⎭

Of the psychological difference (which belongs to physics) and the metaphysical, which is not drawn from experience.

Morality [*Sittlichkeit*], that is, freedom under laws, is the characteristic
of a person.

217

[What is transcendental philosophy?]

21:9 [Ist fascicle, (half-)sheet I, page 1]

[*Top margin*]
Transition to the limit of all knowledge – God and the world.
The totality of beings, God and the world, presented in a synthetic system of the ideas of transcendental philosophy in relation to each other, by, etc.

[*Main text*]

I

In the order of the system of synthetic knowledge through *a priori* concepts (that is, in transcendental philosophy) the principle which provides the transition to the completion of the system is that of transcendental theology in the two questions:

1
What is God?

2
Is there a God?

§

The concept of *God* is that of a *person* – hence, that of a being who has rights, but against whom no other possesses right; of whom there may be either only one or else a species (God or gods) who must, nevertheless, possess personality, a will [*Willkühr*] – without which quality, they would not be gods but idols (*idola*), that is, things [*Sachen*].

21:10 [*Next to it, in the margin*]
Such a person cannot be several (in the plural); that is to say, if there is a God, then he is likewise singular in his person, and there are not many gods, because the concept of several would be quite identical. One would worship different gods, and their worship would be *superstition* and *idolatry*, which would be satanic.

218

§

God and the world are thought as members of the division of existing beings, of which each contains numerical unity (singularity) in itself; that is, one can as little speak of gods and worlds as of spaces and times, for these are all only parts of one space and one time.

Just the same is true of experience: in relation to whose magnitude one cannot depend upon experiences but only on experience as absolute unity. For absolute completeness of perceptions cannot occur, for that would be empirical, and hence stand under the suspicion of some deficiency; there thus remains nothing *a priori* except a principle of the possibility of experience.

In the concept of God, one thinks a person – that is, a rational being who, *first,* possesses rights, but, *second,* without being restricted by duties, restricts all other rational beings through commands of duty.

{To bring about the highest object of moral-practical reason in the world – *God* and the *world* form the objects of reason's willing. The totality of things: *ens summum summa.*} 21:11

[Right of the deleted passage]

In the world as a whole of rational beings there is also a being consisting in [*von*] moral-practical reason, and, consequently, an imperative of right: Thus, however, there is also a God.

[Main text continued]

Such a being is the most perfect in respect of every purely thought quality (*ens summum, summa intelligentia, summum bonum*). All these concepts are united in the disjunctive judgment: *God* and the *world* – in the real division of the negative or *contrarie oppositum*, which the totality of beings comprehends.

Both are a maximum: the one determined according to degree (qualitative), the other according to volume [or] space (quantitative); the one as object of pure reason, the other as sense-object. Both are infinite: the first as magnitude of appearance in space and time; the second according to degree (*virtualiter*), as limitless activity with regard to forces (mathematical or dynamic magnitude of sense-objects). One as *thing in itself* or *appearance.*

A being who *perceives* – has feeling, understanding, personality, and *rights* without *duty.*

A plurality of gods is as little thinkable as a plurality of worlds, but only one God and one world; both ideas depend necessarily upon each other. *Ens summum, summa intelligentia, summum bonum* (understanding, judgment, reason). Technical-practical and moral-practical reason and the principle which combines both in one idea. One cannot express the supreme intelligence through reason, since the latter consists only in the capacity to infer – that is, to judge mediately.

21:12   In moral-practical reason there lies the categorical imperative to regard all human duties *as* divine commands.

[*Margins*]
Technical-practical reason contains skill and arts. Moral-practical, duties.

The complex of all beings as substances is God and the world. The former [the latter?] is not coordinated as an aggregate with the latter [the former?], but subordinated to it in its existence, and combined with it in one system; not merely technically but moral-practically – which characteristic endows it with the quality of being a person.

Self-love (in soul and body) is not generally true or permissible; but benevolence toward oneself, without pleasure, is. But not hatred.
Heat is not radiant (*radians*),[128] but rather, the body is absorptive in relation to it – or exhaling, but not evaporating.

Personality is the characteristic of the being who has rights, hence, a moral quality. Consciousness of this quality in the subject belongs to moral-practical, not technical-practical reason, even when (and *insofar as*) it stands under duties. Does not have merely *technical*-[practical] but also *moral*-practical reason.

Spinoza's idea of the highest being – of intuiting all supersensible beings in God. Moral-practical reason. *Transcendental idealism.*
    Ens summum and *ens entium.*

Reason is only a mediately judging understanding. For the rule, and subsumption under it (its *casus*); namely, the conclusion, does not add anything further, but is only stated explicitly as inference or conclusion. The formula does not increase the content.

Herr von Hess and Prof. Kraus. Herr Schultz or Poerschke and Chaplan [Wasianski].[129]

21:13   [Ist fascicle, (half-)sheet I, page 2]
Transcendental philosophy thinks under the concept of God a substance endowed with maximum existence, with regard to all *active* properties (reality), independent of all sensible representations (pure rational representations *a priori*). It is a self-knowing supreme being (*ens summum, summa intelligentia, summum bonum*) adequate to all the true purposes of man (from understanding, judgment and reason) in an active relation to

the whole of all the objects of sensible representation; so that the division is made: God and the world in relation to each other.

Both are thought as a highest by **transcendental idealism,** according to which the possibility of objects of representations precedes as elements of knowledge, and what is subjective (according to *Spinoza's* conception) is intuited in God, whom reason makes for itself. The problem is thus: First, what is God? (What is understood by this concept?) Second question: Is there a God? (For gods cannot be thought of without contradiction, because the totality of given objects, thought together, does not permit plurality, and, if God is worshipped and his law obeyed, then such a plurality would represent idols.)

There exists a categorical imperative in the mind [*Gemüth*] (*mens,* not the *anima*) of every man in which a rigorous command of *duty* [shows] the transgressor his own reprehensibility (unworthiness of being happy); and, if abstraction is made from sensible appearance, not only is the transgressor's worthiness of being happy denied him, but he himself condemned through an irrevocable verdict (*dictamen rationis*). Not technical-practical but moral-practical reason absolves or condemns.

Nature deals despotically with man. Men destroy one another like wolves. Plants and animals overgrow and stifle one another. Nature does not observe the care and provision which they require. Wars destroy what long artifice has established and cared for. 21:14

A being who is originally universally law-giving for nature and freedom, is God. Not only the highest *being,* but also the highest *understanding – good* (with respect to holiness). *Ens summum, summa intelligentia, summum bonum.* The mere idea of him is likewise proof of his existence.

Among all the characteristics which are attributable to a thinking being, the first is to be conscious of oneself as a *person:* That is, according to transcendental idealism, the subject constitutes itself *a priori* into an object – not as given in appearance, in the *transition from the metaphysical foundations of natural science* to physics, but as a being who is founder and originator of his own self, by the quality of personality: the "*I am.*" As a man, I am a sense-object in space and time and, at the same time, an object of the understanding to myself. [*I*] *am a person;* consequently, a moral *being who has rights.*

The understanding (*mens*) is the faculty of deciding immediately, independent of sensible representations, and can be attributed to God. Reason, which only judges mediately, through inferences, is not original, but derivative.

It is not the principle of benevolence, directed toward happiness, but [the principles] of right which command categorically.

Of the allowable circle of connection in the extremities of forces.

A body can be an *ens simplex* as to its quality, e.g. *sulphur;* its product through combustion, on the other hand, a *compositum,* like *sulphuric acid.*

221

What is *obligated* is outside me, as a rational subject *which yet belongs to the world.* The world is the totality of sense-objects, not so much the outer as the inner.

21:15   [*Left margin*]

Transcendental idealism is the mode of representation which makes concepts, as elements of knowledge, into a whole – as a system of the possibility of synthetic *a priori* knowledge from concepts.

First the moral-practical, then the technical-practical reason. God and the world.

The transcendental idealism of that of which our understanding is itself the originator. Spinoza. To intuit everything in God. The categorical imperative. The knowledge of my duties as divine commands (expressed according to the categorical imperative).

The transcendental idealism of prescribing to reason synthetic *a priori* propositions *from concepts* (such as the categorical imperative is): *dictamen rationis* – not what we ought to *think* but what we ought to do.

The transition from the metaphysical foundations of natural science to physics takes place according to *a priori* principles; for the possibility of *experience,* indeed, which is an absolute whole – not a compiled (*compilatio*) *aggregate* which can be patched together out of perceptions. *Observatio et experimentum* presuppose a formal whole of possible experience as unity.

Reason precedes, with the projection of its forms (*forma dat esse rei*) because it alone carries with it necessity. *Spinoza.* The elements of knowledge and the moments of the determination of the subject through them. (To intuit everything in God.)

One cannot prove the *existence of God,* but one cannot avoid proceeding on the principle of such an idea, and assuming duties to be divine commands.

The concept of God is the concept of an *obligating* subject outside myself.

21:16   [Ist fascicle, sheet II, page 1]

2
GOD
AND
THE WORLD

Introduction

I.

The system of knowledge which formally (thus *a priori*) precedes experience and contains the conditions of the possibility of experience in general, divides into two main branches: nature and freedom, both of which must be treated theoretically and practically; the product of technical-practical or moral-practical reason and their principles

$$\left(\begin{array}{l} \text{inclination and morals } [Sitten] \\ \\ \text{instinct – understanding} \end{array} \right) \quad \text{emerges.}$$

II.

The concept of freedom is not the basis on which the concepts of right and duty can be founded, but the reverse: The concept of duty contains the ground of the possibility of the concept of freedom, which is postulated through the categorical imperative. It is utterly impossible to unite the principle of causal relations in the world with freedom; for that would be an effect without a cause.

If I *ought* to do something, then I must also be *able* to do it, and what is absolutely incumbent upon me, I must also be capable of performing.

The property of a rational being, to possess freedom of the will in general (independence from the incentives of nature), cannot be directly proved as a causal principle, but only indirectly, through its consequences; insofar, that is, as it contains the ground of the possibility of the categorical imperative.

III.

21:17

A being for whom all human duties are likewise his commands, is God. He must be capable of everything, since he wills everything which duty commands. He is the highest being with respect to power, and, as a being who has rights, a living God in the quality of a *person*. A single God, like the object of his power, subordinate to him: one world.

IV.

These concepts are altogether contained analytically in the idea of the highest being, which we ourselves have created; but the problem of transcendental philosophy still remains unresolved: *Is there a God?*

•*Cosmotheology*• V.

There is an object of moral-practical reason which contains the principle of all human duties "as if divine commands," without it being the case that one may assume, for the sake of this principle, a particular substance existing outside man.

223

VI.

Cosmotheology. An idea of the unity of the connection of intuition with concepts, according to Spinoza.

[*Top margin*]

Transcendental philosophy is the principle of synthetic *a priori* knowledge from concepts.

(1) Transition from the metaphysical foundations of natural science to physics. (2) Transition from physics to transcendental philosophy. (3) Transition from transcendental philosophy to the system of nature and freedom. (4) Conclusion. Of the universal connection of the living forces of all things in reciprocal relation: God and the world.

[*Right margin*]

Philosophy – metaphysical and metaphysics

Mathematics and physics

Space and time

God and the world: the supersensible and the sensible being in the totality of things (*universum*), represented systematically in synthetic relation to each other.

21:18   Space is not a *being*, nor is time, but only the form of intuition: nothing but the *subjective* form of intuition.

Not atomism (corpuscular philosophy, *atomi ac inane*). In full space, yet all-penetrating of it, through motion – partly progressive, partly oscillating.

There are not experiences, but only experience and what it teaches (which presupposes *a priori* a form of experience). But many perceptions, indeed, which stand in relation to experience through observation and experiment. Hippocrates.

(1) Metaphysics, (2) transcendental philosophy, (3) physics, (4) *dynamica generalis*, which [presents] the laws of the moving forces, as they stand in relation to one another in *empty* space.

The living bodily being has a soul (*animal*). If it is a person, then it is a human being.

[*Right of IV, V, and VI*]

The highest principle of the system of pure reason in transcendental philosophy, as reciprocal relation of the ideas of God and the world. Not that the world is God, or God a being in the world (world-soul); but the phenomena of causality are in space and time, etc.

An immaterial and intelligent principle as substance is a spirit (*mens*).

The animal.

Nature *causes* (*agit*). Man *does* (*facit*). The rational subject acting with

consciousness of purpose *operates* (*operatur*). An intelligent cause, not accessible to the senses, *directs* (*dirigit*).

God and the world. Freedom and nature. The latter with personality –
or *natura bruta* in contrast with intelligent nature.

Knowledge through reason, laws for reason, man as person or as sense-
object.

The products of nature are in space and time, those of freedom, under
the laws of moral-practical reason (*dictamina rationis practicae*).

[*Above VI*]   21:19
Newton's attractive forces through empty space.
How is empty space itself perceived, for the forces cannot be, indepen-
dently, without physical reality?

[*Below VI*]
There is a God, not as a world-soul in nature, but as a personal
principle of human reason (*ens summum, summa intelligentia, summum
bonum*), which, as the idea of a holy being, combines complete freedom
with the law of duty in the categorical imperative of duty; *both technical-
practical* and *moral-practical* reason *coincide* in the idea of God and the
world, as the *synthetic unity of transcendental philosophy.*

[. . .]ᵃ and empirical personality (*altos videt sub pedibus nimbos et rauca
tonitrua calcat*).¹³⁰

God is not the world-soul.

Spinoza's concept of God and man, according to which the philosopher
intuits all things in God, is enthusiastic [*schwärmerisch*] (*conceptus fanaticus*).

[Ist fascicle, sheet II, page 2]

{*Cosmotheology*

God and the world. A system of transcendental philosophy, of technical-
theoretical and moral-practical reason.

The concept of God is that of a being as the highest cause of world-
beings and as a person. How the freedom of a world-being is possible
cannot be proved directly; it would only be practicable in the concept of
God, if he were assumed.}

I
God

The categorical imperative leads first to the concept of freedom, the
possibility of which property of a rational being we could not otherwise

ᵃ Word illegible.

225

21:20 suspect. These commands are divine (*praecepta inviolabilia*), that is, permit no mitigation, and the judgment of condemnation is pronounced upon their transgression, through man's own reason, just as if addressed by a moral power which executes the judgment.

The highest level of progress in the system of pure reason: God and the world.

The whole of the supersensible and of the sensible object, represented in logical and real relation to each other.*

These representations are not merely concepts but, at the same time, ideas, which give the material to synthetic *a priori* laws from concepts, and so do not merely emerge from metaphysics but found transcendental philosophy.

Each of the two contains a maximum, and there can only be one of each. **"There is one God and one world."**

a

The first object [*Gegenstand*] sets itself above things as objects [*Sachen*] through *personality* – that is, through the sublime quality of *freedom,* to be itself an *original cause:* a property and capacity whose possibility cannot be *directly* either proved or explained, but which conclusively validates its reality indirectly, through the incontrovertible dictates of reason in the *categorical* imperative.

The principle of the knowledge of all human duties *as* (*tanquam*) universally valid commands, that is, *in the quality* of a highest, holy and powerful law-giver, raises the subject thought thereby to the rank of a single, powerful being: That is, the existence of such a being cannot be concluded from the idea which we ourselves think of God, but yet we may infer as [if] there were such a being – with the same force as if such a being (*dictamen rationis*) were combined in substance with our being – to the same consequences.*b*

21:23 [*Top margin*]
What is merely subjective in sensible representation is feeling.

[*Under "I God"*]
•The highest standpoint of transcendental philosophy is that which unites God and the world synthetically, under one principle.•
Nature and freedom.

---

* The logical relation is that of identity and difference; the real that of action and reaction with respect to the causality of the subjects.

b Kant's paragraph continues on page 3.

226

[*Left margin*]

Difference between the *principles* and *laws* of technical-practical or moral-practical reason.

The concept of freedom emerges from the categorical imperative of duty. *Sic volo sic iubeo stet pro ratione voluntas.*[131]

The possibility of such a property as freedom does not emerge analytically, but synthetically, in transcendental philosophy, and is the law of the latter.

The thinking subject also creates for itself a world, as object of possible experience in space and time. This object is only one world. Moving forces are inserted in the latter (e.g. attraction and repulsion) without which there would be no perceptions; but only what is formal.

World is the complex (*complexus*) of things in one space and one time; thus, 21:24 since neither are something given objectively, in appearance. God is a rational concept of freedom, insofar as there lies in him a principle of the connection of the manifold which only pertains to a *person*. Concept of duty. The concept of *freedom*, which points in the direction of the concept of duty, is that of a person – both of man in the world and of God. With respect to the world, a *technical*-practical; with respect to God, a *moral*-practical concept.

There are *gods* as little as there are *worlds;* rather, *one* God and *one* world. Transcendental *cosmology* and transcendental *theology* (cosmotheology). Not the highest being (*ens summum*), but the being of all beings (*ens entium*).

The *totality* of things (*omnitudo*) is, therefore, not yet represented as a *whole* of the united objects (distributive or collective: thus, *logical* or *real* unity). In intuition (space and time) as appearance (mathematically).

Analogy between attraction and light, where seeing precedes the light, and, of the former is not operative in space, then neither is the latter. Illumination in empty space. Double concept of reflection.

Seeing is repulsive – like touch.

[Ist fascicle, sheet II, page 3]   21:21

And the cosmotheological proposition: "There is a God," must be honored and obeyed in the moral-practical relation just as much as if it were to be expressed by the highest being, although no proof of it takes place in technical-practical respect, and to believe or even wish for the appearance of such a being would be an enthusiastic delusion – taking ideas as perceptions.

It can be said without qualification: "There are not gods; there are not worlds," but rather: "There is one world and there is one God" in reason, as a practically-determining principle.

There is a fact of moral-practical reason: the categorical imperative, which commands for nature freedom under laws and through which freedom itself demonstrates the principle of its own possibility; the commanding subject is God.

This commanding being is not outside man as a substance different from man. [It is, rather,] the counterpart to the world represented as the complex of all sensible beings (their totality), as the counterpart [of God] in space and time, as absolute *a priori* unity in intuition. Like God (as the supersensible principle which combines the manifold of the world through reason) the world is thought *a priori*, as absolute unity. These two ideals have practical reality.

A being which includes the whole of all possible sense-objects, is the *world.* (A being in relation to whom all human duties are likewise his commands, is God.)

God and the world are ideas of moral-practical and technical-practical reason, founded on sensible representation; the former contains the predicate of personality, the latter that of . . . Both together in one system, however, and related to each other under one principle, [are] not substances outside my thought, but rather, [they are] the thought through which we ourselves make these objects (through synthetic *a priori* cognitions from concepts) and, subjectively, are self-creators of the objects thought.

21:22 The moving forces which are causal principles contain the representations of God, the world, and my subject of intuition and feeling, as moving forces in the world. The two [namely, God and the world], united in one concept, [contain] the intuition of nature in space and time, feeling and the spontaneity of connection of both into a system of technical-practical and moral-practical reason through freedom (spontaneity and receptivity, both combined in a system). God, the world, and I, who combine both objects in one subject. Intuition, feeling, and the faculty of desire. God, the world (both outside me) and the rational subject which connects both through freedom. (Not substance.) Spinoza's transcendental idealism which, taken literally, is transcendent, that is, an object without a concept: representing the subjective as objective.

[*Margins*]

God and the world are, according to their idea, two heterogeneous beings, not in analytical unity (identical); nevertheless, they could be thought in synthetic unity according to principles of transcendental philosophy. How, then, does their combination acquire reality?

The totality of things (*universum*) contains God and the world. **World** means the *whole* of sensible beings.

There is here then a relation of two heterogeneous objects, a relation of efficient causes (*nexus causalis*), indeed; if the *totality* of beings is thought, however, then this is subjective rather than objective (lying not in the things but in the thinking subject): the highest good (the original and the derivative).

228

The two principles: that of moral-practical and the principle of technical-theoretical reason (to which mathematics also belongs) together form the complete unity.

Knowledge of all human duties *as* divine, not [knowledge] of a substance.

God is the subject of the categorical imperative of duties, and these are therefore called divine commands.

The division into God and the world is not analytic (logical) but synthetic: that is, through real opposition.

Three principles: God, the world, and the concept of the subject which   21:23
unites them and brings synthetic unity into these concepts (*a priori*) insofar as reason makes this transcendental unity itself. Aenesidemus. *God, the world, and I; God,* the *world,* and the human *spirit,* as that which combines the former two: moral-practical reason with its categorical imperative.

The intelligent subject which grounds the combination of God with the world under a principle.

The highest nature
The highest freedom
The highest good (blessedness)
(happiness)

1. The question: Is there a God? One cannot prove such an object of thought as substance outside the subject: [It is,] rather, thought.

[Ist fascicle, sheet II, page 4]   21:24

GOD, THE WORLD AND THE CONSCIOUSNESS
OF MY EXISTENCE IN THE WORLD
IN SPACE AND TIME.
THE FIRST IS NOUMENON, THE SECOND
PHENOMENON, THE THIRD CAUSALITY
OF THE SUBJECT'S SELF-DETERMINATION INTO
CONSCIOUSNESS
OF HIS PERSONALITY: THAT IS, OF FREEDOM
IN RELATIONS OF THE TOTALITY OF BEINGS
IN GENERAL.

I   21:25
There is a God

There is a being in me, which is different from me and which stands in an efficient causal relation (*nexus effectivus*) toward myself (*agit, facit, operatur*);

229

itself free (that is, not being dependent upon the laws of nature in space and time) it judges me inwardly (justifies or condemns); and I, man, am this being myself – it is not some substance outside me. What is most surprising is that this causality is a determination [of my will] to action in freedom ([that is], not as a natural necessity).

This inexplicable inner characteristic reveals itself through a fact, the categorical imperative of duty (*nexus finalis:* God; *effectivus:* the world) whether it is affirmative or negative (command and prohibition).* The spirit of man (*mens*), under a compulsion which is only possible through *freedom.*

It is, however, if one judges directly according to the principle of self-activity, completely impossible to think for oneself a law of self-activity from freedom; for every act of the latter would be effect without cause. For this reason it has been frequently opposed. But self-activity from freedom can and must be conceded indirectly,† as a consequence of the categorical imperative (which is incontrovertibly true) and all human duties, as divine commands, must be obeyed unconditionally.

Freedom of the will [*Willkühr*] is a fact which cannot be attributed to the object as a natural being; but, yet, it is a principle of causality in the world, and appears to contain effect without cause in its very concept. That which commands as a person (categorical imperative), hence as God, hence *as if* a person.

21:26

All knowledge consists in the capacity to *think, intuit,* perceive, and know in experience, and, as efficient cause, is the system of technical-practical or moral-practical reason: not for metaphysics, but for transcendental philosophy. The latter contains synthetic *a priori* principles from concepts, not merely from intuitions; it contains, subjectively in human reason as an absolute whole, a genealogical tree of such principles, whose roots ramify into branches, and a tree of knowledge of quite different kinds: nature and freedom, the world and God. Not a system of nature but of thought.

[Left margin]

The thoroughgoing determination of oneself in experience as unity, [is] existence. But not God's.

All expressions of moral-practical reason are divine (*dictamina sacrosancta*) because they contain the moral imperative (the categorical) and, thereby, alone prove the reality of freedom. But it is not God in substance whose existence is proved.

---

* As is found in the Decalogue, for instance.
† Indirect proof is a mode of proof or examination in which it is inferred apodictically from the consequences of that which is to be proved to its ground.

Freedom under laws which reason prescribes to itself: the categorical imperative in transcendental philosophy.

Transition from the metaphysical foundations to transcendental philosophy.

A concept is enthusiastic if that which is in man is represented as something which is outside him, and the product of his thought represented as thing [*Sache*] in itself (substance). *Principia sunt dictamina rationis propriae: leges communes.*[132]

[Ist fascicle, sheet III, page 1]   21:27

3
SYSTEM OF TRANSCENDENTAL PHILOSOPHY IN THREE SECTIONS

[*Top margin*]

God, the *world*, universum, and I myself, *man*, as moral being.

God, the world, and the inhabitant of the world: man in the world.

God, the world, and that which thinks both in real relation to each other: the subject as rational world-being.

The *medius terminus* (copula) in judgment is here the judging subject (the thinking world-being, man in the world). Subject, predicate, copula.

[*Main text*]

I
God

§1

The concept of such a being is not that of substance – that is, of a being which exists independent of my thought – but the idea (one's own creation, •thought-object, *ens rationis•*) of a reason which constitutes itself into a thought-object, and establishes synthetic *a priori* propositions, according to principles of transcendental philosophy. It is an ideal: There is not and cannot be a question as to whether such an object exists, since the concept is transcendent.

§2

There is, however, in moral-practical reason, a principle of duty: That is, the categorical imperative, according to which reason is absolutely (unconditionally) commanding over all incentives of sensibility (nature) even

231

21:28 when in antagonism to the latter. [Reason] is an effect in the world, without cause, as it would appear; there are, indeed, actions from freedom to which we are determined and compelled, which form of causality appears to contain a contradiction with itself, and, moreover, its possibility is absolutely incomprehensible (*sic volo sic iubeo stet pro ratione voluntas*). In this freedom and independence from all natural influence and direction, a divinity may rightly [be seen] – not of man, however, since divinity is the highest thinkable and, likewise, supremely powerful [*breaks off*]

[*Next to it, in the margin*]
Not a sensible object, a person, rather, what itself thinks (*non dabile sed cogitabile*)

§3

According to this principle, all human duties can, at the same time, be expressed as divine commands (by the principle's formal aspect) even if no such cause, determining reason, were to be assumed as substance. From the practical point of view, it is one and the same thing whether one founds the divinity of the command in human reason, or founds it [in] such a person, since the difference is more one of phraseology than a doctrine which amplifies knowledge.*

§4

The critique of pure reason divides into philosophy and mathematics.
The former, in turn, into metaphysics and transcendental philosophy.
The latter [namely, transcendental philosophy] into the ideas of theoretical and practical reason. •Nature and freedom.•
I: man. Phenomenon, noumenon. The object in appearance and the thing *in itself.*
(The totality of beings, regarded analytically or synthetically (*omnia, aut universum*).)

21:29 [*Margins*]
Objects of thought are: (a) a being (b) a thing [*Sache*] (c) a person.
The highest is: *ens summum – summa intelligentia, summum bonum.*
How is the concept of freedom possible? Only through the imperative of duty which commands categorically.
God, a threefold person, according to [his] powers; not in three persons, which would be polytheism.

---

* The expression *as* divine commands can here [be translated] by *tanquam* (as if) or else by *ceu* (absolutely) [*breaks off*]

No world-material can either *come to be* or *cease to be.*

What compels from us the idea of *God?* No concept of experience, no metaphysics. What presents this concept *a priori* is transcendental philosophy.

The concept of duty. The latter, however, presupposes the concept of the freedom of a causality, whose possibility [can]not be explained, but rests on the capacity of the categorical imperative.

[*Between §2 and §3*]

God, the *world,* and *man* as a person: that is, as a being who unites these concepts.

[*Next to it, right margin*]

Ideas are self-created subjective principles of the power of thought: not fictions but thought.

God is not the world soul.

What unifies the *universum* (not *mundus*), *mens,* insofar as it has personality.

Pluralitas mundorum but *unitas universi.*

The *totality* (*universum*) is to be distinguished from the *world,* of which there can be many. The former belongs to ideas, and to transcendental philosophy.

The *totality* of things (as the one whole): *universum.*

God and the *world,* and the spirit of man which thinks both (*mens*).

The power of thought must precede.

To totality of beings (*universum*). God and the world.

Are thoughts prior to the thinker? Is light prior to the seer? Attraction.

[*Bottom margin*]

Whether there is a threefold or a fourfold form of immateriality. *Spiritus (animantis), animae et mentis (dido).*

[Ist fascicle, sheet III, page 2]   21:30

The *totality* of beings (the *universum*). The latter divides into God and the [*breaks off*]

§5

The reality of the concept of freedom can, thus, only be presented and proved *indirectly,* through an intermediary principle, rather than *directly* (immediately). Likewise the proposition: "There is a God," namely, in human, moral-practical reason, [as] a determination of one's actions in the knowledge of human duties *as* (as if) divine commands – "we are

233

originally of divine race"[133] with regard to our vocation and its dispositions, and the to us incomprehensible capacity of freedom places us infinitely outside the sphere of [*breaks off*]

§6

That which can be thought but not given in perception (*cogitabile, non dabile*) is a mere *idea*, and, if it deals with what is a maximum, then it is an *ideal*. The highest ideal as person (of whom there *can* only be a *single* one) is *God.*

§7

The world (which is also called nature, thought substantively) is the whole of sense-objects (*universum, universitas rerum*). These objects are things [*Sachen*] in contrast to persons.

Taken in this sense there can, thus, only be one world, since the totality is only one; the plurality of worlds (*pluralitas mundorum*) signifies only the multiplicity of many systems, of which there may be an innumerable amount, together with their different forms and real relations (their effects in space and time). •God is not an *inhabitant of the world*, but, rather, its *owner.* As the former (as sensible being) he would be the world-soul, belonging to nature.•

21:31
§8

In this relation, there must, however, be a means of the combination of both [ideas] into an absolute whole – and that is *man* who, as a natural being, has at the same time personality – in order to connect the principle of the senses with that of the supersensible.

§9

From which determinations of the faculty of representation does the system arise? And can the completeness of its elements be formed, insofar as one analyzes that whole found *a priori* in us and develops its formal element from one's own reason? Lichtenberg. Aenesidemus. *Architectonic* of pure reason. Its highest standpoint of speculative (not yet practical) philosophy; from *specula* – view from a height over the plain of experience, not touching or testing by tapping, but gazing about oneself into the distance. Difference between technical-practical and moral-practical reason (skill, prudence, wisdom – *vision* and *touch*).

[*Margin, next to §6*]

God, the world, and man as (*cosmopolita*) **person** (moral being), as sensible being (inhabitant of the world) conscious of its freedom; the rational sensible being in the world.

[*Margin, next to §7 and §8*]

God, the world, and man: a sensible-practical being in the world (architectonic).

A *cosmotheoros*[134] who creates the elements of knowledge of the world himself, *a priori*, from which he, as, at the same time, an inhabitant of the world, constructs a world-vision [*Weltbeschauung*] in the idea.

[*Margin, next to §9*]

The difference between fragmentary and systematic aggregation (from a principle); from which difference the possibility of experience (which is, in turn, what raises a multitude of perceptions into experience) also emerges.

[*Below §9*]   21:32

It is necessary in practical reason's doctrine of purposes to proceed not from parts to the whole, but analytically, from the idea of the whole to the parts.

The world in space and time, and the moving forces in empty space, which, if the central body ceases, are nothing.

Second, freedom as effect without cause.

Faculty of thinking which is not yet substance.

Externality [*rest illegible*]

[Ist fascicle, sheet III, page 3]

TRANSCENDENTAL PHILOSOPHY'S HIGHEST STANDPOINT
GOD, THE *WORLD*, AND THE THINKING BEING IN THE WORLD (*MAN*).

I
God

§1

Even if God is to be regarded in philosophy merely as a thought-object (*ens rationis*), it [is] nevertheless necessary to present the latter and to enumerate all the predicates of pure reason attributed to it, which emerge from this idea analytically. Such a thought-object must necessarily be presented, whether or not there may [be] such a substance, which [contains] in its concept the idea of a person, uniting both the highest technical-practical and moral-practical perfection, and the causality appropriate to it; this cannot be ignored, whether one assumes that such a substance exists or not. Even if there are "fools who have said in their heart: There is no God,"[135] they may well be *unwise*, although they are nevertheless free to be *agnostic* about this concept and what it contains (although not willfully) just as the *Critique of Pure Reason* would have it, which cannot be ignored by any philosopher, either in theoretical or in practical use.

21:33   §2

The second merely analytical proposition which follows from the former concept is that, if it is admitted that there be a God, it follows identically from this that there is a single God; since the totality of things (which is single and of the same quality) allows of no plurality, and, hence, it cannot be said (or even thought) that there are *gods*. For the concept or the idea of God is (1) that of a highest being (*ens summum*) (2) of a highest being of the understanding, that is, of a person (*summa intelligentia*) (3) of the original source of everything which may be an unconditional purpose (*summum bonum*). The ideal of moral-practical reason and of all that which can serve as a rule for the latter: the archetype (*archetypon*) and *architect* of the world, although that can serve only in infinite approximation. We see him as in a glass: never face to face.[136]

He is not the world-soul (*anima mundi*), not a world-spirit (*spiritus*, not *demiurgus*) as subordinate world-builder [*Weltbaumeister*].

[Right margin]

The concept of this being represents a thought-object (*ens rationis*), as the highest being with respect to every quality (*ens summum, summa intelligentia, summum bonum*). The first in power, the second in knowledge (as omniscient), the third in all-wisdom: that is, in that which belongs to all true purposes. If such a being exists, it can only be single; there are no gods, but, rather, what are assumed in plurality as such (if God is thought (worshipped) as the ideal of the greatest perfection) are idols (godlings, not gods). The maximum of every kind, if it signifies a *totality*, can only be one; in the logical opposition of this concept [namely, God] with that of the world, which, as universum, also signifies an absolute totality, only one world can be thought. The plurality of worlds (*pluralitas mundorum i.e. universitatis rerum*) is a contradiction in itself.

21:34   God, the world, and the creator (*architectus*). The latter, however, is not the Demiurge: a mechanically acting principle.

Man is subject and object of knowledge to himself. (Spinoza) World is absolute, since space and time are one.

236

Animals can be *made* by God, because there is, indeed, in them a *spiritus* and even *anima* (*immateriale*), but not *mens*, as free will.

Whether God could also give man a good will? No, rather, that requires freedom.

[Ist fascicle, sheet III, page 4]

{THE HIGHEST STANDPOINT OF
TRANSCENDENTAL PHILOSOPHY
IN THE SYSTEM OF THE TWO IDEAS
BY

GOD, THE WORLD, AND THE SUBJECT WHICH
CONNECTS BOTH OBJECTS,
THE THINKING BEING IN THE WORLD.
GOD, THE WORLD, AND WHAT UNITES BOTH
INTO A SYSTEM:
THE THINKING, INNATE PRINCIPLE OF MAN IN
THE WORLD (MENS).
MAN AS A BEING IN THE WORLD,
SELF-LIMITED THROUGH NATURE AND DUTY.

I
God

All three concepts are ideas:* that is, pure (not empirical, adopted from the perception of given representations) cognitions, self-created through reason.}

THE HIGHEST STANDPOINT OF   21:35
TRANSCENDENTAL PHILOSOPHY
IN THE TWO MUTUALLY RELATED IDEAS,
GOD AND THE WORLD

[*Next to the above heading, in the margin*]
Newtonian attraction through empty space and the freedom of man are analogous concepts to each other: They are categorical imperatives – *ideas*.

§1

They are both thought (*a priori*) rather than *given* (empirically); in real relation, indeed, for the foundation of a system of ideal intuitions. What is

---

* An ideal is an invented sense-object, which, however, in virtue of its perfection, is taken for a mere idea.

postulated is not the existence of the latter's objects, but (only subjectively) the representation of them as mere thought-objects (*entia rationis*) in one doctrinal system. Both present, singly and together, a *maximum* – and, therefore, an absolute *individual* (*unicum*): *If there is a God*, there can only be *one* God, and, if there is a world outside my thoughts (that there is a world, however, [is] given categorically, rather than hypothetically), then only *one* world (*universum*) can be thought. The world – *universum*. Whether the world has limits, is on a par with the question whether space has limits; for the latter cannot be delineated by any object determining the senses. If gods are spoken of, then these are only *idols* (*idola*), and, if it is a question of *worlds*, then these are only *masses:* that is, limited parts of the infinitely distributed matter occupying space (*corpora*).

§2

By *God*, one understands a person who has rightful power over all rational [beings]. This concept presents a maximum (*potestatis legislatoriae*): a being "before whom every knee should bow, of things in heaven, and things in earth, etc.," the highest being, the holy, who can only be single.

21:36   No active opposition between God and the world takes place.

The concept of freedom is founded on a fact: the categorical imperative.

§3

The question which first arises: From where does this concept come to us? It is not a hypothetical concept, in order to support other propositions, but is thought as self-subsisting (absolutely) although not meant as if such a being thereby exists. The concept is problematic. A problematic being would be something quite different – as, for instance, caloric, which is only a place holder, impermissibly used as a hypothesis for one's own (and others') temporary satisfaction.

Twofold self-knowledge: as [knowledge of a] thing in the world, which [is] *a priori* constitutive; and empirical [knowledge] [*breaks off*]

§4

The concept of the world is the complex of the existence of everything which *is* in space and time, insofar as empirical knowledge of it is possible. Under it, human actions: *agere, facere, operari*. The question is, whether *free* actions of man can also fall under it. But there is a fact here: the categorical imperative.

The Ten Commandments are altogether negative. The categorical imperative is only the principle of freedom.

[*Left margin*]

Man, as animal, belongs to the world, but, as person, also to the beings who are capable of rights – and, consequently, have *freedom* of the will. Which ability [*habilitaet*] essentially differentiates him from all other beings; *mens* is innate to him.

God, the world, and I: the thinking being in the world who connects them.

God and the world are the two objects of transcendental philosophy; 21:37 thinking *man* is the subject, predicate and copula. The subject who combines them in one proposition. These are logical relations in a proposition, not dealing with the existence of objects, but merely bringing what is formal in their relations of these objects to synthetic unity: God, the world, and I, man, a world-being myself, who combines the two.

There is one God and one universe. The totality. *Pluralitas mundorum* is not *universorum* (*contradictio in adjecto*).

God, the world, and the free will of the rational being in the world. All are infinite.

Freedom lies in the categorical imperative and its possibility transcends all grounds of explanation from nature. All human duties have thus been regarded as superhuman (that is, as divine) commands. It is not as if a particular person had to be presupposed to promulgate these laws; they lie, rather, in moral-practical reason. There is such a reason in man: Moral-practical reason commands categorically, *like* a person, through the imperative of duty.

Integrity is not the opposite of depravity (perversity) but of loss (as of a limb) – and of imperfection by deprivation.[137]

[*Bottom margin*]

The question whether God could not give man a better will would amount to this: that he should make it the case that [man] wills what he does not will. It operates in terms of a concept of time which is based on phenomena. From a noumenal point of view, the question would be: whether another will is thinkable in place of this one?

Whether immortality can be included *a priori* among the characteristics which belong to freedom? Yes, if there is a devil. Since the latter has reason, but not infinity.

[. . .]

21:40   [Ist fascicle, sheet IV, page 1]

[. . .]

First note

Transcendental philosophy is the system of synthetic *a priori* cognitions
from concepts, insofar as the latter is founded in itself. It contains the
elementary representations, not as perceptions which are empirically aggregated (*compilatio*), but an *a priori* principle, under which what is formal
in the composition of the manifold [founds] the totality of things (*omnitudo*), as a whole (*totum*) in unconditional unity [*breaks off*]

Second note

Each of these objects is absolutely one (*unicum*). If *God* is, he is only one.
If there is a *world* in the metaphysical sense then there is only one world;
and if there is *man* he is the *ideal*, the archetype (*prototypon*), of a man
adequate to duty.
[. . .]

21:41   *[Right margin]*
[. . .] We do not derive the data of intuition from sensible representations
(neither from impressions nor concepts); rather, it is we who first provide
the data out of which cognitions can be woven (into the cognitions possible from them): e.g. attraction, for the sake of determinations and laws of
its relation in space and time. *He who would know the world must first
manufacture it* – in his own self, indeed.

                                                        Lichtenberg[138]

    1st division – God
    2nd   – –   – the world
    3rd   – –   – what unites both in a system. Man in the world.
    God, the inner vital spirit of man in the world.

21:44   [Ist fascicle, sheet IV, page 2]

[. . .]

[Left margin]
  Worm – amanuensis[139]

Titlesheet and Preface
  The world as *universum*

In all these objects, a maximum: idea, *ergo unicum* in all three cases.

1. theoretical-speculative [reason]
2. technical-practical [reason]
3. moral-practical reason

From intuitions, *a priori* concepts, and ideas.
The idea of freedom leads, through the categorical imperative, to God.

1. speculative [reason]
2. practical [reason]
3. technical-practical [reason]
4. moral-practical reason in one system.

[. . .]

[Ist fascicle, sheet IV, page 4]   21:50

I

God

What does reason think in the *idea of God?*
A being who *knows* everything, is *capable* of everything, and *wills* what is good (*ens summum, summa intelligentia, summum bonum*). The *highest wisdom.*

Definition

What do I think under the concept of God? A being of the greatest perfection, a being who knows everything, and is capable of everything, and contains personality in his self-consciousness (*ens summum, summa intelligentia, summum bonum*), and is the originator of all other things.

Spinoza. The enormous idea of intuiting all things, and *oneself, in God* – transcendent, not merely transcendental, and immanently objective (in itself).

Question: Do God and the world form a *system* together, or is only the doctrine of the connection of the two subjectively systematic?

[*Left of the above*]
•Axiom, theorem, problem and conclusion [*Folgerung*].•

Axiom

The concept of God is a principle of moral-practical reason: the knowledge of all human duties, to regard them as divine commands.

241

[*Left and right of "Theorem"*]

Transcendental philosophy commences from what is subjective in reason, from the spontaneity of synthetic principles, through *ideas*. Transcendental idealism.

Theorem

There is in man an active, but supersensible principle which, independently of nature and the causality of the world, determines nature's appearances, and is called freedom.

21:51   [*Right of the above*]

The *veto* and *iubeo* in the pure imperative of duty.

The categorical imperative realizes the concept of God, but only in moral-practical respect, not with regard to natural objects.

God and man, both *persons*. The latter is *bound to duty*, the former *commands duty*.

The totality of beings (*universum*), God and the world, represented as united in a system of the ideas of transcendental philosophy. Technical-practical, moral-practical reason, freedom of man, and hence the *categorical* imperative: **God**. Space (*a priori* intuition) is *subjective, appearance*.

Ideas are images [*Bilder*] (intuitions), created *a priori* through pure reason, which, [as] merely subjective thought-objects and elements of knowledge, precede knowledge of things. They are the archetypes (*prototypa*), by which Spinoza thought all things had to be seen, according to their forms, in God: that is, in what is formal in the elements out of which we make God for ourselves.

God is a being who only has *rights* and no *duties* (only against himself) and is a person who is holy for himself. Freedom – man [a being] who has rights but *also* duties – third, unconditional duties, indeed. Man, as *world-citizen*, who, under the divine régime, is necessarily subject to both [rights and duties], as in a state.

Transcendental idealism. *Mere* space is not therefore an *empty* space. The latter would be something positive. The former is that from which *abstraction* is made.

N.B. Space (in the world) and time (in the subject who determines space inwardly) come first, as *a priori* forms, and furnish self-made concepts, from whose elements knowledge emerges. Attraction through empty space (*actio in distans*, according to Newton); freedom, which postulates a principle of causality in the world (as effect without cause) merely
21:52   by its *veto* in the categorical imperative: [Both] lie outside the world, influencing it. Receptivity for knowledge (*receptivitas*) is founded on the faculty of creating receptivity in oneself – Lichtenberg.[140]

The oath: *by God,* or, by the *living God,* is presumption if it is given in connection with empirical truthfulness (that is, in connection with natural objects).

God and the world. A system of ideas in the highest standpoint of transcendental philosophy.

(These ideas of God and the world lie necessarily and *a priori* in reason, and this division [is] *a priori.* (Lichtenberg))

The genius appropriate to mathematics is quite different in species from that fixed by nature for philosophy: Reccard and Kästner.[141]

[*Right of the above:*]
The one relates to art and skill (for arbitrary ends), the other to *wisdom* – to the *final end.*

The *difference* between the totality of beings and the **universe** [*Weltall*], of which God can be part.

Receptivity – spontaneity.

[*Top margin*]
God and the World. A System of Ideas in the Highest Standpoint of Transcendental Philosophy, presented *by,* etc.

God and the World
the Totality of Beings
presented in a System in the Highest Standpoint of Transcendental
Philosophy

Is the reason for the totality of beings (*universum*) that a single being must found all existence? There can [be] worlds, but only one *universum* [*breaks off*]

[*Left margin, next to "God is a being"*]
His name is *holy,* his honor is worship, and his will almighty, and he himself is idea. His kingdom in nature is still to come, however.[142]

[*Left and bottom margin*]
Transcendental philosophy is the science of pure synthetic *a priori* knowledge from concepts.

A. Which concepts does the idea of God contain, and where does the call to man come from to establish such an idea as indispensable to reason? Or is it a free, problematic invention, and its object a hypothetical thing, like caloric? Herein the question remains unresolved: Is there a God? Yet can it be said that, if God is, then he is only *one?* 21:53

243

God represented as a *person* – but not a corporeal being – spirit. Hence not gods (idols: bodies not spirit). I, man, belong to the *world*-whole, and he is *part* of it. And yet, he is a *person*.

B. There is a world. *Idealism* and transc[endental] *egoism* cannot abandon the objective reality of sensible representations (hence, experience); for it is one and the same thing to say: There *are* such objects, or: *I am a subject* to whom the state of my representation delivers such a lawlike chain of the manifold, which we call *experience.* There can be *worlds* (*mundi*) in space, and yet only *one world* (*universum*) exists.

[. . .]

21:59   [Ist fascicle, sheet V, page 2][143]

Title-Sheet

The Highest Standpoint
of Transcendental Philosophy
in the
System of Ideas: *God,* the *World,* and
Man in the World,
Restricting Himself Through Laws of Duty,
presented
by

The Totality of Beings
God and the World
in a System of Ideas
of Transcendental Philosophy,
    presented.

Introduction

Transcendental philosophy is autonomy, that is, a reason that determinately delineates its synthetic principles, scope, and limits, in a complete system.

Transcendental philosophy commences from the *metaphysical foundations of natural science,* [and] contains the *a priori* principles of the latter's *transition to physics* (and its formal element); without turning into heteronomy, it [then] progresses to physics, as to a principle of the possibility of experience through which the whole of knowledge becomes an aggregate of perceptions; finally, it progresses (as an asymptotic approximation to a proof *from experience* itself) to experience. [. . .]

21:61   [*Left margin*]

Experience, as ground of the proof of the truth of empirical judgments, is

244

never more than an asymptotic *approximation* to the completeness of the possible perceptions which compose it. Is never *certainty*.

Introduction

1. Transition from the metaphysical foundations of natural science to transcendental philosophy.
2. From the latter to the universal doctrine of experience, physics in general, according to its formal conditions.
3. From nature to the doctrine of freedom. Human freedom presupposes the concept of duty, categorical imperative.
4. Progress to physics as a system. God, the *world* and *man* subject to the command of duty.

Man is, on the one hand, a world-being; on the other, however, man devoting himself to the law of duty: a noumenon.

> *totamque infusa per artus*
> *mens agit molem magnoque se corpore miscet.*[144]

[. . .][145]

[Ist fascicle, sheet VI, page 3][146]   21:78

[. . .]

Introduction

There is a *totality* of beings (*entium,* not *rerum,* thing [*Sache*]: for the latter are beings which can be manipulated) and a *universe* of beings. Reason posits this as a thought-object (*ens rationis ratiocinantis*); as a system of things, indeed, but only as subjective, belonging to ideas.

The principle which determines the *whole* of philosophy as in one system, is transcendental philosophy.

Transcendental philosophy is the act of consciousness whereby the subject becomes the originator of itself and, thereby, also of the whole object of technical-practical and moral-practical reason in one system – ordering all things in God, as in one system. (Zoroaster)[147] Analogy with mathematics in space.

Theoretical-practical reason, in conformity with its nature, creates objects for itself, namely, independent ideas – the system of an all-embracing reason which constitutes itself into an object. Transcendental philosophy does [not] occupy itself with something which is assumed as existing, but merely with the human spirit, which [is] its own thinking subject.

Ideas of speculative, aesthetic, and moral-practical reason in a system (*ens summum,* etc.), God, etc. Not metaphysics, but transcendental philosophy.

Synthetic *a priori* knowledge from concepts (philosophy, in contrast to mathematics), that is, transcendental philosophy, is not an aggregate of perception (empirically coordinated) but is the coordination (*complexus*) of ideas in the one system of reason, constituting itself under a principle. The highest existence, the highest power, and the highest will. All unlimited. But only in idea.

21:79 How is the *metaphysician* different from the *transcendental philosopher?* In that the latter addresses merely what is formal, the former what is material (the object, the material).

(Transcendental philosophy is the autonomy of ideas, insofar as they form, independently of everything empirical, an unconditional whole, and reason constitutes itself to the latter as a separate system.) God, world, and the concept of the freedom of rational beings in the world.

Ideas are not concepts, but pure intuitions: not discursive, but intuitive representations, for there is only one such object. (One God, one world (*universum*), and, in the law of freedom, only one principle in the honoring by men in the world of all human duties as divine commands). (It is not appropriate here to assume the existence of a substance with this characteristic.)

The organs of our sense-perception, as feelings, are determined through stimulation of the materials: air, light, and heat. Whether hearing, sight and inwardly feeling one's life (warm or cold) precedes knowledge of their efficient causes?

Of the argillaceous aroma, in breathing on alumina (through decomposition).[148]

Experience can yield no principle, but is only an asymptotic aggregate of perceptions – so it is no principle of transcendental philosophy. The progress and transition to transcendental philosophy takes place from the metaphysical foundations of natural science, to which mathematics also belongs. *Observation and experiment.*

Transcendental philosophy is the subjective principle [of] ideas of objects of pure reason constituting themselves into a system, and of its autonomy according to the concepts: *ens summum, summa intelligentia, summum bonum. World, human duty, and God.*

Transcendental philosophy is the principle of the thoroughgoing determination of reason into theoretical-speculative and moral-practical rea-
21:80 son, founding the unity of the unconditioned whole as the totality (*universum*) of things in their synthetic unity, according to *a priori* concepts of its elements: God, the world, and man in the world subject to the law of duty.

Transcendental philosophy is the absolute whole (system) of ideas; thus it is immediately directed toward objects (*ens summum, summa intelligentia,* etc.) which, independently of experience, are postulated by pure reason as objects [for the sake of] its (experience's) possibility. It contains principles of a *synthetic* cognition from concepts and [is], to that extent, analogous to mathematics – to the latter's formal principles, however, not its material (the object). (Of a philosophical proof of Euclid's 12th proposition.)[149]

[Left and right of "Introduction"]
Philosophy is to be regarded either as the *habitus* of philosophizing or as a work: through which there arises, proceeding from it, a work as a system of absolute unity.

[Right margin]
Doctor Medicinae Reusch, the son of *Professoris Physices* Reusch, will edit the *Intelligenz-Blätter.*[150]
N.B. The melon must be eaten today – with Prof. Gensichen – and, at this opportunity, [discuss] the income from the university.[151]

The return is to be made from the metaphysical foundation of natural science to transcendental philosophy, as a system of the ideas of pure reason insofar as they emerge from reason synthetically and *a priori*. They are God, the *world*, and *man* in the world, determining himself with freedom. The world is here understood not as an object of empirical intuition and experience.

Transcendental philosophy is the system of the ideas in an absolute whole.
God, the world, and the being in the world endowed with free will [*Willkühr*]
With respect to what is formal [in them], the principles are not to be transcendent, indeed, but must be immanent.　　　　　　　21:81

Transcendental philosophy bears this name, because it precedes metaphysics and supplies the latter with principles.

Transcendental philosophy is the philosophical system of knowledge, which presents *a priori* all objects of pure reason necessarily combined in one system.
These objects are God, the world, man in the world, subject to the concept of duty. Totality of beings.

Transcendental philosophy is the system of synthetic knowledge from *a priori* concepts.
It is (or, rather, makes) a system objectively and, at the same time, subjectively. Not mathematical.
Transcendental *ideas* are different from ideals.

247

Man is himself a world-being who constitutes himself into a member. Autonomy of ideas, insofar as they form an independent whole, in contrast to experience.

Religion is conscientiousness (*mihi hoc religioni*). The holiness of the acceptance [*Zusage*] and the truthfulness of what man must confess to himself. Confess to yourself. To have religion, the concept of God is not required (still less the postulate: "There is a God").

Air is a *liquidum*, but not a *fluidum*.

Transcendental philosophy is the principle of *synthetic a priori* knowledge *from concepts* (thereby distinguished from mathematics). How is such a philosophy possible? Through the positing of three objects: God, world, and the concept of duty.

21:82 There are *mathematical* principles in *philosophy as little as* there are philosophical principles in *mathematics*. (Contra Newton's *Philosophiae naturalis principia mathematica*.)

Granite consists of quartz, feldspar and mica. Mica includes muscovite, or Russian glass, of which there are large panes and portholes of seagoing ships.[152]

[Ist fascicle, sheet VI, page 4]

Transcendental philosophy is (1) philosophical knowledge from concepts (and different from mathematics, as knowledge through construction of concepts, as *a priori* principles) (2) different from metaphysics, which forms a particular system; for it contains only the formal element of the principles for the possibility of a system, not the latter itself, according to its content. (3) It is that which founds *a priori* not only *concepts*, as principles, but also *ideas*, which *forms* are supplied through reason. These forms provide the subject with *synthetic* knowledge from concepts; they do not establish a system but emerge *from* a system (*forma dat esse rei*).

Systems can emerge from empirical grounds of knowledge (observation and experiment), namely, from experience; they require as their basis, however, the complete enumeration of forms, which can only emerge from reason (with its absolute necessity); and the philosophy which presents these forms with apodictic certainty is then called transcendental philosophy, since it also contains the objects: *God, world*, and *man* in the world, subject to the principle of duty.

Where does this scale of ideas come from? The *totality* of beings is a concept given *a priori* to reason, arising from the consciousness of myself. I must have objects of my thinking and apprehend them; otherwise I am *unconscious* of myself (*cogito, sum:* it cannot read "*ergo*"). It is *autonomia rationis purae*, for, without that, I would be thoughtless, even with a given intuition, like an animal, without knowing that I am.

21:83 Reason inevitably creates objects for itself. Hence everything that thinks has a God.

Transcendental philosophy is a system of knowledge, which, abstracting from all objects, constitutes the formal element of synthetic *a priori* knowledge from concepts (in contrast to mathematics) into a principle for itself. It abstracts from every object, but is, for that very reason, all the more embracing; as regards the forms of knowledge (as philosophy), all-embracing, and, as regards degree, *apodictic* rather than merely *assertoric* – for in that case it would be concerned only with what is *contingent.*

Transcendental philosophy is, however, also the principle of a system of ideas, which are in themselves problematic (not assertoric) but which must nevertheless be thought as possible forces affecting reason: God, the world, and man in the world, subject to the law of duty.

That which is thinkable without any influence of what is empirical, simply through pure reason, belongs to transcendental philosophy. (1) Absolute totality [*Totalität*]. (2) Freedom (3) Totality [*Allheit*].

(*God and the world outside me and the moral feeling within me.*)

A purely morally good man cannot himself be the originator of his becoming an evil one. He who makes himself into what is evil (originally) is *diabolus.*

It is not even in the divine power to make a morally good man (to make him morally good): He must do it himself.

What is empirical in the system of perceptions – that is, in experience (not experiences in the plural) – is, insofar as it is *made* according to a principle. Observation and experiment.

The being who *knows* everything, *can do* (is capable of) everything and *wills* everything good (which contains true highest purposes) is **God.**

The being which is only possible according to an inner principle of purposiveness has an *immaterial* cause in itself. Organic bodies (plants and animals – also, man), not organic *matters* (the latter are not used at all in the plural, perhaps because they stand in community [with one another] in the universe). There is one space thought *outside* and one time thought inside the subject. 21:84

Transcendental philosophy is the system of ideas which, independently of all given objects, creates objects for itself and delivers to reason a necessary determined whole as the totality of beings.

One must here proceed not from *the one to the many,* but *from the totality to the one.*

Progress *from the metaphysical foundations of natural science to transcendental philosophy.*

nil conscire sibi, nulla pallescere culpa.[153]

Transcendental philosophy is the self-creation (autocracy) of ideas, into

249

a complete system of the objects of pure reason. In the Bible it says: Let us make man, and, behold, every thing was very good.¹⁵⁴

Transcendental philosophy is a principle which constitutes itself, in a system of ideas, into the totality of beings; the latter is not [derived] from experience but is thoroughly self-determining *a priori* for experience and its possibility – [as] an absolute whole of experience. God, the world, and man, subject to the principle of duty, in it.

Transcendental philosophy is the formal system (or the doctrine of the system) of the *ideas* of *pure* (not empirically determinable) reason, *thereby that the subject* makes *itself into an object* (asymptotically); it is the highest standpoint of the *a priori* principle of synthetic knowledge from concepts (not from the construction of concepts – hence, independent of the conditions of space and time) and is different from mathematics. It contains an aggregate: God, world, and *man's* concept of duty, that is, the categorical imperative, whose *dictamen* is a highest being, not a world-being.

God, the world, and man in the world, subject to the concept of duty (as person), are *ideas* which contribute nothing to what is material, but only to the principle of form – like the concept of *freedom*, after the categorical imperative has taught [man] to have regard to it.

21:85 One must say matter, not *matters;* similarly, experience, not experiences [but] the asymptotic approximation to experience (for experiences, so called, are perceptions which lead to experience (*observatio, experimentum*)).

[*Margin* . . .]

21:86 [Ist fascicle, sheet VII, page 1]

7

Transcendental philosophy is the (rational) principle of a system of *ideas,* which are problematic (not assertoric) in themselves (for, in that case, they would be concerned merely with what is contingent); nor do they belong to mathematics, but must, nevertheless, be thought as possible forces, affecting the rational subject: *God,* the *world,* and the subject affected [by] the law of duty: *man* in the world.

As ideas, they cannot contribute anything to the matter of knowledge (that is, to the confirmation of the existence of the object) but only to the

21:87 principle of what is formal, as in the case of the concept of *freedom* according to the categorical imperative. Whether there is a God, whether there are worlds or one absolute world-whole (*universum*), is not here decided.

The progression can take place from the metaphysical foundations of natural science to physics; which progression is founded on empirical principles, and has as its object the possibility of experience (of which there is always only one, and which presupposes a formal *a priori* principle and a system). Observation and experiment, as an aggregate of perceptions, are far from founding the Hippocratic proposition: There is experience.

Transcendental philosophy is that philosophy which proceeds from completely pure philosophy (that is, neither from empirical nor from mathematical principles); it is that synthetic *a priori* knowledge according to concepts [which], as a principle of knowledge of oneself, is self-determining – the subject.

What is, what has been, and what will be, belongs to nature – hence to the world. What is only thought in a concept belongs to appearances. Thence the ideality of objects and transcendental idealism.

Transcendental philosophy is the system of the ideas of the thinking subject, which (system) unites the formal element of *a priori* knowledge from *concepts* (that is, separate from everything empirical) into one principle of the possibility of experience. There can as little be philosophical foundations of mathematics as there can mathematical foundations of philosophy, although Newton unites these two fields.

Spinoza's God, in which we represent God in pure intuition. N.B. Space is also an object of pure intuition, but not an idea.

System of Transcendental Idealism, by Schelling, Spinoza, Lichtenberg, and, as it were, three dimensions: present, past and future.[155]

Transcendental philosophy is the formal element of synthetic *a priori* knowledge from *concepts*, not in order to found an *object*, but *only* to establish completely *the ideas* of them [namely, the objects] *a priori* (in contrast to empirical [philosophy]). What if the idealistic system (that I myself alone am the world) were the only one thinkable by us? Science would lose nothing thereby. What matters is only the lawlike connection of appearances. 21:88

Transcendental philosophy abstracts from all objects, as objects of possible *perception,* and addresses only principles of the formal element of knowledge.

Herr von Humbold[t] has observed in Cumana (Caracas) the remarkable appearance that an *ebb* and *flow* takes place there in the *atmosphere.*[156] The barometer is there in constant motion. The mercury sinks from nine o'clock in the morning until four o'clock in the afternoon. It then rises again: until eleven o'clock; sinks again until four o'clock in the morning and rises again until eleven o'clock. Thus only the *sun* appears to have an influence on this process. Helmont, Claramontan.[157]

Ideas precede appearances in space and time.

Whether everything which acts upon my senses (world) belongs to the world, although not everything which is perceived through them [does]?

Oxygeneity, deoxygeneity and hydrogeneity. Neutralization. Sunlight in an undivided state.

[*Next to the above*]

No. 16 of the *Intelligenzblatt* of the (Erlanger) *Litteratur Zeitung.* Chemical polarity, electrical, galvanic, magnetic, of heat. This One and All, in its purest and freest appearance, is light. Ritter, in Spring 1801.¹⁵⁸

[. . .]¹⁵⁹

21:91   [Ist fascicle, sheet VII, page 2]

Transcendental philosophy is the doctrine of the complex of ideas, which contain the whole of synthetic *a priori* knowledge from concepts in a system both of theoretical-speculative and moral-practical reason, under a principle through which the thinking subject constitutes itself in idealism, not as thing [*Sache*] but as person, and is itself the originator of this system of ideas. (*Ens summum, summa intelligentia, summum bonum.*) To think that One and All in the One is only an idealistic act: That is, the object of this idea which has been created through pure reason, is, as far as its existence is concerned, always a contentless concept. But in moral-practical [reason] this idea has reality, in virtue of the *personality* which pertains identically to its concept.

21:92   The idea of a being who knows everything, is capable of everything, wills everything morally good, and is most intimately present in all world-beings (*omnipraesentissimum*), is the idea of *God.*

That this idea has objective reality – that is, that it has the force appropriate to the moral law [in] the reason of every man who is not wholly bestially crippled – and that man must inevitably confess to himself: There is one and only one God, requires no proof of its existence, as if it were a natural being; its existence already lies, rather, in the developed concept of this idea, according to the principle of identity: The mere form here counts to the being of the thing. The enlightened man can do no other than himself to condemn or to pardon, and that which pronounces this judgment in him (moral-practical reason) can, indeed, be anesthetized through sensible impulses, so that [*breaks off*]

Whether there is a God in nature (as a world-soul) cannot be asked, since this concept is contradictory; but he reveals himself in moral-practical reason and the categorical imperative.

Transcendental philosophy is the system of pure idealism of the self-determination of the thinking subject through synthetic *a priori* principles from concepts; the subject constitutes itself through these principles into an object – the form here amounts to the whole object.

The objects of transcendental philosophy are not objects of perception – that is, this philosophical principle is not empirical – and even the principle of the possibility of experience, as something subjective (of which there cannot be several – not experiences) belongs to transcendental philosophy. Transcendental philosophy contains a system which is enclosed in its own limits, but only as to what is formal in its object (mathematics, although synthetic *a priori* knowledge, is only an instrument for transcendental philosophy).

Transcendental philosophy is synthetic •*a priori*• knowledge •from concepts,• abstracting from all content (that is, all objects); thus merely the formal element of the theoretically-speculatively and morally-practically self-determining subject. (The autonomy of ideas: to found experience as unity, *a priori* – not *from* experience, but *for* experience, not as an aggregate of perceptions, but as a principle.)

Transcendental philosophy is the consciousness of the capacity of being   21:93
the originator of the system of one's ideas, in theoretical as well as in practical respect.

[*Right of the above*]

Ideas are not mere concepts but laws of thought which the subject prescribes to itself. *Autonomy.*

(It is the science of philosophizing about philosophy as a system of synthetic *a priori* principles from concepts.) Transcendental philosophy, regarded subjectively or objectively. In the first case, it is the system of synthetic knowledge from *a priori* concepts. In the second case, it is the autonomy of ideas, and the principle of the forms to which systems with theoretical-speculative or moral-practical intent must conform.

It is not a complex (aggregate) of *philosopheme*, but the principle of an all-embracing system of the *ideas* which constitute philosophy as an absolute (not relative) whole of the principles of philosophizing.

[*Bottom margin*]

To *make* an experience (through observation and experiment) is an asymptotic undertaking. Experiences, matters, worlds in the metaphysical sense, are (like heat) only one, and differ only as more or less (not in quality). (Light in colors permits multiplicity and, hence, requires observation: Heat as material can, like space, only be one.)

[*Left margin*]

Transcendental philosophy is not an aggregate but a system, not of objective concepts but of subjective ideas, which reason creates itself –

not hypothetically (*problematically* or *assertorically*) indeed, but *apodictically*, insofar as it creates itself.

Transcendental philosophy is the capacity of the self-determining sub-ject to constitute itself as *given* in intuition, through the systematic complex of the ideas which, *a priori*, make the thoroughgoing determination of the subject as object (its existence) into a problem. •*To make oneself,* as it were.•

21:94 This philosophy is, thus, an idealism, as a mere principle of forms in a system of all relations.

Of God, world, and the rational being in the world who comprehends them all.

The negative definition of transcendental philosophy is that it is *a principle of synthetic a priori knowledge from concepts* – through which it is, indeed, distinguished from mathematics – yet it does not become comprehensible how such a philosophy as that called transcendental is possible.

That it is only a system of forms is an indication toward thinkable objects, which, however, must be given *a priori* (not empirically) and must also (as regards the matter of knowledge) be capable of being enumerated, since they are to form a closed system.

Beings must be thought who, even though they exist only in the thoughts of the philosopher, yet have normal-practical reality in these latter. These are God, the universe, and man in the world, subject to the concept of duty according to the categorical imperative (consequently, to the principle of freedom).

These objects do not relate merely to ideals – that is, [ideas,] each of which is a *maximum,* and which relate to things outside ourselves – but, especially and primarily, to ideas as forms of knowledge through which the object *constitutes itself* as a thinking being.

What does man make out of himself?

The Academy of Science in Florence.[160]

[. . .]

21:97 [Ist fascicle, sheet VII, page 3]

[. . .]

[*Right margin*]
 System of Transcendental Idealism, by Schelling.
 vide Litteratur-Zeitung, Erlangen No. 82, 83.[161]
 Transcendental philosophy is the absolute principle of determining oneself idealistically into a system of synthetic *a priori* knowledge from concepts (or through them) with regard to the form of self-consciousness.

[. . .]

[Ist fascicle, sheet VII, page 4]   21:99

[. . .]

We can know no objects, either in us or as lying outside us, except insofar as we insert in ourselves the *actus* of cognition, according to certain laws. The spirit of man is Spinoza's God (so far as the formal element of all sense-objects is concerned) and transcendental idealism is realism in an absolute sense.

[. . .]¹⁶²

[Ist fascicle, sheet XII, page 1]   21:155

PHILOSOPHY
AS DOCTRINE OF SCIENCE [*Wissenschaftslehre*]
IN A COMPLETE SYSTEM,
ESTABLISHED
BY

[*Rest of page empty, except right margin*]
   *Estque Dei sedes ubi terra et pontus et aër et coelum et virtus. Superos quid quaerimus ultra Juppiter est quodcunque vides quocunque moveris.*¹⁶³

The love of wisdom is the least that one can possess; wisdom for man the highest – and hence, transcendent. Transcendental philosophy is the progression from the latter to the former.

   The *final end* of all knowledge is to know oneself in the highest practical   21:156
reason.

   Zoroaster: or, philosophy in the whole of its complex, comprehended under a principle.

   Philosophy is directed at the purposes of knowledge as well as the final end of things in general.

   Proem. Knowledge of the science which led to wisdom (historical).

   A. *a priori* knowledge from concepts (philosophy).

   B. *a priori* knowledge in the construction of concepts (mathematics). *The former superior.*

   Elevation of the ideas of pure reason to the self-constituting system of a science, called *philosophy*, which includes even mathematics as its subordinate instrument.

   Nature and freedom are the two hinges (principles) of *philosophy*, founding it. *Physiology* (as pure product of reason) can be either the doctrine of science [*Wissenschaftslehre*] or the *doctrine of wisdom* [*Weisheitslehre*].

   The subjective and the objective elements of philosophy, where transcendental philosophy [*breaks off*]

255

Mathematics is a merely *instrumental doctrine;* but not mere *learnedness.*

Mathematics belongs under philosophy. For it, too, rests (insofar as it is pure) on *space, time,* and on *motion* in space and time (the relation of the two).

Two parts: *physics* and *transcendental philosophy.* The *world* and *God.* As objects in contrast.

Poltron (*pollex truncatus*).[164]

[. . .]

21:6   [Ist fascicle, wrapper, page 3]

[. . .]

Philosophy is rational knowledge: objectively as science (as a science) or subjectively as instruction [*Belehrung*] of oneself.

[. . .]

21:7   Science and wisdom: both from (according to) *a priori* principles.

Philosophy – an *act of cognition,* whose product does not aim merely at science (as a means), but also at *wisdom,* as a purpose in itself – hence [is] directed toward something founded on God himself.

[Ist fascicle, wrapper, page 4]

Without transcendental philosophy one can form for oneself no concept as to how, and by what principle, one could design the plan of a system, by which a coherent whole could be established as rational knowledge for reason; yet this must necessarily take place if one would turn rational man into a being who knows himself.

What necessarily (originally) forms the existence of things belongs to transcendental philosophy.

God, as a holy being, can have no comparative or superlative. There can be only one.

Transcendental philosophy precedes the assertion of things that are thought, as their archetype, [the place] in which they must be set.

[. . .]

Factual notes

1 Page 1 of this leaf is Kant's excerpt from an anonymous review of his *Metaphysical Foundations of Natural Science*. The review appeared in the *Göttingische Anzeigen von gelehrten Sachen*, 191. Stück, December 2, 1786, pp. 1914–18. The anonymous reviewer was Abraham Kästner. (See Oscar Fambach, *Die Mitarbeiter der Göttingischen Gelehrten Anzeigen 1769–1836*, Universitätsbibliothek: Tübingen 1976, p. 134.)

2 The reviewer questions Kant's use of the phoronomic proposition in his proof of proposition 1 of the chapter entitled "Dynamics" ("Matter fills a space, not by its mere existence, but by a special moving force"). Immediately preceding the passage Kant excerpts, the reviewer had written: "Matter fills [a] space, not by [its] mere existence, but [by] a moving force. For its resistance to what will penetrate [its space] alters the latter's motion, and nothing can lessen or destroy motion except motion in the opposite direction. For this the phoronomic proposition is quoted" (p. 1915). Kant's phoronomic proposition states: "The composition of two motions of one and the same point can only be conceived by representing one of them in absolute space while, instead of so representing the second motion, representing a motion of the relative space in the opposite direction and with the same velocity as being identical with the first motion" (AK 4:490).

3 The remainder of this page contains a draft of, and marginal notes for, Kant's preface to the *Critique of Practical Reason*, which appeared in the winter of 1787.

4 Page 1 of this leaf contains a reference to acoustic experiments that the physicist E. F. F. Chladni (1756–1827) performed when visiting Königsberg in February 1794. (On these experiments and on Kant's reactions to them, see E. A. C. Wasianski, *Kant in seinen letzten Lebensjahren*, p. 283.)

5 Kant alludes to phenomena of expansion of organic matter through water, as described especially by Stephen Hales, *Vegetable Staticks*, London 1727 (German translation: Halle 1748). In a footnote to page 4 of draft "γ" (AK 21:263, not included), Kant elaborates that dried pieces of wood, cut into wedges and inserted into the cracks of stones, may break "even millstones" if they are subsequently soaked with water; similarly, roots of trees can seriously damage buildings if they grow into cracks in the building's foundation. (See also AK 21:499.2–9, 22:238n, not included.)

6 Based on a comparison with another Kantian leaf from the time, Adickes dates this leaf summer 1795; see E. Adickes, *Kants Opus postumum*, p. 48.

7 The designation *Oktaventwurf* is Adickes's – referring to the unusual format of the draft; see E. Adickes, *Kants Opus postumum*, p. 55. The numbering of

the text is Kant's. The title "Transition" occurred twice before: Leaf 36, page 2 (AK 21:463–4, not included), is entitled "Transition from the Metaphysics of Nature to Physics" and deals with questions of hydraulics, cohesion, heat, and the peculiar glow of metals. (Page 1 of the leaf contains notes for Kant's *Doctrine of Right* and a reference to his anthropology lectures in the winter semester 1795–6.) Leaf 22, page 1 (AK 21:465–6, not included) is entitled "Transition from the Metaphysics of Corporeal Nature to Physics"; it addresses the question of solidification and the dynamical estimation of the quantity of matter. (Pages 2–4 of this leaf are left empty.)

8   This seems to be either a rhetorical remark, building up to the following discussion, or a slip of the pen, for Kant had already established in earlier drafts that cohesion is possible only through the living force of impact (see leaf 23). The view expressed here, that it is the *pressure* of the ether that makes bodies cohere, was held earlier by Kant himself; it was advanced most prominently by Jacob Bernoulli in *De gravitate aetheris,* Amsterdam 1683. Concerning Bernoulli's theory, J. S. T. Gehler wrote in his *Physicalisches Wörterbuch* (see note 22), vol. 1, p. 516–17: "It remains, however, forever inexplicable how a [kind of] matter that is to penetrate all the intermediary spaces of bodies could exert such a strong excess pressure from without upon the counter-pressure from within."

9   Vital force, or *Lebenskraft,* was postulated by many scientists at the time to explain the phenomena of life. J. D. Brandis, *Versuch über die Lebenskraft,* Hahn'sche Buchhandlung: Hannover 1795, for example, writes with respect to "the motions that take place in organic bodies": "(1) That the cause of these motions seems to be a force which does not permit of being reduced to any physical force known to us; consequently, that we are entitled provisionally to call it a distinct force: we call it vital force, because it belongs only to living organic bodies. (2) This force acts immediately in organic matter, not as the result of the formation of matter, or of [its] organization" (p. 15; see also J. C. Reil, *Von der Lebenskraft,* Halle 1796, and J. F. Ackermann, *Versuch einer physischen Darstellung der Lebenskräfte organisierter Körper,* Frankfurt/Main 1797).

10   Not identified.

11   See note 25.

12   See note 14.

13   "Producing nature" and "produced nature." See, e.g., Baruch de Spinoza, *Ethica ordine geometrico demonstrata,* I, proposition 29 (scholion) and proposition 31.

14   E. Adickes, *Kants Opus postumum,* p. 80, comments: "Kant has in mind P. S. Laplace, *Exposition du système du monde,* which appeared 1796 in two volumes and was translated into German in 1797 by J. K. F. Hauff. The second chapter of Book III is entitled: 'Du mouvement d'un point matériel' ('Von der Bewegung eines materiellen Punkts' in the German translation, the first volume of which is signed 'Easter Fair 1797'.) The French original was briefly advertised in the *Intelligenzblatt* of the *Jenaer Allgemeine Litteratur Zeitung* of December 14, 1796 (p. 1441)."

15   The classificatory systems of natural history (such as, for example, that of Linnaeus) were usually regarded not as natural systems but as (artificial) systems for memory, in the tradition of the classical memory trees and

memory theaters. See, e.g., Kant's *Anthropology From a Pragmatic Point of View*, AK 7:184: "Memorizing *judiciously* is simply memorizing, in thought, the *outline* of the divisions of a system (Linné's, for example) – should we forget anything, we can find it again by enumerating the members we have retained; or memorizing the *divisions* of a whole made visible (for example, the provinces of a country, as shown on a map, which lie north, west, etc.)" (translated by Mary Gregor).

16 In the *Metaphysical Foundations of Natural Science*, proof and observations of proposition 7 of the Dynamics, AK 4:512–15.

17 The former view, that heat consists in the motion of a special substance or material [*Wärmestoff*], was the dominant view throughout the eighteenth century. Kant had long endorsed it, as did the authors of the compendia that he used for his lectures on physics (Erxleben, Karsten). The opposing view, that heat is simply the internal motion of the parts of matter, gained significant support through the experiments that Count Rumford (1753–1814) conducted during the closing years of the century.

In "A Element. Syst 3," AK 22:274.3–10 (not included), Kant quotes from the German translation of the seventh essay of Rumford's *Experimental Essays, Political, Economical, and Philosophical*, London 1797, "Of the Manner in which Heat is Propagated in Fluids," in *Annalen der Physik*, vol. 1, pp. 214–41. (See E. Adickes, *Kants Opus postumum*, pp. 128–30.)

Rumford's results may have contributed to Kant's later view that caloric is problematic and hypothetical – "only a place holder" (Ist fascicle, sheet III, page 4, §3); see also his letter to C. G. Hagen, April 2, 1800, AK 12:301.

18 "To derive everything from nothing, suffices one." *Leibniz's Dyadic* is the name for his binary arithmetic that represents all natural numbers in terms of the numerals 0 and 1: 1 = 1, 2 = 10, 3 = 11, 4 = 100, 5 = 101, 6 = 110, 7 = 111, 8 = 1000, 9 = 1001, 10 = 1010, 11 = 1011, etc. Apart from the mathematical merits of the binary system, Leibniz was interested in the analogy between the origin of all numbers from 1 and 0 and God's creation of all things from nothing. As he explained in a letter to J. C. Schulenburg of March 29, 1698 (see *Gothofredi Guillermi Leibnitii Opera Omnia*, ed. L. Dutens, vol. 3 [*Opera mathematica*], Genevae 1768, p. 350), the dyadic can function as an image of the mystery of creation:

"Atque haec est origo rerum ex Deo, & nihilo; positivo, & privativo; perfectione, & imperfectione; valore, & limitibus; activo & passivo; forma (i.e. entelechia, nisu, vigore) & materia, seu mole, per se torpente, nisi quod resistentiam habet. Illustravi ista non nihil origine numerorum ex 0 & 1 a me observata, quae *pulcherrimum est Emblema perpetuae rerum creationis ex nihilo, dependentiae quae a Deo.*"

["And this is the origin of all things from God and from nothing, from what is positive and privation, perfection and imperfection, value and limitation, what is active and what is passive, form (i.e., entelechy, striving, vigor) and matter or mass, in itself inactive except that it offers resistance. This I have illustrated a little with the origin of numbers from 0 and 1, which I observed. It is a most beautiful symbol of the continuous creation of things from nothing, and of their dependence on God."]

This thought appealed especially to Rudolf August, Duke of Braun-schweig and Lüneburg, with whom Leibniz conversed on the subject. In January 1697, Leibniz accompanied his New Year Congratulations to Rudolf August with the design of a medal with the duke's likeness on one side, and the "image of Creation" in terms of the binary number system on the other. Concerning the inscription on this side, Leibniz writes: "I have thought for a while about the *Motto dell'impresa* and finally have found it good to write this line: *omnibus ex nihilo ducendis SUFFICIT UNUM*, because it clearly indi-cates what is meant by the symbol, and why it is *imago creationis*" (G. F. Leibniz, *Zwei Briefe über das binäre Zahlensystem und die chinesische Philosophie*, ed. Renate Loosen and Franz Vonessen, Chr. Belser Verlag: Stuttgart 1968, p. 21).

The medal was never coined, but Leibniz's letter to the duke was pub-lished in 1720 under the title "Das Geheimnis der Schöpfung," in *Des Freiherrn von Leibniz kleinere philosophische Schriften*, edited by Heinrich Köhler. In 1734, Rudolph August Nolten published a separate edition of the letter. Kant must have known this letter, for the phrase he quotes occurs nowhere else in Leibniz's published writings. Indeed, there is good reason to assume that Kant encountered Leibniz's dyadic early in his career. For in 1742, when he was a student at the University of Königsberg, Kant's teacher Martin Knutzen published an article in which he disputed Leibniz's original-ity with respect to the binary system: "Von dem wahren Auctore der *Arithme-ticae Binariae*, oder so genannten Leibnitzianischen Dyadic," in *Philo-sophischer Büchersaal* 3 (1742), pp. 218–22.

19   "[Constant] dripping wears the stone" – Ovid, *Ex Ponto*, IV, x, 5.
20   Propositions 5 and 6 and their proofs, "Dynamics," AK 4:508–11.
21   See note 27.
22   Johann Samuel Traugott Gehler, *Physicalisches Wörterbuch oder Versuch einer Erklärung der vornehmsten Begriffe und Kunstwörter der Naturlehre mit kurzen Nachrichten von der Geschichte der Erfindungen und Beschreibungen der Werkzeuge begleitet in alphabetischer Ordnung*, Leipzig 1787–95, 5 vols., is frequently used by Kant in the *Opus postumum*. Gehler is critical of Kant's assumption of repulsion as an original force of matter, arguing that apparent repulsion can always be explained by attraction in the other direction, or by other known forces. In his article "Zurückstossen" (vol. 5, pp. 1033–8), Gehler maintains that Tobias Mayer showed the untenability of all known proofs for the existence of original repulsive forces. In particular, he cites Mayer against Kant's claim (in the *Metaphysical Foundations of Natural Science*) that matter cannot by its mere existence prevent another matter from entering into its space but rather requires a repulsive force to do so.
     The article by Tobias Mayer to which Gehler refers, "Ob es nöthig sey, eine zurückstossende Kraft in der Natur anzunehmen" appeared in D. F. A. C. Gren's *Journal der Physik* 7 (1793), pp. 208–37. Kant made an excerpt of this article in R 70, AK 14:499–501.
23   In his article "Zurückstossen, Abstossen, Repulsion" (vol. 4, p. 894), Gehler claims that the behavior of fluids in capillary tubes can be explained indepen-dent of repulsion, by assuming attraction in the opposite direction. More specifically, he maintains that water rises in capillary tubes because the

attraction exerted by the glass ring above the surface is greater than the cohesion of the watery parts with one another. With mercury it is the opposite: There the parts cohere more than they are attracted by the tube, with the result that its surface sinks below the level of mercury outside the tube. (See also the article "Haarröhren," vol. 2, pp. 546–7.)

24 Kant may have in mind Leonhard Euler's *Mechanica sive motus scientia analytice exposita*, Petropoli 1736, of which he owned a copy (see A. Warda, *Immanuel Kants Bücher*, Martin Breslauer: Berlin 1922, p. 34). There Euler writes at §98: "Deinde corpora finitae magnitudinis aggrediemur ea, quae sunt rigida neque figuram suam mutari patiuntur." ["Next we will address those bodies of finite magnitude which are rigid and which do not permit an alteration of their form."]

Kant's point is that "solid" should be contrasted not with "fluid" but with "hollow" – the proper contrary of "fluid" being "rigid." J. S. T. Gehler, *Physicalisches Wörterbuch*, vol. 2, p. 321, had written: "[Fluid bodies] are contrasted with solid bodies (*solida*)." (See also Kant's appendix to S. T. Sömmerring's *Über das Organ der Seele*, Königsberg 1796, AK 12:33n.)

25 That the formation of solid – including living – bodies takes place in a quasi-geometrical manner was a widely held assumption in the eighteenth century. As for living bodies, this view was advocated especially by Albrecht von Haller (1708–77), who in turn drew on G. A. Borelli's (1608–79) and H. Boerhaave's (1668–1738) theories of fibers. In his *Anfangsgründe der Phisiologie des menschlichen Körpers*, Berlin 1759–76, vol. 1, p. 3, Haller writes: "I thus first treat of the fiber, the basic material. . . . For the fiber is for the physiologist what the line is for the geometer, namely, that from which all his other figures are generated." (See also note 66.)

26 Carl Wilhelm Scheele (1742–86), Swedish chemist, coined the term "fire air" for the "respirable" part of the air – the oxygen – which he discovered independently of Priestley. (See Scheele, *Chemische Abhandlungen von der Luft und dem Feuer* [1777].) Gehler, in his discussion of Scheele's discovery, uses the term "empyreal- or fire air" (*Physicalisches Wörterbuch*, vol. 2, p. 372).

27 A mountain in Perthshire, Scotland, next to which in 1774 the Rev. Nevil Maskelyne conducted an experiment to measure its attraction. (Kant's spelling of the mountain's name is incorrect: it is called "Schehallien," meaning [in the Erse language] "constant storm.") Maskelyne contended that "if the attraction of gravity be exerted, as Sir Isaac Newton supposes, not only between the large bodies of the universe, but between the minutest particles of which these bodies are composed, or into which the mind can imagine them to be divided, acting universally according to that law . . . it will necessarily follow that every hill must, by its attraction, alter the direction of gravitation in heavy bodies in its neighbourhood from what it would have been from the attraction of the earth alone, considered as bounded by a smooth and even surface" ("A proposal for measuring the Attraction of some Hill in this Kingdom by Astronomical Observations," *Philosophical Transactions* LXV [1775], pp. 495–9, p. 495). His experiment to test this theory lasted for several weeks and stimulated wide interest. According to Maskelyne, it (a) established that Mount Schehallien exerts sensible attrac-

tion; (b) confirmed Newton's inverse square law; (c) proved the mean density of the hill to be half that of the earth. (See "An Account of Observations made on the Mountain Schehallien for finding its Attraction," *Philosophical Transactions* LXV [1775]), pp. 500–42.) Kant also alludes to this experiment in the IXth fascicle, sheet I, page 2, §4, and at AK 21:352.34 and 429.11 (not included).

28 In opposition to Newton's corpuscular theory of light, Leonhard Euler (1707–83) advanced an undulatory theory according to which light rays are pulsations or vibrations of the ether. See his "Nova theoria lucis & colorum," in *L. Euleri opuscula varii argumenti*, vol. I, Berlin 1746, pp. 169–244, §22:

"Lumen igitur ante omnia simili modo quo sonum per medium quoddam elasticum ope pulsuum propagari statuo; atque cum sonus potissimum per aerem diffundi soleat, lumen per aliud quoddam medium elasticum, quod non solum atmosphaeram nostram, sed etiam universum mundi spatium, quo ultimae stellae fixae a nobis distant, impleat, propagari assumo."

["I maintain that light above all travels through an as it were elastic medium, by means of pulsation, in a manner similar to sound; and just as sound travels mostly through the air, so I take it that light travels through a different as it were elastic medium, which fills not only our atmosphere, but also the entire cosmic space between us and the most distant fixed stars."]

See also his *Lettres à une princesse d'Allemagne sur diverse sujets de Physique et de Philosophie*, St. Petersburg 1768–72, 17–19th letters.

29 This unusual metaphor seems to be an allusion to Fichte's "Second Introduction" to his *Wissenschaftslehre*, published in 1797 in I. Niethammer's *Philosophisches Journal*, vol. 5, pp. 319–78, and vol. 6, pp. 1–40. There Fichte had written: "For me, now, the *Critique of Pure Reason* is in no way devoid of foundations; they are very plainly there: only nothing has been built on them, and the building-materials – though already neatly prepared – lie about on top of one another in a very arbitrary order" (translation by Peter Heath and John Lachs, *The Science of Knowledge*, Cambridge University Press: Cambridge 1982, p. 51n).

That Kant had read Fichte's "Second Introduction" is suggested by his letter to Fichte of (December 1797?), AK 12:222, and explicitly stated by Fichte in his response to Kant's "Open Letter on the *Wissenschaftslehre*" (see note 42) in the *Intelligenzblatt der Allgemeinen Litteratur Zeitung*, Nr. 122, September 28, 1799, pp. 990–2 (see AK 13:548).

30 The dating of this leaf is controversial. It is the address page of a letter to Kant. (Envelopes did not come into use until the early nineteenth century.) Adickes regards it as a "Vorarbeit" to the *Opus postumum* and dates it with four other leaves of the IVth fascicle (Nos. 36, 22, 24, 46), which were written in 1795–6, shortly before the *Oktaventwurf*. He claims that the division of the moving forces of matter on page 2 of this leaf is, by comparison with later drafts, "still very underdeveloped and proves the early origin of the leaf" (p. 53). Burkhard Tuschling has challenged this interpretation (see his *Metaphysische und transzendentale Dynamik in Kants opus postumum*, Berlin/New York 1971, pp. 91n, 125–8), arguing that the content of this leaf

presupposes thoughts developed in "ε 3 and 4"; therefore it can hardly have been written before the summer of 1798.

Adickes provides two additional reasons for the early origin of leaf 6 (not addressed by Tuschling) which, in my view, still fail to support his contention. First, he points out that organically moving forces are here, as Kant says, "passed over or relegated to scholia" – as in the *Oktaventwurf,* but unlike in later drafts. But this is the case with all drafts up to, and including, leaf 7 (AK 21:487.22, not included), which Adickes himself dated August or September 1798. Organic forces first become a topic for the "Transition" in "A Elem. Syst. 1" (October 1798). (Adickes, as p. 54 of his *Kants Opus postumum* makes clear, relied on Reicke's incomplete edition for this argument.)

Second, Adickes claims that leaf 6 agrees "completely" in ink and hand-writing with the first pages of the *Oktaventwurf,* and hence is likely to have originated at roughly the same time. However, a comparison of leaf 6 with 3/4, 5, and 7 (with which I locate leaf 6) showed a remarkable similarity among these leaves, too (as far as I was able to make out in the course of a brief inspection). I am grateful to Albrecht Krause, the present owner of the *Opus postumum,* for permitting me to inspect these leaves. For these reasons, I diverge here from Adickes's chronology.

31 This is the address page of Robert Motherby's letter to Kant of August 11, 1798 (see AK 13:485). Page 3 contains a note for a letter to Christian Garve (see note 33); pages 2 and 4 contain excerpts from Gehler's *Physicalisches Wörterbuch,* on the phenomena of heat, e.g.: "Heat cannot be explained through mere vibration"; "This material [i.e., caloric], which is not entirely hypothetical . . ."; "A space void of heat is not conceivable." See note 56.

32 Leaf 5 is the address page of a letter sent to Kant by the *Königliche Ober-Schulklasse* in Berlin (see AK 13:487). At the order of Friedrich Wilhelm II from March 3, 1789, the secretary of the *Ober-Schulklasse,* Carl Gottfried Schröder, sent Kant a quarterly incremental pay of 55 Thaler from Berlin, which he usually accompanied with a brief official note. (See, e.g., AK 11:534, 12:8, 102.)

33 This is a note for the letter to Christian Garve that Kant wrote on September 21, 1798. It is in response to a letter he had received from Garve two days earlier, together with a book Garve had dedicated to Kant, *Übersicht der vornehmsten Prinzipien der Sittenlehre, von dem Zeitalter des Aristoteles bis auf unsere Zeit.* (See AK 12:252–8.)

34 The mathematician Kant has in mind is Abraham Kästner. In another version of this section (§2) of the Elementary System, Kant writes: "Herr H[of] R[ath] Kästner was the first to demonstrate thoroughly and succinctly the lever without therewith (it appears) bringing into play any physical property, or inner moving force, of matter. A physical lever, however, must have a certain thickness in proportion to the length of its arms, in order not to bend, break, or tear when weights are appended. Herr K., as mathematician, ignored the moving forces required for this" (AK 22:228.23–229.2, not included).

In crediting Kästner with the first mathematically satisfactory demonstration of the lever (that is, of the law of equilibrium of forces on the lever on which the whole of statics is built), Kant follows Gehler's *Physicalisches*

Wörterbuch, article "Hebel," vol. 2, pp. 565–76. Gehler recites the history of the problem from Archimedes to d'Alembert and concludes: "Concerning the inadequacies of the proofs of the first law of statics, d'Alembert rightly remarked (*Traité de Dynamique*, à Paris, 1743, préface) that one had been more concerned with enlarging the system of mechanics than with illuminating its foundations; one always proceeded with this without sufficiently securing its ground. Herr Hofrath Kästner (*Vectis et compositionis virum theoria evidentius exposita*, Lips. 1753) finally overcame this deficiency and offered a fully convincing proof for the law of the lever." See also Gehler's article "Zusammensetzung der Kräfte und Bewegungen," vol. 4, p. 931.

35 Page 4 of "El. Syst. 1" contains a long "Note" on the proper explanation of the rising of water and mercury in capillary tubes, including a citation from a review of J. C. Fischer's *Anfangsgründe der Physik* (1797) in the *Allgemeine Litteratur Zeitung*, July 29 and 30, 1798.

36 As Kant points out in "No 3 β" (AK 22:221.15, not included), this way of determining the degree of cohesion was "already suggested by Galileo." (See Galileo Galilei, *Dialogues Concerning Two New Sciences*, The Macmillan Company: New York 1914, pp. 17–18.)

37 A metallic blue-green longhorn beetle of approximately one inch in length, with steel-blue feelers and legs. A native of Europe, it feeds especially on willows. Its name derives from the musky secretion it discharges. (See note 87.)

38 "Perpetuity is necessity in appearance."

39 "The quantity of motion in the world, if one adds those that go in one direction and subtracts those that go in the opposite direction, do not alter [the quantity of motion] in the universe." See I. Newton, *Philosophiae naturalis principia mathematica*, London 1687, p. 16 (corollary III to the 3rd axiom or law of motion). See also leaf 35, page 1 (AK 21:439.18–22, not included); and *Metaphysical Foundations of Natural Science*, AK 4:562–3.

40 "Transition into a different sphere" – Aristotle's term for what nowadays might be called a category mistake; see Aristotle, *Posterior Analytics*, I, 75A and *De Caelo*, I, 1, 268b.

41 "On account of, not through another part of the same system."

42 See Kant's Open Letter on Fichte's *Wissenschaftslehre*, AK 12:370–1, which is signed August 7, 1799: "I hereby declare that I regard Fichte's *Science of Knowledge* as a totally indefensible system. For the pure science of knowledge is nothing more nor less than mere *logic*, and the principles of logic cannot lead to any material knowledge. Since logic, that is to say, *pure logic*, abstracts from the content of knowledge, the attempt to cull a real object out of logic is a vain effort and therefore a thing that no one has ever done" (translated by A. Zweig, *Kant's Philosophical Correspondence*). Kant's Open Letter appeared on August 28, 1799, in the *Intelligenzblatt der Allgemeinen Litteratur Zeitung*, No. 109, and was reprinted in the *Intelligenzblatt der Erlanger Litteratur Zeitung*, No. 27, September 14, 1799 and the *Oberdeutsche Allgemeine Litteratur Zeitung*, No. 115, September 27, 1799. (See note 110.)

43 Petrus Camper (1722–89), a Dutch anatomist.

Gerhard Lehmann, in his note to this passage in the Academy edition (22:805), refers the reader to Camper's *Über den natürlichen Unterschied der*

Gesichtszüge, 1792, §3. However, there is no discussion of anthropolites in §3 or elsewhere in Camper's book. Rather, the passage Kant has in mind seems to be from an article Camper wrote for the Academy of Science in St. Petersburg:

"Convictus etiam cum maxime sum, orbem nostrum variis illis, ac horrendis catastrophis fuisse expositum aliquot seculis, antequam homo fuit creatus: numquam enim hucusque, nec in ullo museo, videre mihi contigit verum os humanum petrifactum, aut fossile, etiamsi Mammonteorum, Elephantorum, Rhinocerotum, Bubalorum, Equorum, Draconum, seu Pseudoursorum, Leonum, Canum, Ursorum, aliorumque perplura viderim ossa, et eorum omnium haud pauca specimina in Museo meo conseruem!"

["I am also most convinced that our earth has been prey to various of these terrible catastrophes several centuries before man was created: for I have not yet had the opportunity of seeing a real petrified or fossilized human bone in any museum, although I have seen a great many bones of mammoths, elephants, rhinoceroses, gazelles, horses, dragons or pseudo-bears, lions, dogs, bears and other [animals], and I have preserved quite a few specimens of each of these in my museum."]

"Complementa varia acad. imper. scient. Petropolitanae communicanda," in *Nova acta academiae scientarium imperialis Petropolitanae*, 1784 (1788), p. 251. See Adickes, AK 14:619n.

44 Johann Gottfried Herder (1744–1803) was a student of Kant's in 1762–4 but later became increasingly hostile to the Kantian philosophy, especially after Kant reviewed his *Ideen zur Philosophie der Geschichte der Menschheit* in 1785. In May 1799, Herder published his critique of Kant, *Verstand und Erfahrung: Eine Metakritik zur Kritik der reinen Vernunft*, to which Kant here refers. The Kantians responded promptly: Kiesewetter's *Prüfung der Herderschen Metakritik zur Kritik der reinen Vernunft* appeared in the same year in two volumes; in the following year, Kant's colleague F. T. Rink edited *Mancherley zur Geschichte der metacritischen Invasion*, Königsberg 1800. It contained a previously unpublished piece by Herder's then-deceased friend J. G. Hamann (1730–88) and tried to establish that Herder had plagiarized Hamann's text.

45 "Form gives being to a thing" – a phrase of the scholastics; see, e.g., Aquinas, *Summa Contra Gentiles*, II, 58: "Cum igitur a forma unaquaeque res habeat esse," or "De Principiis Naturae ad Fratrem Silvestri," *Opera omnia*, Musurgia: New York 1950, vol. XVI, p. 338: "simpliciter loquendo, forma dat esse materiae."

See also AK 21:637.11–3 (not included): "*Forma dat esse rei:* that is, the *a priori* principles of composition precede the empirical concepts of the composite, which in this manner alone becomes a determinate object (thing [*Sache*])."

46 See note 134.

47 The following text is a copy, by an unknown amanuensis, of "Übergang 9," "Übergang 10," and "Übergang 11" of the Vth fascicle (AK 21:554.5– 579.19). The copy leaves out, no doubt at Kant's instruction, pp. 559.4– 568.17 and 573.13–575.28 of the original. The present text includes the additions and corrections Kant made in the text and margins of the copy.

(Except for Kant's deletions, which are too numerous to be indicated here as such.)

48 On this problem, see the recently discovered "Loses Blatt Leningrad 2," which H.-J. Waschkies published in *Kant Forschungen* 1 (1987), pp. 229–30, and which he suggests is a draft for this footnote. It, too, addresses the question whether some elementary mathematical properties can be found discursively, or only constructively. (See note 106.)

49 Jean le Rond d'Alembert (1717–83), French mathematician and editor – with Diderot – of the first eight volumes of the *Encyclopédie*. D'Alembert does not express the view Kant here attributes to him in his *Discours préliminaire de l'encyclopédie*. Nor is it contained in the extensive commentary, added by the translator, of the German edition Kant used (*Abhandlung von dem Ursprung, Fortgang und Verbindung der Künste und Wissenschaften* [1761]; see A. Warda, *Immanuel Kants Bücher*, p. 45.) In fact, the view Kant cites does not sound like d'Alembert at all.

However, the belief that mathematics will soon cease to progress was not uncommon in France at the time: It was held by, for example, Fontenelle, Buffon, Voltaire, Diderot, and even, to some extent, by d'Alembert's own disciple Joseph-Louis Lagrange. It could be that Kant is here simply confusing d'Alembert with his coeditor of the *Encyclopédie*, Denis Diderot (1713–84), who for instance wrote in his *Pensées sur l'interprétation de la nature* (1754), section IV:

"We are approaching the moment of a great revolution in the sciences. Judging from the inclination that minds seem to have for ethics, literature, natural history and experimental science, I would almost dare to predict with certainty that in another hundred years there will not be three great geometricians left in the whole of Europe. Geometry will have stopped short at the point where men such as Bernoulli, Euler, Maupertuis, Clairaut, Fontaine and d'Alembert left it. They will have erected the Pillars of Hercules. No one will go beyond." (Translated by John Hope Mason, in *The Irresistible Diderot*, Quartet Books: London 1982, p. 62. See also Diderot's letter to Voltaire of February 19, 1758: "Le règne des mathématiques n'est plus. Le goût a changé. C'est celui de l'histoire naturelle et des lettres qui domine." ["The reign of mathematics is no more. The fashion has changed. It is natural history and literature that dominate."])

Because there is no specific reference to astronomy or its instruments of observation in Diderot, it may be that Kant has still another passage in mind. It seems more likely, however, that Kant, who obviously is writing from memory, conflates the views of d'Alembert, Diderot, and a passage from the commentary added to the German translation of the *Discours*. To d'Alembert's claim (§25) that astronomy is most worthy of our study because of the magnificent spectacle that it presents to us, the translator adds in his "note": "Furthermore, in no other science are the observations as accurate as in this one, *because its instruments have been brought to the greatest perfection*" (p. 80, italics added).

There is, however, one passage in d'Alembert's *Discours* that comes close, not to the letter but to the *spirit* of Kant's criticism of Kästner: "Thus of all the sciences that pertain to reason, Metaphysics and Geometry are those in which imagination plays the greatest part. I ask pardon of those superior wits who are detractors of Geometry; doubtless they do not think of themselves so close to it, although all that separates them perhaps is Metaphysics. Imagination acts no less in a geometer who creates than in a poet who invents. It is true that they operate differently on their objects. The first shears it down and analyzes it, the second puts it together and embellishes it. It is true, further, that these different ways of operating stem from different sorts of minds, and for this reason the talents of a great geometer and those of a great poet will perhaps never be found together. But whether or not they are mutually exclusive, they have no right to hold one another in contempt" (translated by Richard N. Schwab, The Library of Liberal Arts: Indianapolis 1963, pp. 51–2).

50 Abraham Gotthelf Kästner (1719–1800), mathematician in Göttingen (see notes 1 and 34), whom Kant once called "the Nestor of all philosophical mathematicians in Germany" (AK 11:186). In 1790, Kästner had contributed several articles to the *Philosophisches Magazin,* edited by Johann August Eberhard, one of Kant's major opponents. Kästner was also a well-known epigramatist.

51 Kant alludes to three epigrams Kästner published in the "Göttinger Musen-almanach," *Poetische Blumenlese für das Jahr 1797,* Göttingen 1797, pp. 84, 100, and 122:

> *Brüdermörder*
> Des Sultans grausames Geboth
> Streckt jüngre Brüder hin, um sicher zu regieren:
> Die Aner ganz allein zu führen,
> Verlangt der Philosoph der ältern Brüder Tod.
>
> [*Fratricides*
> The Sultan, to secure his rule,
> Had his younger brothers cruelly killed;
> Philosophers slay their older kin
> So they alone can lead the school.]
>
> *Vom ewigen Frieden*
> Auf ewig ist der Krieg vermieden,
> Befolgt man, was der Weise spricht;
> Dann halten alle Menschen Frieden,
> Allein die Philosophen nicht.
>
> [*Of Eternal Peace*
> Eternally all war will cease
> If we but heed the wise man's thought;
> Then all men will live in peace,
> Except philosophers, in squabbles caught.]
>
> *Die Unwiderleglichen*
> Von Jedem, der euch widerspricht,
> Sagt ihr verachtungsvoll: Der Mann versteht uns nicht!
> Könnt ihr nun nicht verständlich schreiben,
> So mögt ihr ungelesen bleiben.

[*The Irrefutable Ones*
Of those whose views yours contradict
You say with contempt: our sense he's missed.
But if you cannot sensibly write,
Your texts should never see the light.]

(translated by David Wellbery)

Although not mentioned by name, there is little doubt that Kant is the intended addressee of these epigrams: It is Kant who had declared that there was "no such thing as metaphysics" before him (AK 4:257), and who brought out a *Streitschrift* against J. A. Eberhard when the latter challenged this view: *On a Discovery According to Which Any New Critique of Pure Reason is Rendered Superfluous by an Earlier One* (1790).

Kant is also the "wise man" whose treatise, *Zum ewigen Frieden*, to which Kästner alludes in the title of the second stanza, had come out in the fall of the previous year. Finally, Kant could also not fail to refer the third epigram to himself. In 1790, Kant had asked Kästner to be the arbiter in his disputes with Eberhard (see AK 11:186). Kästner declined but gave Kant the advice: "If your efforts are being misunderstood, I should think that this could be avoided by means of a clarification and determination of the words and expressions [being used]" (see AK 11:214). Two and a half years later Kant sent Kästner his *Religion Within the Limits of Reason Alone*. In his accompanying letter he pointed out that, in accordance with the "prudent recommendation that you made at the time," he now aimed at a more popular language in his works (AK 11:427). As the epigram "The Irrefutable Ones" suggests, however, neither Kant's *Religion* nor any of his later works produced a conversion in Kästner. At least this is how Kant saw it. In another version of this long footnote he remarked with regard to Kästner's criticism: "All of this, however, is not in fact directed (as chicanery) against the study of philosophy in general . . . but rather against the . . . new or critical [philosophy], which finds it impossible to rest content with a revision or restoration of the old Wolffian [philosophy] that was current in his day" (AK 21:243.25–244.26, not included).

52 During the first two decades of his career, Kästner used Wolff's mathematical textbooks as compendia for his lectures. Then he gradually replaced them with many long-winded volumes of his own. In the preface to his *Anfangsgründe der Arithmetik* (1758) Kästner writes: "Germany will still remember the Baron von Wolff with great admiration when the names of most of his detractors survive only in the catalogues of insects [*Insektenverzeichnisse*] diligently compiled by German scribes. It is greatly indebted to him for the expansion of reason, and of mathematics, which makes up a large part of reason" (p. 5).

53 See note 89.

54 "Existence is thoroughgoing determination"; see note 60.

55 "Permanence is necessity in appearance."

56 In draft "No 3η" of the IIIrd fascicle (AK 21:303.11–12, see also 480.28–9 not included), Kant had written: " 'A space void of heat is not conceivable.' (Gehler) *Why not?*" The reference to Gehler is to vol. 4 of the *Physikalisches*

Wörterbuch, p. 546: "Since it [i.e., the caloric] penetrates all materials, a space void of heat is therefore as physically impossible as a space void of air would be if there were no containers impermeable to air." See note 31.

57 The *angulus contactus* "is one [i.e., an angle] formed by the contact of a straight line with a curved [line]" – e.g., the tangent and a circle. Christian Wolff, *Mathematisches Lexicon, darinnen die in allen Theilen der Mathematick üblichen Kunst-Wörter erkläret, und zur Historie der mathematischen Wissenschafften dienliche Nachrichten ertheilet, auch die Schriften, wo iede Materie ausgeführet zu finden, angeführet werden*, Leipzig 1716, p. 67. See also Euclid's *Elements*, Book 3, Proposition 16.

58 "The One and All," or *hen kai pan*, is the phrase Ephraim Lessing (1729–81) used in a conversation with Friedrich Heinrich Jacobi (1743–1819) to characterize his own Spinozism. Jacobi's subsequently published account of this conversation (*Über die Lehre des Spinoza in Briefen an den Herrn Moses Mendelssohn*, 1785) led to the famous *Spinoza-Streit* (pantheism debate) and subsequent Spinoza renaissance in late eighteenth-century Germany. By the time Kant was writing, the phrase had became the general slogan of the German neo-Spinozists.

59 See also the chapter headings of the subsequent pages (not included): "The Supreme Principle of the Elementary System of the Moving Forces of Matter" (AK 21:591), and "Proof of the Existence of the Caloric as the Supreme Principle of the Transition from the Metaphysical Foundations of Natural Science to Physics" (AK 21:594, see 600).

60 See Christian Wolff, *Philosophia prima sive ontologia*, Frankfurt and Leipzig 1729, §226: "Quicquid existit vel actu est, id omnimode determinatum est." ["Whatever exists or is actual is thoroughgoingly determined."]

The converse form seems to originate with Alexander Gottlieb Baumgarten, *Metaphysica*, Halle and Magdeburg 1739, §152: "Singularia sunt interne prorsus determinata, hinc actualia." ["Individuals are completely determined internally, hence actual."]

61 In this sheet five additional leaves are inserted.

62 Page 7 of this sheet contains the remark: "Stäudlin's *Sittenlehre Jesu* given to Herrn Inspector Ehrenboth." K. F. Stäudlin's *Geschichte der Sittenlehre Jesu*, volume one, came out in the spring of 1799; the author announced it to Kant in his letter of December 9, 1798 (see AK 12:270). Friedrich Ludwig Ehrenboth, overseer of the charity schools in Königsberg and one of Kant's table companions, died on January 3, 1800.

Page 12 of this sheet is a draft of Kant's letter to Friedrich Theodor Rink, August 8, 1799 (see AK 12:283).

63 Page 1 of (half-)sheet II and page 1 of (half-)sheet III contain reflections on smallpox vaccination. They were initiated by a letter from Fabian Emil Reichsgraf zu Dohna of August 28, 1799 (see AK 12:283–4), in which he inquired about the passage on smallpox in Kant's *Metaphysics of Morals*, AK 6:424.

64 In 1794, Erasmus Darwin (1731–1802), the grandfather of Charles Darwin, published his *Zoonomia, or the Laws of Organic Life;* a second volume appeared two years later. A German translation of the *Zoonomia* by J. D. Brandis appeared in 1795–9. Darwin's aim in this work was to "reduce the facts belong-

ing to ANIMAL LIFE into classes, orders, genera, and species; and, by comparing them with each other, to unravel the theory of diseases" (vol. I, p. 1).

According to Darwin, a living organism is capable of four different modes of motion or action, corresponding to four different "faculties" that can be excited: "These are the faculty of causing fibrous contractions in consequence of the irritations excited by external bodies, in consequence of the sensations of pleasure or pain, in consequence of volition, and in consequence of the associations of fibrous contractions with other fibrous contractions, which precede or accompany them. These four faculties of the sensorium during their inactive state are termed irritability, sensibility, voluntarity, and associability; in their active state they are termed as above, irritation, sensation, volition, association" (vol. I, p. 32).

65 John Brown (1735–88), Scottish physician who founded the Brunonian system of medicine, according to which all diseases consist in excess or deficiency of excitation of the body by external stimuli (sthenic or asthenic diseases): "As there is always some excitability, however small, while life remains, and the action of the exciting powers in one degree or another is never wanting, the conclusion from that *fact* is, that they are all endowed with more or less of stimulant power, and that it must be either excessive, in due proportion, or deficient" (*Elementa medicinae* [1780], English translation by the author, London 1788, part I, chapter III, xix, p. 8; a German translation was published in 1795).

Life, for Brown, is consequently a "forced state," resulting from the stimulation of the excitable organic tissue by means of external or internal stimuli, thus keeping the organism from "dissolution" (p. 59). In vehement opposition to the then-standard medical practice of bloodletting and "other evacuations" that result in weakening the organism, Brown argued that "a vast number of affections" can be cured by subjecting the body to an increased variety of stimulating powers (p. xi). Applying these insights to himself, Brown claimed to have removed the fits of gout that had long plagued him by going "no further than the use of wine, and other strong drink . . . then seasoned meat . . . then opium and other stimuli" (ibid.).

For several decades, Brown's system polarized the medical world; it was especially popular in continental Europe. His influence on the young Schelling is well known. Frederick the Great as well as Napoleon counted themselves among his followers. In 1802, opposing groups of students (and professors) battled for two days in the streets of Göttingen over the merits of the Brunonian system, until they were eventually dispersed by a troop of Hanoverian horses. Kant's judgment was more balanced: "One can concede this much: that Brown has impeccably presented, as far as its *formal element* is concerned, the concept of the system of the moving forces of human life; for this is an *a priori* and purely theoretical concept. As far as the *material* and practical *element* is concerned, however, [. . .] he has suggested frightful means to this end, both with respect to quality and quantity. Disregarding these, the merely *empirical* principles of his theory of medicine, one cannot deny that his principle of division follows the right clue, which he derives purely from reason and which is capable and worthy of refinement in light of praxis" (R 1539 [after July 7, 1798], AK 15:963).

However, Kant did not entirely "disregard" the "material and practical element" of Brown's theory either: For years he took "a few drops of rum on sugar à la Brown" (E. A. C. Wasianski, *Immanuel Kant in seinen letzten Lebensjahren,* p. 292; see also p. 231, and Kant's letter to J. B. Erhard of December 20, 1799, AK 12:296).

66 Albrecht von Haller (1708–77), Swiss anatomist, physiologist, botanist, physician, and poet. (Haller was one of Kant's favorite poets whom he quoted on numerous occasions.) After studying medicine with Boerhaave in Leiden, Haller traveled and wrote poetry for some years before settling in Bern as a general practitioner. In 1736, he accepted the chair in anatomy, botany and clinical surgery at the newly founded University of Göttingen. In the course of over a hundred experiments, he examined systematically all parts of the human or animal body with respect to their "sensibility" (ability to transmit stimuli) and "irritability" (contractibility of muscle fibers).

In 1753, Haller published his results in *De partibus corporis humani sensilibus et irritabilibus,* a treatise often regarded as the birthplace of modern science of life. In the same year he returned to Bern, having turned down offers from some of the leading European universities and royal courts. Over the next years Haller completed his monumental *Elementa physiologicae corporis humani,* in eight volumes (1759–66), which brought him world fame and consolidated his reputation as one of the most versatile minds of his time. (See note 25.)

67 In the bottom margin of this sheet Kant noted: "Newspaper from [publisher] Nicolovius on the revolution in Paris." Adickes, *Kants Opus postumum,* p. 145, suggests that Kant is referring to Napoleon's coup of the 18th and 19th Brumaire (November 9 and 10) 1799, which led to Napoleon's consulate.

Kant's note should also be compared with an entry in the travel diary of the Heidelberg theologian Johann Friedrich Abegg (1765–1840), who had visited Königsberg in the previous year. Abegg records under June 1, 1798, a conversation with Johann Brahl, a journalist and close acquaintance of Kant. Brahl said "that he [i.e., Kant] loves the French cause with all his heart" and continued: "Incidentally, he is so anxious for political news that Nicolovius has to send him the proof sheets of the *Berliner Zeitung* which he receives by mail the evening before it comes out; and if he cannot read [them] himself, he often sends me a billet afterwards, asking me to report whether anything significant has happened" (J. F. Abegg, *Reisetagebuch von 1798,* Insel Verlag: Frankfurt am Main 1987, pp. 147–9).

68 At Kant's suggestion, Jacob Sigismund Beck (1761–1840), a mathematician and one of Kant's former students, wrote *Erläuternde Auszüge* – explanatory excerpts – of Kant's critical writings. The third volume, published in 1796 and devoted to the *Critique of Pure Reason,* was subtitled "The One Possible Standpoint from which Critical Philosophy is to be Judged." Beck had come to believe that the method of the first *Critique,* especially its sharp separation of Aesthetic and Analytic, was largely responsible for the fact that it had been widely misunderstood. To give an accurate account of the emergence of an object of consciousness, Beck maintained, we must not begin with the opposition of sensibility and understanding but must transpose ourselves into the "original mode of representing." Beck thus provided an account of the

Critique that "reverses" its method, by putting the reader right away at "the very topmost point of the employment of the understanding": "the postulate of original representing" (pp. 138–40). Original representing, in Beck's sense of the term, is the synthesizing activity, the original positing on which all objects, even our concepts, depend (p. 153):

"There really is no original representing 'of an object', but simply an original representing. For whenever we have the representation of an object, it is already every time a concept, that is, it is already always the attribution of certain determinations by means of which we fix for ourselves a point of reference. . . . Accordingly, space itself is original representing, namely, the original synthesis of the homogeneous" (pp. 140–1). "[T]he transcendental statement, 'The understanding posits a something originally', is what first of all gives sense and meaning to the empirical statement, 'The object affects me'. For the first statement is the concept of the original representing itself in which all the meaning of our concepts has to be grounded. Indeed, the concept I have of my understanding as a faculty in me, even the concept of my own *ego*, receives its sense and meaning in the first instance from this original positing" (p. 157, translated by George di Giovani, in *Between Kant and Hegel*, SUNY Press: Albany 1985).

In this context, see also Kant's correspondence with Beck, especially his letter of July 1, 1794, where Kant writes: "We can only understand and communicate to others what we can *make* ourselves" (AK 11:515). See also R 6353 and R 6358, AK 18:679 and 683–4.

69 The main part of this page contains a draft of Kant's preface to Reinhold Bernhard Jachmann, *Prüfung der Kantischen Religionsphilosophie in Hinsicht auf die ihr beygelegte Ähnlichkeit mit dem reinen Mystizism*, Königsberg 1800. Kant signed the final version of the preface on January 14, 1800 (see AK 8:441).

70 The Prince of Palagonia, Ferdinando Francesco Gravina Agliata, became famous outside Italy through the travel journals of Patrick Brydone (*Voyage en Sicile et à Malte, fait en l'année 1770*, two volumes, Amsterdam 1776), and of the French painter and engraver Jean Houel (1735–1813). In his journal, Houel reported on his visit to the prince's villa at Bageria (Sicily), which was decorated with statues of fabulous creatures that "exceed the imagination of painters and poets": human torsos fitted with the wings of birds and fishtails, with limbs of quadrupedal animals, the trunks of elephants, the tusks of boars, the claws of vultures, and the tail of a monkey or a fox (see Jean Houel, *Voyage pittoresque des îsles de la Sicile, de Malte et de Lipari*, Paris 1782, pp. 41–50). Houel's account of his visit to the prince's palace was reported in several German journals and newspapers, which regarded the prince's statues as the ultimate in tastelessness and barbarism. From 1797 to 1806, a German translation by J.-H. Keerl of Houel's *Voyage pittoresque* appeared in five volumes. (See also Kant's *Anthropology*, AK, 7:175.)

J. W. Goethe, who visited the prince's villa on April 9, 1787, while traveling through Italy, felt similarly repelled. He published his impressions of the visit in 1817 in his *Italian Journey*.

71 Page 3 of this sheet contains in the right bottom corner the following deleted note: "To draw from Herrn Nicolovius the first payment *ad rationem* of the

honorarium for the *Anthropology:* 60 fl. in mid February." Nicolovius was the publisher of Kant's *Anthropology;* the second "improved" edition came out in 1800. In his letter to Nicolovius of March 28, 1800, Kant requested another part payment of 60 fl. (See AK 12:300).

72 See note 64.

73 William Cullen (1710–90), Professor of Medicine in Edinburgh, tried to arrange diseases "like systems of Botany," by genera and species. His *Nosology: or, a Systematic Arrangement of Diseases, by Classes, Orders, Genera, and Species,* was first published in Latin in 1785. Greatly admired by many of his contemporaries for its advances in the classification of diseases, the work nevertheless lacked a clear principle of classification. For this Cullen was increasingly attacked by John Brown, who developed his own system in growing opposition to his former teacher and mentor (see note 65).

74 See note 65.

75 "Nature does not proceed by leaps" – a Latin Proverb. See also C. Linnaeus, *Philosophia Botanica,* Stockholm 1751, §77, p. 27.

76 "The turning point."

77 Friedrich Hildebrandt (1764–1816), Professor of Medicine, Chemistry, and Physics in Erlangen. In his *Lehrbuch der Physiologie,* Erlangen 1799 (2nd ed.), §72, Hildebrandt criticizes the assumption that a special vital force (see note 9) must be assumed to explain the phenomenon of life: "To conceive of something under the name of vital force that is distinct from the matter of living bodies is not only unnecessary, but in no way explains the secret of life. We therefore take the vital force to be a *property of living matter itself,* and inseparable from it."

More specifically, Hildebrandt denied that the manifold activities of a living body can be the direct effects of one and the same force. Rather, he assumed these activities to be the combined effects of different mechanical and chemical forces, which as such also exist in inorganic nature but which in living bodies are coordinated and arranged in unique ways.

78 "The encircling Styx confines them" – Virgil, *The Aeneid,* 6, 439. Styx is the principal river of the underworld, flowing nine times around its perimeter.

79 See notes 34, 50, 51.

80 "Philosophical principles of applied mathematics."

81 "Either philosophical or mathematical principles of natural science."

82 "To yoke griffins with horses" – Virgil, *Eclogae,* 8, 27.

83 "Special physiology of the kingdoms of nature"; see note 84.

84 See C. Linnaeus, *Systema naturae per regna tria naturae,* Leydae 1735.

85 According to various chemical theories of the time, "Earth, oil, salt and water are the four principles that produce [*bilden*] the [organic fiber]." J. D. Brandis, *Versuch über die Lebenskraft,* p. 4.

86 "Cat-gold" [*Katzengold*] and "cat-silver" [*Katzensilber*] are medieval names for the mineral nowadays known as muscovite (see note 152). J. F. Blumenbach still lists "cat-gold" and "cat-silver" under *Glimmer* (mica) in the second edition (1782) of his *Handbuch der Naturgeschichte.* The names are dropped in later editions of the text.

87 Blumenbach describes the color of *cerambyx moschatus* (see note 37) as "dark green and blue, like tarnished steel"; see his *Handbuch der Naturgeschichte,* second edition 1782, p. 334.

88 In 1795, Friedrich Schiller (1759–1805) sent Kant the first two issues of *Die Horen* in the hope of winning Kant as a contributor for the journal. The second issue contained an anonymous article "Über den Geschlechtsunterschied und dessen Einfluss auf die organische Natur." In his reply to Schiller, Kant wrote of this article: "The organization of nature has always struck me as amazing and as a sort of chasm of thought; I mean, the idea that fertilization, in both organic realms [of nature], always needs two sexes in order for the species to be propagated. After all, we don't want to believe that Providence has chosen this arrangement, almost playfully, for the sake of variety. On the contrary, we have reason to believe that propagation is not possible *in any other way*. This gives us a glimpse of something inestimable [*eine Aussicht ins Unabsehliche*], out of which, however, one can make nothing at all – as little as out of what Milton's angel told Adam about the creation: 'Male light of distant suns mixes itself with female, for purposes unknown' " (AK 12:11).

The anonymous author of this article was Wilhelm von Humboldt. The passage in Milton that Kant refers to is from *Paradise Lost*, Book VIII, 148–52:

> and other suns perhaps
> With their attendant moons thou wilt descry
> Communicating male and female light,
> Which two great sexes animate the world,
> Stor'd in each orb perhaps with some that live.

89 *Anima mundi* – world soul, *anima bruta* – a dull soul. Although the term "world soul" has a long philosophical history and had occasionally been used by Kant before (see *Critique of Pure Reason*, A641/B669 and *Critique of Judgment*, §72, AK 5:392) its frequent occurrence in the later parts of the *Opus postumum* seems to be occasioned by F. W. J. Schelling's *Von der Weltseele, eine Hypothese der höheren Physik zur Erklärung des allgemeinen Organismus*, published in 1798. For Schelling, the world soul is the unconsciously producing principle that "underlies the continuity of the organic and inorganic world and connects the whole of nature to a universal organism": "[W]e thus recognize in it anew that being that the philosophy of the ancients grasped intuitively as the *common soul of nature*, and that some physicists of the time took to be one and the same as the underlying, form-giving ether" (*Schellings Werke*, edition Schröter, Beck: Munich 1927, vol. 1, p. 637).

A detailed study of the extent of Kant's familiarity with Schelling's work is still a desideratum. He owned Schelling's *Vom Ich als Prinzip der Philosophie*, Tübingen 1795 (see A. Warda, *Immanuel Kants Bücher*, p. 54); he also owned various issues of the *Philosophisches Journal einer Gesellschaft Teutscher Gelehrten*, in which Schelling's "Abhandlungen zur Erläuterung des Idealismus der Wissenschaftslehre" appeared in 1796–7, although anonymously. And he was certainly aware of the rave reviews Schelling's works received in the *Erlanger Litteratur Zeitung* (see notes 155, 161). There Schelling was heralded as a new genius and as the most promising representative of the (Kantian) dynamical theory of matter: "Herr Schelling . . . is one of our truly first-rate thinkers, a true universal genius" (*Intelligenzblatt* No. 2, January 12, 1799); Schelling "had the great, ingenious idea of extending transcendental idealism to a *system of the whole of knowledge*, that is, of establishing that system not only *in general* but *in deed.* . . . Whoever lays claim to the title of *Naturphilosoph* must study the writings of these two scholars [i.e., Kant and Schelling]" (No. 226, November 17, 1800, p. 1803).

The latter passage is in reference to Schelling's *System des transzendentalen Idealismus*, which was published in 1800. So was his *Zeitschrift für speculative Physik;* Schelling's *Ideen zu einer Philosophie der Natur* had come out in 1797.

90 A reference to the famous experiments in which Lavoisier (1743–94) decomposed water by percolating it through an incandescent gun barrel filled with iron rings. As his biographers testify almost unanimously, Kant followed with indefatigable interest the revolution in chemistry that took place during the last decade or so of his life. In 1796, he requested "two lectures" from his friend and colleague, the professor of medicine, Carl Gottfried Hagen, "in which he [i.e., Hagen] conducted all the experiments on which Lavoisier bases his theory, and the doctrine of the composition of different bodies according to it." (See *Neues allgemeines Journal der Chemie,* 2 [1804], p. 240 – although this information comes from an obituary of Kant, signed by the editor of the journal, A. F. Gehlen, it is most likely that his informant was Hagen himself, a frequent contributor to whom Gehlen also dedicated the journal: "to his teacher and friend, as a sign of his gratitude and love.")

Another chemical experiment that Hagen performed for Kant in 1800 is documented through Kant's letter to Hagen of April 2, 1800, and Hagen's reply of April 12 (see AK 12:301–2). Wasianski also had to build for Kant an instrument to measure the electricity of the air (electrometer); much to Kant's disappointment, it did not function as planned. (See E. A. C. Wasianski, *Immanuel Kant in seinen letzten Lebensjahren,* pp. 281–3.)

91 The margin contains an excerpt of a review of E. Tourtelle's *Eléments de médicine théorique et pratique,* 3 vols. 1799, published in the *Jenaer Allgemeine Litteratur Zeitung,* January 30, 1800, pp. 258–61 (see E. Adickes, *Kants Opus postumum,* p. 148).

92 See *Metaphysical Foundations of Natural Science,* Phoronomy, Explication 1, AK 4:480.

93 The German word *Leib* means "human body" – usually in contrast with the soul. In the Eucharist, *Leib Christi* is German for *corpus Christi;* see Matthew 26:26: "And as they were eating, Jesus took bread, and blessed it, and brake it, and gave it to the disciples, and said, Take, eat; *dies ist mein Leib* [this is my body]."

94 Materials are "the counterparts of the moving forces of matter."

95 Kant is referring to Dietrich Tiedemann's *Theätet oder über das menschliche Wissen, ein Beitrag zur Vernunftkritik* (1794), a work critical of Kant's philosophy. In 1798, Johann Christian Friedrich Dietz responded with *Antitheätet oder Versuch einer Prüfung des von dem Herrn Hofrath Tiedemann in seinem Theätet aufgestellten philosophischen Systems.* Kant had a copy of this text in his library (see A. Warda, *Immanuel Kants Bücher,* p. 48). Dietz's book in turn gave rise to Tiedemann's *Idealistische Briefe als Antwort auf mehrere gegen den Theätet gerichtete Einwürfe* (1798), in which he defended his position against Dietz. Tiedemann was not, however, an idealist, but a rather naive and dogmatic realist: He chose the title *Idealistic Letters* simply because his arguments were directed against Kant's critical idealism.

96 Literally: "the latter [is] the former." A term of Aristotelian logic (see *Prior Analytic* II, 64b, 28–33) to designate the logical fallacy that consists in using what is to be proved in the steps of the proof.

97 "Through respective positing alongside and successively."

98 On page 4 of "Insertion II" (AK 22:25.18–21, not included) Kant had written: "Thus the synthetic principles *a priori*. Space, as physical [*körperlicher*] space, has three dimensions; it has three limits – the plane, the line, and the point, which latter signifies no magnitude but only a place in space."

99 See note 28.

100 Kant often uses the term "demiurge" to contrast the "creator of the world" with God as the highest *moral* being. See for instance the following deleted passage in "Übergang [1]" (AK 21:214.35–7, not included): Speaking of the unity of the final end of all organic bodies in "a single supreme cause of the world," Kant points out that this supreme cause "may here be called demiurge since no reference is being made here to any moral end."

101 Kant is most probably thinking of Michelangelo. The sculptor is reported to have "seen" *David* hidden in the block of marble offered him in 1501; and when once asked how he had carved *La Notta*, Michelangelo replied: "I had a block of marble in which was concealed the statue which you see there – the only effort involved was to take away the tiny pieces which surrounded it and prevented it from being seen. Every piece of stone or marble, whether large or small, has a statue or effigy within it – but of course one must know exactly how to carve away only that which hides the statue, and this is very dangerous in that one may take away too much or too little. For anyone who knows how to do this, nothing could be easier" (manuscript by Nicholas Audebert, British Museum; cited in Giovanni Papini, *Vita di Michelangelo nella vita del suo tempo*, Milan 1949, p. 324, translation by Loretta Murnane [1952], p. 275).

Michelangelo's theory of sculpture also found expression in his *Sonnets:*

Non ha l'ottimo artista alcun concetto,
Ch'un marmo solo in sè non circonscriva
Col suo soverchio, et solo a quello arriva
La man che ubbidisce all' intelletto.

[The marble not yet carved can hold the form
Of every thought the greatest artist has,
And no conception can yet come to pass
Unless the hand obeys the intellect.]
                    (translated by Elizabeth Jennings)

Sì come per levar, donna, si pone
In pietra alpestra e dura
Una viva figura,
Che la più cresce u'più la pietra scema

[Just as by cutting away, O Lady, one extracts
from the hard alpine stone
a living figure which alone
grows the more, the more the stone diminishes.]
                    (translated by Sidney Alexander)

The image of a statue concealed in a stone or block of marble can already be found in Aristotle, *Metaphysics*, III. v. 6, 1002 a 21–3: "Moreover every kind of shape is equally present in a solid, so that if 'Hermes is not in the stone', neither is the half-cube in the cube as a determinate shape" (translated by Hugh Tredennick).

102 Christoph Meiners (1747–1810), Professor of Philosophy at Göttingen and one of Kant's more vehement opponents. Kant seems to be referring to Meiner's *Allgemeine kritische Geschichte der ältern und neuern Ethik oder Lebenswissenschaft nebst einer Untersuchung der Frage: Gibt es dann auch wirklich eine Wissenschaft des Lebens? Wie sollte ihr Inhalt, wie ihre Methode beschaffen seyn?* The first volume came out in time for the Easter Fair of 1800; Kant owned a copy of it (see A. Warda, *Immanuel Kants Bücher*, p. 52). A review of Meiner's book appeared in the *Göttingische gelehrte Anzeigen*, 90. Stück, June 7, 1800.

103 "No divine influence is absent, if we only had the sense to see this" – manuscript variant of Juvenal, *Satires*, X, 365.

104 A "separate life," or "life of its own": the ability of a part of a plant or animal to stay alive after being severed from the main organism. See R 1530, AK 15:957: "The life of an animal is an absolute unity of the self-moving forces of matter. Here the parts may have a *vita propria.*"

105 The view that each material process in the body is presided over by a special vital principle or *archeus*, was (in the modern period) advanced most prominently by Jean Baptista van Helmont (1577–1644), who in turn drew on the teaching of Paracelsus (1494–1541) and on cabbalistic ideas. For van Helmont, the *archeus* contains all the formative and functional principles of the organism and of its organs; as such it is distinct from both the sensitive soul (*anima sensitiva*), which guides the lower forms of cognition and volition, and from the mind (*mens*), our link with the divine spirit, the world-soul.

106 See also R 11 (1800), AK 14:52: "How one can demonstrate, fully rigorously though not in Euclidean fashion, the proposition: 'If two parallel lines are intersected by a third [line], etc.', by means of a philosophical mode of representation, by concepts, forgoing construction."

For a detailed discussion of Kant's theory of parallel lines and its historical background, see E. Adickes's notes to R 5–11, AK 14:23–52.

Whereas Kant's initial interest in this subject was probably stimulated by his colleague J. Schultz's "new proof" of Euclid's 11th proposition (see J. Schultz, *Entdeckte Theorie der Parallelen nebst einer Untersuchung über den Ursprung ihrer bisherigen Schwierigkeit*, Königsberg 1784), Kant's return to this issue in the *Opus postumum* may be in response to Christian Gottlieb Selle (1748–1800) – see R 6352, AK 18:678: "Of the analogy between the parallel lines and Selle's principle of universal empiricism." A convinced empiricist, Selle had criticized Kant's philosophy on various occasions. When in 1797 he became director of the *Philosophische Klasse* of the Berlin Academy of Science, he advertised the following prize-essay competition for the year 1799: "The Royal Academy of Science does not share the opinion of those who regard it as proven by mathematics that there are pure subjective representations. It is *convinced*, rather, that there are important arguments to the contrary [*wesentliche Gegengründe*] which have not yet received any satisfactory reply; and that there is no lack of strong reasons *for* [*assuming*] *the general empirical origin of all our cognitions* which may only, perhaps, not yet have been presented in their strongest light."

Kant made a copy of this announcement (AK 18:677). On the cover of the IVth fascicle, he also wrote: "That according to Selle not a single synthetic proposition would carry necessity" (AK 21:338.4–5, not included).

107 "Beings are either things or intelligences."

108 "Conceptual totality is generality – the encompassing totality is totality [proper]."

109 "I am thinking, but I don't know myself yet."

110 Aenesidemus is the main author in a fictional correspondence, written by Gottlob Ernst Schulze and published anonymously in 1792 under the title *Aenesidemus oder über die Fundamente der von dem Herrn Professor Reinhold in Jena gelieferten Elementarphilosophie: Nebst einer Verteidigung des Skeptizismus gegen die Anmassungen der Vernunftkritik.* This text, an attack on the philosophies of Kant and Reinhold from the side of skepticism, played a significant role in the formation of post-Kantian idealism. Through Aenesidemus, Schulze argued that the *Critique of Pure Reason* had failed to refute Hume's skepticism; it fundamentally presupposed what Hume had questioned. According to Schulze, "neither about the existence or non-existence of things in themselves and their properties, nor about the limits of human knowledge" had the *Critique* established anything with certainty (p. 24).

Kant had hoped that his colleague Johann Schultz would reply to Schulze's *Aenesidemus* in a third volume of his *Prüfung der Kantischen Critik der reinen Vernunft.* (See AK 19:317.28–30: "Notify preacher Mellin that the third part of the *Prüfung* will rebut the objections of Maimon and Aenesidemus.") Yet Schultz, who was also friends with Fichte, was reluctant to write a third volume of his *Prüfung:* Fichte's distinction between those who understand the spirit of Kant's work and those who only follow its letter seems to have dampened Schultz's initial enthusiasm, as he was likely to be seen as falling into the latter category. It may be for this reason that Kant wrote his Open Letter against Fichte's *Wissenschaftslehre* (see note 42). This is at least strongly suggested by a letter from Kant's colleague Rink to Charles de Villers of April 18, 1801: "Schultz is now actually working on the continuation of his *Prüfung,* but age, ill health, and various official duties are creating many obstacles for him. For quite some time he was unwilling to proceed with the work, not wanting to be saddled with the label, made fashionable by Fichte, of literalist [*Buchstäbler*], and this circumstance then provided an occasion for Kant's well-known declaration against Fichte. Since that time Schultz has once again taken pen to hand" (*Altpreussische Monatsschrift* 17 [1880], p. 288–9).

However, Schultz's third volume of the *Prüfung* never appeared.

111 Literally, "the theory of freedom." But Kant is perhaps thinking more specifically of J. A. H. Ulrich's *Eleutheriologie oder über Freiheit und Notwendigkeit,* which was published in Jena in 1788 and which contained a strong criticism of Kant's doctrine of freedom. Kant had requested that his former pupil and colleague C. J. Kraus write a review of Ulrich's book; he himself supplied a draft text that Kraus used in his review. For this reason,

Kraus's review is reprinted in the Academy edition of Kant's works, AK 8:453–60. It originally appeared in the *Jenaer Allgemeine Litteratur Zeitung*, no. 100, April 25, 1788.

112 "The highest being, the highest intelligence, the highest good."

113 The Acts of the Apostles 17:28: "For in him we live, and move, and have our being; as certain also of your own poets have said, For we are also his offspring."

114 At the bottom of the margin Kant wrote: "Lampe is to be informed that since he does not stop boozing from morning to night, not only his quarterly pay but also his bonuses will be withheld this week." To Kant's great regret, Martin Lampe (1734–1806), his servant of forty years, had to be dismissed in January 1802. (See note 162.)

115 "A dictate of practical reason."

116 The Epistle of Paul the Apostle to the Romans 2:15: "Which shew the work of the law written in their hearts, their conscience also bearing witness, and their thoughts the mean while accusing or else excusing one another."

117 "There is no valid inference from possibility to existence."

118 Exodus 20:12–13: "Honor thy father and thy mother: that thy days may be long upon the land which the Lord thy God giveth thee. Thou shalt not kill." See Deuteronomy 5:16–17.

119 The Epistle of Paul the Apostle to the Philippians 2:10: "That at the name of Jesus every knee should bow, of things in heaven, and things in earth, and things under the earth."

120 "The duties of humanity and justice, taken widely and strictly (properly determining)."

121 See Ovid, *Fasti*, VI, 15–16: "Est deus in nobis; agitante calescimus illo; impetus hic sacrae semina mentis habet." [There is a God within us. It is when he stirs us that our bosom warms; it is his impulse that sows the seeds of inspiration.] (Translation by J. G. Frazer.)

122 The following text is written on a letter from Wasianski to Kant, December 19, 1801 (see AK 12:329–30).

123 The claim that, according to Spinoza, we perceive everything in God, including ourselves, is repeated many times in the later parts of the *Opus postumum*. Although Spinoza does not exactly say this, his program to view everything *sub specie aeternitatis* could be said to renew the old requirement to perceive all things in God. See his *Ethica*, I, proposition XV: "Whatever is, is in God, and without God nothing can be, or be conceived"; and part II, proposition XX: "The idea or knowledge of the human mind is also in God."

Adickes's claim (*Kants Opus postumum*, p. 762) that "in all these passages, Kant confuses Spinoza with Malebranche," can hardly be upheld.

124 After Lichtenberg's death in 1799, his son Ludwig Christian Lichtenberg and Friedrich Kries began to edit Lichtenberg's *Vermischte Schriften* (1800–6). The second volume contained Lichtenberg's previously unpublished reflections on philosophy, especially on Kant's critical idealism. The editors sent a copy of the text to Kant in mid-1800, prior to publication, in order, according to an entry by Wasianski on the cover, to use in their edition whatever comments Kant might make. Although he did not comply with the editor's wishes, Kant studied Lichtenberg's text thoroughly (see R 6369,

AK 18:693–4, and D. Minden, "Der Humor Kant's im Verkehr und in seinen Schriften," *Altpreussische Monatsschrift* 8 [1871], pp. 343–61).

Lichtenberg's reflections show him to be very sympathetic to Kant's transcendental idealism. With regard to Spinoza, Lichtenberg writes that Spinoza "thought the greatest thought that has ever entered a man's head" (p. 9), and: "If the world continues to exist a countless number of years, then the universal religion will be a refined Spinozism. Left to itself, reason leads to nothing else, nor is it possible that it should lead to anything else" (p. 55).

125   Olaus Römer (1644–1710), Danish astronomer, gave the first scientific estimation of the speed of light. Observing that the eclipses of the first satellite of Jupiter occurred at longer intervals when Jupiter and the earth moved further away from each other than when both planets were closest, he explained this by assuming that light requires a finite time to travel from the satellite to the earth. Based on his observations of the eclipses, he calculated that it takes eleven minutes for light from the sun to reach the earth.

126   Proverbs 1:7: "The fear of the Lord is the beginning of knowledge: but fools despise wisdom and instruction."

127   "Man is a rational animal" – Seneca, *Epistulae ad Lucilium*, Epistula xli, sec. 8.

128   Carl Wilhelm Scheele, in his *Chemische Abhandlung von der Luft und dem Feuer* (1770), §§55–8, pp. 57–64, distinguishes two "types of heat": one that immediately mixes with the surrounding air, another that travels in straight lines without (immediately) fusing with its medium, thus permitting reflection by a metal mirror. Because of the similarity of its behavior with that of light, Scheele calls the latter type of heat "radiant heat" (p. 63). His theory is discussed approvingly in Gehler's *Physicalisches Wörterbuch*, vol. 4, p. 441 ("Verbrennung") and pp. 553–4 ("Wärme").

129   A list of luncheon guests to be invited:

Jonas Ludwig von Hess (1756–1823), a former second lieutenant in the Swedish army, matriculated in the University of Königsberg on October 11, 1800. In January 1801 he received a doctorate in medicine; his dissertation *De actione venenorum in corpus humanum* was dedicated to Kant. He left Königsberg for Hamburg in February 1802 (see AK 12:334–5), from where he provided Kant with wine and smoked meats.

Christian Jacob Kraus (1753–1807), Professor of Practical Philosophy and Political Sciences in Königsberg. A brilliant former pupil of Kant, Kraus had received the chair in philosophy at the age of 28. Close to Kant for many years, Kraus's intellectual independence and growing dislike for purely theoretical philosophy eventually led to strains in their relationship and kept him at a distance from his former teacher. As this note (and others in the first fascicle) show, however, late in Kant's life Kraus returned to his teacher's luncheon table.

Johann Schultz (1739–1805), a court chaplin and professor of mathematics whom Kant once regarded as one of the best philosophical minds in the area (see AK 10:133). Schultz's review of Ulrich's *Institutiones logicae et metaphysicae* was instrumental in Kant's decision to rewrite the transcendental deduction of the categories for the second edition of the *Critique* (see AK 4:474–6). In his response to Schlettwein, Kant recommended Schultz as the person who understood his writings the way he himself wanted them to be understood (see AK 12:367). See also note 110.

Karl Ludwig Poerschke (1751–1812), Professor of Philosophy and Poetics at the University of Königsberg and a weekly guest at Kant's table. In his own philosophy, Poerschke sympathized with Fichte (see J. F. Abegg, *Reisetagebuch von 1798*, p. 246). His *"Weihegedicht"* for King Friedrich Wilhelm III's birthday on August 3, 1801, is used by Kant as the wrapper for fascicle XI.

Ehregott Andreas Christoph Wasianski (1755–1831), a former student and amanuensis of Kant, since 1786 deacon in Königsberg. During the last years of his life, Kant formed a close relationship with Wasianski. In the winter of 1801, he handed over his financial affairs to Wasianski and nominated him as his *executor testamenti* (AK 12:386); from then on, Wasianski looked after the decrepit philosopher almost daily. After Kant's death, Wasianski published his highly informative account of Kant's last years: *Immanuel Kant in seinen letzten Lebensjahren.*

130   "Under his feet he sees the deep thunderclouds and tramples on the hoarse thunder" – a free rendering of Statius, *Thebaid*, II, 35–40.

In a personal note to his own copy of *Immanuel Kant in seinen letzten Lebensjahren*, Wasianski wrote: "Heavy thunderstorms and fire alarm, never frightened him [i.e., Kant] – *Sapiens videt altos sub pedibus nimbos et rauca tonitrua calcat.*" (See P. Czygan, "Wasianskis Handexemplar seiner Schrift: 'Immanuel Kant in seinen letzten Lebensjahren,' " *Sitzungsbericht der Altertumsgesellschaft Prussia*, Heft 17, Königsberg 1892, p. 129.)

131   "I will it, I thus command, let my will stand for a reason" – Juvenal, *Satires*, Satura vi, 223. In earlier years, Kant had cited this phrase to characterize the procedure of the mathematician; see, e.g., R 2930, AK 16:579: "The mathematician, in his definition, says: *sic volo, sic iubeo.*"

132   "Principles are dictates of one's own reason, laws are valid universally."

133   "Τοῦ γὰϱ καὶ γένος εἰμέν" – Aratus, *Phaenomena*, line 5: The sentence Paul the Apostle quotes in Acts 17:28 (see note 113).

134   "*Cosmotheoria* is the doctrine of the physical constitution of the heavenly bodies, their structures, decorations, and inhabitants; e.g. that the moon is a body like our earth, fitted with mountains, valleys, oceans, atmosphere, and so on, in which presumably rational creatures live as well" (Johann Heinrich Zedler, *Grosses vollständiges Universal Lexicon aller Wissenschaften und Künste, welche bishero durch menschlichen Verstand und Witz erfunden und verbessert worden*, vol. 6, Halle und Leipzig 1733, p. 1417).

E. Adickes, *Kants Opus postumum*, p. 140, suggests that Kant takes the word from Christiaan Huygens's posthumously published *Cosmotheoros, oder weltbetrachtende Muthmassungen von denen himmlischen Erdkugeln und deren Schmuck* (1698, second German edition 1743).

135   The Psalms 14:1: "The fool hath said in his heart, There is no God. They are corrupt, they have done abominable works, there is none that doeth good." The fool's assertion also figures as a premise in Anselm's proof for God's existence (see *Proslogion seu Alloquium de Dei existentia*, caput II).

281

136 Paul to the Corinthians, I, 13:12: "For now we see through a glass darkly, but then face to face: now I know in part; but then shall I know even as also I am known."

137 See Kant's *Metaphysics of Morals*, §6, AK 6:423: "It is a form of partial self-murder to deprive oneself of an integral part (or mutilate oneself)" (translation by Mary Gregor). See also §5, AK 6:421.

138 See Lichtenberg's *Vermischte Schriften*, vol. 2, pp. 64–6: "To know *outer* objects is a contradiction; it is impossible for man to get out of himself. If we believe we see objects, we see only ourselves. We cannot actually know anything in the world but ourselves, and the alterations that occur within us. . . . Because these alterations do not depend on us, we attribute them to other things outside us, and say there are things outside us. One ought to say *praeter nos*, but under the *praeter* we subsume the preposition *extra*, which is something entirely different; that is, we conceive these objects in space outside us. This is obviously not sensation, but seems to be something woven most intimately into the nature of our sensuous faculty of knowledge; it is the form under which that representation of *praeter nos* is given to us – the form of sensibility."

139 The amanuensis whom Kant considers here – and again on page 4 of sheet V of the Ist fascicle, AK 21:72.1 (not included) – seems to be Friedrich Wilhelm Worm, who matriculated in the University of Königsberg on March 16, 1799. See *Die Matrikel der Albertus-Universität zu Königsberg i. Pr.*, edited by Georg Erler, Leipzig 1911–2, vol. 2, p. 1189 (Kraus reprint, Liechtenstein 1976, p. 647). These notes (together with the following table of contents) suggest that at this time (March 1801) Kant was still hoping to publish his work.

140 See Lichtenberg's *Vermischte Schriften*, vol. 2, pp. 92–3: "One of the greatest mainstays for the Kantian philosophy is the *certainly true* observation that we too are something, no less than are the objects outside us. Thus if something affects us, the effect does not depend on the effective thing alone, but also on that which it affects. Both are, as with an impact, at once acting and receiving; for it is impossible that a being could receive the sensations of another without the principal effect appearing mixed. I should think a *tabula rasa* is in this sense impossible, for in every effect the affecting thing is modified and whatever issues from it is received by the other, and vice versa."

141 Gotthilf Christian Reccard (1735–98), Professor of Theology and pastor in Königsberg. From 1775 to his death, he was also rector of Kant's old school, the *Collegium Fredericanum*. With his theological work Reccard combined a lifelong interest in natural history and especially in astronomy: In the attic of his parsonage he had a small observatory. Many of his publications combine his scientific and theological interests.

For Kästner, see notes 1, 34, 50, 51.

142 Matthew 6:9–10: "Our Father which art in heaven, Hallowed be thy name. Thy kingdom come. Thy will be done in earth, as it is in heaven." See Luke 11:2.

143 Sheet V is not in the usual *Schönschrift* of the other sheets in this fascicle; it seems to be a scratch sheet. The sheet number "V" on top of page 1 was clearly added later.

144 These are the opening lines of Anchises's speech in which he tells the order of things; see Virgil, *The Aeneid*, Book VI, 724–7:

> To begin: the heavens, the earth, the watery
> wastes, the lucent globe of moon, the sun, the stars,
> exist through inward spirit. Their total mass
> by mind is permeated: hence their motion.
> (translation by Frank O. Copley)

These lines are also the motto of Darwin's *Zoonomia*. Kant quotes this passage again in the VIIth fascicle, sheet V, page 5, in the margin of which he writes: "*agere, facere, operari*, live, move, and have our being. Transcendental zoonomy" (AK 22:62.16, not included).

145 In the bottom margin of this page, Kant notes: Adrastea. *Adrastea* is the name of a journal that Herder began to publish in 1801. The first issue was advertised on April 1, 1801 in No. 61 of the *Intelligenzblatt* of the *Allgemeine Litteratur Zeitung*, pp. 489–90. After Herder's death in 1803, the journal was briefly continued by his son but soon ceased publication.

146 Page 2 of this sheet contains a passage from Schiller's *On the Aesthetic Education of Man: In a Series of Letters*. It is not marked as a quotation, and it was first identified as such by Karl Vorländer, "Ein bisher noch unentdeckter Zusammenhang Kants mit Schiller," *Philosophische Monatshefte*, 30 (1894), pp. 57–62. The passage Kant quotes is the following.

"At this point we must remind ourselves that we are dealing with a finite, not with an infinite, spirit. The finite spirit is that which cannot become active except through being passive, which only attains to the absolute by means of limitation, and only acts and fashions inasmuch as it receives material to fashion. Such a spirit will accordingly combine with the drive toward form, or toward the absolute, a drive toward matter, or toward limitation, these latter being the conditions without which it could neither possess nor satisfy the first of these drives. How far such opposed tendencies can coexist in the same being is a problem which may well embarrass the metaphysician, but not the transcendental philosopher. The latter does not pretend to explain how things are possible, but contents himself with determining the kind of knowledge which enables us to understand how experience is possible. And since experience would be just as impossible without that opposition in the mind as without the absolute unity of the mind, he is perfectly justified in postulating both these concepts as equally necessary conditions of experience, without troubling himself further as to how they are to be reconciled" (translation by E. M. Wilkinson and L. A. Willoughby, Oxford 1967, p. 133, amended).

Schiller had written to Kant on June 13, 1794, inviting him to become a contributor to *Die Horen*, which Schiller planned to edit (see note 88). Failing an answer, Schiller wrote again on March 1, 1795, this time accompanying his letter with the first two issues of the *Horen*, which contained the first installments of Schiller's *Letters on the Aesthetic Education on Man*. In his reply of March 30, 1795, Kant is noncommittal about his contribution to *Die Horen* but praises Schiller's *Letters*, promising that he will "study them and give you my thoughts about them" (AK 12:11). This does not seem to have happened, but since the quoted passage is from the nineteenth letter, whereas the issues Schiller sent Kant only contained the first sixteen letters, Kant must have acquired and studied further copies of Schiller's journal.

147 Kant is in all likelihood thinking of Anquetil du Perron's edition of the Zoroastrian *Zend-Avesta*. His former publisher Hartknoch had brought out a German translation of it by J. F. Kleuker (3 vols., Riga 1776–8). We also know from J. G. Hasse, *Letzte Äusserungen Kants*, p. 16, that this work was a frequent topic of their lunchtime conversations. The title may have suggested to Kant an affinity with his own efforts at the time: *Zend-Avesta, Zoroasters lebendiges Wort, worin die Lehren und Meinungen dieses Gesetzgebers von Gott, Welt, Natur, Menschen; ingleichen die Ceremonien des heiligen Dienstes der Parsen usf. aufbehalten sind.*

Zoroaster, as "lawgiver," unites in one system the rules of "God" and of the "world," that is, the moral and religious laws (vol. 2) and the "cosmogony" of the Parsees (vol. 3). For Kant, it is "man as thinking being in the world" who unites the two fundamental yet "heteronomous" ideas of transcendental philosophy – God and the world – in one system. In positing itself as both a physical and a moral being, man thinks both God and world in "real opposition" and yet combines "both objects in one subject" (Ist fascicle, sheet II, page 3). In this way, the principles of theoretical and practical reason, hence the laws of the phenomenal and noumenal realms, are combined into the system of transcendental philosophy.

Since man in this sense, as the "copula" between God and world, is "the *ideal*, the archetype (*prototypon*), of a man adequate to duty" (Ist fascicle, sheet IV, page 1), Zoroaster can perhaps be seen as representing that ideal: "*Zoroaster:* the ideal of the physical [theoretical] as well as moral-practical reason united in one sense object" (AK 21:4.16–7, not included).

148 See J. F. Blumenbach, *Handbuch der Naturgeschichte*, ch. XII, v: "Many alluminous fossils, when breathed on, emit a peculiar argillaceous aroma. The softer ones generally adhere to the tongue, and many absorb water, thereby becoming tenacious."

149 See note 106.

150 Karl Reusch (1776–1813), oldest son of Kant's colleague, the professor of physics Carl Daniel Reusch (1735–1806). Karl Reusch had attended Kant's lectures in 1793–4, then studied medicine in Berlin and Vienna where he worked with Georg Joseph Beer and Franz Joseph Gall. In 1800, he returned to Königsberg and set up himself as a general practitioner. Kant, eager to hear about Gall's craniology and especially about the new theory of galvanism that Reusch applied to medicine, frequently invited him to his luncheon table (see Christian Friedrich Reusch, "Historische Erinnerungen," *Neue Preussische Provinzial-Blätter* 6 (1848), pp. 293–4). In 1801, Reusch became editor of the *Intelligenzblatt* of the *Königsbergische Gelehrten und Politische Zeitung*.

151 Johann Friedrich Gensichen (1759–1807), since 1795 Professor of Mathematics in Königsberg. A former student of Kant, Gensichen was particularly close to Kant during the last years of the philosopher's life. In 1798, Kant bequeathed his library to Gensichen.

The phrase "income from the university" concerns the *Special Salarien Etat* of the Prussian government, according to which the university had to report the entire income of their employees from time to time so that the civilian budget for the province could be determined. As accountant of the University of Königsberg, Gensichen was responsible for collecting the required information. The present inquiry seems to be for the new budget 1801–7 that was confirmed on June 1, 1801. See A. Warda, "Ergänzungen zu E. Fromms zweitem und drittem Beitrage zur Lebensgeschichte Kants," in *Altpreussische Monatsschrift* 38 (1901), pp. 418–21. (I owe this information to Werner Stark.)

152 Practices in mineralogical classification have changed since Kant's day in such a way as to allow only a free translation of this sentence: "Granit bestehend aus Quarz, Feldspat u. Glimmer enthält im Glimmer die Mica welche im russischen Glas davon es grosse Tafeln und Fenster der Seeschiffe giebt anzutreffen."

Kant is probably referring to an article in Fr. von Zach's *Monatliche Correspondenz zur Beförderung der Erd- und Himmelskunde,* May 1801 (see note 156) in which the problem of the proper classification of the mineral "Glimmer" is discussed. See, e.g., p. 495: "*Glimmer (Mica),* a member of the clay family, whose popular name 'Russian Glass' was occasioned by its customary use in that country as a surrogate for glass, especially in ships' port-holes, lanterns, and so on." ("Auszug aus einem astronomischen Tagebuche, geführt auf einer Reise nach Celle, Bremen und Lilienthal im September 1800.")

"Russian glass" is the mineral muscovite, $KAl_3Si_3O_{10}(OH)_2$, a member of the mica [*Glimmer*] group, characterized by a highly perfect cleavage that allows it to be split into excessively thin, clear, and transparent sheets. The mineral was named in 1850 by E. S. Dana from another of its popular names, Muscovy-glass, after the Russian province Muscovy.

153 See Horace, *Epistulae,* I, 1, 60: "Hic murus aenus esto: nil conscire sibi, nulla pallescere culpa." [Be this our wall of bronze: to be conscious of no guilt, not to turn pale with any guilt.]

154 Genesis 1:26–31: "And God said, Let us make man in our image, after our likeness. . . . And it was so. And God saw everything that he had made, and, behold, it was very good."

155 Kant's sentence is ambiguous: "System des transsc. Idealisms durch Schelling, Spinoza, Lichtenberg u. gleichsam 3 Dimensionen: Die Gegenwart, Vergangenheit u. Zukunft." It also permits the following rendering: "System of transcendental idealism by Schelling, Spinoza, Lichtenberg, and, as it were, three dimensions: present, past, and future." In this case, the three names would represent past, present, and future states of the system of transcendental idealism, and in the literature this is always assumed to be Kant's meaning.

I diverge from this reading for the following reason: Two pages later Kant explicitly refers to a review of Schelling's *System des transzendentalen Idealismus* (1800) in Nos. 82 and 83 of the *Erlanger Litteratur Zeitung.* This review, which appeared on April 28 and 29, 1801, contains a lengthy discussion of the emergence of the three temporal dimensions in Schelling's theory of self-positing. Thus, for example, the reviewer writes: "The ideal I, as the originally positing I, has posited, with this original positing, everything that is and will be. But it cannot intuit itself as such without finding itself in the present. Consequently, there arises for it the idea of a necessary succession. . . . This is the present, through which inner intuition as time, and outer intuition as space arise – without being intuited as such by the I. If they are to be intuited as such, the present must be conjoined with the past and the future, i.e. time must be intuited as extended magnitude, hence as synthetically united with space" (pp. 654–5).

Kant's use of the terms "present, past, and future" – especially in that order – suggests that he is here also thinking of (the review of) Schelling's book, rather than about three stages of transcendental idealism. (Lehmann, who subscribes to the standard view, assumes that Kant has made a slip of the pen, and that "present" should go with "Lichtenberg," "past" with "Spinoza," and "future" with "Schelling"; see AK 22:796, note to 21:87.29–31.)

156 Alexander von Humboldt (1769–1859), who traveled through South America in 1799–1804, reported his observations in two letters of September 1 and November 17, 1799, to Fr. von Zach, who published them in his *Monatliche Correspondenz zur Beförderung der Erd- und Himmelskunde*, vol. 1, Gotha 1800, pp. 392–425 (see Rink's note in Kant's *Physical Geography*, AK 9:233). The passage Kant quotes is on pp. 411–13; it is also printed in the *Annalen der Physik* VI (1800), p. 188. There is an error in Kant's transcription: On the second day, the barometer rises again until nine o'clock, not eleven.

Hasse, in his memoir of Kant's conversations with his luncheon guests at the time, recalls: "Of Hornemann's and von Humboldt's journeys he [i.e., Kant] spoke so often" (*Kants letzte Äusserungen*, p. 31n). Hornemann traveled through Africa at the same time; his experiences were also reported in the *Monatliche Correspondenz*.

157 Kant's reason for recording these two names is unclear. Jean Baptista van Helmont (1577–1644), alchemist, philosopher, medical man, and a follower of Paracelsus. Van Helmont introduced the term *gas* for the third state of aggregation. With respect to living things, he often spoke of the *archeus* as the vitalizing principle (see note 105).

Scipio Claramontius (1565–1653), Italian philosopher, mathematician, and priest. Kant owned his book *De universo*, Coloniae Agrippinae, 1644 (see Warda, *Immanuel Kants Bücher*, p. 27). Claramontan's scientific works are discussed in A. Kästner's *Geschichte der Mathematik*, vol. 4, Göttingen 1800, pp. 120–23.

158 An excerpt from a brief article by Johann Wilhelm Ritter, "Chemische Polarität im Licht. Ein mittelbares Resultat der neuern Untersuchungen über den Galvanismus," in No. 16 of the *Intelligenzblatt* of the *Erlanger Litteratur Zeitung*, April 18, 1801, pp. 121–3.

Ritter reports of his experiments to demonstrate that at both ends of the prismatic spectrum, there are more (invisible) colors, and he concludes: "Sunlight in an undivided state is a neutralisation of the two ultimate determining grounds of all chemical activity: oxygenity and deoxygenity equals hydrogenity. . . . It will be the result of an extensive empirical [*faktisch*] investigation to demonstrate, according to their respective principles, the polarity of chemistry, electricity, galvanism, magnetism, heat, etc., as One and the Same in All. This One and All in its purest, freest manifestation is light – a proposition that can no longer be deemed a mere opinion" (p. 123).

159 Farther down on this page, Kant notes: "Yesterday, that is, Monday, July 27 [1801].

160 Kant's colleague F. T. Rink, the editor of *Mancherley zur Geschichte der metacritischen Invasion* (1800; see note 44), reports in the preface to this work (p. xviii): "that the Italian Academy of Literature, Science and the Arts elected [Kant] as one of its twenty foreign members on April 4, 1798."

161 See note 155.

162 On sheet X, page 1, Kant wrote the following (deleted) passage: "Lampe forced a bonus for the first quarter of 1802 from me yesterday, and forced me to enter it on my writing-slate, with my own hand" (AK 21:128).

Martin Lampe, Kant's servant for forty years, was dismissed in January 1802. When asked by his friends for the reason, Kant gave no explanation: "Lampe has so offended me that I am ashamed to say" (Wasianski, *Immanuel Kant in seinen letzten Lebensjahren*, p. 260). But the passage from sheet X, together with one of Kant's *Gedächtniszettel* (memory note), permit a reconstruction of the event that led to Lampe's dismissal. (The *Gedächtniszettel* was first published as "Beilage B" in A. Warda, "Die Kant-Manuskripte im Prussia-Museum," *Altpreussische Monatsschrift* 36 (1899), pp. 337–67.)

Lampe received for his services a quarterly payment of 10 thaler, plus an occasional bonus, "so that he shall neglect nothing in the observance of his duties" ("Beilage B," p. 349). In the summer of 1801, Kant apparently lost track of the payments. According to the *Gedächtniszettel*, he paid Lampe's salary for the quarter "June, July, August," but then again, one month later, for the quarter "July, August, September." Lampe also managed to get from Kant no less than 10 bonuses of 2 thaler each between June 2 and August 20.

In November 1801, Kant asked Wasianski to take care of his financial affairs and instructed Lampe to receive his pay from Wasianski. (See Wasianski, pp. 246–9, 256–60.) Because this put an end to his bonuses, in January 1802 Lampe must have forced from Kant another bonus, and made him enter the amount in the list of expenditures. Lampe's dismissal led to significant changes in Kant's daily life (see Wasianski, pp. 256–64); in a way, it also marked the end of Kant's "coherent" work on the *Opus postumum*. Kant's loyalty to Lampe continued, however: On condition that he never set foot into Kant's house again, Lampe received a lifelong annual pension of 40 thaler. On page 3 of the same sheet (X) of the Ist fascicle, Kant wrote melancholically, "A brain [*Kopf*] – a brush [*Pinsel*, from *Einfaltspinsel*, a simpleton]. A brain is one who can do something original [*aus eigenen Kräften*]. A brush, one who must be led by the hand" (AK 21:134; see also *Critique of Judgment*, §47, 5:308, and *Anthropology*, §49, 7:210).

See note 114.

163 Lucan, *Pharsalia*, ix, 578–80: "Has God any dwelling-place save earth and sea, the air of heaven and virtuous hearts? Why seek we further for deities? All that we see is God; every motion we make is God also" (translation by J. D. Duff).

164   Hasse, (*Kants letzte Äusserungen*, pp. 14–15), reports that in 1803 Kant began to tire of life. In the course of one of their conversations, Kant said: "Life is a burden to me; I am weary of carrying it. If the angel of death were to come to me tonight and call me away, I would say: Praise be to God! I am no *poltron;* I still have strength enough to take my own life, but I would consider it immoral. Anyone who kills himself is just a scoundrel, throwing himself on the scrap heap.... *Poltron* is actually *pollex truncatus* (a dissevered thumb). Those who were recruited cut off their right thumbs out of fear of military service, so that they would be unable to place the charge on the priming pan and would, therefore, be useless to the service; that is why they were called *pol-troncs*, that is, *poltrons.*" (See also Kant's *Anthropology*, AK 7:256n.)

Glossary

affect	*affizieren*
alteration	*Änderung; Veränderung*
analysis	*Scheidung*
apparentness	*Apparentz*
attraction	*Anziehung*
authority	*Befugnis*
brittle	*spröde*
caloric	*Wärmematerial; Wärmestoff*
change	*Wechsel*
characteristic	*Merkmal*
coercible	*sperrbar*
cohesion	*Zusammenhang*
combination	*Verbindung*
combine	*verbinden*
command(ment)	*Gebot*
command of duty	*Pflichtgebot*
commission and omission	*Tun und Lassen*
compilation	*Stoppelung*
composition	*Zusammensetzung*
connection	*Verknüpfung*
contact	*Berührung*
corpuscle	*Körperchen; Korpuskel*
demonstrable	*erweislich*
density	*Dichtigkeit*
desire	*Begierde*
dissolution	*Auflösung*
doctrinal system	*Lehrsystem*
ductile	*streckbar*
elementary system	*Elementarsystem*
endure	*fortwähren*
ether	*Äther*
excitability	*Erregbarkeit*
exhaustible	*erschöpfbar*

expansion	*Ausspannung*
expansive force	*Ausspannungskraft*
fabric	*Gewebe*
fantasize	*schwärmen*
feign	*dichten*
fiber	*Faser; Strahl*
final end	*Endzweck*
fluidity	*Flüssigkeit*
fluxionary	*fluxionistisch*
formation	*Bildung; Gestaltung*
formative force	*bildende Kraft*
formative means	*Bildungsmittel*
friction	*Reibung*
general physics	*allgemeine Physik*
impact	*Stoss*
impel	*antreiben*
impulse	*Antrieb*
incentive	*Triebfeder*
insert	*hineinlegen*
intermediate space	*Mittelraum; Zwischenraum*
invent	*dichten*
irrevocable	*unablenkbar*
lamina	*Blättchen; Platte*
luminosity	*Lichtreiz*
luster	*Glanz*
material	*Stoff*
mediating concept	*Mittelbegriff*
necessitation	*Nötigung*
nonbeing	*Nichtsein*
occupy	*einnehmen*
original	*ursprünglich*
original being	*Urwesen*
penetrative force	*durchdringende Kraft*
piecemeal	*stückweise*
plates	*Blätter*
posit	*setzen*
precipitation	*Niederschlag*
presentation	*Darstellung*
pressure	*Druck*

primary material	*Grundstoff; Urstoff*
primordial	*uranfänglich*
propagation	*Fortpflanzung*
pulsation	*Klopfung*
rarefaction	*Lockerheit*
reaction	*Gegenverhältnis; Gegenwirkung*
repugnance	*Abscheu*
repulsion	*Abstossung; Zurückstossung*
rigid	*starr*
segment	*Scheibe*
self-positing	*Selbstsetzung*
sensible	*sinnlich; spürbar*
solid	*fest*
sound	*Schall*
special physics	*besondere Physik*
superficial force	*Flächenkraft*
tendency	*Bestrebung*
texture	*Gefüge*
thing in itself	*Ding an sich*
thing [*Sache*] in itself	*Sache an sich*
thoroughgoing determination	*durchgängige Bestimmung*
thought-object	*Gedankending*
totality	*All, das; Allheit*
transcendent	*überschwenglich*
transition	*Übergang; Überschritt*
ubiquitous	*allgegenwärtig*
unify	*vereinigen*
velocity	*Geschwindigkeit*
vibration	*Erschütterung*
viscosity	*Klebrigkeit*
vital feeling	*Lebensgefühl*
vital force	*Lebenskraft*
whole	*Ganze, das; Gesamtheit*
world-system	*Weltsystem*

GERMAN-ENGLISH

abgesondert	*separate, isolated*
Abriss	*outline*
Abscheu	*repugnance*
abschiessen	*discharge*

absichtlich (gebildet)	*(arranged) intentional(ly)*
Abstossung	*repulsion*
Äther	*ether*
affizieren	*affect*
All, das	*totality*
allbefassend	*all-embracing*
allbegreifend	*all-comprehending*
allbewegend	*all-moving*
allgegenwärtig	*ubiquitous*
Allgemeingültigkeit	*universal validity*
Allgemeinheit	*universality; generality*
Allheit	*totality*
allverbreitet	*universally distributed*
allvermögend	*omnipotent*
Anbeginn	*outset*
Anlage	*disposition*
Annäherung	*approach; approximation*
Anschauungsart	*mode of intuition*
anschiessen	*crystallize*
antreiben	*impel*
Antrieb	*impulse*
Anziehung	*attraction*
Aufgabe	*problem*
aufheben	*abolish*
Auflösung	*dissolution; resolution*
Ausdehnung	*expansion; extension*
Ausspannung	*expansion*
Befugnis	*authority*
Begierde	*desire*
Berührung	*contact*
Beschaffenheit	*property; characteristic; constitution*
beschränken	*restrict*
Bestandstück	*component*
Bestimmung	*purpose; determination; vocation; function*
Bestrebung	*tendency*
Bewegungskraft	*motive force*
bildende Kraft	*formative force*
Bildungsmittel	*formative means*
Blättchen	*lamina*
Blätter	*plates*
Darstellung	*presentation*
dehnbar	*stretchable*
Dichte	*density*
dichten	*feign; invent*

292

Druck	pressure
durchdringen	penetrate; permeate
durchgängig	thoroughgoing
einnehmen (Raum)	occupy (space)
einsaugen	absorb
Einteilung	division; differentiation
Einzelheit	individuality
Einzigheit	uniqueness
Empfänglichkeit	receptivity
Endzweck	final end
erfüllen (Raum)	fill (space)
Erkenntnis	knowledge, cognition
Erkenntnisstück	cognition, element of knowledge
Erregbarkeit	excitability
erschöpfbar	exhaustible
Erschütterung	vibration
erteilen	communicate; transmit
Faser	fiber
fest	solid
Flächenkraft	superficial force
flüssig	fluid
Formale, das	formal element
Ganze, das	whole
Gattung; -sbegriff	genus; generic concept
Gebot	command; commandment
Gedankending	thought-entity; figment of the imagination
Gefüge	texture
Gesamtheit	whole
Geschwindigkeit	velocity; speed
Gesinnung	character; disposition
Gestaltung	formation
Gewebe	fabric
Gewicht	weight
Glanz	luster
gleichartig	homogeneous
gleichförmig	uniform
Grenze	limit; boundary
Grösse	magnitude; quantity; size
Grundstoff	primary material
herausheben	extract
hineinlegen	insert; put in

Inbegriff	*complex; sum*
Klopfung	*pulsation*
Körperchen	*corpuscles*
Körperwelt	*world of bodies*
Lebensgefühl	*vital feeling*
Lebenskraft	*vital force*
Lebensprinzip	*vital principle*
Leere, das	*void: the empty*
Lehrsatz	*theorem; proposition*
Lichtreiz	*luminosity*
Lockerheit	*rarefaction*
Maschinenwesen	*mechanism*
Materialien	*ingredients*
Menge	*amount; quantity; number; multitude*
Mittelbegriffe	*mediating concepts*
Naturding	*thing of nature*
Naturkunde	*study of nature*
Naturwissenschaft	*science of nature; natural science*
Nötigung	*necessitation*
ortverändernd	*displaceable; locomotive*
Pflichtgebot	*command of duty*
Potenz	*power*
Raumesgrösse	*spatial magnitude*
Raumesinhalt	*volume*
Reibung	*friction*
reinlegen	*insert*
Sache an sich	*thing [Sache] in itself*
Satz	*proposition; principle; thesis*
schätzen	*[direct:] measure; [indirect:] calculate; estimate*
Schall	*sound*
Scheibe	*slice; segment*
Scheidung	*analysis*
Schranke	*bound*
schwärmen	*fantasize*
Schwere	*gravity; heaviness*
setzen	*posit*
sperrbar	*coercible*
spürbar	*sensible*

starr	*rigid*
Stelle	*position; location*
Stoff	*material*
Stoppelung	*compilation*
Stoss	*impact*
Strahlen	*fibers, rays*
Triebfeder	*incentive*
Tun und Lassen	*commision and omission*
Übergang	*transition*
überschwenglich	*transcendent*
unablenkbar	*irrevocable*
Unding	*impossibility; absurdity; nonentity*
uranfänglich	*primordial*
Urheber	*author; originator*
ursprünglich	*original*
Urstoff	*primary material*
Urwesen	*original being*
Veränderung	*alteration*
verbinden	*combine*
Verbindung	*combination*
verbreitet	*distributed*
verdrängen	*drive out*
vereinigen	*unite*
Verknüpfung	*connection*
Vernunftschluss	*syllogism*
Wägbarkeit	*ponderosity*
Wärmestoff; Wärmematerial	*caloric*
Wechsel	*change*
Zurückstossung	*repulsion*
Zusammenhang	*cohesion*
Zusammensetzung	*composition*
Zweck	*purpose; end*
Zweckmässigkeit	*purposiveness*
Zwischenraum	*intermediate space*

Concordance

AK 21 pages	This volume pages	AK 21 pages	This volume pages
6.12–13	256	241.1–17	79
7.1–18	256	307.20–312.15	23–6
9.9–37.29	218–39	373.1–376.18	10–12
40.1–12	240	378.7–379.6	12
41.16–27	240	386.27–389.11	12–4
44.10–23	240–1	402.11–412.9	14–22
50.1–53.14	241–4	415.1–416.5	3
59.1–26	244	417.1–10	4
61.11–26	244–5	453.18–460–4	5–9
78.1–85.4	245–50	474.1–478.26	39–42
86.20–88.25	250–2	481.25–484.7	43–4
91.15–94.25	252–4	521.1–527.16	34–8
97.23–29	254	548.14–551.6	79–81
99.18–22	255	551.26–553.17	81–2
155.16–156.27	255–6	581.12–587.4	90–3
181.5–186.12	58–61	589.9–590.12	94
206.25–231.7	62–77	601.5–605.13	95–7
231.27–233.14	77–8		

AK 22 pages	This volume pages	AK 22 pages	This volume pages
11.1–13.4	170–1	353.6–356.11	113–15
28.1–29.15	171–2	356.24–359.13	115–17
30.23–34.8	172–5	367.1–368.4	117–18
36.10–39.5	175–7	372.29–373.33	118–19
40.1–41.6	177–8	377.5–378.24	119–20
43.7–44.28	178–9	383.5–384.29	120–1
48.10–60.25	210–17	405.14–409.10	121–4
76.4–89.12	185–94	413.1–417.10	179–82
95.5–101.3	194–8	418.6–421.30	182–5
104.1–105.29	198–9	433.25–436.31	159–61
115.5–131.6	200–9	439.1–445.21	161–5
135.1–136.13	45	446.25–450.11	165–7
138.1–139.23	46–7	451.1–452.22	168–9
141.1–142.19	47–8	453. 1–455.23	124–6
146.1–147.16	48–9	456.14–461.29	126–30
148.6–149.6	49–50	463.1–467.8	130–2
188.1–19	50–1	473.20–476.12	133–4
189.20–194.15	51–4	477.14–481.23	134–7
199.15–201.6	54–5	487.27–495.12	137–42
206.1–215.30	23–34	496.1–505.13	142–8
239.5–242.23	55–8	506.14–509.20	148–50
282.12–283.31	100–1	511.10–517.15	150–4
291.12–292.14	101–2	517.25–519.12	154–5
294.27–295.20	102	524.1–526.4	155–6
298.19–301.15	102–4	528.15–530.18	157–8
317.20–322.30	105–8	535.16–536.5	158
324.4–327.3	108–10	543.1–555.10	82–90
340.19–344.28	110–13	609.25–612.7	97–9

Index

NAMES

Abegg, J. F., 271
Ackermann, J. F., 258
Adickes, E., xvi, xxi–xxiv, xxvi–xxvii, xlviii, xlix, li, lii, liii, 257, 258, 262–3, 265, 271, 275, 277, 279, 281
Aenesidemus, 196, 198, 229, 234, 278
Alembert, J. L. d', 83, 264, 266–7
Anselm of Canterbury, 281
Aquinas, T., 265
Aratus, 281
Archimedes, 264
Aristotle, 264, 276, 277
Arnoldt, E., xviii–xx, xlix, li

Baum, G., lii
Baumgarten, A. G., 269
Bayerer, W. G., lii
Beck, J. S., xxxvi–xxxvii, xxxix, liv, lv, 114, 271–2
Beer, G. J., 284
Berkeley, G., xxxi–xxxiii
Bernoulli, J., 258, 266
Blumenbach, J. F., 273, 284
Boerhaave, H., 261, 271
Borelli, G. A., 261
Brahl, J., 271
Brandis, J. D., 258, 273
Brown, J., 103, 122, 270–1, 273
Brydone, P., 272
Buchenau, A., xxii–xxiv, li, lii
Buffon, G. L. L., Comte de, 266

Camper, P., 66, 67, 264–5
Chladni, E. F. F., 257
Clairaut, A. C., 266
Claramontius, S., 251, 286
Classen, A., l
Cullen, W., 122, 273
Czygan, P., 281

Dana, E. S., 285
Darwin, E., 122, 269–70, 283
Descartes, R., 52
Diderot, D., 266
Diels, H., li

Dietz, J. C. F., 275
Dilthey, W., xxi
Dohna, F. E., Reichgraf von, 269

Eberhard, J. A., 267–8
Ehrenboth, F. L., 269
Epicurus, 69
Erdmann, B., li
Erhard, J. B., 271
Erxleben, J. C. P., 259
Euclid, 188, 247, 269, 277
Euler, L., 32, 35, 261, 262, 266

Fichte, J. G., 262, 264, 278, 281
Fischer, J. C., 264
Fischer, K., xv, xviii–xx, xlix, l, li
Fontaine, B. F. L., 266
Fontenelle, B. L. B. de, 266
Friedrich Wilhelm II, king of Prussia, 263, 270
Friedrich Wilhelm III, king of Prussia, xvii, xxvi, 281

Galileo, 113, 135, 157, 264
Gall, F. J., 284
Garve, C., xvi, xlviii, 44, 263
Gehlen, A. F., 275
Gehler, J. S. T., 32, 258, 260, 261, 263–4, 268–9, 280
Gensichen, J. F., xlviii, 247, 284–5
Goethe, J. W. von, l, 272
Gossler, G. von, xix, xlix
Gravina Agliata, Ferdinando Francesco, prince of Palagonia, 120, 272
Gren, D. F. A. C., 260
Guttmann, B., li

Haensell, P., xviii–xx, xlviii
Haering, T., lii
Hagen, C. G., xxvi, 259, 275
Hales, S., 257
Haller, A. von, 103, 104, 261, 271
Hamann, J. G., 265
Hartknoch, J. F., 284

299

SUBJECTS

phoronomic proposition, 3
phoronomy, 3, 29
pleasure, 145, 201, 220
ponderability, 11, 17, 45–6, 57
ponderosity, 11–13, 17, 19, 30
predicable, 7, 193
pressure, 3, 5, 10, 12, 14–15, 19, 24–6, 28–31, 35, 46–8, 121, 131
prime mover, 55, 68–9, 72, 82
principle: constitutive, 57; physical-cosmological, 94; of principles, 106; regulative, 57; teleological, 146; transcendental, 128, 159–60, 164, 167, 179; vital, 64, 137
propagation, 12, 39, 53, 103; by two sexes, 85, 142, 145, 163, 187
prudence, 44, 177, 234

religion, 248
revolutions of earth, 57, 65, 67
rigidification, 16, 24, 32, 35

schematism, 139, 141, 142
self-affection, 104, 106–7, 109, 117, 119, 121–2, 126–7, 129–31, 134–6, 142, 149, 167, 174, 176, 186, 191
self-intuition, 163, 165, 167
sickness, 118, 128, 132, 145, 197
soul, 8, 16, 118, 149, 182–3, 195, 214, 220; immortality of, 17, 239
sound, 43, 51, 141, 155, 158–9; and tones, 43, 157, 198
space: as idea, 134; as posited, 163. *See also* time and space
stratification, 24, 35–6
sulphur, 221
sulphuric acid, 221
System of Transcendental Idealism, 251, 254
systematics of nature, 145, 147

theology, 8; transcendental, 9, 218, 221
thing in itself, 173, 175, 179, 183, 185, 200, 202–3; as corrrelate for pure understanding, 174; as determinable, 183; as not

object, 173, 179–80; as position only, 173; subject as, 172–4, 180–1, 186; as subject's own activity, 176; as thought-entity only, 173–4, 176, 180–1, 184
time and space: as acts of power of representation, 193; as products of imagination, 176, 185; as thought-objects, 180
topic, 40, 103, 115
transcendental philosophy: as archetype, 256; as autonomy, 244, 246; in contrast with metaphysics, 187, 246–7; founds mathematics, 185; highest standpoint of, 226, 235, 237, 243–4, 250; key to, 175; negative definition of, 254; possibility of, 159, 161–2; principle of, 167, 182, 192; problem of, 133, 158, 171–2, 176, 179, 183, 223; as self-creation of ideas, 249; as self-determination, 252, 254

unity: collective, 81, 86–90, 93, 95, 98, 217, 227; distributive, 81, 86, 90, 93, 217, 227
universality: analytic, 188; collective, 96, 98, 122; discursive, 111, 121, 187, 190; distributive, 96, 98, 122; intuitive, 111, 121, 187, 190; synthetic, 188

vita propria, 182

weighing, 13, 19, 29, 55, 57
weight, 4, 8–10, 17, 19–20, 29–30, 34–5, 45–6, 48–9, 66
wisdom, 176–7, 215, 234, 236, 241, 243, 255–6; doctrine of, 83, 138, 255; as highest principle of reason, 177
world: as maximum, 213, 219, 226, 238; singularity of, 205, 210–12, 219, 223, 227, 234, 240, 244; as whole of sense-objects, 200, 210–12, 227–8
world-soul, 85, 147, 149, 186, 195, 197, 215, 224–5, 233–4, 252
world-system, 30, 42, 53–5, 86, 104

zoonomy, 103–4